THIRTY YEARS OF LABOR

1859 - 1889

THIRTY YEARS OF LABOR

1859 - 1889

By

TERENCE V. POWDERLY

[1890]

REPRINTS OF ECONOMIC CLASSICS

AUGUSTUS M. KELLEY · PUBLISHERS
NEW YORK · 1967

First Edition 1889
Revised & Corrected Edition 1890

Reprinted 1967 by
AUGUSTUS M. KELLEY PUBLISHERS

Library of Congress Catalogue Card Number
66-21692

PRINTED IN THE UNITED STATES OF AMERICA
by SENTRY PRESS, NEW YORK, N. Y. 10019

9/67- #12.50- c.1

F.A.WEHRMAN - COL. O.

THIRTY YEARS OF LABOR

1859 to 1889,

IN WHICH THE HISTORY OF THE ATTEMPTS TO FORM ORGANIZATIONS OF
WORKINGMEN FOR THE DISCUSSION OF POLITICAL, SOCIAL
AND ECONOMIC QUESTIONS IS TRACED.

————————

THE NATIONAL LABOR UNION OF 1866,

THE INDUSTRIAL BROTHERHOOD OF 1874,

AND

THE ORDER OF THE

KNIGHTS OF LABOR OF AMERICA AND THE WORLD.

————————

THE CHIEF AND MOST IMPORTANT PRINCIPLES IN THE PREAMBLE OF THE
KNIGHTS OF LABOR DISCUSSED AND EXPLAINED, WITH VIEWS OF
THE AUTHOR ON LAND, LABOR AND TRANSPORTATION.

————————

BY T. V. POWDERLY.

————————

REVISED AND CORRECTED 1890.

————————

PHILADELPHIA, PA.

PREFACE.

Three years ago it was suggested to the author that he write a book on the labor question. The stirring events of that year, in labor circles, attracted the attention of all classes toward the labor problem, and for the first time in the history of America did the industrial question assume such proportions as to become the theme of conversation in public and private. Taken up with the affairs of the organization of the Knights of Labor, the author could not, in justice to the charge intrusted to his keeping, devote the necessary time to the compiling of the work required of him. During the hours which have flown since 1886 the material has been gathered on which the following pages have been written, and although the time in which the work was done was stolen, here and there, as occasion presented itself to the author, the subjects treated in these chapters have had his earnest attention for the last fifteen years.

Within the period of three years many books have been written on the labor question by men who were interested in the subject. Any one of them would win a place for itself on the shelves of any library under the name of its author, but several of them were published and advertised in such a way as to create the impression that the author of THIRTY YEARS OF LABOR was either associate author or in some way concerned in their publication. This is the first and only book that has been written by the undersigned; it is the only one in which he is or was interested, directly or otherwise. He does not make this statement for the purpose of detracting from the merits of other works on the subject, but merely to state a fact in connection with his name, which has been made use of for advertising purposes; he would advise all to read these books, for they deal with times and subjects which he does not touch upon in these pages.

The necessity for organization among producers becomes clearly discernible when one takes note of the tendencies toward centralization of power in the hands of those who control the wealth of the country.

Combinations, monopolies, trusts and pools make it easy for a few to absorb the earnings of the workers, and limit their earnings to the lowest sum on which they can sustain life. Combination, in America, is heartless in the extreme, and has reached a point where it hesitates about going still further only through the fear of crowding the poor to a condition "where the brute takes the place of the man." And yet these combinations and pools are educators; they are teaching the American people that if a few men may successfully corner the results of labor, and the wealth to purchase them, there is no just reason why the many may not do so for the benefit of all, through agents of their own selection. Natural opportunities are being controlled, monopolized and dwarfed by artificial means; production is limited because consumption is checked through poverty. To free the earth and its treasures, and allow man to have free access to his natural rights, is the aim of organization to-day. Bitter was the opposition shown to governmental control of corporations a few years ago; to-day that opposition is insignificant compared with what it was even five years ago. This result is due to the marching and counter-marching of the Knights of Labor, Farmers' Alliances, Patrons of Husbandry and kindred organizations. The organization of labor means far more in 1889 than it even shadowed in 1859; then the supplication was: "Give us an advance in wages and shorter hours of toil, and we will be content with our stay on earth." To-day the demand is: "Give us the earth and all that it can produce, for to no man, or set of men, belongs the right to monopolize it or its products. We do not mean to deprive any man of his natural rights to the soil, but we do intend to oblige every man to render an equivalent for that which he receives by establishing an equitable standard of taxation."

As to the manner in which these pages have been written, it becomes the author to say but little. He is painfully conscious that they contain numerous imperfections, that they will not be regarded with favor by many, and that others will be disappointed on reading them. He is also conscious that there are thousands entertaining the same views that he does who could have placed them before the world in a far more pleasing and comprehensive manner. His aim has been to tell the story of one movement in a given direction for a short period of time, and his greatest trouble was to keep from diverging. There is so much to say that, when the closing lines were written, the author felt that only a beginning had been made and that he should proceed. The merest outline has been given ; the great' strikes and upheavals were briefly referred to—their discussion has been deferred until justice can be done the subject.

The author has not aimed at rhetorical effect; it has been his aim to answer a number of questions concerning labor organizations which have been put to him within the last three years; he has avoided saying what has been written before as far as he could. If the reader discovers any reasoning in conflict with his own, let him not resort to abusive epithets in order to disprove what is said in these pages; rather let him show wherein the error exists, that others may profit thereby. If the reader can show wherein the author has erred, it is his duty to do so, for by that means the cause of truth will be advanced. The author felt that it was his duty to unveil the early history of the Order of the Knights of Labor, dispel the mystery which enshrouded it, and disprove the oft-repeated assertion that it was of foreign origin and an offshoot of the International of Europe. Well aware that it will meet with adverse criticism, the author takes consolation in the knowledge that the productions of the brightest minds have met with the same reception; he does not expect to receive any more consideration than they.

He might have made these pages more interesting had he spoken in detail of the various men who were actors in the scenes referred to, but the limits within which this may be done with propriety and without giving offense are so circumscribed that he deemed it best to speak only of their deeds. They will be satisfied to know that they were right, although it cost them many a comfort and pang.

> "To brave opinion's settled frown,
> From ermined robe and saintly gown,
> While wrestling reverenced error down."

T. V. POWDERLY.

SCRANTON, Pa., July 4, 1889.

CONTENTS.

The Old Order Changes.

The Awakening.

Searching for the True Path.

MAKING PROGRESS.

THE STORM BREAKS.

MEASURES BEFORE MEN.

Early effort to make name public—Attempts to form national head—Proceedings of early convention—Call for convention January 1, 1878—The convention at Reading, Pa.—The General Assembly organized—List of Representatives—U. S. Stephens elected Grand Master Workman—Charles H. Litchman elected Grand Secretary — Constitution adopted – The Preamble of the Industrial Brotherhood adopted - Measures adopted to provide a revenue—No money in the treasury—Adoption of a seal—"That is a most perfect form of government in which an injury to one is the concern of all "—The Preamble a call to action—Mismanagement of public affairs to be remedied—Constitution and supplies issued to the Order—The gallows in Schuylkill County, Pa.—Molly Maguires—Attack upon the Order by a clergyman—Call for a special session of the General Assembly—The reasons for it—The propositions submitted— Richard Griffiths—The first and second sections of the Preamble discussed – Knowledge the standpoint for action—The aid of Divine Providence invoked to enslave the laborer—"Servants, obey your masters "—" Does the Almighty favor the rich ?"—The difference between the real and the sham in religion— The monuments of the past not erected to the memory of the workmen—The slayers of men remembered and rewarded, while the builders of cities and homes are consigned to oblivion—The politician's indifference to the wishes and welfare of the people—The people to blame—Politics to be discussed by workingmen—Education the watchword—Parties good only as they serve the people—The G. M. W. replies to a " prominent Democrat "—Labor Party not likely to become a success — The interest centres in the candidate—The G. M. W. makes a political speech—Is asked to make others—His reply to committee at Philadelphia—The influence of corporations in elections—Men compelled to vote as corporations dictate—The voter must be allowed to deposit his ballot free from interference or scrutiny—Traders at the ballot-box are traitors to the State—Make election day a national holiday—The General Assembly passes resolution favoring it—The Preamble to be discussed at all meetings.

THE LABOR BUREAU.

The third section of the Preamble—Changed to suit the conditions under which the Knights of Labor worked—The establishment of the Labor Bureau—Its first effects on the workingman –Its benefits as compared with the hardships brought about by its introduction—The employers opposed to making returns of their business affairs—Corporations intended to benefit the public—Hon. M. A. Foran presents a bill to create a Bureau of Labor—The establishment of Bureaus in various States—A National Labor Bureau established at Washington –Powderly and Jarrett applicants for the position of Commissioner of Labor—Employers send in remonstrance against Powderly's appointment— Jarrett's name sent in to the Senate—Its withdrawal—Appointment of Carroll D. Wright—Benjamin F. Butler recommends Wright—The Senate attempts to divert the work of the National Bureau from its proper course—Gathering divorce statistics—Workingmen indignant—The General Assembly instructs the Legislative Committee to work for a Department of Labor—Establishment of a Department of Labor at Washington—What is hoped for from the Labor Bureaus—Old-time slavery as compared with the new.

LAND—TRANSPORTATION—TELEGRAPHY.

Land agitation began when the Federal Constitution was adopted—The Pre-emption Acts—Resolution adopted by the Free-soil Democracy in 1852—Galusha A. Grow introduces Homestead Law—President Buchanan vetoes it—Passes Congress and is signed by President Lincoln—First grant to a railroad in 1833 —The Union Pacific chartered—Land grabbing under way—The declaration of

THE CIRCULATING MEDIUM.

INTRODUCTION OF FOREIGN LABOR.

Co-operation Under Difficulties.

The Eight-hour Problem.

ANARCHY AND THE KNIGHTS.

IMPROVEMENTS(?).

THIRTY YEARS OF LABOR.

THE OLD ORDER CHANGES.

Here the free spirit of mankind, at length,
Throws its last fetters off; and who shall place
A limit to the giant's unchained strength,
Or curb his swiftness in the forward race?—*Bryant.*

Until quite recently the movements of workingmen in the direction of organization did not attract much attention. The historian did not feel called upon to take more than a passing glance at labor societies until within the last five years. Associations of workmen were confined principally to the trades, while the great mass of the laboring men were not counted or considered in the make-up of the labor organizations of the past. No trade organization ever succeeded in gathering within its folds all who followed a special calling, and as a natural consequence no particular organization was considered formidable enough to attract public attention for any fixed period. On the other hand, no concentrated effort of the various organizations of labor ever assumed sufficient proportions to be regarded as having a bearing on the relations existing between employer and employe. The concentration of wealth in the hands of a few has grown very rapidly during the last decade; so alarming and aggressive have been the movements of the owners of wealth that the alarm which was sounded by a few leaders of thought less than thirty years ago has been taken up and echoed throughout the whole land within the last five years. During that period several distinguished authors have written histories of the movements of workingmen in past ages and centuries. To these writers we are deeply indebted for very valuable information concerning the early history of the Guilds and Trade Unions of Europe and America.

It is not the intention, in this work, to enter into an elaborate discussion of the various phases of the Labor question. Neither is it the design to launch into a philosophical treatise on the subject. What is intended is simply to trace a movement which had its origin within the last thirty years, and follow it up to a point where the public is already familiar with it. Other writers have sketched the doings of several organizations. In the chapters to follow the work in one given direction will be traced, and only such associations as were instrumental in lending aid or strength to the movement in question will be introduced or referred to. To give the history of each organization would not be possible in the few pages of which this work will be made up, and, inasmuch as other writers have devoted a great deal of time and space to trade organizations and their efforts, these pages will be devoted chiefly to the causes which led to the introduction to the world of industry of the Order of the Knights of Labor.

Organizations of workingmen have in one form or another existed for centuries. Under various names the mechanics of the world have at times been associated together. At no time in the history of mankind have the various branches of labor been banded together in one organization, although many attempts have been made to bring about such a result. The number of organizations of artisans never was very large until the beginning of the present century, for the reason that men and women were not divided in their occupations as they have been since that time. The necessity for organization was not so apparent when the number of occupations which the toilers followed was so limited.

To illustrate: The man who was called a shoemaker thirty years ago made shoes; the man who claims to be a shoemaker to-day makes only a part of a shoe. What was once a trade in itself is now a multiplicity of trades. Once there were shoemakers, now we have beaters, binders, bottomers, buffers, burnishers, channelers, crimpers, cutters, dressers, edge-setters, eyeleters, finishers, fitters, heelers, lasters, packers, pasters, peggers, pressers, rosettemakers, stitchers, treers, trimmers, welters and several other workers at the shoe trade, and they all call themselves shoemakers.

What is true of the shoemaking trade is also true of other trades, only there are fewer subdivisions in the other occupations. Half a century ago the traveler found the village blacksmith-shop, the wayside shoe-shop, and the country tailor-shop on every hand. The ring of the anvil, the song of the tailor and the sound of the shoemaker's hammer could be heard at every corner. The traveler of a half-century ago made use of the stage coach, the private conveyance belonging to himself or neighbor, or else he used only those powers of locomotion with which he was gifted by nature. To-day we travel by means of the elegant passenger coach drawn by the swift-running locomotive; soon we will be flying through space aided by electricity or the flying machine. If the traveler of the present day and generation could take time to scan the country he traverses, he would not find the slightest trace of the old-fashioned blacksmith-shop, nor would the shoe and tailor-shop greet his fleeting vision.

This change is not attributable to chance, nor did it come about all at once or because the toilers were ashamed of the old-fashioned methods of earning a living. The march of invention had started, and with it began the sharp competition between the men and women of toil. The competition was not between man and man so much as between man and the machine. The locomotive was in its infancy. The steam engine, as an aid to navigation, played but an insignificant part. Steam was at that time beginning to make itself known. It was scoffed at by some, ignored by others and treated with contempt by many who thought that "the old way was the best, and that new-fangled notions could never do away with the good old plan." Soon the roar of escaping steam was heard throughout the land, and mingled with the hissing sound we heard the hum of many machines that were up to that time only in embryo, or unknown to mankind.

The mighty trip-hammer began its work with steam as an assistant; the lathe, that was up to that time propelled by water, hand or foot-power, took on new speed under the impulse given to it by steam. The man who stood by the lathe held the tool against the revolving metal or wood, and pressed against it that he might make his power felt. To-day he fastens the tool in a "rest," moves the shifter and looks on while steam does the work. The McKay stitcher, up to that time unknown, has appeared on the scene, with scores of other machines, to make shoes more rapidly, and the old-fashioned shoe-maker "waxes his end" no more.

One blow from the mighty steam hammer does the work of ten hours' hard effort on the part of the blacksmith with his hand hammer. One hour of the planing or slotting machine, and the result of a week of hard labor on the part of the machinist who works by hand is piled up around the machine. One machine is set in motion in the woolen mill, and fifty employes stand still to look on while it does the work which their united effort once performed. One iron man is set in motion, and three moulders cease to toil in order that the machine may have work to do.

The plowing machine, the reaping machine, the binder, the grain sower take to the field, and hundreds of men turn away from the farm to seek employment in the cities, where other machines have thrown other men and women out of employment. The old sailing vessel has gone to rest, and the mighty steamer plows the deep; the sailing vessel, with its fifty passengers and three months' voyage across the ocean, gave way long ago to the steam propeller, a six days' passage and fifteen hundred passengers.

The old-fashioned carrier system has disappeared; the letter, as a medium of rapid communication between men, has given way, except among the poor toilers, and the electric telegraph makes miles inches between nations. A flash of electricity, and our crowded centres of trade are filled by poor foreigners from other lands, who come to find that they are crowding on the heels of other unemployed ones who came before. The electric machine in the hands of the wealthy does the bidding of the monopolist in the twinkling of an eye, while the letter of warning sent by the poor man to his friend across the sea does not leave our shores until the poor unfortunate has taken shipping from his old home at the bidding of wealth, which, ever greedy for more, cares but little how many bodies and souls are lost, so that a dollar more is gained.

The millionaire, tottering on the verge of the grave, will attempt to stay the hand of time for "just a minute," in order to add one more dollar to his store. even though that dollar is taken from between the pinched, slender fingers of the starving needle-woman, whose " daily bread" may not come until to-morrow in consequence of man's greed and inhumanity.

With the introduction of labor-saving, or, more properly speaking, wealth-producing inventions, which, by the way, are often labor-making inventions as well, began the building of railways through new and old countries. The old government road was abandoned, but it did not give way to the government railroad, for shrewd, discerning men saw in the establishment of the railway a chance to reach out for the acres of the people; the opportunity was not thrown away, and soon the monopolization of earth began. Government aid was invoked to assist in getting access to the land, but the aid was given to those who had no personal use for it. It was given to speculators and shrewd manipulators. Willing tools were found in the halls of Congress, who, for their own aggrandizement and the country's misfortune, lent themselves to the service of mammon, and gave away the heritage of the whole people. Bills were passed, laws were enacted and measures taken to aid in the construction of railways through the Western States and Territories.

There was no talk then of a "paternal government," although the grants of land that were given to railway corporations were given for "the public good." Every speech made in the halls of Congress in behalf of a grant of land to a corporation had as its basis "the public good," and, under that plea, millions of acres of the people's lands were given away. Recent developments have shown that the contracts under which a great deal of this land was bestowed have been either totally ignored or outrageously violated.

With the introduction of machinery, large manufacturing establishments were erected in the cities and towns. Articles that were formerly made by hand were turned out in large quantities by machinery; prices were lowered; and those who worked by hand found themselves competing with something that could withstand hunger and cold and not suffer in the least. The village blacksmith-shop was abandoned, the roadside shoe-shop was deserted, the tailor left his bench, and all together these mechanics turned away from their country homes and wended their way to the cities wherein the large factories had been erected. The gates were unlocked in the morning to allow them to enter, and when their daily task was done the gates were closed after them in the evening.

Silently and thoughtfully these men went to their homes. They no longer carried the keys of the workshop, for workshop, tools and keys belonged not to them, but to their master. Thrown together in this way, in these large hives of industry, men became acquainted with each other, and frequently discussed the question of labor's rights and wrongs. They saw that they no longer were engaged in that competition which is " the life of trade;" they realized that it was a competition which ultimately meant death to manhood and independence, unless through some means it became directed into a different channel.

With the absorption of the land, farming on a large scale came into vogue. The produce once sent to market from many farmers began to come in under the control of syndicates; these syndicates of farmers lived in large cities, and many of them never saw a farm. When machinery began to make itself felt the farm was not forgotten.

A man with a team of horses or a yoke of oxen did good work once in plowing three acres of soil in two days; five acres in as many days were regarded as very rapid work. The three-gang or double-furrow plow does the same amount of work in one day. The steam plow has superseded the double-furrow plow, and makes it possible for one man to do in one day what he formerly did in thirty days. One man now plows for thirty, twenty-nine men leave the furrow to make room for steam.

Once the farmer sowed the seed while walking from side to side across the newly-plowed acres; the seed is now placed in a hopper, a child mounts the box, manages the team, and in one day as great a quantity of seed is scattered over the surface of Mother Earth as it formerly required ten men to sow; ten more of the toilers of earth turn from the soil to seek a livelihood elsewhere.

All the way through, from one end of the farm to the other, machinery has displaced from ten to thirty, and in some instances fifty per cent. of those who worked the farms; planting corn, sowing grain, planting potatoes and gathering the harvest is now done by machinery, and the farmer who cannot afford to use the machine is haunted by the fear that his farm must pass into the hands of another, or else go to swell the acres of the " syndicate " with whom he has been competing. While the craftsmen were bidding farewell to their old-fashioned workshops, preparatory to entering upon a life inside of factory walls, the man who tilled the soil began to look toward the city and town for something to do.

On public works, and in mills and factories, it became easy for one man to do the work of ten and sometimes twenty, or even fifty. On the farm one man took up the work where from ten to fifty laid it down. In the factory, the hours of labor were reduced a mere trifle after a bitter struggle on the part of those who did the work; but the reduction in the hours of labor does not begin to compare with the reduction in the purchasing capacity of those who make, buy, eat and wear the product of toil. The farmer still walks the furrow and scatters the seed from sun up to sun down as before, unless he is the fortunate possessor of machinery, and can hire others to manage it.

The year 1859 came upon the people of the United States and found them suffering and in distress. Beggars and tramps began to ask for bread. In every large city and town numbers of people were without employment. Warehouses filled to overflowing, everything cheap, and little or nothing to buy with. Bankruptcy stood at the nation's gate. The panic of 1857 had reduced many to beggary. The rapid march in inventions, which had just begun, had increased the producing capacity of the people of the United States, while nearly everything that entered into consumption was being imported in large quantities.

The people had not as yet become accustomed to the new order of things; it was a common thing to hear men and women say when asked to purchase a machine-made article: "Give me the hand-made article; the machine does not do the work as it should." The merchant frequently heard the words: "Give me the imported article; this country cannot do as good work as the old world yet."

While machinery was forcing itself into prominence and forcing men into idleness at the same time, it was working in competition with machine-made articles from across the water; it was making a name in opposition to the "imported article;" the result was that the shelves were piled high with the product of toil, home-made and imported, and men walked the streets in vain searching for employment, with no money to buy the wares that lay rotting or rusting on the shelves.

Competition between man and man is healthy to both, but competition between man and the machine is injurious to the former. He who offered to sell his labor after the introduction of machinery could not hope to compete with a fellow-man in the work he proposed to do; he was forced to compete with a machine, or a whole row of machines, being managed by boys or girls who worked for inadequate wages. With the erection of the factory commenced the combination of capital and capitalists.

Every two, three, ten or fifty men, who united their wealth for the purpose of instituting a manufacturing establishment, formed a combination of employers, and to that extent were members of a union whose object was to make profit from the sale of their product, and to secure from other men as much labor as possible, at the lowest rate of compensation.

For one workingman to attempt to successfully compete with a union of that kind was sheerest nonsense; such a thing was, and is, an impossibility. Competition soon took on a double significance; it began to be waged between the men who labored and the men who employed labor. In former times men of equal ability and attainments competed with each other and achieved success, or experienced failure, according to their merits. Beneath the shadow of machinery merit went for naught so far as man's natural ability to perform labor was concerned. It was of the latter-day competition that Louis Blanc said about that time:

"The principle on which modern society rests is that of isolation and antagonism; it is that of competition. Let us consider a little what such a principle can carry in its train. Competition is the perpetual and progressive increase of poverty. Instead of associating forces that they may produce the most useful results, competition perpetually places them in a state of warfare, and reciprocally annihilates them, destroying one by the other. * * * * * What fortunes are formed solely of ruins? And of how many tears is often composed the good fortune of those we call happy? Is it, then, a good state of society which is so constituted that the prosperity of one fatally corresponds with the sufferings of others? Is that a principle of order, of conservation of wealth, which makes of society a disorderly confusion of forces, triumphing only by the incessant destruction of opposing forces? Competition is a source of general impoverishment, because it induces an immense and continual loss of human labor; because, every day, every hour, everywhere, it reveals its empire by the annihilation of vanquished industry; that is to say, by the annihilation of capital, of raw material, of time, of labor employed. I do not hesitate to assert that the mass of wealth thus devoured is so great that any one who could at a glance measure it would recoil with horror. Competition is a source of general impoverishment, because it delivers up society to the gross government of chance. Is there under this system a single producer, a single laborer, who does not depend on the closing of some distant factory, on a failure which takes place, on a machine suddenly discovered and placed at the exclusive disposition of a rival? Is there a single producer, a single laborer, whose good conduct, foresight or wisdom can guarantee him against the effects of an industrial crisis?"

After the formation of unions of capitalists began the formation of labor unions, and away back in the early days of the Republic we can trace the organization of crafts here and there for their own advancement and protection. Step by step the organization of labor unions can be traced, until the year 1859 found men of all callings looking about them for a relief from idleness and want.

Isolated organizations of mechanics were scattered all over the country, but no very successful efforts at forming a national union of any one trade was made until 1859. On the 3d of March of that year the various unions of machinists and blacksmiths came together in the city of Philadelphia and organized the first national union of these trades. Perhaps it would be well to quote the words of one of those who took a part in the formation of the Machinists' and Blacksmiths' Union, when stating his reasons for the organization of these trades. He said :

"Unfair dealing on the part of employers had long been a grievance with the men. The baneful system of paying in orders was common. The taking on of as many apprentices as could possibly be worked was considered the indubitable right of every employer, who, through the possession of labor-saving machinery, found it an easy matter to get as much work out of the apprentice as he formerly exacted from the journeyman. The peremptory dismissal of workmen was another; hence, in dull times, men with families to support would find themselves out of work, while the shops, whose doors were closed to them, were filled with apprentice boys. This inordinate rush of apprentices was remonstrated against in vain.

"The writer of this was one of some twenty young men kept at work after the great financial crash of 1857, while there were sixty apprentices employed. Over one hundred and fifty journeymen had been discharged from that shop within two months. The extra amount of suffering in Philadelphia that winter caused the formation of the first Machinists' and Blacksmiths' Union of Pennsylvania, in the spring of 1858. The organization had no well-defined plan of action, but they felt that something must be done or their trade, already low, would soon be the lowest of all mechanical callings. They realized that, if the welfare and interests of three thousand men in that one city could be trifled with by the one hundred employers, without their being able to make even the show of resistance, they would soon be but little better than slaves.

"It must be borne in mind that a marked difference had come over the employers during the same time. In the early days of mechanism in this country but few shops employed many men. Generally the employer was head man ; he knew his men personally ; he instructed his apprentices, and kept a general supervision of his business. By that means every workingman knew his employer, and, if aught went astray, there was no circumlocution office to go through to have an understanding about it. But as the business came to be more fully developed, it was found that more capital must be employed ; and the authority and supervision of the owner or owners must be delegated to superintendents and under foremen. In this manner men and masters became estranged and the gulf could only be bridged by a strike, when, perhaps, the representatives of the workingmen might be admitted to the office and allowed to state their case. It was to resist this combination of capital which had so changed the character of the employers that led to the formation of the union."

Before the adjournment of the Machinists' and Blacksmiths' Convention a preamble was adopted, to be sent out to all members of these trades wherever found to be in need of organization. It was afterward published in the preface of the Constitution of the Order, and remained as promulgated by the convention of 1859. The following is the preamble:

WHEREAS, In the present organization of society, capital and labor being, as a matter of necessity, united in all kinds of productive industry (and, as is generally the case, represented by different parties), it has come to pass: That, in consequence of the smallness of the number representing capital, their comparative independence and power, their ample leisure to study their own interests, their prompt co-operation, together with the aid of legislation, and last, but not least, the culpable negligence of the working classes themselves; that notwithstanding their joint production is amply sufficient to furnish both parties the necessaries, comforts and luxuries of life, yet the fact is indisputable that while the former enjoy more than their share, the latter are correspondingly depressed; and

WHEREAS, The machinists and blacksmiths have in several localities effected an organization of their trades by the formations of unions for their mutual benefit and protection, and as the experience of our trades fully demonstrates the great utility of our International or Central Organization, and the said unions have elected delegates to form and compose such Central or International Organization: Therefore, we, the delegates-elect, do ordain and establish the following as the Constitution of the International Union of North America.

And we hereby proclaim to the world that, so far from encouraging a spirit of hostility to employers, all properly organized union recognize an identity of interests between employer and employe, and we give no countenance or support to any project or enterprise that will interfere with the promotion of perfect harmony between them.

In the same year, 1859, the owners of iron foundries in the Eastern and Middle States issued a call for the purpose of forming a National Founders' League. Local strikes were in progress in several places, and the founders determined to send abroad for moulders to come to the United States and take the places of the striking mechanics. Carefully watching the progress of the strikes, the condition of his trade and the efforts of the Founders' League was a moulder named William H. Sylvis, who inaugurated a movement early in the year to bring about an understanding between the various branches of the Moulders' Union, with a view to having them united in a national organization. His efforts were eminently successful, for on the 5th of July, 1859, the Iron Moulders' Convention assembled in the city of Philadelphia and effected a permanent organization.

From the address issued by that convention to the moulders of the United States some extracts are taken which give an idea of how the industrial situation was regarded at that time by one of the brightest minds in the labor movement, for the address was prepared and read to the convention by Mr. Sylvis:

" Labor has no protection—the weak are devoured by the strong. All wealth and all power centre in the hands of a few, and the many are their victims and their bondsmen.

" So says an able writer in a treatise on association, and, in studying the history of the past, the impartial thinker must be impressed with the truth of the above quotation. In all countries and at all times capital has been used by those possessing it to monopolize particular branches of business, until the vast and various industrial pursuits of the world have been brought under the immediate control of a comparatively small portion of mankind. Although an unequal distribution of the world's wealth, it is perhaps necessary that it should be so. To attain to the highest degree of success in any undertaking, it is necessary to have the most perfect and systematic arrangement possible; to acquire such a system, it requires the management of a business to be placed as nearly as practicable under the control of one mind; thus concentration of wealth and business tact conduces to the most perfect working of the vast business machinery of the world."

That statement is in itself sufficient to show that the parent of the Iron Moulders' Union was possessed of a mind so liberal, so broad and expansive that, while condemning capital for its grasping selfishness, he realized the necessity for the concentration or centralization of business tact and ability as well as capital at the head of manufacturing and mercantile concerns. That statement plainly indicated that Mr. Sylvis was not averse to what is so often termed "one-man power." He knew that, to keep a manufacturing establishment or a business of any kind running in proper order, all of the parts must be in hearty accord with the one selected to manage the business as president or director. It was because he wanted labor to profit by the example thus set by capital that he so forcibly called the attention of the convention to that particular point. He fully realized the possibilities of capital properly directed, and sadly confessed that the probabilities were that capital would not deal justly by labor so long as labor took no steps to command a just recognition of its rights. In witness whereof, I quote still further from the address:

" And there is, perhaps, no other organization of society so well calculated to benefit the laborer and advance the moral and social condition of the mechanic of this country, if those possessed of wealth were all actuated by those pure and philanthropic principles so necessary to the happiness of all; but, alas! for the poor of humanity, such is not the case."

Further on in the address the greed of capital is arraigned in such terms as tend to show that Mr. Sylvis foresaw that the cause of all laboring men was identical. He did not undertake to demonstrate that the interests of labor and capital were identical, but he forcibly pointed out to his craft the necessity for a clearer understanding between the various branches of toil. In proof of this, let the remainder of the address speak:

" Wealth is power, and practical experience teaches us that it is a power too often used to oppress and degrade the daily laborer. Year after year the capital of the country becomes more and more concentrated in the hands of a few, and, in proportion as the wealth of the country becomes centralized, its power increases, and the laboring classes are impoverished. It, therefore, becomes us, as men who have to battle with the stern realities of life, to look this matter fair in the face; there is no dodging the question; let every man give it a fair, full and candid consideration, and then act according to his honest convictions.

"*What position are we, the mechanics of America, to hold in society?* Are we to receive an equivalent for our labor sufficient to maintain us in comparative independence and respectability, to procure the means with which to educate our children and qualify them to play their part in the world's drama? or must we be forced to bow the suppliant knee to wealth, and earn by unprofitable toil a life too void of solace to confirm the very chains that bind us to our doom?

"In union there is strength, and in the formation of a national organization, embracing every moulder in the country, a union founded upon a basis broad as the land in which we live, lies our only hope. Single-handed we can accomplish nothing, but united there is no power of wrong we may not openly defy. Let the moulders of such places as have not already moved in this matter organize as quickly as possible and connect themselves with the national organization. Do not be humbugged into the idea that this thing cannot succeed.

"We are no theorists; this is no visionary plan, but one eminently practicable. Nor can injustice be done to any one; no undue advantage can be taken of any of our employers. There *is* not, *there cannot be,* any good reason why they should not pay us a fair price for our labor. If the profits of their business are not sufficient to remunerate them for the trouble of doing business, *let the consumer make up the balance.*

"The stereotyped argument of our employers, in every attempt to reduce wages, is that their large expenses and small profits will not warrant the present prices for labor; therefore, those just able to live now must be content with less hereafter.

"In answer, we maintain that the expenses are not unreasonable, and the profits are large and, in the aggregate, great; there is no good reason why we should not receive a fair equivalent for our labor. A small reduction seriously diminishes the already scanty means of the operative, and puts a large sum in the employer's pocket. And yet some of the foundry proprietors would appear charitable before the world. We ask: Is it *charitable,* is it *humane,* is it *honest,* to take from the laborer, who is already fed, clothed and lodged too poorly, a portion of his food and raiment and deprive his family of the necessaries of life by the common resort—a reduction of his wages? It must not be so. To rescue our trade from the condition into which it has fallen and raise ourselves to that condition in society to which we, as mechanics, are justly entitled, and to place ourselves on a foundation sufficiently strong to secure us from further encroachments, and to elevate the moral, social and intellectual condition of every moulder in the country, is the object of our international organization; and to the consummation of so desirable an object, we, the delegates in convention assembled, do pledge ourselves to unceasing efforts and untold sacrifices.''

So well were the assembled delegates pleased with the address that they adopted it as the preamble to the Constitution which they framed at that convention. It has stood well the test of years, for it still adorns the first pages of the Constitution of the Iron Moulders' International Union of North America. That same preamble was afterward adopted by the Association of Erie Railway Employes in 1869, and still later by the Amalgamated Association of Iron and Steel Workers of the United States; the latter organization still continues to fight its battles under that same declaration of principles.

Although Mr. Sylvis saw the absolute necessity for a closer bond of union between all crafts and callings, he was not successful in impressing his views upon the minds of the delegates who assembled at the first convention of his trade. He continued, however, to agitate the question and worked unceasingly to bring the matter into prominence. He opened up a correspondence with the leading men in other trades, and, for the purpose of securing their co-operation, he went before men who were in no way allied to the cause of the workingman except through sympathy.

With the members of the trade unions of that day the wage question was paramount. Briefly stated, the time of every session of the convention, of every trade organization, was taken up in discussing two measures—the question of wages and the regulation of the number of apprentices, other things being of secondary consideration.

It became necessary for the organizations of labor to elect men to office who could devote all their time to the duties assigned to them; they saw that, in order to properly compete with capital, labor must keep its agents actively at work in its interests. This soon brought the men of ideas in each organization into contact with each other, and soon an agitation began which had for its object the bringing of economic, political and social questions prominently before the workingmen of America.

The vast majority of the men who became members of the labor organizations, which were established soon after the disastrous panic of 1857, did not realize that the daily wage of the workman was not the most important question with which he should deal, nor would the workman of that day tolerate a discussion of any length on any other subject in the society to which he was attached. It had not yet dawned on his mind that, no matter how much his wage was increased, the price of living went up accordingly, so that at the end of the year the purchasing power of his savings was no greater than before.

The first departure from the old track was when the field of inquiry was invaded by those who began to question whether the hours of labor were not too long and wearisome. I. S. Cassin, who had been elected the first President of the Grand Union of Machinists and Blacksmiths at the convention of March, 1859, in presenting his report to the convention of 1860, called attention to the eight-hour question by suggesting that the matter be brought before the Congress of the United States. So far as can be ascertained that was the first intimation, on the part of a member of a trade organization, that Congress should take official notice of the regulation of the hours of labor.

The subject of shorter hours having been broached, it soon became a fruitful theme for discussion in the various branches of the Machinists' and Blacksmiths' Union; the agitation soon spread to other organizations and took up a great deal of their time and attention. The ice once broken and attention having been directed toward other than the wage question, the eight-hour problem, the establishment of labor journals and the question of co-operation became food for debate and thought by members of trade unions.

The discussion of questions of a political character was not tolerated in any of the trade unions of that day; the word "politics," if mentioned in a union, would raise such a storm about the ears of the offender that he at once repented of his temerity and resolved to sin no more.

The Civil War, whose mutterings had been reverberating through the United States, came upon the mechanics of America at a time when they were putting forth every effort to perfect their separate unions. The war, when it broke out, found among those who were most bitterly opposed to it the trade unionists of North and South; they saw in the coming struggle a menace to the welfare of the country which they would turn aside if possible. The bonds of fraternity between the mechanics of the United States was a means of causing some of the leading trade unionists to call a convention for the purpose of expressing the disapproval of the workingmen of the attempts to foment sectional strife and bitterness.

The convention was held in Philadelphia on the 22d of February, 1861, and was called to order by William H. Sylvis, who was among the most prominent in the agitation. From an old issue of the *United Mechanics' Own*, then the only labor paper published in the United States, is copied a letter published by Mr. Sylvis, under date of February 12, 1861, in which he said:

" We are going to have a workingmen's national convention in the city on the 22d.   The call has been issued by the workingmen of Kentucky, and should be responded to by the workingmen of all sections of the country.   Under the leadership of political demagogues and traitors scattered all over the land, North and South, East and West, the country is going to the devil as fast as it can.   And, unless the masses rise up in their might and teach their representatives what to do, the good old ship will go to pieces.   We hope to see every State represented in the coming convention, if by only one man ; but let each State send as many as possible."

At the convention which assembled in Philadelphia on the 22d, and which was well attended, a committee of thirty-four was appointed to sit and arrange for public demonstrations after the adjournment of the convention.   Writing of this committee on the 23d of March, Mr. Sylvis said :

" The business of this committee is to perfect and perpetuate an organization among the industrial classes of the city and State, for the purpose of placing in positions of public trust men of known honesty and ability ; men who know the real wants of the people, and who will represent us according to our wishes; men who have not made politics a trade; men who, for a consideration, will not become the mere tools of corporations and aristocratic monopolies ; men who will devote their time and energies to the making of good laws and direct their administration in such a way as will best subserve the interests of the whole people."

Among those who took an active interest in the work of the convention was a garmentcutter named Uriah S. Stephens, who, commenting on the work which it attempted to do, wrote the following: " It is too bad that the popular mind is not more fully in accord with the sentiment which is abroad among enlightened workingmen.   Had caste not closed the eyes of so many to the true, real worth of the workers of the United States, more than toilers would have assembled at the convention.   It failed in bringing about the desired result, but it *did not meet in vain.*"   His words were prophetic, for that small, determined band of men laid the foundation for a grander structure than they dreamt of erecting when they were called together.

THE AWAKENING.

Through decades, ages, centuries,
The mind was led to cross and stake;
It struggled, lived and moved the world,
And mankind is at last awake.

For several years prior to 1861 the constitutional right of man to "life, liberty and the pursuit of happiness" was being discussed by men of advanced ideas, and a public opinion was being moulded which held that property in man was iniquitous and degrading; that it was entirely inconsistent with the "Bill of Rights," dangerous to morals, and a standing menace to the liberties of the toiling masses in all parts of the United States. The time had gone by when the American people believed that a nation should be regarded as the exclusive property of those who rule its political destinies.

The experience gained since the establishment of the Republic was of a most beneficial character, and it was not thrown away on the reading workingman. He had learned to know that the right of kings to waste the substance of the people in riotous living, under the shadow of divine authority, was a myth, and that the doctrine once held to be sacred was deserving only of the hatred and scorn of all lovers of equity and fair dealing. The rudiments of the science of co-operation in the affairs of government by all the people were being learned.

That a portion of the dwellers on the soil should be bound down in chains, and continue to remain in that condition for any length of time after the doctrine of industrial emancipation had been launched before the people, was inconsistent with every consideration of justice; it was totally at variance with every aspiration of the men who pioneered the movement which had for its ultimate aim the establishment of a system which would make the statement "that all men are created equal" a brilliant, blazing truth instead of a mere empty sound.

"Life, liberty and the pursuit of happiness" are words that were being read and studied by the mechanics of the United States. Every time that these words were read they took on a deeper meaning. Liberty to live meant more than to be a slave to the whim or caprice of any man. The man who held ownership in his fellow-man had the right to so misuse that fellow-man as to deprive him of life, and, while the conditions of servitude were somewhat different between the white toiler of the North and his sable brother of the South, yet the result was the same when the master decided to use his power. Shutting off the supply of food from the black slave while holding him to the plantation was no worse than the discharge of the white mechanic and the sending of the blacklist ahead of him when he left his home to seek for employment elsewhere.

Only a change of color made it possible for the Southern slave-owner to rule, with power most absolute, the destinies of his bondman. The white mechanic felt that only a change of conditions was necessary to place him in the same category with the colored man. No wonder then that the desire to secure freedom for all the inhabitants of the United States began to grow among the members of labor organizations, and gave them renewed zeal in the work of emancipation. The right to live, the right to work and the liberty to work for home and family instead of for a master is inherent in man, but the mechanic could not feel secure in that right while the slave-owner had it in his power to hold one portion of mankind in serfdom the most degrading and brutalizing.

The anti-slavery agitation and the organization of the mechanics of the United States kept pace with each other; both were revolutionary in their character; and though the agitations differed in methods, the ends in view were the same, viz.: the freedom of the man who worked. Though both were revolutionary in character, one agitation reached the climax, burst into flame, was fought out upon the battle-field and resulted in victory for the black slave, whose walk to liberty was tracked in the blood of millions whom he had never known.

Daniel Webster once said, in speaking of the anti-slavery movement: "It is a succession of lectures in school-houses, the mere efforts of a few hundred men and women to talk together, excite each other, arouse the public, and its only result a little noise." The lectures were not only held within, but they were heard beyond the walls of the school-houses; the efforts of a few hundred men and women to talk together caused thousands to think together; they did excite each other, and they aroused the public from its slumbers as did Paul Revere when he rode through the valleys and over the hills on that eventful night years ago to warn the slumbering people of their danger. But the result was not a "*little* noise," for when the smoke of battle had blown away, when the sharp crack of the rifle and the mounted gun had ceased, when the terrible sounds of human butchery no longer echoed through the land, and the roll of the drum for the last time called the troops together in grand review, it was told on the pages of history that the rule of the lash was over, that the cry of the bleeding slave that had ascended to heaven for mercy had been stilled in justice, and that human slavery in the United States was dead.

Revolutions are not manufactured or made to order; they are never successfully planned or deliberately entered upon; they do not come at the bidding of one man or one set of men; they grow and then come.

A revolution which bursts to-day is apt to have had its origin away back in the past, and the leader who mounts to power and fame on the crest of the revolution of to-day may owe his elevation to a brain that has ceased to think, a voice that speaks only from between the leaves of books, a man whose mortal part has gone to rest between coffined walls.

Wherever a few honest, earnest men or women gather together to deliberate upon and investigate an injustice, there will be found the beginning of a revolution. When the convention which assembled in Philadelphia on the 22d of February, 1861, selected the committee of thirty-four, it laid the foundation for a revolution yet to come, but a revolution that is working its way upward and onward to the goal of man's ambition without the aid of fire or sword.

It was a difficult thing to convince the rank and file of the trade unions of that day that there existed the slightest necessity for an understanding, even, between the different trade organizations. Many of the members of these organizations seemed to regard themselves as being hired for life; they were content with demanding and obtaining from their masters better conditions in the regulation of workshops and wages; beyond that they did not think they had a right to venture, and many workmen could not be induced to enter a labor organization for fear of being required to go that far. This condition of affairs had a most disheartening effect on the leading men of the trade organizations, who clearly foresaw that to allow such erroneous ideas to prevail would entail endless misfortune upon the workingmen over whose affairs they were chosen to preside.

While such men as Sylvis were struggling, on behalf of their constituents, to reach a higher ground on which to base the just claims of labor, their best efforts were being retarded by the men for whom they battled. It was the hope of the men who were in the fore-front of labor's hosts but little over a quarter of a century ago that the toiler would heed the call to reach forth and take not only the ballot, but the man it placed in power, and make use of both for the common good. It is on record that when the circular which called attention to the proposed formation of the National Labor Union was read before a subordinate branch of a trade union, the president of the national body to which the union was attached was denounced most bitterly in a set of resolutions which were denominated by the framers as " a set of ringing and timely resolutions which called the head of the order back to first principles, and taught him not to attempt to lead the rank and file into the tortuous paths of politics." The efforts of those who stood on the watch-tower were neutralized, but still they fought their way, manfully, vigorously and intelligently, even though they were not as successful as they, in the first flush of enthusiasm, believed that they would be. It is the part of wisdom for a man to refrain from entering

a contest or a controversy when the odds are sure to be against him.
If he permits his good sense to be overruled by the taunts or jeers of
bystanders or friends, he is sure to enter a losing game. If he stands
in dread of losing prestige by reason of a failure to show his strength
or courage by engaging in a struggle of any kind, and for these reasons
enters upon a struggle, he enters it with the chances against him. In
such a predicament as that just pictured did the trade-union leader
often find himself in the early days of trade unionism in the United
States. The word arbitration was as yet unspoken; successful efforts
at conciliation were unknown; neither employer nor employe thought
of employing such weapons except in the rarest of cases. The strike,
which was, at first, forced on the workmen in order to get a hearing,
soon became the recognized weapon of defense with organized and
unorganized workmen. Whenever a dispute arose between the
employers and workmen, the latter crowded excitedly to the meeting-
room of the union, if they were organized; if they were not organized,
they would begin at once to look about for some means of gaining
admission to a society. No matter what efforts would be made by the
officers to restrain the men, they felt that to lose a moment would
imperil their prospects. It very seldom happened that the strike was
averted; and once entered upon, whether legally or otherwise, the
chief officers of the union were expected to approve of it. If a word
of caution came from headquarters it was regarded as cowardice; if
the executive intimated that the men were wrong, it was whispered
that he had sold out to the "boss," and the whisper once started
gained in volume and sound until it became both loud and threatening.

It required the presence of a brave man at the helm to succeed in
impressing it upon the minds of the laboring men that the strike was
not the only remedy; but brave men were found in every trade union,
who, having studied the question more closely than the rank and file,
whose long hours of hard labor did not allow them much of leisure in
which to read or study, came to the front and took the ground that
laboring men had the same right to study social, economic and political questions that their employers had, and that, until they did so act,
their condition would continue to grow worse instead of better.

It was through the efforts of such men that the convention of the
Machinists' and Blacksmiths' National Union, which met in 1863,
appointed a committee to sit during recess and request the other
National and International Trade Unions to appoint similar committees to meet with them and draw up a plan for the formation of a
National Trade Assembly, to facilitate the advancement of the
interests of labor by the formation of subordinate Trade Assemblies.
When this proposition came before the convention of the Iron Moulders' Union in 1864, it was recommended by the President, Mr. Sylvis,

as "being well worthy of the highest consideration of the convention, and should be acted on favorably."

The convention adopted the resolution without any serious objections, and the committee was appointed to meet with that from the Machinists' and Blacksmiths' Union and other trade unions. With the exception of the two unions named, no other organization took official action on the matter, and it died without issue. During the first years of the Civil War the various trade organizations made no progress, and most of them were entirely dismembered. The mechanics from every large centre enlisted in the army, and among those who were foremost would be found the officers of the local union. It is on record, in Philadelphia, where one union enlisted to a man; the entry made upon the records of the union reads: " It having been resolved to enlist with Uncle Sam for the war, this union stands adjourned until either the union is safe or we are whipped."

In consequence of the disturbed state of the country, and the changes which were being made everywhere in the methods of conducting business, the trade organizations became almost a thing of the past until it was made apparent to the mechanics that their labor was not appreciated by their employers. They saw a condition of affairs surrounding them which rendered it absolutely necessary that steps should be taken to protect the laborer from the encroachments of unscrupulous employers, political hucksters, and land and money speculators.

While the Civil War was in progress, if the President of the United States called for troops, the workingmen patriotically responded. If more troops than responded to the call were necessary, a draft was ordered and more men were taken from the forge, factory, mine and farm. It is true that men from other walks in life enlisted and did good service in the Union cause, but the great bulk of the army was made up of workingmen.

While the workingmen were enlisting in the service of their country, the bankers and owners of gold were working their way into Congress; many of them had closed their vaults and refused to loan a dollar to the government except at the very highest rate of interest. They suspended payment and made every effort to depreciate the United States currency, and when the war ended they had control of Congress. A speaker on the floor of the House of Representatives said, after looking around him: " I see the representatives of eighty banks sitting as members of this House."

These men enacted such legislation as was beneficial to themselves; they diminished the volume of currency and reduced the price of labor and property; they demanded gold bonds for their almost worthless paper, and changed the terms of contracts to give themselves gold instead of currency. Everything that entered into consumption in the poor man's home was heavily taxed in order to pay for gold. Monopolies were born and nourished, and the Congress of the United States gave them millions of acres of the nation's land.

Two dollars during the war would not purchase as much as one dollar before the breaking out of the struggle, and, until the working-men of the nation made a vigorous protest against the system of adhering to the ante-bellum price-list for labor done, the employers took no steps to advance the wages of their employes. The agitation for an increase in the prices paid to labor soon gained headway, and became successful without much effort; men were scarce, owing to the vast number who were required to serve as soldiers; work was plenty, and the increased earnings of the workingmen soon enabled them to live comfortably and save a great deal of the money which they received.

With the beginning of the agitation for increased wages began the reorganization of the unions that had languished or dwindled down during the early days of the war; the interest thus begun continued until the close of the rebellion, and greatly encouraged the men who had been so actively engaged in the organization of labor in 1859-'60 and 1861.

With the ending of the Civil War came the discharge, from the armies of the North and South, of upward of two millions of men who had been doing the work of destruction for four years. While in the army they were non-producers, but others were producing for them; when discharged from the army they at once entered into competition with the men who had remained at home. Those who returned to the walks of peace after the war flocked to the cities and towns in search of employment, where they were forced to the conclusion that, while the war for the preservation of the Union was over, the battle for the preservation of life itself was still being waged with unrelenting fury.

The summer of 1865 saw four millions of men standing where there was room for but two millions. Dull times were coming fast; distress was making itself felt in many places. Those who had served as soldiers in the Northern army had received such small pay that they had saved nothing, and the soldiers of the Southern army had served for nothing. The soldier of the Civil War had no opportunity, while in the service, of paying any attention to his private interests, and many a discharged veteran would have had to walk to his home in the North had the government not furnished him with transportation to his destination.

The soldiers had no opportunity while the war was going on to engage in the profitable business of " blockade running;" they could not interest themselves in contracting with the government for the sale of "shoddy" clothing; they were denied the privilege of making cheap shoes for large prices to sell to the government for the use of its soldiers; they were not permitted to engage in speculation in gold, for Wall Street had a monopoly of that; they had no chance to engage in the gambling and speculation which began to run riot while the very life of the nation was hanging in the balance, and while they were periling life, limb and happiness to maintain the unity and honor of the nation; consequently they were through sheer necessity obliged to offer their services to employers for less than half what they were worth in order to maintain life, and wherever they did find employment it was where others had been displaced.

An advertisement for a mechanic, that would, during the war, run a whole week before an applicant would make his appearance, would bring a dozen to the door of the factory or mill, before the ink was dry on the paper in which it appeared, in the autumn of 1865. With so many men competing for the same position, it became an easy matter for the employer of labor to dictate what wages he should pay.

It then began to dawn on the minds of the wage-earners that other remedies than the strike and the regulation of the apprenticeship question must be applied, and those who advocated organization on a broader basis than that on which the trade union was founded at last secured an audience to listen to them.

What failed of accomplishment in 1864 received its first impetus in 1865, when that small but determined band of men, headed by Captain Richard F. Trevellick of Detroit, met in the city of Louisville, Ky., to discuss the best means of securing the attention of the trade unions to matters of greater concern than they had heretofore considered. Twelve men assembled in Louisville, representing none of the organizations to which they were attached; they came together after corresponding for some time, and met there to take counsel from each other in the hope of arriving at some conclusion that would enable them to arouse the toiler to a true sense of his surroundings.

Trevellick was at that time President of the Ship Carpenters' Union; Burleigh of Indiana was a member of the Machinists' and Blacksmiths' Union, as was Bailey of Missouri; John Blake of Chicago was one of the owners of the *Workingmen's Advocate;* William H. Gudgeon of Cincinnati, Ohio, was of the Shipwrights' and Calkers' Union, as was Thomas K. Knowles of Buffalo, N. Y.; John W. Krepp was a glasscutter from Pittsburg, Pa.; Whittier of Massachusetts was a member of the Carpenters' and Joiners' Union; Sinsnick of Detroit came from the printing office, and was a member of the Printers' Union; Clafflin of St. Louis, Mo., was a carpenter; Boyer of Kentucky and William Harding, coachmaker, of Brooklyn, N. Y., made up the twelve men who took the first step beyond trade lines in the organization of labor in America. These men adopted no platform at that meeting, but united in issuing a call to all organized bodies of workingmen to meet the following year in Baltimore, Md., for the purpose of perfecting an organization.

It was decided at the meeting to send Trevellick to the South for the purpose of making an attempt to rekindle the fires of organization that had died out during the war. On the 26th of March, 1866, William Harding and William H. Sylvis held a conference with some others and decided upon the date of the Baltimore meeting. A call was issued to all organizations to send delegates to Baltimore on the 20th of August following. It is not known whether it was contemplated by those who issued the call to engage in politics from a party stand-point, but that it was the intention to take political action in some manner or other is evident from the call which went forth. After reciting the recent depressions in the labor world and the evils which beset the mechanic from the overcrowded markets, it says: " The agitation of the question of eight hours as a day's labor has assumed an importance requiring concerted and harmonious action upon all matters appertaining to the inauguration of labor reforms, and it is essential that a national congress be held to form a basis upon which we may harmoniously and concertedly move in its prosecution."

Sixty-four representative men assembled in Baltimore to attend the first convention. Among them were John Hinchcliffe of Illinois; J. C. C. Whalley of Washington, D. C.; Thomas Dolan of Detroit, Mich.; A. C. Cameron of Illinois; William Cathers of Baltimore, Md.; William Harding of Brooklyn, N. Y.; Thomas A. Armstrong of Pennsylvania; John Ennis of New York City ; Edward Schleger of Illinois; John Oberly of ———; Phelps and Gibson of Connecticut, and many other well-known reformers.

When the convention assembled, Mr. Sylvis, through whose efforts more than those of any other man the meeting was successfully called, could not attend on the account of illness. Mr. William Cathers of Baltimore called the body to order and read the call under which the delegates assembled. A. C. Cameron, editor of the *Workingmen's Advocate*, nominated John Hinchcliffe of Illinois as temporary president of the assemblage.

The discussion took a wide range, embracing such questions as related to eight hours, trade unionism as a means of elevating the workingmen, co-operation, the currency and national debt questions, and the swindling of the people in the rapid absorption of the public lands. Such questions as these were entirely new to many of the delegates, who vigorously protested against allowing the debates to extend any further than the eight-hour subject; but there were students in the convention who determined that it would not adjourn until at least a few of the evils which oppressed the people had been thoroughly ventilated.

As the debates progressed a desire on the part of some to advise that political action be taken by the industrial masses made itself manifest. A recommendation was offered which contained the following words: "That no workingman should vote for any aspirant to public office who fails to pledge himself to the eight-hour doctrine." It is true that all who were present at that meeting were unanimous in the opinion that an industrial party should be formed, but the majority did not deem it prudent or advisable to inaugurate such a movement at that time; they realized how hard it was to secure the attendance of the representatives of the trade organizations, and those who did not belong to such organizations did not insist on or advise the formation of a political party at that session.

One of those who advocated the immediate organization of a party said, during the debate on the resolution to form a National Labor Party, that he wanted "a specific and decisive plan of action which could not be misunderstood. A new party of the people must and will be in the minority when first formed. But what of that? Persever.ance will win converts, and time will bring victory; and if we are unwilling to make a sacrifice of time and employ persistent effort, we are undeserving of victory now or hereafter. It is useless to hold conventions if we fear to rub against the time-honored prejudices of those who would be with us to-day but for those prejudices. A new party must be formed if we would win any lasting results, and it must be composed of the elements of American labor. We are shy of fighting the old political parties, but should not be so. If we are right, and I believe we are, let us go ahead. The Free-soil Party originated with a few hundred votes, but had it not been formed Lincoln would never have been President of the United States. This is a central committee of labor, and it must propose some definite plan of action for the future. A political question is one that is always decided at the ballot-box, and here must this question be met."

While many eloquent and forcible speeches were made in behalf of the resolution, it failed of adoption by a large vote. When the body adjourned, it had adopted as a name for the future the National Labor Union. The preamble adopted declared that the "rapid and alarming encroachments of capital upon the rights of the producing classes of the United States have rendered it imperative that they should calmly and deliberately devise the most effective means by which the same may be arrested."

In the resolutions which were adopted it was declared: "That the first and grand desideratum of the hour, in order to deliver the labor of the country from this thraldom, is the enactment of a law whereby eight hours shall be made to constitute a legal day's work in every State of the American Union." Resolutions favoring other reforms were adopted, and workingmen were advised to watch more carefully the men who were elected to legislative positions. Co-operation was recommended; the support of the newspapers devoted to the interests of the industrial masses was also recommended. A resolution which pledged the support of the members to the "sewing-women and daughters of toil of the United States" was adopted after a stormy debate. The tenement-house evil, which had at that early day began its work of death, was denounced, and reforms advocated. A resolution which declared that the whole of the public domain should be disposed of to actual settlers only was passed without a dissenting vote.

When the Committee on Trade Unions and Strikes made its report a lengthy discussion ensued, but the report was adopted. It recommended the organization of all workmen into unions of their trades and the association of all who had no trades into general labor unions, a more rigid enforcement of the apprenticeship system as a preventive against filling shops with "botch mechanics," and the establishment of workingmen's lyceums and reading-rooms.

In regard to strikes the committee reported as their "deliberate opinion that, as a rule, they are productive of great injury to the laboring classes; that many have been injudicious and ill-advised, and the result of impulse rather than principle and reason; that those who have been the fiercest in their advocacy have been the first to advocate submission; and on these grounds recommend that they be discountenanced, except as a last resort and after all means of effecting an amicable settlement have been exhausted;" and that each Trade Assembly appoint an Arbitration Committee for the settlement of all disputes between employer and employed, "by the earlier adoption of which means we believe the majority of the ill-advised so-called strikes would have been prevented."

The convention elected J. C. C. Whalley of Washington, a printer and a man of scholarly attainments and great executive abilities, as president. A committee that had been appointed by the convention waited on President Johnson to present to him a copy of the proceedings of the congress. John Hinchcliffe was chairman of the committee, and acted as the spokesman when introduced to the President, who, in responding to the address of the committee, said that he was in thorough sympathy with them on the questions of convict labor and the reservation of the public lands, and showed them his message to Congress, in which he said, after calling attention to the successful operation of the Homestead Act: "The homestead policy was established after long and earnest resistance. Experience proves its wisdom. The lands in the hands of industrious settlers, whose labor creates wealth and contributes to the public resources, are worth more to the United States than if they had been reserved as a solitude for future purchasers."

Before adjourning, the convention, which did not adopt a platform, appointed a committee to prepare and present to the next meeting a declaration of principles. This committee consisted of A. C. Cameron, Chairman; R. F. Trevellick, who at that time was in the South and could not attend the convention; John W. Krepps, Thomas A. Armstrong, John Hinchcliffe, William Harding, ———— Phelps, and one or two others.

•On the 14th of December following a convention was called at Ionia, Mich., for the purpose of acting in concert with the National Labor Union. This convention drew up a platform, adopted and published it to the world on December 18, 1866. The chairman of the committee which drew up the platform was R. F. Trevellick, who was elected delegate to the Chicago Convention and there presented the platform of the Michigan State Convention, which, with the substitution of the word national for State, was adopted by that body.

From the adjournment of the Baltimore Convention to the assembling of the Chicago meeting but little was done in the way of organizing branches of the National Labor Union. In fact, there was little or no interest shown in the work by the members of trade unions, who gave what time they could spare to the building up of the organizations of their own particular occupations.

It was found when the convention of the National Labor Union met in Chicago in 1867 that no progress had been made in the way of organizing subordinate labor unions. The Baltimore Convention made no provision for the raising of a revenue with which to push the work of organization, and, while it set forth certain principles, it took no steps to put any of them in practical operation. With the exception of calling on the President of the United States, there was no effort made in the direction of agitation. All the work fell on the shoulders of a patient, hard-working few, who labored zealously, and were instrumental in bringing the convention together in Chicago. That body, when assembled, saw a great many of the men who had been at the meeting the year previous, but they were not encouraged by the sight of as many new faces as they had hoped to see.

It was at this convention that the first reference was made to the establishment of a National Labor Bureau. To William H. Sylvis belongs the credit of making the recommendation favoring its establishment by Congress. The financial feature was discussed at this session, and, although it met with a formidable opposition at first, it passed by a handsome majority, after its advocates were accorded an opportunity of expressing themselves freely upon the subject. While this meeting approached nearer to perfection than its predecessor, it was found after adjournment that little that was practical had been done to assist in the work of organizing during the year, and, as a consequence, the work between the adjournment of the convention and the convening of the next session of the National Labor Union, which was held in New York City in August, 1868, was insignificant. The agitation was not in proportion to the actual work which was done, for no steps that could be taken were left untrod to bring the principles of the union before the world.

The number of labor papers in existence at that time was exceedingly limited; those that were being published received but little encouragement, and the subscription lists were in proportion to the encouragement. Up to this time a persistent silence had been observed by the daily press of the land as to the real aims of the organization. Its name was seldom mentioned in the papers except in terms of ridicule or reproach.

The right of the workingmen to take action on the subject of the currency of the United States was at that time seriously questioned. It was an unpardonable offense to suggest to Congress that it should take notice of the "issue of legal-tender paper money or an issue of government bonds bearing a low rate of interest." The name of the association had been extensively advertised, however, between the sessions of 1867 and 1868, particularly among workingmen.

A public meeting in the interest of labor at that day was a novelty, and the man who had the temerity to address such a gathering would be sure to meet with a storm of abuse and ridicule. It made no difference what was said or done at a meeting of workingmen, the report of the proceedings in the papers of the following day would be the same. The meeting would be characterized as a "gathering of the rag-tag and bob-tail of the community;" "the worst element was out last night to hear a kid-gloved, oily-tongued, sleek-faced demagogue hold forth in an incendiary, blood-curdling speech on the rights of horny-handed workingmen."

The editorials of the papers of that day, after giving a burlesque description of the meeting and the speaker, would sometimes suggest that such meetings should be frowned down, suppressed or discountenanced by the better element of society. Instances are not rare where personal violence has been hinted at as a preventive of such meetings. Among the names applied to labor speakers of that day we find: "Communist, socialist, Molly Maguire, incendiary, blood-and-thunder spouter, hungry-looking loafer, a sinister-faced wretch whose company could be dispensed with in this community, a fellow whose appearance suggested a recent visit to the penitentiary; a fellow who violently gesticulated and frothed at the mouth for half an hour without saying anything; and a blatherskite, who had the audacity to stand before a body of workingmen to tell them of their wrongs, while he himself was dressed in a suit of broadcloth. Such creatures should be treated as they deserve by the honest toilers, and sent out of town in a suit of tar and feathers." These and many more choice epithets were applied to those who spoke from the public platform in that early day of labor reform. Not only was the speaker abused and ridiculed, but the chairman of the meeting was discharged in nearly every instance, and many of those who attended were "spotted" and stood in fear and trembling for many a day after the meeting was held. Neither prejudice, abuse, ridicule, blacklisting nor the many methods which were resorted to to stem the tide of agitation proved effectual, and from stage to stage the work of educating the laboring man to a sense of his duty to himself was continued by the few who had taken up the gauntlet in defense of the poor.

From the time the National Labor Union was first organized, those who had been instrumental in bringing it before the public had busied themselves in agitating for the enactment, by the United States government, of a law establishing the eight-hour system among the employes of the government. It was strictly enjoined upon those who were present at the convention at Chicago to call upon or write to as many Congressmen and United States Senators as possible, and to urge others to do the same. Communications appearing from time to time in the press advising and urging the nomination of a labor ticket, to be run in the next presidential campaign, were invariably coupled with the demand for the short-hour working day. In this way the eight-hour movement received an impetus which had its effect on the legislation of that year.

The views of leading labor advocates were asked for by members of the National Legislature, and bills were introduced having the establishment of the eight-hour day in view. It was claimed that if the government would set the example by limiting the number of hours to eight, it would have a salutary effect on the employers of labor throughout the nation. With the government operating its works on the short-hour plan, it was supposed that in time the factories of the land would adopt the plan and establish the system everywhere.

On the 25th of June, 1868, after a long and bitter debate, Congress passed a law which declared eight hours to be a legal day's work for employes of the government. The law will be found in the "Revised Statutes of the United States." It is in the following language:

Section 3738. Eight hours shall constitute a day's work for all laborers, workmen and mechanics who may be employed by or on behalf of the government of the United States.

The passage of this law had a good effect on the agitation which was carried on during the remainder of that year, and called the attention of workingmen to the necessity for organization as a means of improving their condition.

This was the first thing that attracted the attention of the leading papers to the movement, then going on among the organized trades, for the establishment of a national organization that would embrace all branches of toil. Up to this time silence was the rule in dealing with the question of organization; the success which attended the efforts of those who advocated the eight-hour system before the United States Congress caused some alarm in manufacturing circles for awhile, but the movement had not reached such proportions as would justify either employer or press in making an attack upon it.

When the National Labor Union assembled in convention in New York in 1868 considerable interest was manifested in its deliberations by men in various walks of life. It was not because the organization was expected to strengthen the political parties of that day that this interest was shown. The one-absorbing question with many who assembled in New York at that meeting was: "Will the National Union advocate the formation of a separate and independent political party before it adjourns?"

It was plain to most of the delegates that many of the reforms that were advocated must be brought to an issue through political action; as a consequence, those parts of the platform of 1867 that favored measures requiring political action were bitterly opposed by many delegates who were so firmly wedded to party that the thought of voting for any but the regular candidate, even though his election would assure the passage of the desired measure, seemed like a sacrilege.

Partisan prejudice was at that time strongly bedded in the workingmen, and it required an education, which they had not then received, to enable them to philosophically view the introduction of measures which might one day force them to take action against the party to which they were at that time attached. They could not tolerate the idea of defiling labor by bringing it into contact with politics. Politics meant corruption and fraud. Why should workingmen have anything to do with politics except as members of a party?

There were trade unionists at that time who had been engaged in politics for years on their own account. They were not acting under any instructions from the unions they belonged to when they took political action; and it was well for them that their fellow-members were not aware of the extent of their bargaining, for it was a notorious fact that many men of pretended influence in trade unions had traded on that influence with both of the political parties. Such men were bitterly opposed to the introduction of any resolution to a labor society that would tend to weaken their allegiance to the party of their choice. Politics were bad and politicians were corrupt, but, as bad and corrupt as they were, they were none too bad or corrupt to prevent many of those who were loudest in their opposition to politics among workingmen from selling their votes and pretended influence to those who were foolish enough to buy. Among this latter class of workingmen the planks in the platform of the National Labor Union, which suggested political action, were particularly distasteful. The influence of this class of reformers was exercised in the various trade unions of the land. Political measures being new, and up to that time supposed to be foreign to the trade unions, these men had but little trouble in defeating resolutions which favored connection with the National Labor Union. In many of the unions that had affiliated with the National Union were men who secretly antagonized the movement. It was of this class that Mr. Sylvis must have been thinking when, in 1868, he wrote :

" The very greatest drawback to the labor reform movement is the fact that the trade unions hold themselves aloof from it. This is not only a singular, but a very unfortunate fact. If it were possible to make all the trade unions in the country see the importance of this movement, and appreciate the fact that if we can succeed in establishing our monetary system as the law of the land it would so change the whole face of society as to do away with the necessity for trade unions entirely, there would be no trouble to accomplish the whole labor-reform movement in a very short time. I have long since come to the conclusion that no permanent reform can ever be established through the agency of trade unions as they are now and have been conducted. They are purely defensive in their character ; and experience has taught all of us who have been for any considerable time connected with them that to keep them alive at all requires a continued struggle and a vast expenditure of time and money. The organization I have the honor to represent has spent money enough within the past ten years to have effected an entire revolution in our monetary system, and secure whatever Congressional legislation we may need. Within the past ten years we have spent a million and a half of dollars ; and to-day we have the same struggles to maintain ourselves we ever had, and there will be no end to it until the workingmen of the country wake up to the necessity of seeking a remedy through the ballot-box. All the evils under which we groan are legislative ; that is, they are the result of bad laws, and there is no way to reach the matter and effect a cure but by a repeal of those laws, and this can only be done through political action."

In the convention of 1868 were men who favored immediate political action on an independent basis ; there were men who advocated the reverse, and claimed that the workingmen should not take political action at all ; and there were a number of men in the convention, wise, cautious and farseeing, who saw that to take action either way would not result in harmony, and they advocated the adoption of a platform containing such measures as were political in their nature without suggestion as to how they were to be enacted into law. It was the belief of the men who took the conservative middle ground that education would in time bring these measures prominently to the front, and make friends for them with men of all parties. It mattered little to

them what the name of the party was, so long as it took up and advocated measures of relief for the suffering poor. When the convention
reached this frame of mind the adoption of a declaration of principles
became easy of accomplishment. Those who objected to it on the
grounds above set forth withdrew their opposition, and the convention
approved of the platform.

After the platform was adopted the discussion on the formation of a
political party was resumed, and the convention resolved that the
organization should be continued in its present form for some time to
come. It was also decided to instruct the officers-elect to work for the
formation of a new party, to be composed of all classes and grades of
laboring men—"from mill, mine, factory, forge and farm."

A feature which was discussed at that session with considerable
warmth was that which related to the workingwomen of the land.
Up to that time the admission of women to labor societies was
unknown, and the innovation on a time-honored custom was not
hailed with any degree of enthusiasm by many who ardently advocated
the right of man to all the blessings of earth. The resolution, which
was finally adopted, received the opposition of those who were not
partial to its adoption for a long time after the convention adjourned.

This convention elected William H. Sylvis, President, and instructed
him to proceed with the work of organizing subordinate branches of
the National Labor Union throughout the United States.

The platform on which the association entered upon its third year
is as follows:

"PLATFORM OF THE NATIONAL LABOR UNION.

" We hold these truths to be self-evident: that all people are created
equal; that they are endowed by their Creator with certain inalienable rights; that among them are life, liberty and the pursuit of happiness; that, to secure these rights, governments are instituted among
men, deriving their just powers from the consent of the governed.

" That there are but two pure forms of government: the autocratic
and the democratic. Under the former, the will of the individual
sovereign is the supreme law; under the latter, the sovereignty is
vested in the whole people; all other forms being a modification of
the one or the other of these principles; and that ultimately one or
the other of these forms must prevail throughout all civilized nations,
and it is now for the American people to determine which of those
principles shall triumph.

" That the design of the founders of the Republic was to institute a
government upon the principle of absolute inherent sovereignty of the
people, that would give to each citizen the largest political and religious liberty compatible with the good order of society, and secure to
each the right to enjoy the fruits of his labor and talents; that when

the laws are enacted destructive of these ends they are without moral binding force, and it is the right and duty of the people to alter, amend or abolish them and institute such others, founding them upon the principles of equality, as to them may seem most likely to affect their prosperity and happiness.

"Prudence will indeed dictate that important laws long established should not be changed for light and transient causes; and experience has shown that the American people are more disposed to suffer, while evils are sufferable, than to change the forms and laws to which they have been accustomed. But when a long train of legislative abuses, pursuing invariably the same object, evinces a design to subvert the spirit of freedom and equality upon which our institutions are founded, and reduce them to a state of servitude, it is their right, it is their duty, to abolish such laws and provide new guards for their future security. Such has been the patient suffering of the wealth-producing classes of the United States, and such is the necessity which constrains them to put forth an organized and united effort for maintaining their natural rights, which are imperiled by the insidious schemes and unwarranted aggression of unscrupulous bankers and usurpers by means of unwise and corrupt legislation.

"We further hold that all property or wealth is the product of physical or intellectual labor employed in productive industry, and in the distributions of the productions of labor; that laborers ought of right, and would, under a just monetary system, receive or retain the larger proportion of their productions; that the wrongs, oppressions and destitution which laborers are suffering in most departments of legitimate enterprise and useful occupation do not result from insufficiency of production, but from the unfair distribution of the products of labor between non-producing capital and labor.

"That money is the medium of distribution to non-producing capital and producing labor, the rate of interest determining what proportion of the products of labor shall be awarded to capital for its use and what to labor for its productions; that the power to make money and regulate its value is an essential attribute of sovereignty, the exercise of which is, by the Constitution of the United States, wisely and properly granted to Congress; and it is the imperative duty of Congress to institute, upon such a wise and just basis that it shall be directly under the control of the sovereign people who produce the value it is designed to represent, measure and exchange, that it may be a correct and uniform standard of value, and distribute the products of labor equitably between capital and labor according to the service of labor performed in their production.

"That the law enacting the so-called national banking system is a delegation by Congress of the sovereign power to make money and regulate its power to a class of irresponsible banking associations, thereby giving to them the power to control the value of all the property in the nation, and to fix the rewards of labor in every department of industry, and is inimical to the spirit of liberty and subversive of the principles of justice upon which our democratic-republican institutions are founded, and without warrant in the Constitution ; justice, reason and sound policy demand its immediate repeal, and the substitution of legal-tender Treasury notes as the exclusive currency of the nation.

" That this monopoly is the parent of all monopolies—the very root and essence of slavery—railroads, warehouses and all other monopolies, of whatever kind and nature, are the outgrowth of and subservient to this power, and the means used by it to rob the enterprising, industrial, wealth-producing classes of the products of their talents and labor.

" That as government is instituted to protect life and secure the rights of property, each should share its just and proper proportion of the burdens and sacrifices necessary for its maintenance and perpetuity; and that the exemption from taxation of bank capital and government bonds, bearing double and bankrupting rates of interest, is a species of unjust class legislation, opposed to the spirit of our institutions and contrary to the principles of sound morality and enlightened reason.

" That our monetary, financial and revenue laws are, in letter and spirit, opposed to the principles of freedom and equality upon which our democratic-republican institutions are founded. There is in all their provisions manifestly a studied design to shield non-producing capital from its just proportion of the burdens necessary for the support of the government, imposing them mainly on the industrial, wealth-producing classes, thereby condemning them to lives of unremunerated toil, depriving them of the ordinary conveniences and comforts of life, of the time and means necessary for social enjoyment, intellectual culture and moral improvement, and ultimately reducing them to a state of practical servitude.

" We further hold that, while these unrighteous laws of distribution remain in force, laborers cannot, by any system of combination or co-operation, secure their natural rights; that the first and most important step toward the establishment of the rights of labor is the institution of a system of true co-operation between non-producing capital and labor ; that, to effect this most desirable object, money— the medium of distribution to capital and labor—must be instituted upon such a wise and just principle that, instead of being a power to centralize the wealth in the hands of a few bankers, usurers, middlemen and non-producers generally, it shall be a power that will distribute products to producers in accordance with the labor or service performed in their production—the servant and not the master of labor. This done, the natural rights of labor will be secured, and co-operation in production and in the distribution of products will follow as a natural consequence. The weight will be lifted from the back of the laborer, and the wealth-producing classes will have the time and the means necessary for social enjoyment, intellectual culture and moral improvement, and the non-producing classes compelled to earn a living by honest industry. We hold that this can be effected by the issue of Treasury notes, made a legal tender in the payment of all debts, public and private, and convertible, at the option of the holder, into government bonds, bearing a just rate of interest, sufficiently below the rate of increase in the national wealth by natural production as to make an equitable distribution of the products of labor between non-producing capital and labor, reserving to Congress the right to alter the same when, in their judgment, the public interest would be promoted thereby ; giving the government creditor the right to take the lawful money or the interest-bearing bonds at his election, with the privilege to the holder to reconvert the bonds into money or the money into bonds, at pleasure.

" We hold this to be the true American or people's monetary system, adapted to the genius of our democratic-republican institutions, in harmony with the letter and spirit of our Constitution, and suited to the wants of the government and business interests of the nation ; that it would furnish a medium of exchange, having equal power, a uniform value, and fitted for the performance of all the functions of money, coextensive with the jurisdiction of government ; that, with a just rate per cent. interest on the government bonds, it would effect the equitable distribution of the products of labor between non-producing capital and labor, giving to laborers a fair compensation for their products and to capital a just reward for its use ; remove the necessity for excessive toil, and afford the industrial classes the time and means necessary for social and intellectual culture. With the rate of interest at three per cent. on the government bonds, the national debt would be liquidated within less than thirty years, without the imposition or collection of a farthing of taxes for that purpose. Thus it would dispense with the hungry horde of assessors, tax-gatherers and government spies, who are harassing the industrial classes and despoiling them of their subsistence.

" We further hold that it is essential to the happiness and prosperity of the people and the stability of our democratic-republican institutions that the public domain be distributed as widely as possible among the people, a land monopoly being equally as oppressive to the people and dangerous to our institutions as the present money monopoly. To prevent this, the public lands should be given in reasonable quantities, and to none but actual occupants.

" We further hold that intelligence and virtue in the sovereignty are necessary to a wise administration of justice ; that as our institutions are founded upon the theory of sovereignty in the people, in order to their preservation and perpetuity, it is the imperative duty of Congress to make such wise and just regulations as shall afford all the means of acquiring the knowledge requisite to the intelligent exercise of the privileges and duties pertaining to sovereignty; that Congress should ordain that eight hours' labor, between the rising and setting of the sun, should constitute a day's work in all government works and places where the national government has exclusive jurisdiction; and that it is equally imperative on the several States to make like provision by legal enactment. Be it therefore unanimously

"*Resolved*, That our first duty is now to provide, as speedily as possible, a system of general organization in accordance with the principles herein more specifically set forth, and that each branch of industry shall be left to adopt its own particular form of organization, subject only to such restraint as may be necessary to place each organization within line, so as to act in harmony in all matters pertaining to the welfare of the whole, as well as each of the parts; and that it is the imperative duty of each individual, in each and every branch of industry, to aid in the formation of such labor organizations in their respective branches, and to connect themselves therewith.

"CO-OPERATION.

"*Resolved*, That in co-operation, based upon just financial and revenue laws, we recognize a sure and lasting remedy for the abuse of the present industrial system; and that, until the laws of the nation can be remodeled so as to recognize the rights of men instead of classes, the system of co-operation, carefully guarded, will do much to lessen the evils of our present system. We, therefore, hail with delight the organization of co-operative stores and workshops, and would urge their formation in every section of the country and in every branch of business.

" WOMAN'S LABOR.

"*Resolved*, That with the equal application of the fundamental principles of our republican-democratic government, and a sound monetary system, there could be no antagonism between the interests of the workingmen and workingwomen of this country, nor between any of the branches of productive industry, the direct operation of each, when not prevented by unjust monetary laws, being to benefit all the others by the production and distribution of the comforts and necessaries of life; and that the adoption by the national government of the financial policy set forth in this platform will put an end to the oppression of workingwomen, and is the only means of securing to them as well as to the workingmen the just reward of their labor.

"*Resolved*, That we pledge our individual and undivided support to the sewing-women and daughters of toil in this land, and would solicit their hearty co-operation, knowing, as we do, that no class of industry is so much in need of having their condition ameliorated as the factory operatives, sewing-women, etc., of this country.

"CONVICT LABOR.

"*Resolved*, That we demand the abolishment of the system of convict labor in our prisons and penitentiaries, that the labor performed by convicts shall be that which will least conflict with the honest industry outside of the prisons, and that the wares manufactured by the convict shall not be put upon the market at less than the current market rates.

"IMPROVED DWELLINGS FOR LABORERS.

"*Resolved*, That we would urgently call the attention of the industrial classes to the subject of tenement-houses and improved dwellings, believing it to be essential to the welfare of the whole community that a reform should be effected in this respect, as the experience of the past has proved that vice, pauperism and crime are the invariable attendants of the overcrowded and illy-ventilated dwellings of the poor; and urge upon the capitalists of the country attention to the blessings to be derived from investing their means in the erection of such dwellings.

"INTELLECTUAL IMPROVEMENT.

"*Resolved*, That the formation of mechanics' institutes, lyceums and reading-rooms and the erection of buildings for that purpose are recommended to workingmen in all cities and towns as a means of advancing their social and intellectual improvement.

"REMEDY FOR INSUFFICIENT WORK.

"*Resolved*, That this Labor Congress would most respectfully recommend to the workingmen of the country that, in case they are pressed for want of employment, they proceed to become actual settlers; believing that, if the industry of the country can be coupled with its natural advantages, it will result both in individual relief and national advantages.

"*Resolved*, That where a workingman is found capable and available for office, the preference should invariably be given to such person."

A circular was issued soon after the adjournment of the convention by the president, in which he urged the immediate formation of local branches of the union. The document circulated principally among workingmen who were fortunate enough to be members of trade organizations. Among the many who knew nothing about the organizations of their trades the circular never circulated. The laws of most of the trade unions at that time forbade the discussion, or even the mention, of political matters in their meetings; and as the circular issued by Mr. Sylvis strongly urged the formation of a new party, it was not received with any degree of enthusiasm among mechanics who were members of trade unions. The subjoined extract from the circular in question will explain why it was not received with any warmth by those who were opposed to political action :

" The convention resolved to proceed at once to the organization of a ' Labor Reform Party, having for its object the election of representative men to our State and national councils.' The organization of a new party—a workingman's party—for the purpose of getting control of Congress and the several State Legislatures, is a huge work ; but it can and must be done. We have been the tools of professional politicians of all parties long enough. Let us now cut loose from all party ties and organize a workingman's party, founded upon honesty, economy and equal rights and equal privileges to all men. The day of monster monopolies and class legislation must come to a close. Let our motto be, ' Our God, our country, our currency.' Money has ruled us long enough, let us see if we cannot rule money for a time. We want equal taxation upon all property according to its real value, no matter whether it be in the shape of houses, lands or government bonds. Let our cry be REFORM—down with the moneyed aristocracy and up with the people. Now let every man and woman go to work. Do not wait. Remember that ' procrastination is the thief of time.' Let each one start out with a determination that we will make the President in 1872, and that between now and then we will control Congress and the State Legislatures. If we will but set out in earnest to accomplish this great work obnoxious laws will soon disappear from our statute books, plain, practical laws for the protection and encouragement of the deserving will take their place, and the drones who fatten upon the earnings of the poor will be compelled to make an honest living or starve. Don't let us wait to be pushed into a corner. Stop acting on the defensive—take the aggressive ; make war upon every opposing power ; have faith in the right, and success will come. I ask every one who may have a suggestion to make or a question to ask to put it on paper and send it to me. I shall proceed, with the aid of others, to adopt a system of operations as fast as possible."

The next convention of the National Labor Union was held in Cincinnati in the early part of the year 1869. It bore but little resemblance to the largely attended and enthusiastic gatherings of 1866, '67 and '68. Very few new faces were to be seen, and the greater number of those who had attended previous sessions were absent. Notwithstanding the discouraging reports which were made by the officers and delegates, it was resolved to continue to push the organization forward and to begin operations in the South at once. Richard F. Trevellick was elected President, and entered upon the discharge of his duties as hopefully as though he had a constituency running up into the millions, and as readily as though there were thousands in the treasury.

Immediately after the adjournment of the convention Mr. Trevellick started on his Southern trip, accompanied by Mr. Sylvis; the latter was at that time President of the Iron Moulders' International Union.

It was the intention to work jointly for the good of both organizations, but the apathy displayed by those who should be most enthusiastic and most deeply interested in the work of organization proved such a barrier to their progress that the work performed by Trevellick was not productive of much good. The seeds of dissolution had been sown, the novelty which attended the first appearance of the National Labor Union had worn off, and the interest died away even while these brave, earnest men were putting forth their best efforts to build the organization up in strength and usefulness. It was not in the power of any man or set of men to overcome the obstacles which presented themselves at every step. There was not a dollar in the treasury when the Southern trip was contemplated, and when Sylvis and Trevellick started on their journey it was with the knowledge and understanding that they would have to defray their own expenses. With them it was a labor of love, and the sacrifice they made was trifling compared with the work for humanity which they hoped to accomplish. The future, which seemed brightly opening up before them, was full of grand possibilities for the American workingman.

Although the proceedings of the National Labor Union had never been published for distribution, the work which had been done, and the effort which was at that time being made by the prominent men in the movement, brought the platform of the organization prominently before the people, and leading men in both parties began to examine and study the principles on which the National Labor Union laid claim to public favor. Students among workingmen laid the document carefully away among their papers to be referred to at frequent intervals for instruction and inspiration.

Once fairly before the people and undergoing the ordeal of investigation, the evil influences of the political trader began to make themselves manifest. Men who were anxious for notoriety and political preferment sought entry to the organization and began to advertise their membership to the workingmen of their localities, in the hope that such action on their part would assist them in a political way. This had a discouraging effect on the earnest men who had pioneered the movement, and who had given careful thought and years of toil to the rearing of the structure. They saw the very men who would profit most by the success of the association—the workingmen—turn away from it because it suggested to them that their safety lay in an honest administration of the political affairs of the government by the chosen servants of the people. They did not understand the needs of the hour, they rated good and bad as one in politics, and they looked with suspicion on everything that suggested political action.

This apprehension, or distrust, on the part of the workers was not without cause. On many an occasion they had been duped by office-holders who had professed friendship for the claims of labor up to the day of election, and at the closing of the polls forgot all the promises they had given to the laborer. Duplicity among politicians had so long been the rule that the name politician was at that time synonymous with rogue or thief. In too many cases the application of these terms was just and proper; but the evil, corrupting effects of dishonesty on the part of public servants had well-nigh worn out the patience of the people. They certainly caused the name of politician to be regarded with scorn by toilers throughout the land.

The office-seeker at that time loved the workingman for the votes he gave—only this and nothing more. When he saw the friends of labor organizing a National Labor Union, which held out a hope that the worker would eventually strive to better his condition in a political way, he at once became an applicant for membership in the local union next to him. If he did not know how to gain admittance, he always found some recreant member who felt more of a regard for the party to which this self-constituted workingman belonged than he did for the Labor Union, and in this way his name would be brought up for election. If objections were raised on account of past political treachery to labor's interests, the excuse would be made that he was reforming and would soon cast off the shackles of his party to work unselfishly for the interests of the industrial classes.

When this class of men gained admittance to the National Labor Union they at once set to work to create dissension among the members by hinting that the officers were robbing them; that they were being petted and courted by politicians; that they were selling out the interests committed to their charge; that they were seeking to divide the workingmen and make them powerless by withdrawing them from the parties that would one day reform every abuse if allowed to do it without the intervention of officious labor reformers, who, having worked all their lives in the shop, knew absolutely nothing about politics or their management.

By this system of deception the artful, cringing scoundrels who professed friendship for the workingmen, aided by knaves in the ranks of labor, soon gained a foothold in the National Labor Union sufficiently strong to neutralize in a month the work that such men as Sylvis and Trevellick had been doing for years. Pliant tools in the ranks of labor aided them, and soon the power of the organization began to wane until it finally disbanded.

The convention which met in Cincinnati in 1869, at which Mr.

Trevellick was elected President, was but the shadow of what it ought to have been, while the one held the succeeding year in St. Louis, Mo., was insignificant in point of numbers, and scarcely any better in point of enthusiasm.

When the last session adjourned, it had made some additions to the platform. They were published, but the work of the association, so far as active effort in the field of organization was concerned, was at an end, and the year 1872 saw the death of the National Labor Union, which, in 1868, had given promise of so much that was good to the laboring men of America. Were an epitaph to be written for the society, " Murdered in the house of its friends " would be a line most appropriate with which to begin. Men strong of heart, giants in intellect, determined and honest as ever breathed, had stepped forward in the ranks of labor and had given to the toiler a weapon with which to smite his enemy. These were the pioneers. They were few. Men, honest of heart and good in intention in the ranks of labor, listened to the voice of the slanderer, the political demagogue, the self-seeking fellow-toiler, the jealous-minded and the paid emissary of wealth. They were many. The many overruled the few, took from their hands labor's best defense, and while listening to the voice of the siren, who sings sweetest when her heart is full of hate, they said each trade for itself, each one for himself, each organization for itself; and, while proclaiming their ability to stand alone, began to quarrel among themselves and fall, one by one, victims of their own jealousy and carelessness.

Additional resolutions were adopted at the Cincinnati and St. Louis sessions of the National Labor Union, but were never given to the public for want of funds to publish them. They are as follows:

"*Resolved*, That the claim of the bondholders for payment of it (gold of that class of indebtedness known as 5-20 bonds, and the principal of which is legally and equitably payable in lawful money) is dishonest and extortionate; and hence we enter our solemn protest against any departure from the original contract, by funding the debt in long bonds, or in any increase of the gold-bearing and untaxed obligations of the government.

"*Resolved*, That justice demands that the burdens of the government should be so adjusted as to bear equally on all classes and interests; and that the exemption from taxation of government bonds, bearing extortionate rates of interest, is a violation of all just principles of revenue laws.

"*Resolved*, That Congress should modify the tariff so as to admit free the necessaries of life, and such articles of common use as we can neither produce nor grow ; also to lay duties for revenue mainly upon articles of luxury, and upon such articles of manufacture as (we having the raw material in abundance) will develop the resources of the country, increase the number of factories, give employment to more laborers; maintain good compensation, cause the immigration of skilled labor, the lessening of prices to consumers, the creating of a permanent home market for agricultural products, destroy the necessity for the odious and expensive internal taxation, and will soon enable us to successfully compete with the manufacturers of Europe in the markets of the world.

"*Resolved,* That the public lands of the United States belong to the people, and should not be sold to individuals, nor granted to corporations, but should be held as a sacred trust for the benefit of the people, and should be granted, free of cost, to landless settlers only, in amounts not exceeding one hundred and sixty acres of land.

"*Resolved,* That the treaty-making power of the government has no authority in the Constitution to "dispose of" the public lands without the joint sanction of the Senate and House of Representatives.

"*Resolved,* That as labor is the foundation and cause of national prosperity, it is both the duty and interest of the government to foster and protect it. Its importance, therefore, demands the creation of an executive department of the government at Washington, to be denominated the Department of Labor, which shall aid in protecting it above all other interests.

"*Resolved,* That the protection of life, liberty and property are the three cardinal principles of government, and the first two more sacred than the latter; therefore, money necessary for prosecuting wars should, as it is required, be assessed and collected from the wealth of the country, and not be entailed as a burden on posterity.

"*Resolved,* That we are unalterably opposed to the importation of a servile race, for the sole and only purpose of tampering with the labor of the American workingmen.

"*Resolved,* That the rights and interest of all useful industries are unitary, and, to be successful, must make common cause against their common enemies—unprincipled capitalists, dishonest legislators, and all monopolists of the products of human labor.

"*Resolved,* That we cordially invite and entreat all classes of workers—common, agricultural and skilled laborers—and all persons who sympathize with our efforts to protect and improve the condition of the producing classes, to unite heartily with us in placing in office men who truly represent the substantial interests of the whole country.

"*Resolved,* That we view with apprehension the tendency to military domination in the Federal government; that standing armies are dangerous to the liberties of the people; that they entail heavy and unnecessary burdens on the productive industries, and should be reduced to the lowest standard.

"*Resolved,* That the Union was sustained in the late struggle by the working classes, the citizen-soldiers of the Republic, who, when the battle was over, returned to the private walks of life and the productive industries, whereby the expenses of the war are being paid, the government supported, and the wealth of the country increased; that the officers of the army, who receive the highest pay and do the safest work, get all the honors and the highest pensions, do the least and get the best accommodations, and are now clamoring for positions which are sinecures, resisting the efforts to retire the surplus and to reduce their pay, demanding the continuance of a standing army beyond our necessity ; and that all this shows that patriotism is in the people, ambition and plunder in the officers, injustice and ingratitude in the government.

"*Resolved*, That we recognize in agricultural labor the base of all our supplies, and this interest is second to no other; and that we specially and heartily invite the farmers and workingmen with us in our efforts to improve ourselves and the country.

"*Resolved*, That what we call common or unskilled labor is an essential and indispensable element of support and wealth, and we cordially invite its co-operation in our efforts to improve the condition of the productive classes.

"*Resolved*, That inasmuch as both the present political parties are dominated by non-producing classes, who depend on public plunder for subsistence and wealth, and have no sympathy with the working millions beyond the use they can make of them for their own political and pecuniary aggrandizement; therefore, the highest interest of our colored fellow-citizens is with the workingmen, who, like themselves, are slaves of capital and politicians, and strike for liberty.

"*Resolved*, That the Indian has the same normal rights as any other type of the people; that he has an original and inalienable right to maintain his tribal condition ; and that any attempt on the part of government to force on him an unwilling citizenship is grossly unjust, and a blow at individual liberty.

"*Resolved*, That the management of our Indian affairs is wasteful, abortive and destructive of its own objects, and demands an immediate and radical reformation.

"*Resolved*, That women are entitled to equal pay for equal services with men ; that the practice of working women and children ten to fifteen hours per day, at starvation prices, is brutal in the extreme, and subversive of the health, intelligence and morality of the nation, and demands the interposition of law.

"*Resolved*, That we reaffirm our position in favor of the necessity and justice of the reduction of the hours of labor, as well as the obligation of all able-bodied persons to contribute to useful labor an equivalent for their support."

Almost simultaneously with the promulgation of these resolutions came the collapse of the organization, and those who would have published them to the world with favorable comment, had the society been strong in membership and treasury, scrupulously excluded all mention of them from the columns of the press.   It is well worth the time and patience of the student to read carefully the platform and additional resolutions of the National Labor Union, as they furnish a key to the condition of affairs of that day, and show conclusively that these early pioneers in the labor-reform movement were gifted with prophetic vision, for they clearly foresaw the evils which menaced the Republic, and which, though apparently insignificant at that time, were destined to develop and stretch out on every hand, gaining strength and power as they grew in years.

It will be borne in mind that these resolutions were written before the age of invention and electricity had given to wealth its present wonderful and matchless advantages.   They are all the more astonishing because of their accurate description of the condition of affairs which followed, and which we contemplate without wonder at the present day.

SEARCHING FOR THE TRUE PATH.

Never yet
Share of truth was vainly set
In the world's wide fallow.
After hands shall sow the seed,
After hands from hill and mead
Shall reap the harvest yellow.— *Whittier.*

It is a noticeable fact that while the efforts of the owners of capital are redoubled in the direction of entrenching themselves more securely in their possessions, while they leave nothing undone to add to their possessions, the men of labor neglect their organizations and pay no heed to the future. Steady employment at fair wages to-day drives all thought of loss of time, reduction of wages and poverty from the minds of the laboring men of America. Although times were not particularly brisk, they continued fair during the years 1870, '71, '72 and the early part of '73.

The power and usefulness of the National Labor Union having died away, its members became hopeless of accomplishing any lasting benefit or reform. Those who were members of trade unions took but little interest in these societies, and a consequent falling off in membership began to make itself manifest during the years 1872 and 1873. Many mechanics who had never belonged to a labor organization, having heard of the National Labor Union, began to make inquiries as to the existence of labor societies. The officers of trade unions clearly foresaw the danger to be apprehended from a continuation of the apathy which had fallen upon the members of these organizations.

The Presidents of the Machinists' and Blacksmiths' Union and the Coopers' International Union, whose headquarters were at Cleveland, Ohio, held a consultation and agreed to unite in issuing a call to the officers of all labor societies in the United States and Canada. Through the columns of the journals of the societies above mentioned the following call was issued:

"INDUSTRIAL CONGRESS.

"There will be an informal meeting of the Presidents of the National and International Trade organizations of America in Cleveland, Ohio, on the 19th of November, 1872, for the purpose of taking the initiative steps looking to the formation of an Industrial Congress of North America, to be composed of *bona fide* representatives of *bona fide* labor organizations. It is to be hoped that there will be a representative from every National or International Trade Union in America present at the meeting on the 19th inst.

" The principal object in the formation of an Industrial Congress is to unite the workingmen of America more closely, and through a unity of action on their part secure to themselves and their children the fruits of their labor, now enjoyed by those who have thus far succeeded by the aid of corrupt legislation to rob and plunder instead of laboring honestly for a livelihood. The informal meeting will no doubt result in issuing a call for a general meeting, to be composed of representatives of all labor organizations wishing or feeling disposed to send a representative.

" If the meeting on the 19th inst. will so decide we expect to see a larger meeting of *bona fide* representatives of workingmen than any ever held upon this continent. We make the announcement in order to prepare our unions and give them time for reflection and a full expression to their views upon this important matter."

The call, which was mailed to the officers of other labor organizations, was written by M. A. Foran, and was signed by him and two others—John Fehrenbatch and William Saffin; the latter was then President of the Iron Moulders' International Union. On the 19th of November only two men attended the conference, Messrs. Foran and Fehrenbatch.

These two men resolved to give an expression of their views to the members of their respective organizations, and to members of organized labor generally, through the columns of the journals which were published by them. Their efforts were not in vain, for the presidents of other labor organizations, who were editing journals in the interests of their societies, took upon themselves a portion of the burden, and by patient effort succeeded in calling a convention together in Cleveland on the 15th of July, 1873. The only labor organization in America that pronounced against the movement was the Brotherhood of Locomotive Engineers, with headquarters in Cleveland, and presided over at that time, as Grand Chief Engineer, by Charles Wilson.

This congress remained in session for several days and drew up a plan of action to be pursued during the coming year. No Constitution was adopted, at least none was issued until the following year. The officers who were elected to manage the affairs of the organization until the convening of the next congress were men of known ability and integrity. Their names and the positions to which they were elected were:

President—Robert Schilling of Ohio.
First Vice-President—Warrick J. Reed of Virginia.
Second Vice-President—Edward Sniggs of New York.
Third Vice-President—Hugh McLaughlin of Illinois.
Recording Secretary—Solluna Keeffe of Pennsylvania.
Treasurer—James Atkinson of Ohio.

The convention adjourned to meet in Rochester, N. Y., on the second Tuesday in April, 1874   Before concluding its labors, the convention adopted a platform or series of resolutions, from which the following extracts are taken :

" WHEREAS, The recent alarming development and aggressions of aggregated wealth, which, unless checked, will inevitably lead to the pauperization and hopeless degradation of the toiling masses, render it imperative, if we desire to enjoy the blessings of the government bequeathed to us by the founders of the Republic, that a check should be placed upon the power and unjust accumulation of wealth. and a system adopted which will secure to the laborer the fruits of his toil ; and

" WHEREAS, This much-desired object can only be accomplished by the thorough unification of labor, and the united efforts of those who obey the divine injunction, ' In the sweat of thy face shalt thou eat bread;' and

" WHEREAS, While we recognize in the ballot-box an agency by which these wrongs can be reduced when other means fail, yet the great desideratum of the hour is the organization, consolidation and co-operative effort of the producing masses, as a stepping-stone to that education that will in the future lead to more advanced action, through which the necessary reforms can be obtained ; and

" WHEREAS, While we fully recognize the power and efficiency of trade and labor unions, local and international, as now organized, in regulating purely trade matters, yet upon all questions appertaining to their welfare, as a whole, the influence of these organizations without closer union must prove comparatively futile.   Therefore

"*Resolved*, That we submit to the people of the United States the objects sought to be accomplished by the Industrial Congress."

Twelve separate demands were made and submitted with the above preamble.   They were all approved without alteration or amendment at a subsequent meeting, and will appear in their regular order later on.

When installed into office as President of the Congress, Robert Schilling opened up an active campaign, and proceeded to sow the seed from which it was hoped the new organization would take root. He encountered a great deal of opposition from members of trade unions, who thought they saw the old National Labor Union's recommendation to take political action creeping to the front in the new organization.   Some of the men who were elected deputies to aid the president in his work failed to render any service at all, and the entire burden fell upon his shoulders.   Without funds or assistance he struggled along until the following year, when he issued the call for the second convention, and sent out the appended circular :

"To All Labor Organizations in the United States.

" On Tuesday, April 14, 1874, the second annual session of the Industrial Congress will convene in the city of Rochester, N. Y. Every organization, having for its object the amelioration of the condition of those who work for a living, is entitled to one representative upon payment of two cents for each of its members, for the purpose of defraying necessary expenses. I deem it entirely unnecessary to urge upon you the necessity of sending a representative. The events of the past few months have fully demonstrated the imperative necessity of a general unity of action among the toilers of the land. This can only be secured through a general congress of representative workingmen, and it is your duty to elect and send these on. Matters of the utmost importance to all workingmen will be considered at the session. Among others, the advisability of forming an organization of labor similar in its form, intents and purposes to the Patrons of Husbandry ; the applicability of the federative principles to trade unions, co-operation, arbitration, prison labor, etc., etc. Let no organization entitled to a delegate fail to elect and send one, so that the session alone, irrespective of its actions, may appear as a grand demonstration, and an emphatic protest of the industrial classes against the injustice done them by the consolidation of monopolies and the legislative powers of the nation.

" Yours in the cause of labor's redemption,

" Robert Schilling,
" *President of the Industrial Congress.*"

Pursuant to announcement the Industrial Congress of the United States convened in the second annual session in the city of Rochester, N. Y., April 14, 1874 ; continued in session four days, and adjourned on the 18th. The officers elected for the coming year were as follows:

President—Robert Schilling, Cleveland, Ohio.
First Vice-President—A. Warner St. John, Carthage, Mo.
Second Vice-President—Jackson H. Wright, Indianapolis, Ind.
Third Vice-President—T. C. Claiborn, Richmond, Va.
Fourth Vice-President—Christopher Kane, Rochester, N. Y.
Fifth Vice-President—O. E. Powers, W. Meriden, Conn.
Secretary—Byron Pope, Cleveland, Ohio.
Treasurer—P. K. Walsh, Cleveland, Ohio.

Deputies were appointed for thirty-one States, with power to organize local lodges of the order. The resolutions adopted at the previous session were amended and subjected to a number of changes. The preamble, or declaration of principles, received more attention at the hands of the convention than the Constitution, for the drafting of the Constitution was left to a committee of seven. Robert Schilling was made chairman of the committee, and to him the other members of the committee assigned the work of preparing and printing the Constitution. All that was done at the convention in the way of making a Constitution was to discuss measures without arriving at conclusions. It was left to the committee to prepare the Constitution, and so arrange it that it would harmonize with the spirit of the debates which took place during the session.

With the declaration of principles the convention was more particular, and to its construction the delegates devoted more time; and though the greater part of the preamble was drawn up by Mr. Schilling, the instrument in full received the sanction of the convention before it adjourned. Many of the delegates who attended that session had in former years been active as members of the National Labor Union. It was one of the latter who offered the platform of the old organization, and moved that it " be adopted by this congress as the declaration of principles under which to fight the future battles of the laboring man." The resolution was debated for some time, and was finally disposed of by referring the whole matter to a select committee, who prepared and presented a platform, which, after some debate on the financial feature, was adopted. Many delegates opposed taking action of any kind, which would appear as though the laboring men were presuming to dictate to the government what should be done in the way of providing a circulating medium or currency for the people of the United States. One delegate from Massachusetts asserted that " the workingmen have no right to interfere with so important a matter as the finances of the nation." The sentiment of the convention was that they should give an expression of opinion of the currency question, and one delegate voiced the sentiments of the majority when he said:

" The wealth producers of this nation are the men and women who dig, delve and spin. Upon their shoulders rests the burden of giving to all the people that which money merely represents—the wealth itself. Without toil there can be no wealth. He who toils is a wealthmaker. Being a wealthmaker, why should he not look after that which he creates? and why should he not look after that which represents the wealth that his hands, his brain, his skill and genius gives to the world? Money is only the representative of value. We make the value. Why, may I ask, should we not see to it that the value is honestly and fairly represented by an honest American currency based upon the real tangible possessions of the people of the United States, instead of a few imaginary golden dollars, which are themselves of no more value than their equivalent in intrinsic worth of any other metal which can be brought out of the earth? If that which comes from the earth, and only a small part of it at that, is what we base our currency upon, why should we not base it upon the whole of the earth within?"

At the close of his speech a vote was taken upon the adoption of the currency plank, and with one dissenting voice it was adopted. A delegate from Massachusetts was the only one who did not favor the measure, and he opposed it to the last.

The document is as follows:

"PREAMBLE OF THE INDUSTRIAL BROTHERHOOD.

" The recent alarming development and aggression of aggregated wealth, which, unless checked, will inevitably lead to the pauperization and hopeless degradation of the toiling masses, render it imperative, if we desire to enjoy the blessings of the government bequeathed to us by the founders of the Republic, that a check should be placed upon its power and unjust accumulation, and a system adopted which will secure to the laborer the fruits of his toil; and as this much-desired object can only be accomplished by the thorough unification of labor, and the united efforts of those who obey the divine injunction, 'In the sweat of thy face shalt thou eat bread,' we have formed the INDUSTRIAL BROTHERHOOD, with a view of securing the organization and direction, by co-operative effort, of the power of the industrial classes; and we submit to the people of the United States the objects sought to be accomplished by our organization, calling upon all who believe in securing ' the greatest good to the greatest number ' to aid and assist us:

" I. To bring within the folds of organization every department of productive industry, making knowledge a standpoint for action, and industrial, moral and social worth—not wealth—the true standard of individual and national greatness.

" II. To secure to the toilers a proper share of the wealth that they create; more of the leisure that rightly belongs to them; more societary advantages; more of the benefits, privileges and emoluments of the world; in a word, all those rights and privileges necessary to make them capable of enjoying, appreciating, defending and perpetuating the blessings of republican institutions.

" III. To arrive at the true condition of the producing masses in their educational, moral and financial condition, we demand from the several States and from the national government the establishment of bureaus of labor statistics.

" IV. The establishment of co-operative institutions, productive and distributive.

" V. The reserving of the public lands, the heritage of the people, for the actual settler—not another acre for railroads or speculators.

" VI. The abrogation of all laws that do not bear equally upon capital and labor, the removal of unjust technicalities, delays and discriminations in the administration of justice, and the adoption of measures providing for the health and safety of those engaged in mining, manufacturing or building pursuits.

" VII. The enactment of a law to compel chartered corporations to pay their employes at least once in every month in full for labor performed during the preceding month in the lawful money of the country.

" VIII. The enactment of a law giving mechanics and other laborers a first lien on their work.

" IX. The abolishment of the contract system on national, State and municipal work.

" X. To inaugurate a system of public markets, to facilitate the exchange of the productions of farmers and mechanics, tending to do away with middlemen and speculators.

" XI. To inaugurate systems of cheap transportation to facilitate the exchange of commodities.

" XII. The substitution of arbitration for strikes, whenever and wherever employers and employes are willing to meet on equitable grounds.

" XIII. The prohibition of the importation of all servile races, the discontinuance of all subsidies granted to national vessels bringing them to our shores, and the abrogation of the Burlingame Treaty.

" XIV. To advance the standard of American mechanics by the enactment and enforcement of equitable apprentice laws.

" XV. To abolish the system of contracting the labor of convicts in our prisons and reformatory institutions.

" XVI. To secure for both sexes equal pay for equal work.

" XVII. The reduction of the hours of labor to eight per day, so that laborers may have more time for social enjoyment and intellectual improvement, and be enabled to reap the advantages conferred by labor-saving machinery, which their brains have created.

" XVIII. To prevail upon the government to establish a just standard of distribution between capital and labor by providing a purely national circulating medium based upon the faith and resources of the nation, issued directly to the people, without the intervention of any system of banking corporations, which money shall be a legal tender in the payment of all debts, public or private, and interchangeable at the option of the holder for government bonds, bearing a rate of interest not to exceed three and sixty-five hundredths per cent., subject to future legislation of Congress."

There was in existence at that time an organization known as the Industrial Brotherhood. A. Warner St. John of Carthage, Mo., was the leading spirit in the society, and saw in the organization which started out from Rochester with so much of promise an ally which he hoped would in time prove of great service to the cause in which he was engaged.　Mr. Schilling conferred with the officers of the Industrial Brotherhood, which at that time had about forty branches in existence, and finally arrived at an understanding by which the name and ritual of the organization then in existence were adopted, and when the Constitution was printed it bore the name of the Industrial Brotherhood.　The two societies became one, and from that time worked under the same code of laws, under the same ritual and declaration of principles.

The ritual provided for the initiation of members regardless of their affiliation with other organizations, and pledged each member to secrecy so far as the workings of the society while in session were concerned.　It pledged every member to work with earnest zeal and to the best of his ability to aid in bringing about the objects of the order as outlined in the preamble.　The candidate for admission was told at the threshold of the organization that, "should you become one of us, you will be required to work with all your strength and energy to secure the ends therein enumerated.　You will be required to lay aside all selfishness and personal motives as we have all agreed to do, because labor can only be elevated by concerted action on the part of all concerned.　The condition of one part of our class cannot be improved permanently unless all are improved together.　From this you will see that the task before us is not an easy one, and in consideration of this fact we will admit none to membership unless they agree to work with heart and hand and with might and main to secure the amelioration of the producing classes."　The candidate would then be asked if he agreed to do as required ; if he consented, he was admitted to membership by being regularly initiated.　After being admitted to full membership, the new member was taken before the president of the lodge, who administered to him the following advice:

"It is now my duty to add a few words of advice.　The great aim and object of our organization is to secure for the industrial classes that position in the world and in society to which they are entitled as the producers of the necessaries and the comforts of life.　It is a strange state of affairs that those who produce nothing, but live on the labor of others, hold the highest positions, are most respected, and can live in ease and luxury, while those who earn their own bread, and the bread of others, in the sweat of their faces, are often suffering from poverty and destitution, and in many cases in old age have no alternative but starvation or the poor-house.　That such a condition of things is manifestly unjust none will deny, and for this reason we demand that worth, and not wealth, shall be the standard of greatness; that individuals shall be treated and respected according to their industrial, moral and social worth, instead of measuring their value by the length of their purses.　To secure these desirable objects we should be willing to labor unremittingly and unselfishly, for only through hard and unceasing work can we expect to eradicate and remove ridiculous prejudices that are now in our way. You have been chosen as one of these workers. See to it that you do not waver in your efforts; allow no wily enemy or ignorant friend, no seemingly insurmountable obstacle, to lead you from the path of duty, but let the redemption of labor from oppression and prejudice be your goal. Let your guides be truth, justice and charity. By truth deceit and hypocrisy will be banished from our midst, sincerity and plain-dealing will distinguish us, and the heart and tongue join in promoting each other's welfare and rejoicing in each other's prosperity. Justice we should be willing to give all, as we demand it for ourselves; and, in being charitable toward the errors or failings of others, we only do that which we desire others to do unto us. I now bid you a hearty welcome to the Industrial Brotherhood, and earnestly hope that you will work with us and for us, and remain of us, until the objects of our associating together are permanently secured, or until you join that great Brotherhood above.''

Constitutions were printed and distributed, rituals were sent to deputies with which to proceed with the work of organization, but the sentiment expressed in the words, "The condition of one part of our class cannot be improved permanently unless *all* are improved *together*," was not acceptable to trade unionists, who were selfishly bound up in the work of ameliorating the condition of those who belonged to their own particular callings alone.

The Rochester Convention selected as a motto, which would, in few words, give a reason for the existence of the organization, the words of Burke: "When bad men combine the good must associate, else they will fall, one by one, an unpitied sacrifice in a contemptible struggle." Bad men had combined to rob the nation of its liberty, to rob the children of America of the lands to which an all-wise Providence had called them; to take from labor the very crust it held between starving fingers; to stifle the cry of distress that it might not ascend on high to speak against the greed of man ; to gamble in food, in money, and life itself. Good men and true were required to battle against such iniquities as these, and for that reason the Industrial Brotherhood was formed, for that reason did it select that motto.

The deputies who were elected to carry forward the work of organization made little or no headway. They were commissioned by the president, as follows :

Alabama—Thomas Casey, Montgomery.
California—William Dunn, Sacramento.
Colorado—Isaac Seely, Denver.

Connecticut—O. E. Powers, West Meriden.
Delaware—Francis Bonner, Wilmington.
Florida—J. McKay Smith, Milton.
Georgia—John A. Warren, Rome.
Illinois—B. J. Murphy, Chicago.
Indiana—Jackson H. Wright, Indianapolis.
Iowa—Jacob Goehring, Davenport.
Kansas—Charles H. Messinger, Leavenworth.
Kentucky—Maurice Coll, Louisville.
Louisiana—Richard Swann, New Orleans.
Maryland—John Matthews, Baltimore.
Massachusetts—George E. McNeill, Cambridgeport.
Michigan—P. Dwyer, Detroit.
Minnesota—E. A. O'Brien, Minneapolis.
Mississippi—James C. Greener, Water Valley.
Missouri—William T. Blaetterman, St. Louis.
Nebraska—John Tracy, Omaha.
New Jersey—John G. Drew, Elizabeth.
New York—George Blair, New York.
North Carolina—Charles W. Winn, Wilmington.
Ohio—David A. Plant, Columbus.
Pennsylvania—John Siney, St. Clair.
South Carolina—William H. Pratt, Helena.
Tennessee—Joseph Hicks, Nashville.
Texas—William Gibbons, Houston.
Vermont—V. C. Meyerhoffer, Rutland.
Virginia—C. W. Thompson, Manchester.
West Virginia—Z. F. Brantner, Martinsburg.
Wisconsin—Hosea P. Osborn, Milwaukee.

The president was vested with the authority to appoint additional deputies as occasion might demand. John Siney, deputy for Pennsylvania, who at the time was President of the Miners' and Laborers' Association, had but little time to devote to the work assigned to him by the Rochester Convention of the Industrial Brotherhood, and President Schilling appointed as deputy for Western Pennsylvania, T. V. Powderly, a machinist, who was at the time employed in the machine shops of the Oil Creek and Allegheny River Railroad Company at Oil City, Pa. The commission was issued on the recommendation of the President of the Machinists' and Blacksmiths' Union, John Fehrenbatch of Cleveland, Ohio. Mr. Powderly was at the time a member of the Machinists' and Blacksmiths' Union. A subordinate lodge of the Industrial Brotherhood was organized in Oil City, and another in Pittsburg, Pa. The commission was issued by Mr. Schilling on the fourth of June, 1874. So far as known this is the only commission that was issued to any but those who were appointed at the convention at Rochester.

The next convention of the Industrial Brotherhood was to be held in Indianapolis, Ind., on the first Thursday before the second Tuesday in April, 1875, but the continued depression in trade and the indifference shown by the mechanics to the work of organization proved fatal, and when the time came to call the convention to order the organization had received its death blow from those who should have been most interested in prolonging its existence.

Once again did history repeat itself; once again did defeat attend the best efforts of good, earnest men, who lived ahead of their time; once again did the employer laugh at the folly of men, who, while clinging to an association which had raised around itself a wall over which those of other trades could not climb, or to which none but the elect of the trade could come, allowed an organization which would bring all men of toil face to face at a point where the scales would fall from their eyes, where they would see their condition as it really existed, to die even while they were crying out against the evils which this association of all others could abolish; once again could it be written on the tombstone of buried hopes and aspirations: " Murdered in the house of its friends."

No matter what objections may have existed, or no matter what opposition may have been shown to the men who made up the conventions of the order, the officers, or the Constitution of the order, it was not a sufficient reason for allowing the association to dwindle away and die of neglect and indifference. The cry raised against the formation of local lodges of the Industrial Brotherhood was: " It's no use in having so many organizations; we have our trade union and that is enough ; we are not in favor of allowing our affairs to be discussed by those who know nothing about them, and WE *will not associate with the common every-day laborers in any organization of labor;* we do not object to meeting with them elsewhere, but to place them on the same level with ourselves is asking too much. Pretty soon they will want to take our places at the bench, and it is time to nip this thing in the bud."

They did nip it in the bud, and at the same time nipped the hopes of the toilers in the bud. The rapid decline of the Industrial Brotherhood had a disheartening effect on the leaders of trade unions, who had hoped to see the new order win its way to favor among the rank and file of their associations. The order had its birth among advanced trade unionists, and trade unionists gave to it the blow that drove it from the field of labor reform. But while the Industrial Brotherhood died, its spirit still lived and took new strength in another and more powerful order of toilers, who, profiting by the errors of the past, began to creep before attempting to walk in the face of opposition from capitalists, suspicion from the general public, and jealousy on the part of those who adhered to trade lines in the ranks of labor.

If the convention which met at Rochester had been composed of men who were not connected with trade unions, if it were possible for such to have the same experience in the affairs of labor as trade unionists had acquired, there is no doubt but that, as a separate organization, the Industrial Brotherhood would have made more progress than it did. The principles enunciated were so broad and liberal as to appeal to the sympathies of workingmen generally, but those who had never been connected with organizations of any kind understood little or nothing of the tendency toward centralization of wealth. The opposition to labor organization, even on the part of those who worked for a livelihood, caused men to look askance at every effort in the direction of combination.

The men who were instrumental in calling the convention were trade unionists. They were sincere and active workers in the unions to which they were attached, and they could not consistently or conscientiously advocate the exclusion of trade unionists as such from the Industrial Brotherhood, since their intention was to bind trade unions, as well as men, together.

It is easier to bind men whose interests are identical together than to cause associations, whose selfish interests are paramount, to come together and become a part of a united whole. Old ties must be sundered or strained, old forms must give way or submit to radical alterations, recognized principles of trade regulations must be modified to meet the ever-coming changes. These things were not understood, and the men selected to sow the seeds of the new organization known as the Industrial Brotherhood were obliged to travel over fields whose soil was already sown with another kind of grain. To induce one to take root while the other was growing was next to impossible; and even though it had been done, it is a question if the result would not have proved disastrous to both the old and new orders.

But the principles of the Industrial Brotherhood were not permitted to die out of sight. The papers of that day gave wide circulation to the work that was done at Rochester. The Philadelphia *Ledger*, in commenting on the work done, said :

"Altogether this is the best specimen of a platform we have seen for a good while—best in its clearness and force—best in its freedom from inflated nonsense, mere " bunkum," or artful demagogical appeals to passion or prejudice. Some of the demands may be debatable ; none of them can be stigmatized as unreasonable ; and most of them are perfectly right."

The platform was copied far and wide. It was read by men who, though they were not members of any organization, felt that there was much food for reflection in what had been given out by the Rochester Convention. Isolated organizations of different branches of trade were scattered all over the United States. Some of them were slumbering, others dying, and none of them flourishing. It is for the purpose of scanning the progress made by one of these associations that we now turn back the pages of history for a few years in order that the connection between the organization of the past and present may be traced; that the preamble, issued from the convention of the Industrial Brotherhood in 1874, may be followed through the years in which it lay dormant until it was adopted, given new life, and sent out to the world by another organization that has made these principles known wherever men and women toil for bread, wherever they meet to discuss their rights and wrongs, for they have been translated into every language now spoken and are in the hands of workingmen in all quarters of the globe.

MAKING PROGRESS.

Standing still is childish folly,
Going backward is a crime:
None should patiently endure
Any ill that he can cure;
Onward! keep the march of time.—*Mackay.*

Among the local societies organized in Philadelphia during the Civil War was an association of garmentcutters. The demand for clothing to supply the wants of the army had brought to the front the speculator in shoddy, who attempted to palm off his worthless wares on the government and public. The great demand for clothing and the inducements offered to contractors created a corresponding demand for tailors, and drew the attention of men to that trade who had never sewed a stitch or even pricked the finger-end with the needle as apprentices. The speculation which was indulged in at that period brought rich rewards to those who were directly interested.

When the skilled workmen, those who had spent long years at low wages and had served years as apprentices, saw the inroads that were being made upon the tailoring trade by the introduction of so many incompetent workmen to the bench, they began to question whether it was not time to make an effort to stem the tide of ruin that was setting in against their trade. No action was taken until the employers, encouraged by the work they had done, and in the hope of realizing still greater gains, inaugurated a scheme to reduce the wages of the tailors.

Among those who had been carefully scanning the field of operations and studying the signs of the times were the garmentcutters of Philadelphia, who, as soon as the movement in favor of a reduction of wages made itself visible, called a meeting in the autumn of 1862, and passed resolutions which declared that they were entitled to a fair compensation for labor done, and would accept nothing less. From this meeting grew the organization afterward known as the "Garmentcutters' Association of Philadelphia." It grew in strength and influence. It had on the roll of membership some of the ablest men who toiled for a living in Philadelphia, and it was particularly fortunate in selecting as the first corps of officers the best and brightest men in the craft.

The care and attention which had been displayed in the election of the first set of officers became a precedent by which officers were chosen at following elections, and gave to the association a standing among the garmentcutters which it would not otherwise have had. This association continued in existence for a number of years.

Having served the purposes for which it was first organized, it became a beneficial association, taking care of the sick and disabled members, and assisting many members of the trade who were not in affiliation with the association. In the early spring of 1869, a lack of interest having manifested itself among the members, it was deemed advisable by some to introduce new features and make some changes which innovations in workshop regulation seemed to demand.

One Sunday afternoon two members of the association, Uriah S. Stephens and Henry L. Sinexon, met by appointment and took a walk in the direction of League Island. While sauntering along, Mr. Stephens complained bitterly of the lack of interest manifested by the members of the Garmentcutters' Association. He said: "There is more discussion in the cutting-rooms the day after a meeting than there is at any of the meetings. There is very little interest manifested in the welfare of the society. The members do not seem to have any conception of what organization means. I have been making an effort to have something done that will be of interest to our people, but am becoming disgusted with the manner in which they receive it. The organization cannot last long; it will go to pieces; and I want to get together some of the broad-minded, thinking members and see if something cannot be done to formulate a plan to prevent this loud talking in the cutting-rooms. Why, the floor-walkers, who are not connected with the society in any way, carry every day to the counting-rooms all that has been done in our organization, and they pick it up by hearing our loose-mouthed members discussing it at the bench."

Mr. Sinexon asked his companion if he had given any thought to the formulation of any plans. The reply was: "No, but I am determined to make an effort to institute something different. When the dissolution takes place I shall make an effort to get some good men together and originate something that will be different from what we have ever had."

Mr. Sinexon then discussed the features of the various societies with which he was connected, and contrasted their aims and methods with those of the association of garmentcutters. He said: "I have been looking all my life for something that will be advantageous to the masses; something that will develop more of charity, less of selfishness; more of generosity, less of stinginess and meanness, than the average society has as yet disclosed to its members. I cannot find it, for from none of the societies with which I am connected can I carry home the feeling that I would wish to bring with me. We want to establish a society that will place man and his needs at the forefront instead of the dollar he pays in."

In this way these two men discussed various measures of reform for several hours, and finally parted with the understanding that each was to invite a chosen few to meet at a certain spot in Fairmount Park on the following Sunday. The meeting in the park was attended by eight or nine of the older and more reliable of the Garmentcutters' Association. They agreed to draw up plans for the organization of a new order, and to submit them at a subsequent meeting. On several Sundays these meetings were held in the park. The men who met would take three of the park benches and place them in the form of a triangle. They would then sit on the inside of the triangle, and each one would read off the plans he had drawn up during the week. Mr. Stephens usually occupied the post of honor in the centre, and at the close of each meeting all papers would be placed in his possession for consideration. Should it happen to rain while they were in session, they would seek the shelter of one of the park buildings, and there continue to perfect their plans. They continued to meet in this way for months. When the weather grew too cold for them to meet in the park they held their sessions in the homes of the members until their plans were well matured.

On December 9, 1869, a resolution was offered at a meeting of the Garmentcutters' Association: "To dissolve and divide the funds among the members in good standing." The motion met with but little opposition, and its passage was practically unanimous.

Immediately after the dissolution of the Garmentcutters' Association, several members from among those who had made a study for several months of the best means of inaugurating a new movement among the garmentcutters met in the hall of the American Hose Company, on Jayne Street below Seventh, and proceeded to organize by electing James L. Wright as Temporary Chairman and Robert McCauley as Temporary Secretary. After a free and deliberate discussion of the subject of organization, the question was put to each person present: "Have you any objections to connect yourself with a secret organization?" The following answered in the negative by stating that they had no objections to offer: James L. Wright, William H. Phillips, U. S. Stephens, Robert McCauley, William Cook, James M. Hilsea, Joseph S. Kennedy, Robert W. Keen and David Westcott.

Mr. Keen was then placed in charge of the door, a pledge of secrecy was administered to all present, and a password was given out to be used on subsequent occasions. Various plans were considered, and the measures which had been under discussion for months by the few who had busied themselves with the work of bringing the new order into being were referred to a committee consisting of U. S. Stephens, R. W. Keen, David Westcott, Joseph S. Kennedy, James M. Hilsea, James L. Wright and Robert McCauley, with instructions to meet and prepare, from the documents placed in their possession, a secret work, such as would be suitable for the government of such a body. It was agreed at this meeting that no further mention would be made to any one who was not present, except those who had taken part in the preliminary discussions which had taken place in the park and at other places.

When that meeting adjourned it was to meet again in the same hall on the 23d of December of the same year. When the second meeting was called to order, the Committee on Secret Work made a partial report, which was the only subject discussed. James L. Wright occupied the chair at this meeting.

The third meeting was held at the house of Joseph S. Kennedy on December 28, 1869. At this meeting the name of the new association was made a subject for discussion, and it was decided to call it the KNIGHTS OF LABOR, and the local name of the body was to be Garmentcutters' Assembly. It was reported that a room could be secured in the United States Engine House at Fourth and Vine Streets, and Messrs. Keen and McCauley were appointed to engage the room. The committee made a partial report, and recommended a form of obligation to which U. S. Stephens, R. W. Keen, James L. Wright, James M. Hilsea, Joseph S. Kennedy, William Cook and Robert McCauley subscribed.

This meeting began the permanent organization of the first Assembly of the Knights of Labor. At the next meeting, which was held in the room which had been secured in the United States Engine House, on December 30, 1869, the Committee on Ritual reported progress, and G. W. Cook, H. L. Sinexon, W. C. Yost, Samuel Wright, G. W. Hornberger and James Barron were elected to membership.

On January 6, 1870, the first regular officers were elected, after the Committee on Ritual recommended what titles the officers should be known by. It was decided to call the retiring presiding officer Venerable Sage, the presiding officer Master Workman. The next officer in rank to be known as Worthy Foreman. The other officers were to be known as Worthy Inspector, Unknown Knight, Recording Secretary, Financial Secretary, and Treasurer. James L. Wright, who had occupied the position of presiding officer, was appointed Venerable Sage, and Uriah S. Stephens was elected the first Master Workman for the year beginning January, 1870.

It had often happened, during the experience of the founders of the Knights of Labor, that men who were given to the practice of indulging in strong drink had brought disgrace on societies to which they belonged by frequenting saloons on the meeting nights of their societies, and who either became drunk and disturbed the harmony of the meeting, or else presented the spectacle to the world of going direct from the meeting-room to the saloon, from whence they did not come until they were in such a condition as to reflect no credit on themselves or anything with which they were connected. Being composed of sensible, reasoning men, the new organization determined that nothing would be left undone to make the meetings pleasant and profitable. It was resolved to offer a substitute for the amusement which men sought in saloons, and combine sociability with business, by setting apart a time during each meeting when refreshments would be served.

After a certain portion of the proceedings of the meeting would be transacted, usually after the initiation of new candidates, the Master Workman would declare that the meeting would take a recess for refreshments. Hot coffee, sandwiches, cake and lemonade would be served during recess, and, when the regular order of business would be resumed, the bills for the same would be passed upon and ordered paid. Through this practice, and through the watchful care of the members, no newly-initiated candidate was permitted to spend any time in a saloon until he became thoroughly conversant with the purposes of the society, and understood the importance of keeping his business, as well as that of the society, from those who were not members.

At a meeting held in February, 1870, it was decided to fix the initiation fee at $1, and on May 5, of that year, the first newspaper advertisement ever published under the auspices of an Assembly of the Knights of Labor was ordered by the Garmentcutters' Assembly. It appeared in the *Ledger* of May 10 and 11, 1870, and read as follows:

FOUNTAIN OF POWER—*K. of L. Officers and Representatives.*—A special meeting will be held on Thursday, 12th inst., to act on first report from State Labor Union, giving aid to Garmentcutters' Branch; to resist the attempt of certain oppressive houses in the trade to reduce the wages of skilled workmen; secondly, shall the patronage of industrials be given to establishments that refuse just remuneration? By order.　　　　　　　　L. A. SMITH, *M. E. W.*

When the meeting assembled, May 12, the Master Workman explained that he signed the advertisement L. A. Smith because it was not advisable to have his own name appear, for the reason that he was known so well in the craft that it would not have the same effect as though the announcement was made over the signature of some one unknown to the majority of employers. It was also advisable to have it appear that there was a strange or new organization in existence in the city, one which had connection with a national association. The initials, L. A., signified "Labor Advocate;" and the letters, "M. E. W.," were suggested by Mr. Sinexon, and by him interpreted to mean "Most Excellent Workman." When these explanations were made, the Assembly ratified the action of the Master Workman, and passed a vote of thanks for the effort which had succeeded in bringing together so large a meeting.

William Fennimore became a member of the Assembly on January

20, 1870, and contributed largely to the successful career of the association.

On June 6 a special committee of five was appointed on ritual. The committee consisted of Messrs. J. M. Hilsea, Joseph S. Kennedy, H. L. Sinexon, Robert McCauley and Robert W. Keen.

At the first meeting in July, 1870, a discussion arose as to the best means of securing members, and it was thought by some that it would be well to remove at least a portion of the secrecy which surrounded the member when asking a workman to join. The following motion was entertained by the chair on the evening of July 14, and after a sharp debate was voted down:

"To allow members to disclose to such persons as they wished to propose the existence of this Order."

At a subsequent meeting, held on August 11, Mr. McCauley made a motion which received the approval of the Assembly. It is in the following language:

" That a member of this Assembly have the privilege to reveal his membership in this organization to those he desires to obtain for members; *provided always, however*, that he does not reveal the name or names of any other person or persons who are members of this organization, according to the terms of the obligation."

The adoption of this regulation allowed the member more freedom, and as a consequence he could go further into detail when asking a person to become a member of the society.

The idea of extending the benefits of the organization to others than garmentcutters was first introduced at a meeting of the Assembly on July 28, 1870. A motion was made to "strike out the words Garment-cutters' Assembly," but it did not prevail. The idea was suggested by a member who believed that the doors of the association should be thrown open to workingmen of every trade or calling.

On October 5, 1870, the first death occurred in the Assembly. Henry A. Sennig was the first member of the Knights of Labor that an Assembly was called upon to mourn. A memorial service was held, and the portrait of the deceased was placed in the minute book of the Assembly.

On October 20 the first person not a garmentcutter was proposed as a sojourner in Assembly No. 1. In order to spread the benefits of organization among workingmen, it was allowed to initiate good men of all callings, and to allow them the benefits of association on the same footing with the garmentcutters, except in deciding trade matters. Sojourners were not required to pay any dues until such time as enough of their own calling had been initiated to form a separate Assembly. The sojourner was admitted that he might become a missionary among his fellow-tradesmen; he was to be an instructor and an organizer.

This departure from the original plan of the Assembly was the first real step in advance of the old system of organization that was made, and from October 20, 1870, dates the history of the Order of the Knights of Labor as something in advance of, and differing from, the exclusive trade union. From its inception Assembly No. 1 was more exclusively a trade organization than any trade union that had ever existed in the United States. None but garmentcutters who could prove that they had served a stated term as apprentices were admitted. The principles of co-operation and assistance were to be confined to a few who could pass examination as first-class workmen. The real work of Knighthood had not yet started, and the founders of the first Assembly, with the exception of Uriah S. Stephens, William Fennimore and Henry L. Sinexon, were as much interested in trade matters as any person who belonged to a trade union. Compared with the trade unions of that day, the first Assembly of the Knights of Labor was far behind them in toleration and fellowship.

The idea which Stephens and Sinexon discussed at the outset was not put in practice until the adoption of the motion, made by the latter, threw open the doors for the admission of other workmen than garmentcutters. From that moment began the progressive work of the Knights of Labor.

The ideal organization for which the workers in the National Labor Union and the Industrial Brotherhood had sought in vain loomed up before the eyes of those who were members of the new Order in 1870. From that moment organization took on a new significance and assumed more dignified and important proportions. Trade lines were no longer powerful enough or sufficient to compass the toilers who sought protection, as much from their own errors, through their ignorance of the rights and duties of each other, as from the encroachments of unscrupulous employers. The secrecy which enshrouded the new Order made it difficult to organize, and it was a process slow of operation to propose, elect and initiate a candidate.

As secretly as they worked, the operations of the members could not be screened from the public gaze. On October 27, 1870, it was reported to the Assembly that "one of the members had been so indiscreet as to reveal to several persons not only the existence of this organization, but also part of the machinery and the benefits to be derived therefrom, as well as the names of the members."

A committee was appointed to wait on the offending member, but no action was ever taken to prevent a repetition of the transgression, and the member who had violated his obligation made satisfactory excuse to the committee and was forgiven on promise not to repeat the offense.

When a member found a man who was considered worthy of

admission, he was questioned as to his opinions concerning the elevation of labor, and if his sentiments were found to be in accord with the objects of the society his name would be brought before a meeting of the organization, the local name of which was "Garment-cutters' Assembly, No. 1." A committee would be appointed to make an investigation into the qualifications of the person proposed. The member who proposed the candidate was not allowed to act on the committee, for the reason that he might be swayed or influenced by friendship in making his report. When the committee reported, the candidate was balloted for; if rejected, no further mention was made of the matter to any one. The candidate would be kept in ignorance of what had transpired; and the members, even those who had voted against his admission, would treat him with the same consideration in the workshop as before.

If the candidate was elected, the friend who proposed him would on some pretext invite him to a meeting, a party, a ball, or a gathering of some kind, and manage to secure his presence at the regular meeting-place of the Assembly on the night of initiation; and when the candidate for the first time learned that he was to enter a society as a new member, he was at the same time led to believe that his friend had also been invited there for the same purpose; so that, in case of failure to initiate, the elected one would not even then know that his friend was connected with the society.

This method of securing members was kept up for several years, and became the rule with all future Assemblies. The reason for this extreme secrecy was because it was claimed that open and public associations had, after centuries of toil and struggle, proved to be failures in one way or another. It was also claimed that when the association worked openly, so that its members might be known to the public, it exposed them to the scrutiny and, in time, the wrath of their employers. It was deemed best to work in such a way to avoid comment and scrutiny.

The troubles which were at that time attracting attention toward the coal fields from which Philadelphia received its principal supply of fuel also influenced the members of the new Order. Through open and public association the men of the coal fields allowed desperate men to gain admittance to their societies; and among the latter was the detective, who, in order to earn his salary, added to his treachery the crime of perjury and murder in order to make out a case against his fellow-men.

Where associations of workingmen are working openly, it matters but little what laudable object they may have in view, men can always be had for a price who will deliberately enter a society as though actuated by the best of motives, and, after ingratiating themselves in the good graces of the members, become leaders only to lead to ruin and death. Such things have been done in Pennsylvania, and it was to avoid the repetition of such a catastrophe that the first Assembly of the Knights of Labor assumed the garb of secrecy, which it wore until, with the rest of the Order, it cast the outer covering aside and announced to the world that there was such an organization as the Knights of Labor working for the emancipation of the wage-earner.

The seed that is carelessly sown, or scattered over the surface of the earth, is at the mercy of every wind. It may for a time take root, but so long as it is unprotected it can never be expected to grow and flourish. The rain, wind and sunshine, elements that would have destroyed it if left exposed at the outset, will contribute to its strength and future life if it is securely screened from exposure by being placed beneath the surface of the earth in the beginning. It was that the organization and its members might be protected as the seed in early spring-time that the veil of secrecy was first adopted; and the precaution was necessary, protection was necessary, not only from the employers, but from men who toiled for a living also.

Jealousy, malice and mean ambition were known to the men of labor as well as to others, and it was for the purpose of keeping profoundly secret their actions from men in their own sphere and calling, as well as others out of it, that the early pioneers of the Knights of Labor hid themselves from public view. They did not adopt the veil of secrecy to promote or shield wrong-doing, but to shield themselves from persecution and wrong.

In using the power of organized effort and co-operation they simply followed the example which capital had previously set; for in all the diversified branches of trade capital had its combinations, and too often, through their operation, had crushed the manly hopes of those who were guaranteed the right to live and be happy under the laws of the land. Humanity was frequently trampled in the dust that money might be exalted to the shrine at which the few worshiped.

It was not the intention to create an antagonism between labor and capital. No conflict with legitimate enterprise was contemplated, but the members realized that men who possessed wealth, in their haste and greed, blinded by self-interest, often overlooked the interests of others less fortunate than they and frequently violated the rights of such as they deemed helpless and defenseless.

Stephens and his co-laborers meant to uphold the dignity of labor and to affirm the nobility of all who earned their daily bread in an honest way, but they swore unending enmity to every form of vice by which the poor were being fleeced for the benefit of the gamblers in the necessaries of life. It was their intention to work for the creation of a healthy public opinion on the subject of labor—the only creator of values—and to advocate the justice of its receiving a full, complete share of the values, or capital, it created. It was furthermore intended to support all laws that were made to harmonize labor and capital; for since labor gave life and value to capital, it was but just to place both upon an equality before the law. Laws which were intended to lighten the exhaustiveness of toil were to be supported and advocated, and new laws were to be advised in the interest of the worker. Every lawful and honorable means was to be resorted to to procure and retain employment for fellow-members; and it mattered not to what country, color or creed the member belonged, if misfortune befell him, he was to receive the aid and comfort of his fellow-members. Strikes were discountenanced; but when it became justly necessary to make use of that weapon, it was intended to aid such members as might suffer loss. In short, it was the intention to extend a helping hand to every branch of trade which formed a part of the vast industrial forces of the country.

Members were not taught that idleness was to be respected in any one, and the newly-initiated soon realized that those who surrounded him were not there to spend their time in frivolous or idle amusement. The new member soon learned that to rescue the toiler from the grasp of the selfish was a work, which, being worthy of the best of the race, was an undertaking in which he might well engage, to the end that he might help to divest labor of the evils to body, mind and estate which ignorance and the greed of man had fastened upon it.

The fundamental principle on which the organization was based was co-operation, not a co-operation of men for the mere purpose of enhancing the value of their combined contributions to any productive enterprise alone, but a co-operation of the various callings and crafts by which men earned the right to remain upon the earth's surface as contributors to the public good. The barriers of trade were to be cast aside; the man who toiled, no matter at what, was to receive and enjoy the just fruits of his labor and exercise of his art whether as a skilled artisan or the humblest of the toilers of the earth.

Such is but an epitome of the aims and objects of the new Order' which had its real beginning when the Garmentcutters' Association voted to admit men of all callings. The old society admitted to membership none but garmentcutters, but a radical change was made in this direction by the new one. It recognized the right of all toilers to combine, and, having admitted that they should do so, it was considered best for all that all should be associated together in one fold, wherein the actions of all craftsmen would be known to each other, and thus avoid those errors of the purely trade society.

In the early stages of organization in the United States, when a trade union felt called upon to take action on a question of any kind, the feelings, wishes or interests of others were never for a moment considered. To illustrate: If the iron moulder had a difference of opinion with his employer, and could not settle it in a reasonable time, he never sought the advice of the machinist to whose hands the castings would go after it left the sand into which it had been run as molten metal by the moulder. When the moulder struck against the decree of the employer, the machinist was forced to stop work; the blacksmith, who did the forging for the same machine that the machinist and moulder were at work upon, suspended operations also; carpenters, who did wood-working in connection with the establishment, had to leave off until the trouble was settled with the moulder. The boilermaker, too, had to submit to a stay of proceedings. In fact, all the employes of that concern were prevented from working at their usual occupations on account of the strike in which they were all concerned, but in which they had no right to have a voice, or to the settlement of which they could not contribute. When the employer had a difference of opinion as to wages, rules or discipline with the machinists in his employ, and in a fit of anger ordered them to quit work until the difficulty was settled, he never took into consideration that he was at the same time depriving men of employment who, while they were concerned in the controversy, had no chance to offer a word of advice or enter a protest against hasty action. Not only did a strike affect the mechanics who were employed in the particular establishment where it originated, but it affected other branches of trade apparently far removed from the scene of conflict.

The shoe manufacturer, who made the shoes which were worn by the men employed in the foundry and machine-shop, soon felt a depression in trade when the men who were on strike absented themselves from his place of business, and no longer purchased so many shoes as before for themselves and families. Then shoemakers were told not to come to work, and they too joined the ranks of the non-producers.

The clerks who stood behind the counters in grocery and dry-goods stores, who in that day felt that they were a step higher in the social scale than the men at the bench in the factory, were dismissed until the strike was ended and the men again were earning money with which to purchase shoes, groceries and dry goods. The factory did not require any fuel while the men were out of work; the shoe-shop, if run by steam, did not require so much coal to make steam; and blacksmith, carpenter, machinist, moulder, shoemaker, clerk, merchant and manufacturer did not purchase coal in such quantities as before the suspension of work.

If the institution which had been thrown idle was a railroad-shop, then the brakesman, the engineer, the fireman, the conductor and the switchman felt the depression when they were informed that they must remain idle until the trouble had been adjusted. The locomotive was run into the round-house, and no longer burned coal. Then the effects of the trouble between the employer and one branch of labor extended to the mines, and the demand for coal was not so great, and more men were told to remain idle until the trouble was settled. More men were thrown idle along the line of the road on which the coal was transported to market.

When the companies who mined coal saw so many men out of employment, they saw an opportunity to reduce wages, and they made the attempt. The result invariably was a strike, which added fresh recruits to the ranks of the unemployed. The trouble did not end there. Factories in other parts of the country suffered for want of coal, and were shut down not alone for the want of coal, but for the want of trade which was lost to them through the idleness of those already mentioned. In other factories wages were reduced, other strikes took place, and more men were placed on the list of non-producers.

Reverse the beginning of the strike, lockout or dispute, and let it start among the miners of coal, and the results would be the same in the end. One strike, if of any consequence at all, begets others, and entails losses on those who are powerless to either stay the hand that stops the first wheel or to give advice to the employer, who too often feels that, in the matter of advice, " it is better to give than receive." Co-operation for a common end was necessary. That common end was to forever stop the suicidal policy that debarred workingmen from entry to the workshop because of a difference of opinion which should have been submitted to a tribunal where the interests not alone of the employer and his workmen would be considered, but a tribunal which would carefully investigate the cause of the strike and the effect of the stoppage of work by one branch of industry upon all others.

It has somewhere been said that the Order of the Knights of Labor grew out of a failure, but the details were not given, and they were not necessary; but the failure hinted at, and the failure which really led to the organization of the Knights of Labor, was the failure of the trade union to grapple and satisfactorily deal with the labor question on its broad far-reaching basic principle: the right of all to have a say in the affairs of one. It was because the trade union failed to recognize the rights of man, and looked only to the rights of the tradesman, that the Knights of Labor became a possibility. Trade rules would not allow a common, every-day laborer to take a place in a shop as a mechanic until he had served an apprenticeship; but the tradesman, who religiously adhered to that doctrine, when on strike against an injustice of any kind or when locked out by his employer, would not hesitate to take the shovel from the lean, half-starved hand of the laborer, and cause two men to stand where there was room for but one. The rights of the common, every-day laborer were to be considered by the new Order, because the members of trade unions had failed to see that they had rights.

The failure of the National Labor Union, the good and noble originators of which strove in vain to make it a power for good, was also a reason why the new organization should enter upon its mission. The founders of the Knights of Labor were fully acquainted with the attempts which had been made by the founders of the National Labor Union to bring tradesmen to a sense of their duty to the whole of labor's forces. They also knew that every effort to bring all branches of trade into closer affiliation had proved a failure through the opposition manifested by the rank and file of the trade unions, and they knew that if their work should be done as openly as was the work of the National Labor Union the same opposition would retard the progress of the movement. The unjust restrictions and greed of capitalists, the tendency to monopoly on the part of large concerns, and the selfishness of the mechanics of America, are the reasons why the Knights of Labor were first organized, and also furnish the reason why the early movement was shrouded in mystery so profound.

It was observed by those who were members of the first Assembly that, when workingmen of whatever calling were engaged in a strike, they could rarely tell the why and wherefore of the strike; they could not say whether the establishment in which they were employed paid better wages than any other, or whether the rules of discipline differed or were more severe in other workshops. The conditions of the workman in his home were seldom considered by the labor organization of that period prior to 1869. The new Order determined to investigate the conditions which surrounded the worker from the time he went to work in the morning until he again presented himself at the door of the workshop to begin the next day's toil.

One of the officers of the Assembly was delegated to ascertain the full facts in regard to the work, wages and manner of living of the laborer. The Statistician, as this officer was called, was required to ascertain the names and locations of all who were members, the amount of money received and spent by them, as well as by the concern for which they toiled. He had the right to call for the assistance of all members in gathering and compiling statistics. It was hoped that the profits of the man whose capital was invested would become known to the public, and that knowledge, coupled with the information which would be gathered by the Statistician of the Assembly, would enable the worker to decide how much of the joint product of his labor and his employer's capital should compensate the worker.

Another reason why the full facts in relation to profits and compensation should be gathered and made known was that a fair and impartial public could accurately decide the justice of every case brought before the tribunal of that healthy public opinion which the new association hoped to create on the subject of labor.

The officer known as Inspector was to keep a record of all employed and unemployed members, the number of unemployed was to be noted at every meeting, their names read off to the Assembly, and questions asked as to where employment could be secured for those who required it. Not only was the Inspector required to know how many were employed, but it was also his duty to know why they were out of employment. The effect was to be traced to its cause so that steps could be taken to remove the cause. All of this came within the domain of Knighthood, and should not be overlooked in particular or detail.

Ignorance of the law of the land, of the every-day affairs of life, was considered a wrong, and it was told to the new member that he should learn to write his name in full, and learn to read it when written. In this way it was hoped all members would be secured against false-hearted friends and designing enemies.

The officers of the Assembly were a Master Workman, whose duty it was to preside over the affairs of the society; a Worthy Foreman, who should perform the duties of the Master Workman in the absence of that officer; a Recording Secretary, to keep a correct account of what transpired at each meeting; a Financial Secretary, who would receive the dues of the members, and keep an account opened between the Assembly and its members; a Treasurer, to whom the Financial Secretary should turn over all money that he received; a Statistician, whose duties are outlined elsewhere in these pages; a Worthy Inspector, whose task is also spoken of; an Unknown Knight, who was to take charge of all applicants for admission, and see that they were properly introduced to the meeting; an Assistant Unknown Knight, whose name indicates what the duties of the position should be; an Almoner, to visit all sick and disabled members and relieve their distress. One feature of the Almoner s duty was indicative of the broad, liberal spirit which animated the movers in the new association; when the Almoner found a brother member in distress, he was authorized to alleviate that distress, and carefully conceal the name of the recipient. When he made his report and stated what he had done with the funds, that was sufficient. No names were asked for. His honor and the care observed in his selection were the only safeguards taken or required by his fellow-members. Confidence in the officers was instilled into the minds of the members by the careful method of selecting them for their important duties.

At a meeting held January 12, 1871, Master Workman Stephens read to the Assembly an annual address, as follows :

" A cycle is ended, the first in our history, and bears its record of labors and toils to the Dead Sea of the past. During the year God's toilers have worked and wept as of yore. The brain has throbbed and the heart has bled for wrongs they were powerless to right. Busy industry has struggled to heap in the lap of the world's commerce the usual amount of values.

> " 'Rich in model and design ; harvest tool and husbandry.
>   Loom and wheel and engin'ry, secrets of the sullen mine,
>   Steel and gold, and corn and wine, fabric rough or fabric fine,
>   Sunny tokens of the line, polar marvels ; and a feast of wonders, out of
>   West and East.'

"And while the toiler is thus engaged in creating the world's values, how fares his own interest and well-being ? We answer, badly; for he has too little time, and his faculties become too much blunted by unremitting labor to analyze his condition or devise and perfect financial schemes or reformatory measures.

" The hours of labor are too long and should be shortened. I recommend a universal movement to cease work at five o'clock on Saturday as a beginning. There should be a greater participation in the profits of labor by the industrious and intelligent laborer. In the present arrangement of labor and capital the condition of the employe is simply that of wage-slavery; capital dictating, labor submitting; capital superior, labor inferior. This is an artificial and man-created condition, not God's arrangement and order, for it degrades man and ennobles mere pelf; it demeans those who live by useful labor, and in proportion exalts all those who eschew labor and live (no matter by what pretense or respectable cheat, for cheat it is) without productive work.

" Living by and on the labor of others is dishonest, and should be branded as such. Labor and capital should treat each other as equals. Let us hint to the world in broad and unmistakable terms our demands. Where lies the fault that this condition of things exists ? Mainly with ourselves. Disjointed, inharmonious, no concert of action, not even much mutual respect; prone to defer to wealth, to respect pretension and bow to assumption, instead of boldly stripping it of its mask and exposing its hideousness.

" What is the remedy ? Cultivate friendship among the great brotherhood of toil; learn to respect industry in the person of every intelligent worker; unmake the shams of life by deference to the humble but useful craftsman; beget concert of action by conciliation, confidence by just and upright conduct toward each other, mutual respect by dignified deportment, and wise council by what of wisdom and ability God in His wisdom and goodness may have endowed us with.

" In our own sphere and circle much has been done in the year that has passed. Much preparation before the foundation could be laid;

much material to be gathered. A retrospect of the year is satisfactory. Several have been steady in their situations, some have been changed to better, and many have been assisted to vacancies they would not have known of. All this and more has been done, and all has tended toward the central point of keeping the remuneration up to a satisfactory standard. Influences are at work to reduce the standard. This must be watched vigilantly, and, if necessary, an effort must be made to counteract the evil by public, open work ; blows in the right place that will tell and hurt, for evils have their vulnerable points and can be reached.

" There is work for the ready hands and willing hearts, and abundant harvest awaits the reaper. Let us be aroused ; labor's interests have suffered long enough, because the interested ones neglect to take care of them ; unwise counsels have too long prevailed ; suspicion and distrust have too long kept us apart ; let us reason together, and let our reasonings bear the fruit of action. Knighthood must base its claims for labor upon higher ground than participation in the profits and emoluments, and a lessening of the hours and fatigues of labor.

" These are only physical effects and objects of a grosser nature, and, although imperative, are but the stepping-stone to a higher cause, of a nobler nature. The real and ultimate reason must be based upon the more exalted and divine nature of man, his high and noble capabilities for good. Excessive labor and small pay stint and blunt and degrade those God-like faculties, until the image of God, in which he was created and intended by his great Author to exhibit, are scarcely discernible, and ignorance boldly asserts does not exist. Time will not permit us to reason out the details or enforce them by argument, but must leave their development to your own thought and investigation. To God and your own best judgment I leave the cause. Prophecy and inspiration assert the ultimate triumph of the principle."

When five Assemblies had been organized a Committee on Good of the Order was formed by selecting three members from each Assembly to meet in joint session for the purpose of discussing the affairs which related to the welfare of the whole. This committee continued in existence until the organization of the first District Assembly, which took place in December, 1873.

At one of the meetings of the Joint Committee on Good of the Order, Mr. Stephens delivered an address upon the duty and purposes of the Assembly. This address was never before given to the public, and is so instructive that it not only deserves to be preserved, but ranks among the best literature of the Order of the Knights of Labor. The address of Mr. Stephens was preceded by a selection, and is as follows:

"THE IDEAL ORGANIZATION.

"'Make for thyself a definition or description of the thing which is presented to thee so as to see distinctly what kind of a thing it is in its substance, in its nudity, in its complete entirety, and tell thyself its proper name, and the names of the things of which it has been compounded and into which it will be resolved. For nothing is so productive of elevation of mind as to be able to examine methodically and truly every object which is presented to thee in life, and always to look at things so as to see at the same time what kind of universe this is, and what kind of use everything performs in it, and what value everything has with reference to the whole, and what with reference to man, who is a citizen of the highest city, of which all other cities are alike families; what each thing is, and of what it is composed, and how long it is the nature of this thing to endure.'—*Marcus Aurelius Antonius.*

"THE CITY OF REFUGE.

"For untold ages men have seen and felt the vice and misery that spring from poverty and an unequal distribution of the wealth produced by labor. They have seen and felt, too, that as the possibilities and privileges go where the wealth goes, so do the burdens of society fall heavier upon them, and with more crushing severity as their just share of wealth recedes and hopelessly eludes their grasp. This has been the travail of the ages as they passed; but the night of agony and despair is rapidly passing away. The day dawning of hope is illuminating the horizon, and as light spreads over the world the masses begin to discern the remedy for the evils under which they have heretofore writhed, and, divesting themselves of the impediments with which they have so persistently burdened themselves, they are pressing toward the gates of the City of Refuge, over which is inscribed, in letters of living light, 'Organization.'

"Within these gates, and as seen from the city side, these letters blaze with the ineffable glory and sparkle with the unutterable truth, Universal Brotherhood. The babel of tongues is hushed within its sacred walls; the discords of party strife are stilled; the war of creeds gives place to the white-robed angel of charity. Creed, party and nationality are but outward garments, and present no obstacle to the fusion of the hearts of the worshipers of God, the Universal Father, and the workers for man, the Universal Brother.

"Men have not been idle in the past, nor unmindful of their duty to themselves and their fellow-toilers. Seer, prophet and apostle have labored and kept vigil by the altar and the way; but the result has mainly been to cry in the wilderness, and foretell of the good time to come in the dim and distant future, and the crown of martyrdom. Statesman, philanthropist and scholar, too, have wrought as best they could; but the surrounding gloom of bigotry, ignorance and selfishness has nullified their efforts, and craft and cunning bore off the rich increase of toil. A fatal want rendered their efforts nugatory, and left the masses hopelessly in the toils of craft, which rioted in the luxury and plenty created by labor. That fatal want was organization—combination—based on high, noble and holy sentiments, the mother of principles, the nurse of reform, a tower of strength in numbers for the weak, a City of Refuge for the persecuted and proscribed.

"In the fullness of time it came, as messiahs have ever come, when the world was ready for them, could receive them; as every epoch has come, when the conditions of growth were favorable; as the leaf in spring, the fruit in summer; as the ingathering in autumn. Our beloved fraternity is here! The world is ready for it. The conditions are favorable to its growth. It has come to stay; it has a work to do; it will do it. God's seal of approval has been set upon it in its increase, and the shape it has given to the thought of the country, everywhere apparent in the hostility manifested by its enemies. Let us but do our duty. Mahomet, whether right or wrong, was one of the most remarkable men in history. He gave to each one of his followers a promise, ' Victory or paradise!' 'and he was successful. We formulate the great universal cry of the toilers of every land—every phase of legalized robbery, as the greater contains the less, as the sum of all evils under which the masses groan, and the sum of all the remedies includes all incidentals—' Land and liberty!'

"The work to which this fraternity addresses itself is one of the greatest magnitude ever attempted in the history of the world. It enters a field occupied by no other organized effort; is engaged in a work essayed by no other instrumentality in existence, that of knitting up into a compact and homogeneous amalgamation all the world's workers in one universal brotherhood, guided by the same rules, working by the same methods, practicing the same forms for accomplishing the same ends. It builds upon the immutable basis of the Fatherhood of God and the logical principle of the Brotherhood of Man. Beyond these two correlated and inseparable truths, it neither seeks nor allows any interference with men's religious faith, or the duty they owe to their family, their country or their God. Inspired by these lofty principles, it moves majestically forward to elevate the race to a higher plane of existence—a truer, nobler development of its capabilities and powers, and a realization of the greatest good possible within the limit of law.

"Its work is the complete emancipation of wealth producers from the thraldom and loss of wage-slavery. The entire redemption of the world's toilers from the political tyranny of unjust laws, and the annihilation of the great anti-Christ of civilization manifest in the idolatry of wealth, and the consequent degradation and social ostracism of all else not possessing it, and its baneful effects upon heaven-ordained labor.

" Civil and religious liberty and theoretical equality before the law we already have in America. That was achieved for us by our revolutionary forefathers, and bequeathed by them as a sacred legacy to us, their descendants and successors. But an accursed slavery, a heaven-denounced tyranny, a degrading, atheistical idolatry, remains, has grown upon us, which it becomes our duty to ourselves, to our posterity, to God and humanity to destroy and utterly annihilate. This we must do for ourselves. If we neglect or refuse to do it, let things remain as they are, we shall justly be the prey of monopolists, the serfs of lords of land, slaves of lords of labor, and victims of lords of law ; be simply bread-winners—that and nothing more; fortunate in succeeding in accomplishing that, and escaping the almshouse and a pauper's grave at last. No higher aspirations of manhood can be indulged, no brighter prospects in the future for ourselves or the children to come after us; no addition to the legacy bequeathed us by our patriotic forefathers, who did what they could in their day for the upbuilding of humanity, but left an unfinished superstructure for those who came after them to complete. This must not be. The possibilities of humanity must not be circumscribed or rendered impossible by mere wealth, the creation of labor, or confined only to the possessors of it, however acquired, thus creating and continuing an aristocracy of the most pernicious kind. Labor must be rendered and esteemed as much a heaven-given ordinance as matrimony, and its increase just as sacred and inviolable to its producer ; and he that degrades or defrauds it rendered as odious and infamous as the licentious libertine. The oppressors of labor should be made to take their proper place with the slaveholder and tyrant of barbarous times, and the corrupt or unfaithful legislator justly placed in the category of fratricides, pirates and outlaws.

" Such is its work, undertaken in the fear and reverence of God, and with the same reliance and trust in His help and approval, and the same unshaken belief in the justice of the cause as our forefathers felt and expressed when they pledged their lives, their fortunes and their sacred honor to achieve the civil and religious liberty of the American colonies.

" Watchman ! what of the night ? The day is dawning, the City of Refuge is in sight. 'And they shall build houses and inhabit them ; and they shall plant vineyards and eat the fruit of them. They shall not build and another inhabit; they shall not plant and another eat.' —*Isaiah.*

" Clear seeing, a clear understanding, must always precede action; for action, to be efficient, must be intelligent.

" In giving a synopsis of its objects and purposes, its benefits and advantages, a manual for the efficient working of its methods, and a realization of the ends sought to be accomplished thereby, it will be necessary to *first define what it is not;* for the reason that many are inclined to draw their ideas, or patterns of societary workings, and methods of operations from the formularies of ' beneficial orders,' and the narrow range of the former trade union.

" The Assembly is neither the *one* nor the *other.* It is as much more and greater as a week's work, with all its attendant interests ; is greater than the giving of a dime for the relief of a fellow-mortal in distress, or aiming to restrict the industry of the world to the production of Chinese fans. As the *whole* is greater than a part, so the Assembly is greater than any organization founded simply to protect *one* interest, or to discharge *one* duty, be it even so great as that of benevolence.

" While it retains and fosters all the fraternal characteristics of the one, and the single trade protection of the other, it gathers into one fold *all* branches into which productive labor is now subdivided, and by the multiplied power of union protects and assists *all.* Isolation in the former method is weakness and invites oppression, and has always experienced its crushing effects. The impregnable strength of compact union deters and prevents assault, ostracism, black-list, martyrdom, and assures victory and triumph.

" The fraternity of the one is here supplemented and intensified by our business and educational purposes, by our world-wide and universal scope, embracing as it does in its care the entire wants and necessities of the worker of to-day in every part of the globe, under every condition of life, industrial and social. Its foundation of *exact methods* produces *exact results;* and the baffling and incomplete effects of the isolated trade society are avoided.

"At the founding of an Assembly the *Title Deed of Heaven to Man* of earth is read. Man's inalienable inheritance to his share for use is set forth. The right to life carries with it the right to the means of living. Human statutes that obstruct or deny these rights are wrong, unjust and must give way, and in time be reversed and obliterated. Man, the child, must come into his inheritance from God, the Father. In Oriental language hill and mountain are metaphorical terms for governments. The peoples composing these governments must have ' clean hands and pure hearts '—*i. e.*, their acts righteous, their principles pure—and they ' shall receive the blessing from the Lord. ' Such, and such alone, are the generation of them that seek Him.' In those rich, poetical languages ' gates ' and ' doors ' refer to instrumentalities —avenues of accomplishment. So, in founding an Assembly, the door is opened, the instrument furnished through which right may be established and justice perpetuated among men. The tabernacle— the dwelling-place of God—is among men. No longer shall men pine for justice or perish for lack of judgment. 'And He will dwell with them, and they shall be His people.'

"'God and Humanity.' How inseparably connected! God, the Universal Father; Man, the Universal Brother! The sacred symbol can never be effaced from the memory, or the sacred obligations we owe one to the other forgotten or neglected, without injury to ourselves.

"The unbroken circle is an impenetrable shield, protecting man in his threefold nature—physical, mental and moral. Golden silence guards the Assembly with the same jealous care that men guard their greatest treasures. Obedience to the 'officers of their choice,' rendered with the same alacrity as at the outposts of 'Honor and Danger,' is rewarded with the cordiality due to fidelity and safety.

"Efficiency should be aimed at in every Assembly. Feeble efforts and feeble means are sure to result in failure. Failure, in this day of great results and gigantic enterprise, should be held as beneath the dignity of workers in a cause so great, a world so full of resources. The equipment should be complete; the location the best for the purpose. All the symbols are important object lessons and have their teachings. All surroundings are inspiring and have an elevating or depressing effect, as they are good or indifferent. Enlightened liberality brings better return than pinching parsimony in equipping the Assembly, and gives stability. Accomplished officers always commit their work to memory. They take the floor and do their work without a book or impediment of any kind. This is the universal custom. The opening service, when well done, has a harmonizing effect, and results in a more pleasant and profitable session. Precision in detail soon leads to efficiency of work in all that is undertaken. In no part of the labors of an Assembly is this more apparent than in the 'covering' of an initiate. First impressions are most indelible. In most men they color and influence their societary life and determine their stability and usefulness. No effort should be spared to render the 'covering' as nearly perfect as possible.

"After the two principal officers at the Base and Capital have given their lectures, the initiate may be taken to an anteroom, where the work of the centre may be communicated by the Venerable Sage, and the important instructions of the Inspector in the secrets of the Master Workman's Roll Book, and the duties of the Almoner and Financial Secretary given. These should never be omitted. In this way the business of the Assembly will be interfered with but a very short time. After receiving the instructions, the initiate can work his way into the sanctuary in the usual manner, and receive the short closing address of the Master Workman. The friendly greetings of the members can follow. But little time of the Assembly proper has been consumed, yet a full instruction has been given. New and forgetful members, if they so desire, can, on permission of the Master Workman, accompany the Venerable Sage and refresh their memories in the unwritten work.

"Dispatch of business depends greatly on the Master Workman. He should call to his assistance as many light-footed and competent brothers as will be necessary to execute trifling duties, without for a moment quitting his station, except some important matter absolutely requires it. When so assisted he should politely give thanks in an audible tone of voice. When officially absent from his station, the Assembly should 'work from the Base,' as per form. The Master Workman, giving one tap, should say, 'The Assembly will now work from the Base,' and send the gavel to the Worthy Foreman by the hand of a messenger. The Worthy Foreman, giving one tap, should say, 'By order of the Master Workman the Assembly will now work from the Base.' Address is then made to, and motions put by, the Worthy Foreman. On again resuming his station, the Master Workman should give one tap and say, 'Work will now proceed in form from the Capital.'

"Time should always be taken to do all things decently and in order. If the world's workers are true to themselves they will not be long confined to evenings, in which the important matters of the industrial world must be hurried through. Shorter hours, 'five days for labor, one day for God and one for humanity,' in every week, will give more time to devote to the momentous interests of the world's redemption.

"It would be to some a startling proposition to hold society meetings in the day-time, on one of the working days of the week. Some would think they could not spare the time, that they could not afford it, etc. All such considerations would be true in relation to a society with circumscribed objects, though they were ever so good and laudable. But the Assembly is not a 'society;' it is a 'business firm,' every member an equal partner, as much so as a bank, a commercial house or a manufacturing establishment. Each one is in duty bound to put in his equal share of *money and time.* Nothing, absolutely nothing, has been done when the officers have been elected, if they are expected to run it and the partners to do nothing, as is the case in mere 'societies.' In this, earnest men quit playing 'society' and get down to *bona fide* work. Just in proportion as a broad, sensible view is taken of the situation of the toiler to-day, and broad, enlightened efforts are made to meet requirements of the situation, will be the benefits derived. 'As ye sow so shall ye also reap' fits exactly here, as much so as it does in the mercantile house, the factory or the bank. There can be no 'silent partners' in this business, and the working world will yet grow up to the *giant idea* that the labor question is the momentous question of the age and overshadows all others.

"Very few men have any just conception of the changed condition that exists to-day between the productive labor of the world (which includes their own, of course) and that which existed before the introduction of machinery production and steam-motive power, and the changed modes of conducting the world's commerce or exchange of products necessitated thereby.

" The individual producer is overwhelmed, lost sight of entirely, in the mighty combination of steam, electricity and paper exchange.

" The power of all these elements in trade have been developed to an almost illimitable degree in the few decades last past, while the power of one set of muscles or one brain (one individual) has remained, and must still remain, stationary. What is the per centum value that one producer sustains to the world's commerce to-day as compared with the value he bore when the world's work was done by muscle, unaided or supplemented by power-driven machinery? What is the secret of this mastery of material over man? Are human souls to grow of less value in exact ratio to the increase of wealth production by inanimate machinery? What will be the effect in a few years, or decades at most, of this domination of soulless material over the destiny of man? It is a question of the moral quite as much as of the material well-being of the race. Both are involved and cannot be separated.

" The answers to these momentous questions cannot be derived from narrow grounds or isolated interests. They must cover all, or they will fail to cover any satisfactorily. Thinking men stand dazed in the presence of the oncoming condition of the toiler involved in the supremacy of mere material wealth, the creation of his own labor. The heroic struggle of the trade unions was but partial and palliative, and contained no promise of ultimate cure. They had their uses, and are to be commended therefor. They taught their lessons to the toiling world, served their purpose, and left a legacy of experience for the guidance of the world to better methods and means more in accordance with the existing order of things to-day.

" These are a few hasty glances at the situation to touch up and sharpen the outlines of the work to be done by the Assembly, and a reminder that the world means business, and that labor efforts must conform to similar standards.

" In the foregoing the founding and opening services were alluded to and the covering instructing touched upon. Let us now take the departments in detail.

" The business of an active Assembly necessitates a large correspondence by the Secretary on matters of importance to the trades and callings of the membership. This correspondence should all be read and properly disposed of by the Assembly before leaving the Secretary's table to take up any other business. This will lead to the methodical disposition of the correspondence, and originate many points of interest and the development of fruitful sources of information. It is the reception of the 'week's mail,' and parceling the contents to the proper 'heads of business' or departments for future action and disposition further on in the session. It gives time for thought by members and consultation by committees, thus avoiding hasty action and immature conclusions. Hasty action and incomplete consideration are the bane of labor councils, and will be as long as they are confined to evening meetings. What would religion be without one day in seven, or one-seventh of the entire time? What would the legislation of a State or nation amount to if done in such a trivial manner? Is the every-day interest of a life-time so small, involving as it does the destiny of the race?

"It is a certain fact that the inventive genius of man and the wealth-producing capacity of the country were enhanced many fold by the adoption of the ten-hour system. What, then, may we not reasonably expect from a further shortening of the hours, or, what would be better, a reduction of the working days to five per week, and a consecration of one whole day to the interests of labor? Committees are the hands of the Assembly by which it works, and the Secretary's table is the place from whence the material is taken and to which the finished work is returned ready for this disposal of the Assembly. He should receive the cordial assistance of every one. His minutes are the crystallized action of the whole Assembly, and should be kept according to the best models and in the technical language of the Order. Any other mode would be as improper as it would for the sailor to conduct the affairs of a ship in the terms of the farm. An efficient navigator will not tolerate the landsman's phraseology on shipboard. Words and terms are more enduring than monuments, and have a direct influence on mankind.

"The Secretary should be stationed within easy, low-toned ear-shot of the Master Workman, and the two should act in perfect accord, for upon these two depend the successful conduct of the session. An efficient Secretary is invaluable, and should not be changed except on death or removal of residence. While the Master Workman is the *head*, the Secretary is the efficient *right hand* of the Assembly. His table should be thoroughly equipped with all the appliances necessary for the faithful discharge of his duties and the rapid dispatch of business. When well supplied with all the appurtenances of the office an active Assembly will keep him busy, and an efficient Secretary will keep the Assembly up to its work. His duties are distinct from that of the Financial Secretary, who is stationed at the Base, in the rear of the Worthy Foreman."

The manuscript of the remainder of the document is so torn and obscured as to be illegible. Sufficient of it is given to make clear the idea of the first Master Workman as to the duties of the officers and members of the society.

At the end of the first year the association had elected one hundred and thirteen candidates and initiated seventy into the mysteries of Knighthood.

On the occasion of the death of John Hobson, who died on March 10, 1871, it was decided to hold a memorial service in the sanctuary of Assembly No. 1, on the evening of March 16. At the meeting at which the motion to hold the memorial service was made, the Master Workman requested that some member volunteer to compose an original poem in commemoration of the services of the departed member. William Fennimore tendered his services, and at the meeting held on the 16th he read a poem, which was inscribed upon the minutes of the meeting. It is as follows:

A FALLEN FRIEND.

We stand to-night, as some will stand again,
    To mourn a friend and brother of the past,
Who formed a link in love's cemented chain,
    Whose weary limbs have found repose at last.

Time's wheels that move with never-ceasing roll,
    Along the shores of ever-ebbing streams,
Have brought another to his journey's goal,
    To sleep the sleep that's undisturbed by dreams.

Once more the cold and raven-colored hand
    Has passed around the sable cup of grief
For us to drink, though labor's tree may stand,
    To weep in sadness o'er the fallen leaf.

His nature social, ever free and kind
    To give instruction or assistance lend,
With mind congenial to congenial mind,
    A hand to grasp the stranger or a friend.

The head that once an active brain possessed
    Is wrapt in slumber never more to wake
To friendship's call; but on its pillow rests,
    Till on his brow the final day shall break.

The eye that beamed with penetrating glance,
    That's faded now and withered with the brain,
Will never more with love and pleasure dance,
    Or weep in sorrow with a brother's pain.

The tongue is palsied, silent is the voice,
    And never more the kind and friendly word,
To make the hearts at home or friend rejoice,
    Will at his home or by his friends be heard.

The heart that throbbed with kindness warm and true
    Has ceased to beat and every pulse is still;
Its warmth is gone, and cold as autumn dew,
    Resistless lies in silence, awe and chill.

The hand that labored long has lost its grasp,
    And in repose is laid upon his breast;
Yet memory holds the strong fraternal grasp
    That linked our hearts in labor or in rest.

Those passive feet have left a vacant place,
  And listening ear will never hear their tread ;
So let us leave with meek, becoming grace,
  Our friend to slumber with the dead.

ADELPHON KRUPTOS, treasured in his heart,
  Was guarded well by silence, truth and trust ;
For never deigning with the gem to part,
  His praise to speak is only speaking just.

Then let us keep his memory ever green,
  In hearts as true as his we meet to mourn ;
Then when we fall by darts that fly unseen,
  True-hearted friends will think of us in turn.

And where kind duty laid with many a sigh
  His weary form in solitude to sleep,
The rose shall borrow from the evening sky,
  Or give its blush for Christian tears to weep.

And autumn winds shall through the branches moan,
  As though in sorrow o'er the silent scene;
And vernal beauty, when the blight is gone,
  Each year renew his grave with living green.

On July 18, 1872, Assembly No. 2 was organized, and those who had been connected with No. 1 as sojourners took leave of the parent Assembly for the purpose of organizing the ship carpenters and calkers of Philadelphia and surroundings. The second Assembly once under way, the work of organization made rapid progress. Thomas Thompson, the Master Workman of Assembly No. 2, was an untiring worker, and left nothing undone to not only strengthen his own Assembly but to organize new ones. It was the practice to propose and initiate all sojourners in Assembly No. 1, and when a sufficient number were enlisted to draw them out or allow them to sojourn to a new Assembly of their own calling.

The organization of new Assemblies did not prevent the workers of No. 1 from initiating persons whose crafts were organized. When a member of No. 1 discovered a man who would make a good member, he proposed his name in No. 1, had him initiated, and then gave him a card with which to gain admittance to the Assembly of his craft.

On December 21, 1872, Assembly No. 3, shawl weavers, was organized. No. 4, carpet weavers, was organized shortly afterward. No. 5, riggers, was founded by U. S. Stephens, March 27, 1873. Assembly No. 6, carpet weavers, was organized at Kensington soon after the founding of No. 5.

A singular incident occurred after the organization of No. 6. One day some of the carpet weavers were returning to the mill, after dinner, when they were accosted by two strangers, who asked if they could get an audience with a number of carpet weavers. On being told that they were talking to carpet weavers, they stated that they were about to start a carpet factory in Leavenworth, Kan., and wished to secure the services of experienced workmen to go there to operate the factory. That evening No. 6 held a meeting. There were just enough members initiated to make up the number required by the men who represented the Kansas firm. They passed a motion to go to Leavenworth in a body, and take the Assembly with them. Every man of No. 6 went to the West, and when they arrived in Leavenworth established an Assembly there under the advice and instructions of Mr. Stephens, who attended the last meeting they held in Kensington prior to their departure.

After the organization of No. 6 Assemblies were instituted very rapidly, and before the end of the year over eighty Assemblies were in operation. No. 7 was composed of stonemasons. No. 8, bagmakers, was organized May 8, 1873; No. 9, machinists and machine blacksmiths; No. 10, stonecutters; No. 11, wool sorters; No. 12, machinists, blacksmiths and boilermakers; No. 13, tin-plate and sheet-iron workers; No. 14, steelmakers; No. 15, patternmakers and moulders; No. 16, shopsmiths; No. 17, machinists, blacksmiths and boilermakers; No. 18, house carpenters; No. 19, bricklayers; No. 20, gold-beaters. Assemblies Nos. 21, 22, 23, 24, 25, 26 and 27 were organized almost simultaneously. No. 28, gold-beaters, was organized in New York City. No. 30 was organized in Wilmington, Del.; it was composed of ship carpenters and calkers. No. 31, of the same calling, was soon after organized in Camden, N. J.

With the organization of Assemblies outside of Philadelphia there arose a necessity for a uniform code of laws, as well as for a printed form of ritual. Up to this time the ritual was not printed. The work was enlarged upon and perfected as the Order progressed. The Committee on Ritual continued to make its reports, adding new forms and ceremonies as the necessity for their use became apparent. It became necessary to have Organizers stationed in the cities and towns where Assemblies were organized to answer the call for organization as it arose. A trusted member of the Order was selected, his name would be submitted to Assembly No. 1, and if it was deemed satisfactory he would be authorized to organize and found Assemblies.

When an Organizer was commissioned in this way he was given a set of numbers which it became his duty to apply to the Assemblies he founded; thus, Nos. 100 to 120 were given to one Organizer, Nos. 121 to 141 were given to another, and in this way the numbers were given out. It was because of this practice that the record of a number of Assemblies could not be obtained when the General Assembly was finally organized. Sometimes the full number would not be filled out by the Organizer, and as a consequence no Assemblies representing such numbers could be found.

THE STORM BREAKS.

Poor naked wretches, wheresoe'er you are,
That bide the pelting of this pitiless STORM,
How shall your houseless heads and unfed sides,
Your loop'd and window'd raggedness, defend you
From seasons such as these?—*Shakespeare.*

In the fall of 1873, Assembly No. 1 appointed a Committee of Progress, consisting of five of the oldest and most experienced members. A request went out to the other Assemblies to take similar action. When the joint committees met they saw the necessity for the institution of a system whereby the representatives of the different Assemblies could meet for the discussion of measures of importance to all. It was decided to organize a District Assembly, and, when all the Assemblies in Philadelphia had instructed their committees to advocate the adoption of the new system, each Assembly elected three delegates to attend a meeting for the purpose of organizing a District Assembly. The preliminary meeting was held on the 18th of December, and the meeting on which the District was organized was held on Christmas day, 1873.

Although the charter of D. A. 1, which was not issued until February, 1878, shows that some of the Assemblies were numbered as high as 262, they were not in existence at the date of organization, but they were attached to the District in 1878, when the first charter was issued. Assembly No. 84 of New Brunswick was organized prior to the formation of D. A. 1, and Assembly No. 88 of Scranton, Pa., was organized shortly afterward.

On October 14, 1874, D. A. 2 was organized in Camden, N. J. It was composed at date of organization of Assemblies Nos. 22, 31, 52, 54 and 60. In two weeks afterward Nos. 66 and 69 were added to the roll of D. A. 2.

In order to save space in writing, and to keep the names of the separate organizations as secret as possible, even among members, it was decided that the Assembly should be known as the " A.," while the District Assembly should be known as the " D. A."

D. A. 2 was organized and founded by Mr. Stephens, and in a short time he was called on to organize some Assemblies in Reading, Pa. It was the custom, whenever any prominent workingman visited Philadelphia, to initiate him into such Assembly as would be in session during his visit. Engineers, and railroad men generally, who were

99

running trains out of Philadelphia, were initiated with the express purpose of having them take the Order to other points. When enough men had been initiated in Reading to form an Assembly, Messrs. Stephens, McCauley and Wright went up one Saturday night and on Sunday organized an Assembly. They returned to Philadelphia on Sunday night, and were at work as usual on Monday morning. They charged nothing for their time or services, and voluntarily contributed their car-fare in order that the new organization might flourish.

The organization having gained a secure foothold in the East, the attention of the active workers was turned toward the West. Pittsburg, constituting a vast hive of industry, was selected as the base of operations for the territory west of the Alleghenies, and the first opportunity which presented itself was taken advantage of by those who had carried on the work from the beginning.

On January 9, 1873, John M. Davis began the publication of the *National Labor Tribune* of Pittsburg, and in a short time run the circulation of the paper up to six thousand, principally among miners and rolling-mill men. On June 25 of that year the miners struck, and about four thousand of the subscribers failed to pay their subscriptions to the paper. The strike continued until October, and when it came to an end it was feared that the paper would do the same for lack of financial support, but Mr. Davis persevered and kept the paper going. He took in as partners Thomas A. Armstrong and Henry Palmer on December 28, giving each a third interest.

While these gentlemen were associated with Mr. Davis he heard of the existence of the organization, and in October, 1874, went to Philadelphia to be initiated. He was taken to Assembly No. 53, cigarmakers, and was admitted to membership in October, 1874. On his return to Pittsburg he at once called together a number of his workingmen friends and organized Assembly No. 81. The Assembly was composed of iron-workers. James L. Wright and Frederick Turner went from Philadelphia to assist in the organization.

The next Assembly was organized at Coal Valley. It was No. 96, and was composed of miners. No. 98, cabinetmakers, was next organized in Pittsburg. Then Nos. 100 and 106; the latter at Gallitzin. Mr. Davis then began to push the organization further westward with the aid of deputies. One of the most active workers among them was L. J. Booker, who traveled through Ohio and Indiana in the interest of the organization.

In March, 1875, Mr. Davis issued a call for a convention of delegates from the Assemblies of Pittsburg and vicinity. All of the Assemblies sent delegates, and it was decided to form a District Assembly, but the convention was in doubt as to the method of procedure. It was not until August 8, 1875, that D. A. 3 was founded. Mr. Stephens responded to the call of Mr. Davis, and performed the founding ceremony. Mr. Booker was elected Corresponding Secretary of the District Assembly, and Mr. Davis was called to the Master Workman's chair.

After the institution of D. A. 3, the officers put forth every effort to spread the Order in all directions. The coke region was organized, Assemblies were founded in Akron, Ohio, along the Ohio and Monongahela Rivers, and in various other parts of the West. During this time an Assembly was organized, through the efforts of Messrs. Davis and Booker, in Rock Springs, Wyoming.

There was much opposition from the start in Pittsburg. It was very difficult to have the proceedings and other work of the District Assembly printed. Absolute secrecy prevailed, and only when Mr. Davis found time to write could he send out instructions to the various Assemblies. He devoted all of his means to the building up of the Order, and traveled from place to place on foot to do the work. Mr. Booker, although a cigarmaker, bought a font of type and set up the proceedings with his own hands. Jealousy and trickery played their parts then as now, and secretly the efforts of the workers of D. A. 3 were opposed; but in the face of all obstacles over one hundred Assemblies were organized previous to January 1, 1876. On June 30, 1876, the last meeting of D. A. 3 was held under its old form, and after two years of struggle the officers of the District were obliged to yield to the pressure which was brought to bear against them.

All of this time there was but one Assembly in Pittsburg — the iron-workers—for the cabinetmakers had disbanded in a few months because the socialistic idea was not more prominent in the Order.

The officers of D. A. 3 were very often embarrassed by reason of the length of time necessary to receive supplies and communications from Philadelphia. They had to make their own passwords, and in many other ways were obliged to depend on themselves for aid which should come from the officers of D. A. 1, who were too busily engaged in the work of organizing the Eastern cities and towns.

In organizing through the West, Messrs. Davis and Booker were obliged to give out numbers to Assemblies and Districts, and in many instances they proved to be duplicates of those given out to Eastern Assemblies by D. A. 1. In rapid succession District Assemblies were organized in Connellsville, Pa.; Akron, Ohio; and along the Kanawha River in West Virginia. The District Assembly organized in Raymond City, W. Va., was No. 5. About the same time a District was founded in Scranton, and was given No. 5 by D. A. 1 of Philadelphia.

The last convention of the Knights of St. Crispen was held in Boston in 1876. The Cincinnati branch of that organization was represented by Joseph N. Glenn, who visited New York on his way to the convention and while there was initiated into the Knights of Labor. When Mr. Glenn returned to Cincinnati he gave a glowing account of the organization he had connected himself with, and on Sunday, April 24, 1877, thirteen shoemakers met in Workman's Hall and organized what was afterward known as Assembly 280. Among the charter members was Hugh Cavanaugh, who had up to that time endeavored to keep alive the local branch of the Knights of St. Crispen. Mr. Cavanaugh has since then devoted his time and energies to the organization of the Knights of Labor.

Desiring to obtain more information the Cincinnati Assembly requested L. J. Booker to visit them, and about the 20th of May, 1877, he went to Cincinnati, attended a meeting of the Assembly there and imparted to the members his knowledge of the workings of the Order.

It was understood that until a national organization was formed, D. A. 1 was to be the recognized head of the Order. All orders were to emanate from that source, and all numbers were to be given out under that authority. When D. A. 3 met with such phenomenal success in organizing new Assemblies and Districts, a jealously sprung up between that body and D. A. 1. For a time this feeling threatened to destroy the chances for a harmonious blending of the various parts of the Order. When the District was organized in West Virginia, D. A. 1 was not notified of it, nor of the fact that the new organization was to be known as D. A. 5; and in ignorance of that fact, as well as of the organization of other Assemblies and District Assemblies, D. A. 1 continued to duplicate the numbers which were given by D. A. 3. D. A. 5 of Raymond City, W. Va , and the District in Scranton, Pa., continued to work under the same number until the meeting of the General Assembly in Reading, Pa., in January, 1878.

On January 23, 1876, Uriah S. Stephens founded D. A. 4 at Reading, Pa. The Assemblies on the roll of the District at date of founding were Nos. 86, 99, 125, 126, 127, 128, 130, 165, 171, 172 and 173 of Reading, 92 of Allentown, 118 of Pottstown, and 129 of Royersford. The Assemblies which were assigned to D. A. 4 by D. A. 1, but not represented by delegates on the evening on which the new District Assembly was founded, were Nos. 90 of Bethlehem, 88 of Scranton, 91 of Allentown, 132 of St. Clair and 133 of Bethlehem, Pa. The parent Assembly in Reading, No. 86, was organized May 19, 1875.

The Master Workman of D. A. 4 was George Rieff; Worthy Foreman, Samuel Burkhart; Recording Secretary, Wesley Horning; Corresponding Secretary, Thomas King ; Treasurer, George Corbett; Financial Secretary, George Reisinger ; and the Venerable Sage of the District was Samuel Whittaker.

D. A. 4 made rapid progress, and in a short time spread over the greater part of the anthracite coal fields. Until the organization of the District at Scranton, all Assemblies organized in the upper anthracite coal fields were attached to D. A. 4 of Reading.

The first Assembly in the Lackawanna Valley was organized May 15,

1875, by Frederick Turner and James L. Wright, who visited Scranton for the purpose of planting the Order in the upper coal fields. Acting under instructions from Mr. Turner, the stationary engineers employed in and around the coal mines held several meetings for the purpose of making arrangements to form a society. But little interest was taken in the enterprise by the engineers, and when Messrs. Wright and Turner went from Philadelphia to organize them there were but eight persons at the meeting. With this number Assembly No. 88 was instituted, and for a long time it was a difficult matter to induce men to join the organization. The extreme secrecy which characterized the early days of Assembly No. 1 was emulated by their pupils of No. 88; in fact, those who were admitted were not told of the name of the society for weeks after they were initiated. None but stationary engineers were admitted for over a year, at the end of which time Messrs. Wright and Turner paid a second visit. This time to found the Assembly. On performing this ceremony they informed the members of No. 88 that they were at liberty to admit men of other trades and callings as "sojourners" and that it was a part of their mission to make Assembly No. 88 the foundation for a powerful association of all trades and callings in the anthracite region.

The first person not a stationary engineer to be admitted was a coal miner. His admission was contested for some time by the members who had not yet realized the necessity for a bond of union between all workingmen. The first Master Workman of No. 88 was John F. Williams, who worked zealously for the success of the Assembly, and after the miners began to gain admittance, he had the satisfaction of seeing other names proposed.

As soon as there were thirty miners enrolled they sojourned and formed an Assembly of that craft in the upper end of the city known as Providence. The number of the new Assembly was 216. It was founded on July 3, 1876, by George W. George, a member of No. 88, who had been commissioned Organizer by D. A. 1, under jurisdiction of D. A. 4 of Reading.

On the founding of Assembly No. 88 it was attached to District 1 of Philadelphia, but was transferred to D. A. 4 of Reading, when that District Assembly was founded. A number of carpenters who had been admitted to No. 88 sojourned from that Assembly on August 29, 1876, and organized No. 217 of Scranton, Pa., with Duncan Wright as Master Workman and George Starkey as Worthy Foreman. A number of the employes of the Dickson Manufacturing Company's Locomotive Works were initiated in No. 88 during the summer of 1876, and on October 14 of that year Assembly No. 222 was organized. On September 6, T. V. Powderly was admitted to Assembly No. 88. He was formerly initiated and instructed in 1874 at Philadelphia, but could learn nothing of the whereabouts of the Order until he was

sought out by a member of No. 88. When Assembly No. 222 was
organized, T. V. Powderly was elected Master Workman; Joshua R.
Thomas, Worthy Foreman, John Fitzgibbons, Recording Secretary.

Organizer George found plenty of work to do after the organization
of No. 222. No. 223 was soon after established in Carbondale.
Assembly No. 224 was organized in Wilkes-Barre, No. 225 at Danville, No. 226 at Dunmore, No. 227 at Scranton; Nos. 228, 229, 230 and
231 were soon organized. When No. 231 was organized the question
of establishing a District Assembly was brought up at a meeting of
representatives from the Scranton Assemblies on January 1, 1877, and
on the 19th of that month the first meeting for the purpose of organizing the District was held in Machinists' and Blacksmiths' Union
Hall, Scranton. Each Assembly was represented by three delegates,
but none of them had ever attended a meeting of a District Assembly,
and, with the exception of expressing their willingness to organize,
no steps were taken in that direction. George W. George was delegated to go to Reading and attend the next session of D. A. 4, and on
his return to issue a call for the delegates to reassemble. The call
was issued for February 24, and on that evening, in the same hall,
D. A. 5, now No. 16, was organized. James Albert Clarke, then
editor of the Scranton *Free Patrol*, and at this writing editor of the
Free Quill, Laurel, Md., was elected District Master Workman;
Edward Black of Wilkes-Barre was elected Recording Secretary;
T. V. Powderly was elected Corresponding Secretary; and Joshua
R. Thomas was delegated to act as Treasurer.

It was voted at the meeting to levy a per capita tax on each
member of one cent per month for organizing purposes. Joshua R.
Thomas was elected Organizer, and deputized to give his whole time
to the work. He at once entered upon the performance of his duties,
and in a short time the work of organization spread through the
whole valley. On July 1, 1877, D. A. 5 had one hundred and seven
Assemblies within its jurisdiction, and, although the work was
carried on at fever heat, not a word concerning the Order was
breathed above a whisper, not a sentence that could be understood
as having a bearing on the organization appeared in the press.

A notice of a reduction of wages, the same to take effect on July 1,
1877, was served on the employes of the Lackawanna Iron and Coal
Company at Scranton. With the promulgation of this notice began an
agitation among the men. No cessation of work took place on July 1,
but iron-workers, who were members of the Knights of Labor, began
at once to take steps to bring their fellow-workmen into the Order.
Wages at the time were low in consequence of the many reductions
which had followed the panic of 1873, but it is not likely that a strike
would have followed had it not been for a train of circumstances
which led up to it.

On July 16 the employes of the Baltimore and Ohio Railroad, who were engaged in transportation of trains at Martinsburg, W. Va., struck against a reduction of wages, which was to take effect on that date. The strike spread along the entire Baltimore and Ohio system, and communicated to the Pennsylvania Railroad on the 19th of July.

The history of that strike has been written by others, and reference to it in these pages is for the purpose of explaining the connection of the Knights of Labor with the great railroad strike of 1877. The men on the Baltimore and Ohio were not organized, and no concert of action was taken by them, although the strike spread with amazing rapidity along the entire system.

On June 1 the Pennsylvania Railroad notified its employes that their wages would be reduced, and at once all railroads centering at Pittsburg began to agitate the question of effecting a restoration of the ten per cent. reduction. On June 2 a meeting of railroad men was held at Allegheny City, and a "Trainmen's Union" was organized. The leading spirit in the movement was R. A. Ammon, better known during the strike as "Boss Ammon," owing to the fact that during one whole day he held absolute sway over the entire affairs of the Pennsylvania Railroad in and around Pittsburg.

The agitation continued until July 19, and at that time was beginning to slumber, when the events on the Baltimore and Ohio Railroad rekindled the fires along the line of the Pennsylvania, and on the 19th the employes of that railroad struck work. There were but few Knights of Labor on the Pennsylvania, and as such none took part in the strike; but the members of the Order in and around Pittsburg took an active interest in the movement, and endeavored to effect a thorough organization of the "Trainmen's Union" with a view to having a uniformity of action. The most active Knights of Labor at the time was Thomas A. Armstrong, editor of the *National Labor Tribune.* He was untiring in his efforts to keep down the boisterous element that flocked to Pittsburg at that time. He held several meetings with the trainmen, counseled moderation, and advised them to avoid contact with the idle element that at the time seemed bent on mischief. The advice that he gave was re-echoed by every member of the Order who had any influence with the strikers. It is but just to the strikers to say that they followed the advice as far as practicable, and, had it been left to them, there would never have been an act of violence committed during the strike.

The discriminations of the Pennsylvania Railroad against the city did not make many friends for that corporation in Pittsburg; and when the riot began it was noticed that business men everywhere expressed sympathy for the striking employes, and in many instances were found among the rioters aiding in destroying the property of the company.

The Pennsylvania Legislature appointed a committee to investigate the cause of the strike throughout the State. Referring to the feeling at Pittsburg, the report of the committee says.

"From the first commencement of the strike, the strikers had the active sympathy of a large portion of the people of Pittsburg. The citizens had a bitter feeling against the Pennsylvania Railroad Company on account of, as they believed, an unjust discrimination by the railroad company against them in freight rates, which made it very difficult for their manufacturers to compete successfully with manufacturers further West, and this feeling had existed and been intensified for years and pervaded all classes. A large portion of the people also believed that the railroad company was not dealing fairly by its men in making the last reduction in wages, and the tradesmen with whom the trainmen dealt also had a direct sympathy with the men in this reduction, for its results would affect their pockets. The large class of laborers in the different mills, manufactories, mines and other industries in Pittsburg and vicinity were also strongly in sympathy with the railroad strikers, considering the cause of the railroad men their cause, as their wages had also been reduced for the same causes as were those of the railroad men, and they were not only willing but anxious to make a common fight against the corporations. This feeling of aversion to the railroad company and sympathy with the strikers were indulged in by the Pittsburg troops to the same extent that it was by the other classes, and, as many of them had friends and relatives in the mob, it is not to be wondered at that they did not show much anxiety to assist in dispersing the crowd and enforcing the law."

On Friday, July 20, a committee of the strikers waited on the Superintendent of the Pittsburg Division of the Pennsylvania Railroad and presented him with a written statement of the demands of the men. The following is a correct copy of the demands:

"BROTHERHOOD OF LOCOMOTIVE ENGINEERS,
PITTSBURG DIVISION NO. 50.
PITTSBURG, Pa., July 20, 1877.

"*To the Superintendent Western Division, Pennsylvania Railroad:*

"1st. We, the undersigned committee appointed by the employes of the Western Division of the Pennsylvania Railroad Company, do hereby demand from said company, through the proper officers of said company, the wages as per department of engineers, firemen, conductors, brakemen and flagmen as received prior to June 1, 1877.

"2d. That each and every employe who has been dismissed for taking part or parts in said strikes to be restored to their respective positions.

"3d. That the classification of each of said departments be abolished now and forever hereafter.

"4th. That engineers and conductors receive the wages as received by said engineers and conductors of the highest class prior to June 1, 1877.

"5th. That the running of double trains be abolished, excepting coal trains.

"6th. That each and every engine, whether road or shifting, shall have its own fireman.

"Respectfully submitted to you for your immediate consideration.

> "J. S. McCAULEY,
> "D. H. NEWHART,
> "JOHN SHANA,
> "G. HARRIS,
> "J. P. KESSLER,
> *"Committee."*

Mr. Pitcairn declined to send this document to the President of the Pennsylvania Company, Thomas A. Scott, and told the committee that the company would not accede to the demands.

Citizens of Pittsburg made an effort to have the company and men agree on some settlement, but the superintendent informed them that the case was in the hands of the State authorities, and that the military would have to settle the matter unless the strikers withdrew from the company's property.

On Saturday night and Sunday, July 21 and 22, about sixteen hundred cars (mostly freight), including many passenger and baggage cars, with all of their contents that remained in them after the raid of the day previous; one hundred and twenty-six locomotives, and all the shops' materials and buildings between Twenty-eighth Street and the Union Depot, were burned.

It is not probable that so many locomotives would have been centered at one point were it not for the interest taken in the shaping of legislation by the agents of the railways during the previous session of the Legislature.

On the 22d of March, 1877, the Governor of Pennsylvania, John F. Hartranft, signed the law of which the following is the preamble and first section:

WHEREAS, Strikes by locomotive engineers and other railroad employes, and the abandonment by them of their engines and trains at points other than their schedule destination, endanger the safety of passengers and subject shippers of freights to great inconvenience, delay and loss. Therefore

SECTION 1. *Be it enacted, etc.,* That if any locomotive engineer, or other railroad employe upon any railroad within this State, engaged in any strike, or with a view to incite others to such strike, or in futherance of any combination or preconcerted arrangement with any other person to bring about a strike, shall abandon the locomotive engine in his charge, when attached either to a passenger or a freight train, at any place other than the schedule or otherwise appointed destination of such train, or shall refuse or neglect to continue to discharge his duty, or to proceed with said train to the place of destination, as aforesaid, he shall be deemed guilty of a misdemeanor, and upon conviction thereof shall be fined not less than one hundred nor more than five hundred dollars, and may be imprisoned for a term not exceeding six months, at the discretion of the court.

The " Tramp Act " of the session of 1876, and the act of which the above is a part, had a tendency to cause workingmen to think that the Legislature of Pennsylvania was in sympathy with the corporations of the State, and a very bitter feeling existed against the corporation in consequence thereof. The tendency of legislation of that day was in accord with the wishes of large corporations, and workingmen generally felt that wealth had as controlling an interest in the halls of legislation as in the workshops which it directly controlled and managed.

The damage to property in Pittsburg alone amounted to $5,000,000, and, taken altogether, it was a costly experiment both for strikers and employers. While the strike might not have taken place, it is certain that loss of life and property would have been avoided had conciliation been called into play in the beginning.

When the news of the strike on the Baltimore and Ohio Railroad, and the one succeeding it on the Pennsylvania, reached Scranton, it found the workingmen in the entire Lackawanna and Wyoming Valleys on the tip-toe of anxiety and expectancy.

On Sunday, July 22, the brakemen on the Delaware, Lackawanna and Western Railroad held a meeting at Scranton and passed the following resolutions :

Resolved, That we, the brakemen of the Delaware, Lackawanna and Western Railroad, know that our wages are not sufficient for the work performed by us.

Resolved, That we, the brakemen of the said Delaware, Lackawanna and Western Railroad, send a committee to confer with the superintendent of the railroad and state our grievances to him.

Resolved, That we ask him to readjust our wages to the rate per day which we received during 1876, and that we send a committee to communicate with the grand officers of the Brakemen's Brotherhood, and to solicit their support.

Resolved, That we ask our superintendent to let us know by six o'clock on Tuesday whether he can comply with our request.

P. FORKIN,
E. McALPIN,
J. GAGHEGAN,
Committee.

William F. Halstead, the Superintendent, received the committee, and informed them that he had no authority to restore the wages as requested, but would take pleasure in presenting their claims to the President of the company, Samuel Sloan. He wired Mr. Sloan and received his reply, which was unfavorable to the employes, in time to lay it before the men on Tuesday afternoon, and on Wednesday morning the running of trains on the Delaware, Lackawanna and Western Railroad ceased. At noon on Tuesday the rolling-mill and steel-mill men employed by the Lackawanna Iron and Coal Company quit work, and increased the number of idle men.

On Wednesday morning the railroad men refused to allow any trains to run on the Delaware, Lackawanna and Western Road, and at ten o'clock that morning detached the passenger coaches from the mail car on the morning train for New York when it reached the Scranton Station. The men telegraphed to Governor Hartranft and the Postoffice Department at Washington expressing their willingness to allow all mail cars to go through. The Governor advised that the mail cars be allowed to run, but the contract which the Delaware, Lackawanna and Western Company had made with the government only called for the carrying of the mails with passenger trains, and the superintendent refused to allow the mail car to proceed without the passenger coaches.

On Wednesday, the 25th, the miners employed by the Delaware, Lackawanna and Western Company held an out-door meeting and passed the following resolutions :

WHEREAS, We, the employes of the Delaware, Lackawanna and Western Railroad Company, believe that we are not getting a just remuneration for our labor, or a sufficient supply for ourselves and families of the common necessaries of life. Therefore

Resolved, That we demand a twenty-five per cent. advance on the present rate of wages ; also, it is further

Resolved, That with the refusal of these demands all work will be abandoned from date, as we have willingly submitted to the reduction without a murmur or resistance ; and finding that it now fails us to live as becomes citizens of a civilized nation, we take these steps in order to supply ourselves and little ones with the necessaries of life.

A committee of six miners waited on the General Coal Agent of the company, William R. Storrs, and laid the resolutions before him for his advice. Mr. Storrs courteously informed the committee that he would present their resolutions to the president of the company, and would give them his answer at the first possible moment. The answer sent from New York by Mr. Sloan, the President of the company, was unfavorable, and the strike of the coal miners was commenced.

The strike in the coal fields took place between the sessions of D. A. 5, and that body, which alone had the right to decide such matters for the government of the Assemblies within its jurisdiction, had no opportunity to deliberate upon the matter until the strike was inaugurated. It would have made no difference in any event, for the wave of excitement was so swift and strong as to carry all obstacles before it, and, had the District ordered the members of the Order not to take a part in the strike, the order could not have been obeyed.

The strike in Scranton began among those who had no knowledge of the Knights of Labor; they were not amenable to the laws of that Order; knowing nothing of its existence, they could not take counsel from its members. The railroads thrown idle, the mines as a necessary consequence could not work for want of cars to take away the coal.

The strike once inaugurated, a joint meeting of the Assemblies located in the city of Scranton was held, and the following resolutions were passed and ordered read at all meetings of the Assemblies represented:

WHEREAS, A general strike has been inaugurated among all classes of workmen in the Lackawanna Valley; and

WHEREAS, Said strike was precipitated upon the miners, laborers, railroad men and mechanics of all grades who are members of the * * * * * without consultation, and before the advice of the * * * * * was asked for or given. Therefore

Resolved, That while expressing our sympathy for the men who are engaged in the strike, while hoping for a settlement of the same upon a basis which will be favorable to their interests, and while counseling moderation in every action which may be taken, we urge upon our members to exercise the greatest caution, so that no evil effects may be visited upon them at the termination of the strike.

Resolved, That we extend our moral aid to those who are engaged in this struggle, and pledge to them our best efforts to bring the strike to a successful termination through counsel and advice.

Resolved, That under no circumstances shall any member of this Order, or other person, have any claims against the Order for injury to interests or estate. Said strike was not entered upon on the order of the * * * * * is not being conducted under its auspices, and the * * * * * will not in any way hold itself responsible for anything that may occur during the continuance of the said strike.

Resolved, That we counsel all members of the * * * * * to refrain from visiting saloons and public houses during the strike, and urge upon them not to attend any out-door or public meetings, except those called at the order of responsible persons, who may be authorized to call such meetings.

Resolved, That we counsel the greatest moderation in speech and action, and urge upon all members of the * * * * * to assist in maintaining the peace and prosperity of the community.

The miners were advised to hold meetings by collieries, and to select representatives to voice their sentiments at a general meeting. It was also ordered that all meetings be held in what was known as the Round Woods, a tract of woodland situated on an eminence above the city. Whenever meetings were held in the Round Woods they were attended by miners who possessed influence enough to at all times prevent the passage of incendiary resolutions or motions. The presence of these men was never necessary to preserve order, for all meetings held in the Round Woods were conducted with due decorum.

On July 31 the brakemen and firemen yielded, and voted to return to work at the old terms. This action, when communicated to the miners, was received with anything but enthusiasm, and many expressed themselves as being unwilling to return until their demands were acceded to. Several prominent miners held a consultation and agreed to issue a call for a meeting at the Round Woods, where the miners, in mass-meeting, could decide for themselves whether to return to work or not.

The notice went out and everything was arranged for the meeting at the Round Woods. Late in the afternoon of the 31st a rumor was circulated that the place of meeting was changed from the Round Woods to the silk-mill. It was stated that there was more room, and that the location was more central than the other. Who started the rumor is not known, but it was industriously circulated through the streets.

The men who had agreed upon holding the meeting in the Round Woods had gone home, and were not consulted as to the change. They alone had the right to call the meeting; but once called, others took it upon themselves to change the place. On the morning of the 1st of August crowds began to assemble both at the Round Woods and at the silk-mill. The meeting at the silk-mill was called for an earlier hour than the other, and before the chosen representatives of the miners had assembled at the Round Woods those who had gone there to attend the meeting had disbanded and gone over to the silk-mill meeting.

Between five and six thousand men assembled at the silk-mill and organized the meeting by selecting a chairman. Several men who were prominent in the Knights of Labor gained the platform after one or two speeches had been made and attempted to address the multitude. The speeches thus far were calculated to appeal to the passions, rather than the reason, of the men, and the Knights intended to advise calm, deliberate action. No action looking to an adjustment of the difficulty between the miners and their employers was taken for the reason that the committee having the matter in hand had not arrived upon the scene. A motion was made that a committee be appointed to wait on the men who were at work in the Delaware, Lackawanna and Western shops, and the rolling-mills, shops and blast furnaces of the Lackawanna Iron and Coal Company. The number stated was twenty-five, but the chairman of the meeting, who was a discreet man, advised that a small committee be appointed, in view of the fact that every man who served on it would be discharged. The advice of the chairman was accepted, and a motion to appoint a small committee was substituted, and would have been carried had it not been for the reading of a letter. A man elbowed his way through the mass of humanity and handed a letter to the chairman to read. He glanced over it and handed it back with a disapproving shake of the head, and proceeded to put the motion, when the bearer of the letter demanded that it be read, as it contained important developments.

The chairman endeavored to suppress it, but the insinuation was made that he dared not allow it to be read, and at once the cry, " Read the letter ! " was taken up, and the voice of the presiding officer was powerless. The man who held the letter mounted the platform and read off the death warrant of one man who was not within a mile of the meeting, and knew nothing about what was going on ; another, who was on the outskirts of the meeting, who had no voice in the deliberations, and went with the crowd through curiosity; and another who led the crowd from the silk-mill until it reached the scene of conflict.

The purport of the letter was that the manager of the Lackawanna Iron and Coal Company, W. W. Scranton, had asserted that he would yet have the men working for three shillings a day, and would have them buried at the base of the culm heaps about the city when they died. The effect of the reading of that letter was exactly what the villain who wrote it anticipated. Whether he was employed by the enemy of the workingmen to write it, or whether it was the product of his own vile brain, the effect was the same ; and if ever man was accountable for the blood of his fellow-man, the writer of that letter stands in the sight of heaven a red-handed murderer.

The meeting broke up in disorder. The last subject before it was the appointing of a committee to wait on the men in the shops, and at once the vast crowd began to move in that direction. The Knights of Labor, who had attended the meeting with a view to heading off any disturbance, at once held a consultation, and determined to lead the men away from the centre of the city, and away from the shops. One man started across the river with the request that the men follow him ; another went up the hill ; and a third started in another direction. Of the number who assembled at the silk-mill about fifteen hundred started in the direction of the shops, and the remainder went in the directions named.

When the strike was inaugurated, the Mayor of Scranton issued a call for assistance and appointed a committee of prominent citizens to advise with him during the crisis. He asked the Councils to appoint a special police force, and to otherwise act in preserving order. The Councils refused to take action, claiming that there was no occasion for it, and that such a step would have the effect of creating a breach of the peace. Committees from the railroad men and miners waited on the Mayor and assured him of their loyalty to law and order, and offered to assist him. He organized what was known to him and its members as the " Scranton Citizens' Corps." This company of men—some fifty in number—organized and established headquarters in the company store of the Lackawanna Iron and Coal Company. They were armed with Remington rifles, furnished by the corporations. No knowledge of their existence was communicated to the public, and on the day of the meeting at the silk-mill, when the crowd of men surged up on the principal street of Scranton, this body of armed men marched from the company store and halted on the street crossing. Whether any cause or provocation existed for opening fire on the unorganized mass will never be known. Certain it is that a body of regular troops would have had no occasion to fire, and had the Mayor openly proclaimed to the citizens that he had called into existence an armed body of men, he would never have had occasion to call for their services.

By many it was believed that the manager of the Lackawanna Iron and Coal Company had written the letter which was read at the silk-mill; and while threats of doing injury to Mr. Scranton were freely made by the angry men who surged up through the archway to the street on that August morning, it is certain that no premeditated or organized attempt at violence was made. Mobs always go on the impulse, and the miscreant who indited the anonymous letter knew that it would inflame the passions of those who heard it read, and incite them to deeds of desperation. Those who know human nature know that when violence is once invoked in a labor trouble, the odds are from that time against the success of the strikers.

It was believed by many that Mr. W. W. Scranton knew of the writing of the letter, but there was no evidence to prove it, or no foundation on which to base the belief except his natural desire to see the men do something desperate that he might have an opportunity to cast odium on their actions and efforts.

When the men reached Lackawanna Avenue, the principal street of the city, the Citizens' Corps had started on its march, and soon came in contact with the mob Some one threw a missile and then a shot was fired. The Mayor had been assaulted, and with blood streaming down his face gave the order to fire. His order was obeyed, and three men were killed and one wounded.

Two events in that unhappy drama were deeply to be deplored: the reading of that anonymous letter, and the secret organization of an armed force by the Mayor, who was assisted by the corporations instead of the legal authorities of the State. The knowledge of the existence of that armed body of men would have prevented the action of that portion of the meeting that would not listen to reason or any other argument save an appeal to force, and the speech made to the Citizens' Corps in the company store by Mr. Scranton would not have been necessary. In his testimony before the Investigating Committee of the Pennsylvania Legislature, page 769 of report, Mr. Scranton testified that he called the Citizens' Corps together, and said: " I did not want any man who was not willing to shoot to kill, and said if there was any man who fired, I wanted him to shoot to kill; that we meant no nonsense. There was only thirty-four of us; there were three or four thousand of the others; and we wanted no fooling. We wanted them to obey orders to the last degree, and when they received orders to fire, to fire to kill."

They fired, and fired to kill. They killed two innocent men, and one who was engaged in leading the men on to destruction.

On that evening Assembly No. 227 was to hold a meeting, that being the regular meeting night. The chief officer of the District issued positive instructions that no more meetings should be held during the excitement. At the next meeting of the District Assembly his action was approved by an unanimous vote.

Only in the direction of counseling moderation and peaceful methods was the influence of the Knights of Labor exercised in the labor troubles of 1877.

The first meeting of D. A. 5, after the inauguration of the strike, was held at Carbondale on August 29. Previous to adjournment the following resolutions were adopted and ordered read in the Assemblies of the District:

Resolved, That we do most earnestly urge upon all Assemblies within the jurisdiction of D. A. 5 to take up the question of the present strike and make it a subject of discussion.

Resolved, That we urge upon our members throughout the District Assembly to use their influence with their fellow-workmen to the end that this prolonged and useless conflict may be brought to a speedy termination. The further continuance of the strike cannot be productive of any good to the workmen of this valley, and we, therefore, advise that all members of the Order in D. A. 5 use every effort to at once set in motion the idle wheels and machinery in mine and workshop.

On October 16 a mass-meeting was held in the Round Woods. The question of resuming operations was taken up, and by an unanimous vote it was decided to return to work at once. The officials of the various companies were advised of the action taken, and on the following day, October 17, after three months of idleness, the miners of the Lackawanna and Wyoming coal fields returned to work on the same terms on which they struck.

D. A. 5 of Scranton was organized February 24, 1877, and on May 5 of the same year D. A. 5 of West Virginia was founded at Raymond City. The Assemblies represented, as recorded on the charter of the District Assembly, were Nos. 158 of Raymond City, 392 of Coalburg, 393 and 395 of Cannelton, and 394 of Lewiston. D. A. 6 was organized at New Haven, W. Va., on October 20, 1877, with the following Assemblies: Nos. 338 of New Haven, 329 of Clifton, and three others whose numbers were duplicated in other parts of the country, and were afterward changed to Nos. 1432, Minersville, Ohio; 1501, Syracuse, Ohio; and 1502, Pomeroy, Ohio.

D. A. 7 of Ohio was organized May 8, 1877, at Akron. It was known to the world as Sciota Assembly. Assembly No. 120 was the first Assembly organized within its territory, and was instituted by Christopher Evans on September 23, 1875. The first Master Workman was Thomas Lawson, and the first Recording Secretary, Wm. Shuttleworth. The Assembly was organized in New Straitsville. The next Assembly in Ohio was No. 169 of Shawnee. It was founded by Thomas Lawson of No. 120 on February 5, 1876. The first Master Workman was William Davey ; the first Recording Secretary, John D. Phillips.

When D. A. 7 was founded it was at a time when every society of workingmen was supposed to be in some way connected with the Molly Maguire organization of Pennsylvania, and wherever a meeting assembled the curious and inquisitive endeavored to learn something of the workings of the society whose name was spoken with dread. David Morgan, a puddler working in the rolling-mills at Akron, was elected the first Master Workman of D. A. 7, and Richard Jones, also a mill hand, and working in the same mill with Morgan, became the first Recording Secretary. This District Assembly continued in existence until 1886, when it became a part of N. T. A. 135.

D. A. 8 was founded September 23, 1877, at Pittsburg, Pa., and was composed of Assemblies Nos. 281, 300, 305, 319, 322 and 484, all of Pittsburg. These Assemblies were composed of men who worked at the glass-blowing trade, and the District Assembly continued in existence until the beginning of the year 1880, when it lapsed. On May 8 of that year the surviving Assemblies, Nos. 300, 305 and 322, merged into one Assembly under the name of Window-glass Workers' Assembly, No. 300. It takes in all who work at the window-glass trade, and is one of the strongest Trade Assemblies in existence.

D. A. 9 was organized on October 23, 1877, at West Elizabeth, Pa., with Assemblies Nos. 96, Coal Valley ; 109, West Elizabeth ; 124, Noblestown ; 140, Walkers Mills ; 147, Fayette City ; 151, Coal Bluff ; 157, Elizabeth ; 162, Monongahela City ; 168, Greenfield ; 178, Hope Church ; and 198, McKeesport.

Of D. A. 10 there is no record either at the General Office of the Order or elsewhere.

D. A. 11 was organized September 11, 1877, at Connellsville, Pa., and was composed, at date of organization, of the following Assemblies : Nos. 234, Frost Station ; 239, Dunbar ; 245, Scottdale ; 279, Connellsville ; 290, Fairchance ; and 297, Mount Pleasant.

D. A. 12 was organized in Youngstown, Ohio, about the same time that D. A. 11 was instituted, but there is no authentic record to be had.

D. A. 13 was organized August 1, 1877, at Springfield, Ill., with Assemblies Nos. 271 of Springfield, 346 of Hollis, 360 of Kingston Mines, 415 of Limestone, and an Assembly from Peoria.

D. A. 14 was organized September 13, 1877, at Knightsville, Ind. Its roll at date of organization had Assemblies Nos. 299 of Cardonia, 303 of Brazil, 318 of Knightsville, 455 of Harmony, and 456 of Carbon.

Fourteen was the highest number assigned to a District Assembly previous to the organization of a national body, which took place in January, 1878.

MEASURES BEFORE MEN.

There is a poor blind Samson in this land,
  Shorn of his strength, and bound in bonds of steel,
Who may, in some grim revel, raise his hand,
  And shake the pillars of this Commonwealth.—*Longfellow*.

No effort to establish a national head, or supreme authority, for the government of the Order of the Knights of Labor was made until 1875. At the first meeting in October of that year a communication from Assembly No. 82, Flint-glass Workers of Brooklyn, N. Y., was read in D. A. 1. It recited the difficulties under which that Assembly labored in securing members, and wound up with a petition asking that D. A. 1, "as the head of the organization," take steps to make the name of the Order public, so that workingmen would know of its existence. No action was taken for several weeks, although a resolution to declare the name of the Order public was offered at the next meeting after the communication had been received from Assembly No. 82. It was not until the matter was pressed by the New York Assembly that a debate ensued in D. A. 1. After much discussion it was resolved not to take action on the matter until all Assemblies had been notified and given an opportunity to vote on the question.

This discussion led to the subject of forming a national or central organization, and after much deliberation a call was issued to all Assemblies, whose addresses could be obtained, to meet in convention in the city of Philadelphia on July 3, 1876. Pursuant to call the representatives of several Assemblies convened at Red Men's Hall, Third and Brown Streets, on July 3, at ten o'clock A. M.

The record of proceedings, while not of sufficient importance as a whole to merit publication, are worthy of reproduction in order that they may be preserved for comparison with the records of the sessions of the General Assembly, which have been held since January 1, 1878. They are not lengthy, and, being the only copy now in existence of the proceedings of the first session at which an attempt was made to establish a national body, they are given in full, as follows:

PHILADELPHIA, July 3, 1876.

In accordance with the resolutions adopted by D. A. 1 for calling a convention in the city of Philadelphia, on the 3d of July, 1876, for the purpose of strengthening the Order for a sound and permanent organization, also the promoting of peace, harmony, and the welfare of its members.

MORNING SESSION.

The convention met and was called to order by Brother James L. Wright of Philadelphia, No. 1.

Motion was then made that Brother George Rieff take the chair as Temporary Chairman; carried. Brother Rieff then took the chair.

On motion, that Brother William Farrell of No. 23 act as Temporary Secretary; so ordered.

On motion, that a Committee of three be appointed on Credentials; carried.

On motion, that a Committee on Permanent Organization, of five, be appointed, carried. Stewart Atkinson, No. 23; Jesse Barnes, No. 58; Henry F. Esmerbrink, No. 118; Edward P. Brenan, No. 79; George C. Bowers, No. 165.

Committee on Credentials—John Kelly, No. 86; U. S. Stephens, No. 1; S. J. Christian, No. 92.

Committee on Credentials presented the following report: That we have received the credentials of the following delegates:

U. S. Stephens,	No: 1, Garmentcutters.
W. Kelley,	86, Reading Iron-workers.
S. J. Christian,	92, Allentown Shoemakers.
Harry S. Rogers,	173, Reading Painters.
William A. Bayes,	28, Reading Boilermakers.
Joseph H. Auchenbach,	171, Reading Heaters and Stovecutters.
James L. Wright,	D. A. 1, Philadelphia.
James McCambridge,	18, Philadelphia House Carpenters.
George E. Rieff,	19, Reading House Carpenters.
Samuel J. Burkart,	D. A. 4, Reading.
Andrew Burt,	95, Pittsburg.
Samuel Lamond,	18, Philadelphia Machinists.
George C. Bowers,	165, Railroaders.
Charles Stroud,	100, Chester Iron Moulders.
Adam Grandes,	129, Philadelphia Iron Moulders.
John Word,	116, Philadelphia Stove Moulders.
Charles F. Miller,	14, Philadelphia Safemakers.
H. F. Elnerbunk,	118, Pottstown Iron-workers.
William Farrell,	23, Philadelphia Carpet Weavers.
Frederick Schauble,	128, Reading Machinists.
Millard F. Smith,	40, Philadelphia Painters.
Charles H. Simmerman,	31, Camden Iron-workers.
E. P. Brenan,	79, Philadelphia Moulders.
Jesse Barnes,	58, Stocking Weavers.
Jonathan Holt,	127, Reading Iron-workers.
James Reaney,	77, Reading Iron-workers.
William Faing,	83, New York and Brooklyn.
Jacob Umstead,	82, Philadelphia Cigarmakers.
John McCormick,	84, Brooklyn Flint-glass Blowers.
C. Ben Johnson,	59, Pottsville, all trades.
Howard Seenley,	101, Allentown Machinists.
Samuel C. Miller,	126, Reading Moulders.
Stewart Atkinson,	D. A. 1, Philadelphia.
George Blair,	156, Brooklyn Boilermakers.
Michael Keating,	174, Greenland, all trades.

Committee on Permanent Organization—That rules governing the House of Representatives are to govern this convention, and on motion nominated the following as permanent officers:

President—JAMES L. WRIGHT of Philadelphia, No. 1.

Vice-Presidents—GEORGE E. RIEFF of Reading, No. 99; SAMUEL LAMOND, GEORGE STROUD.

Secretary—WILLIAM FARRELL.

Assistant Secretaries—MILLARD F. SMITH, JOSEPH H. AUCHENBACH.

Treasurer—JAMES MCCAMBRIDGE.

Doorkeepers—J. FORTNER, SAMUEL BURKHART.

(Signed)   STEWART ATKINSON, No. 23.

JESSE BARNES, No. 58.

HENRY F. EINERBUNK, No. 118.

E. P. BRENAN, No. 79.

GEORGE O. BOWERS, No. 165.

President James L. Wright then took the chair, returned thanks for his election, and made some remarks as to the reason for the calling of the convention.

On motion, that we adjourn to the northwest corner of the room on account of the noise on Third Street; so ordered.

On motion, that a committee of five be appointed to receive all communications; so ordered.

U. S. Stephens, George E. Rieff, S. J. Burkhart, Stewart Atkinson and James McCambridge were then appointed.

On motion, that these five be the Committee on Communications.

On motion, that we devote the balance of the morning session to ten-minute speeches; so ordered

On motion, that the session be from 9 to 12 o'clock A. M., and from 2 to 5 o'clock P. M.; so ordered.

On motion, that we adjourn. The vote was then taken, and, there being a division called, resulted in the motion being lost.

Adjourned until 2 o'clock P. M.

AFTERNOON SESSION.

A brother from No. 82 made a speech, stating that he represented over four hundred men who wanted to have information concerning the workings of the Order.

On motion, the two delegates be allowed to represent No. 82 by one of the brothers, and the other have a seat but no vote.

Amended, that one be allowed a seat and the other represent No. 82; carried. Whereupon the delegates from No. 82 retired for consultation.

The Committee on Communications presented their amendment for action.

On motion, that article first of the amendment, which reads, " That the Master Workman, Worthy Foreman and Worthy Q. be elected and installed once every six months, and that the Master Workman of the District may have the sole power of installing the officers of subordinate Assemblies," be laid on the table.

Brother James McCambridge made a few remarks, giving his own views on the subject of labor and the organization of the Order.

On motion, Brother J. Fortner be allowed the floor. He stated the misunderstanding of New York delegates was owing to the negligence of Brother Turner, and that his Assembly, No. 28, became defunct.

Brother C. B. Johnson was then introduced and called on for his views, but asked to be excused.

Brother Simmerman advocated a very strict set of rules.

Moved and seconded that the amendments to the rules be taken up; so ordered. On motion, the amendments be adopted as read; indefinitely postponed.

Committee on Communications presented the following resolutions:

Resolved, That we, as yet, do not believe that the Order is sufficiently organized to warrant the employment of salaried officers.

WHEREAS, The Constitution and By-Laws governing the different Assemblies of the Knights of Labor are imperfect and do not meet general satisfaction. Therefore, be it

Resolved, That a committee of nineteen be appointed to draft a Constitution for the government of the Assemblies under the jurisdiction of the National Convention, and report in writing to the next National Convention.

Amended, that the committee be nine—that they be five.

Offered as a substitute:

Resolved, That the acting Master Workman and four others be a committee to report, on next Wednesday morning, a draft of Constitution for the governing of the National Convention of the Order.

Time extended fifteen minutes that the Business Committee be substituted for the committee of five; lost.

The substitute was then adopted.

Adjourned.

SECOND DAY.

The second day's session was called to order by the President, James L. Wright.

The roll of delegates was called and the minutes of the last session read and approved.

Brother Holt called for the reading of the following resolutions:

Resolved, That this convention do declare itself the Grand National Convention Assembly of Knights of Labor.

Resolved, That this Grand National Convention is hereby declared the executive head of the Order of Knights of Labor, with power to act only in General Convention.

On motion, action on the resolutions be postponed for the purpose of letting the Committee on Constitution prepare the laws for the convention; so ordered.

The Business Committee recommended the following:

Resolved, That no one shall be admitted to membership in this Order except he be 21 years of age.

Which was amended to read 18 in place of 21 years; postponed.

The Constitution was brought before the convention for action.

Section 1 was then read, and, on motion, the name of North America was adopted.

Section 2 adopted. Article III adopted. Section 4 adopted.

Section 6 was then read, and, on motion, it was referred back to the committee, with instructions to insert a clause to assess a certain sum to bear the expenses of the delegates to this convention; carried.

Articles VII, VIII and IX were adopted. Article X was amended to read Cushing instead of Mathias.

Articles XI, XII and XIII were also adopted.

On motion, that we go into discussion of the subject of who is eligible to become members of the Order. Brothers Simmerman, Rieff, Blair, Johnson and Stephens were appointed a committee.

Brother Wood offered a resolution recommending that no mechanic or laboring man go to work before the regular hours; adopted.

A resolution was then offered that a committee of five be appointed to draft a platform by which every member of the Order may be guided, and submit the same for further action; laid on the table.

A resolution was then offered to make this society a beneficial one; lost.

A resolution—that when this convention adjourns it adjourns to meet at

Pittsburg, Pa., on July 10, 1877. Amended to be 5th instead of the 10th. Laid on the table until to-morrow, to come up at 11 o'clock.

Adjourned.

THIRD DAY.

Convention reassembled at 9 o'clock A. M. President James L. Wright in the chair.

The minutes of the last day's session were read and approved.

On motion, that we take up the resolution relating to the next meeting. Amended to strike out Pittsburg and insert Reading; laid on the table until after the report of the Committee on A. K.

The Committee on A. K. reported. Acted on by sections.

Sections 1 and 2 read and adopted. Section 3 read and adopted.

That the office of Statistician be left discretionary; carried. On motion, that we adopt relating to organizations; carried. On motion, that it be left optional as regards writing of the name by the candidate before being admitted; lost.

The matter of holding the next convention was then taken up.

Amended to strike out the tenth of July and insert first Monday in February; lost. Reamended to read in July, 1877; carried.

On motion, that there be a committee appointed to draft a Constitution for the Districts, to report at the next meeting; carried.

On motion, that there be one delegate from each District, and one from New York. Amended to appoint delegates from this convention; carried. George E. Rieff, D. A. 4, Pennsylvania; George Blair, New York; Charles H. Simmerman, D. A. 2, New Jersey; James L. Wright, D. A. 1, Philadelphia; Andrew Burt, D. A. 3, Pittsburg, were appointed.

Resolution relating to taking political action was offered; lost.

On motion, that the recommendation of the support of labor journals be adopted as read; carried.

On motion, that we go into nomination for Executive Committee, and that they be elected by scratch; carried.

The result of the election—George Blair, 26; Charles B. Johnson, 22; George C. Bowers, 22; J. J. Govan, 18; Andrew Burt, 17.

On motion, that the Constitution and amendements to the A. K. go into effect on the first day of August, 1876. Amended to strike out August and insert September; carried.

A resolution in regard to the organization of Districts, which read as follows: "That any five or more Assemblies may constitute themselves into a District, provided that they are not in arrears to that District with which they were connected; and, provided further, that no two Districts shall be formed in any one congressional district, town or city without the consent of all the Assemblies therein located;" was adopted.

A resolution that all members in good standing be assessed at least ten cents annually for the purpose of supporting the Executive Committee was amended to read five instead of ten cents, and adopted.

A resolution was offered that no one should be admitted to membership in the Order except he be a man of good moral character, sober and industrious, and thoroughly understanding the trade which he follows; carried.

On motion, to grant the Executive Committee power to give the passwords to the Districts, and the Districts to the subordinate Assemblies; carried.

A vote of thanks was tendered the officers by the convention.

Adjourned, to meet in Pittsburg, July, 1877.

WILLIAM FARRELL, *Secretary.*

CONSTITUTION.

Section 1. This organization shall be known to its members as the National League, and to the public, should it be considered expedient to make any of its proceedings public, as the National Labor League of North America.

Sec. 2. It shall be composed of two delegates from each District, and one delegate from each Local Assembly.

Sec. 3. Alterations of the A K., which is hereby declared the supreme law of this League as it is of the Local Assemblies, whose delegates compose it, shall not be made except at the regular meetings of the League, and then only by a two-thirds vote of all the delegates present.

Sec. 4. The object of this League is to bring the Local Assemblies into closer fraternal union with one another, to assist them as far as possible to share each other's burdens, and enable them to agree upon such modes of procedure as will make the members of the Order a band of true pioneers of labor reform, pledged at all times and under all circumstances to do all things lawful and honorable, looking to the elevation of the working class generally.

Sec. 5. The officers of the League shall be a President, Vice-President, Treasurer, Secretary and Doorkeepers, whose duties shall be the same as those appertaining to the same officers in other deliberative bodies, and who shall be elected immediately after the temporary organization of each succeeding convention.

Sec. 6. At each meeting of the convention, immediately after a permanent organization has been effected, the President shall appoint a Finance Committee of five delegates, one of whom shall be the Treasurer, whose duty it shall be to ascertain the cost of the session and assess the same equitably upon all the Assemblies represented.

Sec. 7. Before the adjournment of each regular annual convention there shall be a committee of five appointed, who shall be styled the Executive Committee of the National League, who shall hold office during the year, or until their successors are elected, and shall have power to fill all such vacancies as may, from time to time, occur in their number, provided that no two members of any one Assembly shall at one and the same time be members of the said committee. This committee shall, in the interval between the regular sessions of the League, have sole power to decide, by a majority vote, all disputed points as to the exact meaning of the A. K. or this instrument, said decisions to be operative until the next regular session of the League, and final, unless set aside thereat, which setting aside shall require a majority vote; only any District or Local Assembly in which there may occur any disputes as to the meaning of the A. K. may address any member of the Executive Committee, whose duty it shall be to correspond with his fellow-members concerning the matter in dispute, see that a decision is rendered, and communicate the same to the Assembly interested without unnecessary delay.

Sec. 8. All calls for the convention shall be signed when published by the Executive Committee. Tarnell's Manual shall be authority in all conventions of the League where it does not conflict with this instrument or the A. K.

Sec. 9. District Assemblies shall be organized according as the sessions of the League may, by resolution, determine, and shall be numbered by the Executive Committee.

Sec. 10. All legislative powers not reserved to this League that are consistent with the A. K. are vested in the Districts, and when not reserved by the Districts in the Local Assemblies.

Sec. 11. Conventions shall be held annually at such places and on such days as may, from time to time, be agreed upon by the League; provided, that the Executive Committee may, at their option, and with the consent of ten Local or five District Assemblies, call special sessions at any time or place.

U. S. STEPHENS, *Chairman of Committee on Laws.*

ORDER OF BUSINESS.

1. The convention shall be called to order by the delegate from the senior Assembly represented.

2. Appointment of Temporary Chairman.

3. Appointment of Secretary.

4. Appointment of Committee on Credentials, which committee shall be privileged to report at any time.

5. Report of Committee on Credentials.

6. Election of Permanent Officers.

7. Appointment of Finance Committee.

8. Appointment of Business Committee.

9. Appointment of Committee on A. K., to whom shall be referred, without debate, all propositions pertaining to the A. K.

Each convention shall, under this Constitution, be the pledge of the qualifications of its own members, and shall have power to adopt an order of business to govern its sessions, after the regulations provided for the first day shall have been complied with.

JAMES L. WRIGHT, *Chairman.*

D. A. 3 of Pittsburg was not favorable to the holding of the convention, and did not take the interest in the proceedings that was expected. For some reason not thoroughly understood D. A. 3 and the Assemblies west of the Alleghenies decided to call a national convention at an earlier date than that to which the Philadelphia meeting adjourned.

The chief cause of difference between the Assemblies west and those east of the Alleghenies was owing to the belief that the name of the Order should be made public. At the Philadelphia meeting no action was taken in relation to the matter, although the calling of the convention originated in a debate on making the name public.

The Pittsburg Assemblies were of the opinion that they had done more to spread the Order and to establish it in various parts of the country than D. A. 1, and felt that the call for a general convention should come from them. The feeling of jealousy which had sprung up between the Eastern and Western Assemblies threatened at one time to frustrate the designs of those who were making an honest effort to establish a national head.

On May 14, 1877, a conference was held in Pittsburg, but many of those who had signified a willingness to attend failed to do so, and the meeting fell far short of what was expected. As a literary production, the proceedings of that session are unique and interesting. They are deserving of preservation in their original form for the reason that they were prepared and the type was set by L. J. Booker, who knew nothing about the art preservative until, as a matter of necessity, he conceived the idea of printing the proceedings himself, so that they might not undergo the scrutiny of non-members if sent to a printing office for publication. They are as follows:

FIRST APPROVED OF THE CHARTER CLAUSE.

Preeeding of theConferance Committe

The meeting was called to order by Bro, J. M. Davis Chairman. Bro C A. Broockmeyer Sec pro tem. the Chair stateing the object of the meeting in a long and neat address, stating what is wanted to make the order prosperous, namly. 1st A Charter. 2nd A change in the Ritual. 3th A chang in Signs Grip & c. Each Delegate made statment what he was in stucted to present.

May, 15th The Minuts of the first day's session, where read and approved. The Chair stated the first in order is the election of National Officers. On motion it Resolved' that we go into a election of Officers the following is the result, to be known as For National Master Workman J. M. Davis, of Pittsburgh. For N. W. F. George Blair N. Y. For National Lecturer. G. M. Atkinson, of W. Va. For National Past Workman Bro. Wright of Philadelphia. For N. W. G. Thos R. King of Reading Pa. For N. O. G. R. C. Jones of Akron. N. I. G. Jos N. Glenn of St Louis. For National Organizer Chas A. Broockmeyer. of Charleston. Va. For National Secretary L. J. Booker. of Mt Washington Bro Chas A Broockmeyer, Nationla Treasurer. KANA WA.W Va on motion it was Resolved, That this body, go into revising the Ritual and changing the signs, adodted. motion to procure a Charter, and appoin a committee to attend to the same. the committe to consist of three Brothers living in Pittsburgh, adobted the committe shall consist of Bro Davis Booker, and Bowie. Rerolved, That the name of the Order be public.

On motion the Expulsion Claus where read and approved

On motion it was Resolved, That the Viseting and Traveling Cards have the name of the Order Printed on them

Resolved, That it shall be duty of Past Master Workman, to instruct the new Initiate that are of the Catholic Church, that their is nothing in this Order to prevent him from reciving the Sacrament, and if he considert it his duty to confess to his Father confesser, he may have the power so to do. adobtede Resolved, That three Black Balls rejects, and the candidates can make application to any Assembly within three months by asking permission of the Assembly, from which he was rejected. adobted.

Resolved, That each District Assembly, be taxed   TEN DHLLARS PER ANNUM to defrau the exspences   of   NATIONAL   COUNSEL. and Whereas it is neesary, to have Organizers out, therefor be it Resolved That each Assembly PAY TEN CENTS PER MEMBER ANNUAL, payable Quartly ofall members on the Books, the Organizers to travel North. and South East and West, adobted.

Resolved, That all Assemblies make applecation at once to the NATIONAL SECRETARY, for aCharter, Rituals and Constitutios A full set will be sent for Five Dollars [$5] which contains Four Ritual ten Constituiion one Charter

Notes As money is neated to carry out the plan it is the wish for the Assemblies to sent in the CASH as soon as possible. as 1000 Charters and 10,000 Constitution and 4000 Ritual. will be printed.

Resolved,That the National Secretary shall recive the sum of ONE $100 HUNDERT DOLLARS ANNUM payable quartly.

Resolved, That we adobt the Philadelphia Constitution with amendments,

The new order of business, 1st Reading of Minutes of last stated Meeting 2d Balloting on applicant. 3th Initiation' 4th Collection of dues 6th Unfinished Business. 7th New Business. 8th Dicuss Labor and its Interest. 9th Thus any member know of Brother are Brothers Family in distress. 10th For the Good of the Order. 11 Are their Brothers out of employment. 12th Are you all ready and satisfied to close

Resolved, That nexs our Corferece be held in Washington D. C and the exspence to be paid for the Delegate by N. C.

Resolved, That ex-district and the present district Offices are hereby declared Members of the National Councel.

On Motion the Conference. adjourned to mest the first Monday Jauary 1878 L. J. Booker.　N. C. S.

While D. A. 3 had done excellent work and had made marvelous headway, it lost sight of the fact that the patient years of toil which were given to the laying of the foundation of the Order by the parent Assemblies of Philadelphia were necessary, and that without them no organization could be properly established. The feeling which existed after the closing of the Pittsburg conference was not satisfactory to those who had taken a part in the meeting.

No notice of the Philadelphia Convention had been given to the Scranton Assembly in 1876, and, although a large and powerful District Assembly flourished in the Lackawanna and Wyoming Valleys when the Pittsburg conference was called, the officers of that District were not notified until the proceedings of the conference were mailed to them by the corresponding officer of D. A. 3, who had by merest accident learned of the existence of the Scranton District.

When the Secretary of D. A. 5 of Scranton, T. V. Powderly, received the report of the conference he at once communicated with such members of the Order as had taken part in the various efforts to establish a national body, and at the same time corresponded with D. A. 3, advising that proceedings be stayed until a convention could be called that would be truly representative in its character, one that would speak for all parts of the Order. A correspondence at once sprung up between William H. Singer of St. Louis, Mo., Richard Griffiths of Chicago, Ill.; George Blair of New York, Charles H. Litchman of Marblehead, Mass.; Frederick Turner of Philadelphia; and T. V. Powderly of Scranton. The result of the correspondence was to give to the recognized head of the Order, D. A. 1, a record of such Assemblies as were in existence so far as the addresses could be obtained.

When this work was commenced D. A. 1 decided not to hold the convention in Pittsburg, as agreed upon in the Philadelphia meeting, and postponed the date until September ; but a wave of political excitement swept over the Order about that time, and it was decided to lay aside all differences and unite with the Western part of the Order in holding the meeting in January, 1878. In order that neither Philadelphia nor Pittsburg would have cause for complaint, it was agreed that the meeting should be held in Reading, Pa. To this proposition D. A. 3 consented, and accordingly the following circular was issued by the Corresponding Secretary of D. A. 1 :

" CIRCULAR.

"PHILADELPHIA, August 2, 1877.

*"To the Officers and Members of * * **

" Notice is hereby given that a convention, for the purpose of forming a Central Assembly, will be held in the city of Reading, January 1, 1878, commencing at 10 o'clock A. M., and also for the purpose of creating a central resistance fund, bureau of statistics, providing revenue for the work of organization, establishment of an official register, giving number, place of meeting of each Assembly, etc. Also the subject of making the name public, together with all business appertaining to the perfection of a national body, all of which Assemblies shall vote upon, and instruct their delegates to report to the District Assembly. Each District Assembly shall be entitled to three delegates. States having no District Assembly shall be entitled to three delegates each, who shall be the members of the Organizing Committee in such States; they to receive the instruction from the Assemblies in their respective States. The action of the convention shall be final, hence the importance of all Assemblies discussing at once the subject-matter contained in this circular. Such Assemblies shall take a vote on the subject of making the name public, and report the result for or against to the District Assembly and Organizers, the delegates and Organizers to report to the convention. Two-thirds vote of the membership is necessary to declare the name public. By order of D. A. 1.

"FREDERICK TURNER,
"C. and R. Secretary.

" Place of meeting shall be announced in due time."

The Secretary of D. A. 3, L. J. Booker, forwarded the addresses of such Districts as he had organized to Frederick Turner, and a copy of that circular, together with blank credentials, was mailed to each of them.

On January 1, 1878, the representatives of the various parts of the Order met in Reading, Pa. Richard Griffiths of Chicago, who had been elected by the Chicago Assembly, No. 400, was not present, owing to the fact that he was not provided with the necessary funds by his Assembly, and he could not afford to defray his own expenses. He had deputized T. V. Powderly to represent him should it be decided that representation by proxy would be legal.

The full proceedings of that meeting were published and sent in sufficient quantities to supply every Assembly in the Order. They are still in existence, and it is not necessary to reproduce them here. Reference will be made to such parts as are of the greatest importance only. The following is the list of names and addresses of the delegates attending the Reading Convention :

Beaumont, Ralph, *Shoemaker*, 210 West Hudson Street, Elmira, N. Y.
Bowers, William W., *Moulder*, 119 Rose Street, Reading, Pa.
Boyle, George S., *Engineer*, Hazleton, Luzerne County, Pa.
Burgess, John, *Miner*, Stockton, Luzerne County, Pa.
Burtoft, Edmund, *Miner*, Pike Run, Washington County, Pa.
Byrne, John L., *Miner*, Box 103, Scottdale, Westmoreland County, Pa.
Chisholm, John B., *Miner*, Carbondale Luzerne County, Pa.
Christ, Jacob, *Locomotive Engineer*, Box 316, Waverly, N. Y.
Crowne, Thomas P., *Shoemaker*, 138 Bridge Street, Corner of High, Brooklyn, N.Y.
Gallagher, Hugh, *Miner*, Walker's Mills, Allegheny County, Pa.
Gallagher, Thomas M., *Machinist*, Tower Grove Station, St. Louis, Mo.
Geary, Patrick, *Shoemaker*, Canisteo, N. Y.
Gibson, John A., *Miner*, Knightsville, Clay County, Ohio.
Hamilton, James A., *Printer*, Leetonia, Columbiana County, Ohio.
King, Thomas, *Machinist*, 933 Spruce Street, Reading, Pa.
Lamond, Samuel, *Steam Boilermaker*, 160 North Sixth Street, Philadelphia, Pa.
Laning, John G., *Nail Packer*, Clifton, Mason County, W. Va.
(P. O. address, Box 337, Middleport, Ohic.)
Larkins, Matthias, *Locomotive Engineer*, 2446 Tulip Street, Philadelphia, Pa.
Litchman, Charles H., *Shoemaker*, Box 386, Marblehead, Mass.
McCoy, Charles S., *Glass-worker*, 1003 Carson Street, Pittsburg (South Side), Pa.
McLoughlin, Harry, *Glass-blower*, 1109 Bingham Street, Pittsburg (South Side), Pa.
McMahon, Michael J., *Machinist*, 336 West Seventh Street, Elmira, N. Y.
Powderly, T. V., *Machinist*, Lock Box 445, Scranton, Luzerne County, Pa.
Reiff, George E., *Carpenter*, 430 Woodward Street, Reading, Pa.
Schilling, Robert, *Cooper*, Office *Labor Advance*, Cleveland, Ohio.
Steen, Robert A., *Glass-blower*, 81 Sixteenth Street, Pittsburg (South Side), Pa.
Stephens, Uriah S., *Garmentcutter*, 2347 Coral Street, Philadelphia, Pa.
Thomas, Joshua R., *Blacksmith*, Lock Box 445, Scranton, Pa.
Todd, Robert, *Miner*, Thomastown, Summit County, Ohio.
Van Horn, William L., *Teacher*, Lewiston, Kanawha County, W. Va.
Welch, Morris C., *Miner*, Dunbar, Fayette County, Pa.
Williams, Richard, *Miner*, Audenried, Carbon County, Pa.

When the delegates assembled in Crouse's Hall, 508 Penn Street, Thomas King, Secretary of D. A. 4, and a representative to the convention, called the meeting to order, and nominated Uriah S. Stephens as Temporary Chairman. Robert Schilling nominated Charles H. Litchman as Temporary Secretary, and with these officers the convention proceeded to transact its business. Frederick Turner, who was present, though not in the capacity of a representative, was invited to a seat without voice or vote.

It was voted to call the body, which was then in session, the General Assembly of the Knights of Labor of North America. The names by which subordinate bodies were designated previous to that time were continued. It was at this meeting that the subordinate Assembly was first called Local Assembly, a term which has continued in use ever since.

Two District Assemblies appearing, through their representatives, bearing the number five on their credentials, it was resolved to allow the one which had already procured a seal and other property to retain the number. The Scranton District Assembly surrendered its right to the number, and accepted sixteen, by which number it has been known ever since.

To the titles by which the officers of Local Assemblies were designated was added the word Grand. The chief officer of the General Assembly was to be known as Grand Master Workman, the presiding officer of the District Assembly was to be known as District Master Workman, and the executive of the Local Assembly was to continue in office as Master Workman.

Mr. Stephens was called home before the convention adjourned, but his true worth was known to the assembled representatives, and when the election of officers took place he was chosen Grand Master Workman for the ensuing year, and Charles H. Litchman and Thomas Crowne were delegated to install him in office on their way home.

No nominations were made except in an informal way, each representative casting his ballot for that person whom he believed to be best qualified to fill the position.

The first Committee on Constitution of the Order of the Knights of Labor, appointed by Mr. Stephens, consisted of Representatives Robert Schilling, Chairman; Ralph Beaumont, Thomas King, T. V. Powderly and George S. Boyle. Two members of this committee, Messrs. Schilling and Powderly, were members of the Industrial Brotherhood; and though neither one knew that the other would be present, both brought with them a sufficient number of Constitutions of the Industrial Brotherhood to supply the body   The adoption of the Preamble was left to these two, and a glance at it will show what changes were made in the Declaration of Principles whose history has been traced down from year to year since it was first adopted by the National Labor Union of 1866.

The Committee on Constitution adopted the Constitution of the Industrial Brotherhood so far as practicable. The Constitution, when printed, bore the same legend on the title page as was adopted at the Rochester meeting in 1874. The following is the Preamble adopted at Reading, January 3, 1878:

"When bad men combine the good must associate, else they will fall, one by one, an unpitied sacrifice in a contemptible struggle."

PREAMBLE.

The recent alarming development and aggression of aggregated wealth, which, unless checked, will inevitably lead to the pauperization and hopeless degradation of the toiling masses, render it imperative, if we desire to enjoy the blessings of life, that a check should be placed upon its power and upon unjust accumulation, and a system adopted which will secure to the laborer the fruits of his toil; and as this much-desired object can only be accomplished by the thorough unification of labor, and the united efforts of those who obey the divine injunction that "In the sweat of thy brow shalt thou eat bread," we have formed the * * * * * with a view of securing the organization and direction, by co-operative effort, of the power of the industrial classes; and we submit to the world the objects sought to be accomplished by our organization, calling upon all who believe in securing "the greatest good to the greatest number " to aid and assist us:

I. To bring within the folds of organization every department of productive industry, making knowledge a standpoint for action, and industrial and moral worth, not wealth, the true standard of individual and national greatness.

II. To secure to the toilers a proper share of the wealth that they create; more of the leisure that rightfully belongs to them; more societary advantages; more of the benefits, privileges and emoluments of the world; in a word, all those rights and privileges necessary to make them capable of enjoying, appreciating, defending and perpetuating the blessings of good government.

III. To arrive at the true condition of the producing masses in their educational, moral and financial condition, by demanding from the various governments the establishment of Bureaus of Labor Statistics.

IV. The establishment of co-operative institutions, productive and distributive.

V. The reserving of the public lands—the heritage of the people—for the actual settler; not another acre for railroads or speculators.

VI. The abrogation of all laws that do not bear equally upon capital and labor, the removal of unjust technicalities, delays and discriminations in the administration of justice, and the adopting of measures providing for the health and safety of those engaged in mining, manufacturing or building pursuits.

VII. The enactment of laws to compel chartered corporations to pay their employes weekly, in full, for labor performed during the preceding week, in the lawful money of the country.

VIII. The enactment of laws giving mechanics and laborers a first lien on their work for their full wages.

IX. The abolishment of the contract system on national, State and municipal work.

X. The substitution of arbitration for strikes, whenever and wherever employers and employes are willing to meet on equitable grounds.

XI. The prohibition of the employment of children in workshops, mines and factories before attaining their fourteenth year.

XII. To abolish the system of letting out by contract the labor of convicts in our prisons and reformatory institutions.

XIII. To secure for both sexes equal pay for equal work.

XIV. The reduction of the hours of labor to eight per day, so that the laborers may have more time for social enjoyment and intellectual improvement, and be enabled to reap the advantages conferred by the labor-saving machinery which their brains have created.

XV. To prevail upon governments to establish a purely national circulating medium, based upon the faith and resources of the nation, and issued directly to the people, without the intervention of any system of banking corporations, which money shall be a legal tender in payment of all debts, public or private.

After adopting a Constitution and the Preamble given above, the General Assembly elected the officers for the ensuing term, fixed upon St. Louis as the place to hold the next session, and adjourned with the following corps of officers:

Grand Master Workman—Uriah S. Stephens of Pennsylvania.

Grand Worthy Foreman—Ralph Beaumont of New York.

Grand Secretary—Charles H. Litchman of Massachusetts.

Grand Assistant Secretary—John G. Laning of Ohio.

EXECUTIVE BOARD.

Thomas P. Crowne of New York. *Chairman.*

James A. Hamilton of Ohio, *Secretary.*

John A. Gibson of Indiana.

Robert A. Steen of Pennsylvania.

William L. Van Horn of West Virginia.

The first session of the General Assembly was regarded somewhat in the light of an experiment, and the bodies of which it was made up were not as sanguine of success as the representatives. When the latter reported to their constituencies it was some time before they responded with sufficient enthusiasm to predict the successful continuance of the General Assembly as the head of the Order of the Knights of Labor. The means provided by the General Assembly for the collection of revenue is outlined in the following section:

Section 1. The revenue of the General Assembly of * * * * * shall be derived as follows: For charter to District Assembly, five dollars; for charter and A. K. to Local Assembly, five dollars; for each traveling, transfer or final card issued, ten cents; in addition, all District Assemblies shall pay, in advance, the sum of one cent and a half every three months for every member on the books of the Local Assemblies represented therein.

But few of the representatives, when making their reports, endeavored to impress upon the minds of their constituencies the necessity for a prompt remittance of funds to headquarters in order that the work might be carried on as mapped out at Reading. The proceedings were to be published; constitutions, rituals, blank reports and forms of all kinds were to be printed and mailed.

The salary of the Grand Master Workman was fixed at $200 per annum, the salary of the Grand Secretary at $800 per annum, and the salary of the Grand Treasurer was limited to $50 per annum. Without a dollar in the treasury the first corps of officers undertook the task of placing upon its feet an organization which aimed at the performance of more good to the cause of labor, more of reform and more educational facilities than any other organization that had ever taken up the cudgel in defense of the workingman. It was a herculean task, and none but strong, true men were wanted; none else were put at the head of the Order.

The adoption of a seal for the use of the General Assembly was left to the Grand Master Workman and the Grand Secretary. These officers, soon after the adjournment of the General Assembly, held a conference and adopted a design, which has since then continued in use as the official seal of the Order. The inscription which appears around the edge, " That is the most perfect government in which an injury to one is the concern of all," was taken from the precepts of Solon, the Grecian sage and law-giver.

In the selection of this motto the Grand Officers were not actuated by mere sentiment, or a desire to make use of nicely-worded phrases or high-sounding terms. They studied carefully and well before adopting that motto.

In accepting the Preamble of the Industrial Brotherhood, the convention fully realized that for the most part the reforms which were asked for in that Preamble must one day come through political agitation and action. The chief aim of those who presented the document to the convention was to place something on the front page of the Constitution which, it was hoped, every workingman would in time read and ponder over. It was their hope that by keeping these measures, so fraught with interest to the people, constantly before the eye of the worker, he would become educated in the science of politics to that extent that he would know that those things that were wrong in our political system were wrong simply because he did not attend to his political duties in a proper manner; that the righting of such things as were wrong would not be done by those who had the management of political affairs up to that time, but by himself. " Man, know thyself," is good advice. Man, know thy rights; man, know thy wants; and man, know how to properly and temperately minister to these wants and secure these rights, are words of advice that should also be listened to.

The Preamble to the Knights of Labor is a call to action. The motto of the organization is intended to direct the attention of the member to the form of government, in all the affairs of life, that will be brought about if Knighthood is properly understood by its members and friends.

In the ordinary affairs of labor, in the daily experiences of work-shop life, action is often taken which at first may seem to be trifling and to concern only those who are the immediate participants. It often develops that a trifling grievance in a workshop, if not care-fully and judiciously handled, will involve others far removed from the scene of action. The experiences of the past, the many miserable failures which had attended the efforts of struggling labor organiza-tions of former years, were before the eyes of the men who selected the inscription to place upon the outer edge of the seal, and they had in mind the duty which every workingman owed to his brother man. If an injury to one is the concern of all, is it any more than just to so shape the affairs of government that all may be consulted before action is taken which will affect all ? Is it not equity to allow every man who is concerned to have a voice in the adjustment of such difficulties as will in time be brought to the doors of all ?

It was not contemplated to have all persons act on all matters, but it was the intention to give all an opportunity, through their repre-sentatives, to express an opinion on all matters which would in any way affect or at any time be likely to have a bearing on others outside of the first parties concerned. If an advance in wages became necessary in any department of labor, the old-fashioned remedy for every labor difficulty—the strike—was not to be entered into for the purpose of enforcing the demand for an advance, at least such a step was not to be taken until it had been ascertained how the strike would be likely to affect all the members of the organization; and if it could be demonstrated that others outside of the department involved would be likely to suffer, then the representatives of all the depart-ments, and all those likely to be involved, must first be consulted, and the true state of affairs realized before action should be taken.

In this way, and in this way only, could labor take intelligent action, and it was to the end that the true condition of labor might be known that the various reforms advocated in the Preamble of the Industrial Brotherhood were reaffirmed by the first national conven-tion of the Knights of Labor. The reasons why the separate sections in the Preamble of the Knights of Labor were adopted and kept in the foreground will be explained further on, and for the present they will occupy no more of the time or attention of the reader.

Notwithstanding the fact that there were no funds in the treasury and that the whole of the Order was not represented at the Reading Convention, the Grand Secretary, Mr. Litchman, proceeded with the work, and before the end of March every District Assembly and Local Assembly in the Order was provided with copies of the proceedings of the convention, and sample copies of the Constitution. Blank forms were sent out at the same time on which to make application for charters for the various Assemblies. Samples of traveling and transfer cards were also mailed by the Grand Secretary, and all of this was done before one dollar of revenue had been paid into the treasury.

When the different Assemblies saw that the Secretary was attending to his duty they began to respond, and by the end of the year 1878 every Assembly, whose whereabouts could be ascertained, was in possession of a charter and a sufficient number of Constitutions to supply all members. Confidence in the Order and the Grand Officers was at once established, and the work of organizing new Assemblies was immediately begun.

While the association was working secretly, yet the stir in organizing soon attracted attention, and the first move from the outside against the association came from the church. The events which preceded the erection of the gallows in Schuykill County, Pa., were still fresh in the minds of residents of that place, and one of the first fields that opened up to the Organizer was the middle coal region of Pennsylvania. Everything in the shape of a society, which was at all secret or new, was supposed to be the outcome of Molly Maguireism. It became necessary to allow the name of the Order to become known, but the name was no shield from persecution, misrepresentation and misunderstanding, and soon a scathing denunciation of the association came from the altar of one of the churches in Schuylkill County. The members became alarmed; many left the Order at once; others withdrew temporarily; while others, knowing the justice of the principles, determined to make an effort to have objectionable features, if any there were, removed.

Grand Master Workman Stephens was written to, and after investigation a special session of the General Assembly was called to take action on the matter of placing the aims and objects of the Order in a favorable light before the public. The request for this call came from the middle coal fields of Pennsylvania.

The workingmen of that region were sincerely desirous of having the features of the society properly understood by everybody. They still held in dreadful remembrance the terrible lessons that were taught at the foot of the gallows, when men were strangled whose guilt was never proven, and whose innocence is to this day believed in by those who knew them best. Whether the men who were hanged in Pennsylvania were all guilty of murder is not known, but it is known that men were hung on the testimony of those who were themselves murderers. It is known that that plague spot on American civilization, the Pinkerton detective, had entered the council chambers of the workingmen of Schuylkill County, and, under the guise of friendship, urged the men on to deeds of desperation and blood.

When the final day shall come, and the deeds of all men shall become known, the writer of this believes that no man's hand will be redder, no individual will be steeped more deeply in the guilt and crime for which men died on the scaffold in Pennsylvania, than the men who controlled the corporations which were operating the coal mines at that time. Justice no longer knew an abiding place in their hearts; honesty had given way to make room for the craze for gold, and with one ambition constantly before them, is it any wonder that they cared but little if one of their hired assassins of character swore away the lives of the innocent with the guilty? Men of influence, politicians, business men, clergymen and professional men united in condemning the Molly Maguires, but the voice of him who condemned the outrageous system which made the Molly Maguires possible was never heard above a whisper. Men who had witnessed the terrible scenes of past years knew full well how easy men's lives could be sworn away; and when they saw the same men opposing organization in 1878 they naturally became alarmed, and urged that a special convention be called at once to set at rest the fears of those who were as yet uninitiated. A convention was called as follows:

N. AND H. O.

OF THE

*   *   *   *   *

OF NORTH AMERICA.

PEACE AND PROSPERITY TO THE FAITHFUL.

To the Fraternity wherever found, Greeting:

SPECIAL CALL.

On account of what is believed by many of our most influential members to be an emergency of vast and vital importance to the stability, usefulness and influence of our Order, and in accordance with the power given me by the Constitution, I do hereby call a special session of the General Assembly of the N. and H. O. of the K. of L. of North America, to be held Thursday, June 6, 1878, at the Sanctuary of No. 1, Northwest corner of Sixth and Walnut Streets, Philadelphia, Pa.

The session will commence at 9.30 A. M.

The business is to consider the expediency of making the name of the Order public, for the purpose of defending it from the fierce assaults and defamation made upon it by the press, clergy and corporate capital, and to take such further action as shall effectually meet the GRAVE EMERGENCY.

(Signed)   URIAH S. STEPHENS,

Grand Master Workman.

Issued through the office of the Grand Secretary, and the seal of the General Assembly affixed, this 16th day of May, 1878.

Attest: CHARLES H. LITCHMAN,

Grand Secretary.

[SEAL]

The General Assembly remained two days in session discussing the various plans proposed for the adjustment of the difficulty which had arisen to perplex the officers and members of the Knights of Labor. It was at this session of the General Assembly that Richard Griffiths, afterward elected Grand Worthy Foreman of the Order, first made the acquaintance of the men who composed the supreme law-making body of the Order. He had been elected to attend the Reading Convention, but was not able to defray his own expenses, and as a consequence he was debarred from attending the first session of the General Assembly.

It was decided by the convention that it would not be proper to make any radical changes in the workings of the Order until the various Assemblies had been given an opportunity to take action and give instructions.

The following resolutions were adopted and ordered sent out to the Order at large:

Resolved, That all District and Local Assemblies under the jurisdiction of the General Assembly take into consideration and discuss the propriety of the following propositions:

1. Making the name of the Order public.
2. Expunging·from the A. K. all scriptural passages and quotations.
3. Making such modifications in the initiatory exercises as will tend to remove the opposition coming from the church.
4. Dispensing with the ceremony of founding District and Local Assemblies.

Resolved, That when the General Assembly meets in St. Louis in January, 1879, a vote shall be taken upon each of the above questions, and it shall require a two-thirds vote of the total membership to decide in the affirmative.

The resolutions, which were offered by Representative Powderly, were supplemented by a resolution offered by Representative Litchman, which was also adopted and ordered sent out with the other:

Resolved, That each Local Assembly shall take an informal vote upon each of the above propositions, and shall forward to the Grand Secretary, not later than December 1, 1878, a record of the number of votes in the affirmative and the number in the negative upon each proposition.

This was the first step taken by the General Assembly toward making public the name of the society, and from one stage to another it progressed, until the General Assembly, which met in Detroit in 1881, discarded the veil of secrecy in which the name of the Order was shrouded and declared to the world that there was such an organization in existence as the Knights of Labor. The efforts of the Order to throw off the secrecy in relation to its name will be chronicled in their regu.ar order as the history of the society is unfolded.

It is proper at this time to give the reasons why the General Assembly of the Knights of Labor adopted the Preamble of the Industrial Brotherhood. It is declared in that Preamble that it is the mission of the Order of the Knights of Labor:

" I. To bring within the folds of organization every department of productive industry, making knowledge a standpoint for action, and industrial, moral worth—not wealth—the true standard of individual and national greatness.

"II. To secure to the toilers a proper share of the wealth they create; more of the leisure that rightfully belongs to them; more societary advantages, more of the benefits, privileges and emoluments of the world; in a word, all those rights and privileges necessary to make them capable of enjoying, appreciating, defending and perpetuating the blessings of good government."

In order to successfully reach all who are engaged in "productive industry," it is necessary that the members of the Order should know who may appropriately come under that head. The belief was prevalent, until a short time ago, among workingmen that only the man who was engaged in manual toil could be called a workingman. The man who labored at the bench or anvil, the man who held the throttle of the engine or delved in the everlasting gloom of the coal mine, did not believe that the man who made the drawings from which he forged, turned or dug could be classed as a worker. The draughtsman, the time-keeper, the clerk, the school-teacher, the civil engineer, the editor, the reporter, or the worst paid, most abused and illy appreciated of all toilers—woman—could not be called a worker. It was essential that the mechanics of America should know who were workers. A more wide-spread knowledge of the true definition of the word labor must be arrived at, and the true relations existing between all men who labor must be more clearly defined. Narrow prejudice, born of the injustice and oppressions of the past, must be overcome, and all who interest themselves in producing for the world's good must be made to understand that their interests are identical. All the way down the centuries of time, in which the man who worked was held in bondage or servitude, either wholly or partially, he was brought directly in contract with the overseer, the superintendent or the boss. From these he seldom received a word of kindness; indeed, it was the recognized rule to treat all men who toiled as if they were of inferior clay.

The conditions which surrounded the laborer of past ages denied to him the right to dress himself and family in respectable garb. The coarsest material, made in the most untidy fashion, was considered good enough for him. Not only did his employer and overseer believe that his dress, habitation, furniture and living should be of the coarsest, cheapest material or quality, but he also shared in that belief, and took it for granted that it was ordained of heaven; that the stay of the laborer on earth was only as a matter of convenience for his master; and that he must put up with every indignity, every insult and privation, rather than violate the rules of government, which were held up to him as being as sacred as the Ten Commandments. The Holy Scriptures were quoted to show to the toiler that it was said in Holy Writ that he should be content with his slavish lot on earth in order that he might enjoy an eternity of bliss in a future world, through the portals of which those who held him in subjection could not get a glimpse of the happiness beyond. " Servants, obey your masters," was written on every wall in letters of fire for those who could read, and the story was told and retold to those who could not, until the worker believed that to ask for better things on this earth was almost a sacrilege. It would be flying in the face of Divine Providence to even remonstrate against the injustice which the employer practiced upon the poor laborer.

It was necessary to teach the laborer that it was not essential for him to grovel in the dust at the feet of a master in order to win his title deed to everlasting . bliss in the hereafter; and it cannot be wondered at that many who strove to better the condition of the toiler lost all respect for religion when they saw that those who affected to be the most devout worshipers at the foot of the heavenly throne were the most tyrannical of task-masters when dealing with the poor and lowly, whose unfortunate lot was cast within the shadow of their heartless supervision. Men who kneeled before the altar of the Most High and asked for heavenly grace, men who prayed for their "daily bread," were to be found among those who denied the meanest privileges to the workman; and not only denied to him the right to worship his God in a decent manner, but actually took from his mouth, from the fingers of his half-fed babes, the crust of bread on which they sought to sustain life itself.

It was no wonder that to many workingmen religion seemed to be but a parody when they contrasted their own condition with that of their employers. When they were told that all were children of the same Father, it could not be wondered at that some of them rebelled against the decree which had rung in their ears for centuries: "Servants, obey your masters." "We are children of the one Father, and that Father has given to one brother all the good things of earth, while to us He has given nothing. Can it be possible that Almighty God has ordained that some of His children are but step-children from birth ? Are our souls of as much consequence as those of our employers ? Does the Almighty think more of them than of us ? Does He give all the good things to them, and place it in their power to take everything that we produce without a proper equivalent; and is it essential to the salvation of our souls that we grovel forever beneath the feet of wealth ? "

These questions began to loom up before the children of toil, and then their masters sought to fasten the screws still tighter upon them by bringing to their aid the powers of press and pulpit to convince the laborer that he should not aspire to the good things of earth, but should be content to live in that sphere to which it had pleased his God to call him. Workingmen are very imitative, and they saw that if it was possible for the man of wealth to save his soul while enjoying so much of this world's goods, it was also possible for them to do so, and they determined to take the risk and try to die in sin by acquiring some of the wealth which they had helped to create. When workingmen saw other men feathering their spiritual nests at a salary of from five to fifty thousand dollars a year for little or no labor, they began to believe that so long as they paid heed to the command, "Servants, obey your masters," they would stand but little chance of enjoying anything like ease on this earth, and they resolved, one by one, to test the command by breaking it. They did break it by reaching out for better wages, conditions and shorter hours of toil; but in doing so they ran terrible risks of future punishment, for all of these things were in direct conflict with the wishes of the "masters" whom they were told to obey.

The laborer gradually realized that while the gaunt form of poverty stood in his doorway from one end of the year to the other, and at the end of each year his earthly store was smaller, his family larger and his hunger keener, he was tempted to commit sin in order to get bread for his family and himself. Leaders of workingmen believed that souls could be saved with bread as well as with prayer, and they resolved to make the attempt by bringing the men of toil to a sense of their duty to themselves.

The hope was held out, as a sort of balm to the feelings of the tired wretches who worked and struggled along in poverty, rags, disease and dirt, that when final judgment came it would be "easier for a camel to go through the eye of a needle than for a rich man to gain entrance to the kingdom of heaven." As a recompense for the hours of misery and pain spent on earth, the toiler would have the happiness in the next world of seeing the rich man writhing in hell, while he roamed at will in the realms of eternal bliss. No creed taught this doctrine, no religion said to workingmen that they should look at these scriptural passages in the light in which I have portrayed them, but that these impressions were created on the minds of the workingmen by alleged ministers of God every man who toils can testify.

It then became a question whether to acquire wealth was not a sin, and again the imitative qualities of man came to his rescue. He saw that the minister of the religion which he professed never made calls of a friendly nature on him; his neighbors, who worked where he did, never received a visit from the clergyman; but he saw that the man who could not get into heaven until the camel passed through the eye of a needle was often favored with a visit from the minister who preached poverty and humility as a means of acquiring grace on earth and happiness in heaven.

It became the duty of the workingman's friend to solve the camel question. How was it to be done? To make knowledge a standpoint for action, it was necessary to teach the toiler that it was the uses, the abuses of riches, and the methods by which wealth was acquired, that would be the test when the rich man would enter upon his race to eternity, with the camel as a competitor.

The deep-toned voice of many a minister of God rang out in denunciation of the workingman, who, in his poverty, in his agony, in his very despair, often struck against the systems which crushed him to earth; and there were those in the ranks of toil, who, mistaking the false for the true, railed against religion because some of those who preached it and professed it failed most miserably in the practice of it. Knowledge for the workingman meant that he should be able to detect the difference between the real and the sham. Whenever a learned man said that which did not appear to be just to labor, he was to be questioned, publicly questioned, as to his base of actual facts. All through the centuries toilers have erected the brass and granite monuments of the world's greatness, and have thrown up on hill-side and plain the material for other homes than their own. The weary feet of toil have trodden the earth, and strong hands have formed the pillars of the bondage of old. All along the blood-stained march of the years that have flown the struggling ones have given to earth more of richness in the sweat which fell to earth from their throbbing foreheads; the grain, which lifted its head for long ages of time under the care of the toiler, has been enriched by the sweat, the blood and the flesh of the poor, plodding men of toil. While the sun kissed to warmth and life the wheat and corn which their hands nurtured and cared for, they received the husks and stalks as their recompense for labor done. Their masters took the grain for themselves, but lifted no hand in its production.

At the command of a profligate queen, the most enduring of the monuments of time were erected on the Egyptian sands. One stands by the Seine in Paris, one looks toward heaven on the banks of the Thames in London, and another stands erect to tell the wondering sightseer who visits Central Park, New York, that that which man does on earth will live for centuries after he has passed away. At the decree of Cleopatra, men, made in the same mould as men are made in to-day, wrought with hammer and chisel upon the surface of the stone that still survives to testify to the skill of past centuries. The name of Cleopatra still lives. We may go back among the dust-covered crooks and crevices of time and search for the name, the memory even, of the mechanic whose skill designed the huge stone; we may search for the name of the artisan whose hand in by-gone ages cut into the face of the solid rock the characters which still remain upon its surface. Oblivion, mystery, gloom and everlasting death surround the names of the men who worked out the emblems whose import is as a sealed book to the man who to-day looks in wonder and awe at the imperishable monuments to the genius of that by-gone age. Go to the base of the Pyramids and count the stones over whose peaks the sands of Egypt have failed for centuries to climb, and there, too, will be seen the evidence that man was as skillful in the past as he is to-day; but where is the record which tells the names of the men who erected the Pyramids or the names of those who chiseled out the obelisks of Cleopatra?

Time has marked its furrows upon the surface of the stone without removing the marks of the chisel, but it has obliterated the names, the history and the fame of the workmen who toiled for future ages. Whether freemen or bondmen, no one can tell who did this wonderful work.

In the city of Washington there stands a monument to the memory of the man who gave to the world a hope and to the toiler the right to enjoy political and religious freedom. Ask the guide who attends your visit to that magnificent, awe-inspiring pile, erected in honor of " The father of his country," whose hand placed the first stone in its mortar-bed, and he will stand speechless as the marble itself.

Pass up the East River beneath the " Brooklyn Bridge," on sloop or shallop, ocean steamer or ferry-boat, and, while gazing upward in admiration at the grandest witness to the genius of man that the world has ever produced, ask the names of those who made two cities one with a single span, and silence is the only answer. Look where we will at the mighty structures that attest the triumph of the present over the past, stand in wonder before monuments, the stones of which were cemented in human blood, and inquire who they were that toiled up from corner-stone to cap-piece, and no tongue pronounces their names, no page in history records the story of their achievements. While the names of rulers have been handed down, the names of generals have been remembered for the lives they took and the cities they destroyed, the names of those who ministered to the sum of human happiness in erecting cities and adding to the store of the world's greatness and wealth have been forgotten, the recollection of their deeds have passed away with the entombing of their lifeless clay. Those who destroyed have been remembered; those who constructed have been forgotten.

" Will it be ever thus? " was the question that was asked when it was finally determined that knowledge should in the future be the standpoint for action, and that moral worth—not wealth—should in the future mark the contrast between the workmen of the past and those of to-day.

The rights of the people were usurped, their liberties were being gathered up in the strong hand of wealth, and the fingers of death were being circled around the Constitution of the United States, when it was resolved to make " moral worth—not wealth—the true standard of individual and national greatness." Wealth had bought its way into senate chamber and council hall; it had seated its pliant tool upon the bench, and placed the ermine on the shoulders of its own. Politicians had made pledges only to break them, for they knew that to keep a promise and to break it would win the same reward from the toiler, whose vote was cast for party and not for principle. The politician knew that once seated in office he need not care for the opinion of the laborer; he need not exert himself to do that which was indicated in the platform of his party. The platform itself was a living lie; and while that " sum of all villainies " was allowed to exist on American soil, it contaminated all who came in contact with it, and it sought to come in contact with all men. The Declaration of Independence said one thing, and the people practiced an entirely different thing. All men were declared to be born equal, yet the people of a nation stood by and saw millions born into servitude the most damnable and revolting. This taught politicians to be dishonest, for honesty was banished from the high places.

It came to be the opinion of the partisan that the workingman was his legitimate prey; as much his to command on election day as was the black slave the property of his master on every day. To work, then, meant to be ignorant of what a man's rights were to some degree, and the selfish politician took advantage of everything that offered itself to him. He received bribes as though they were pay for lawful service; he sought not to cover up his crime, for the long, dark days of slavery made it possible for the system of robbery to go on unmolested. Wealth, wrung from the back of the weary, bleeding slave, sat in the halls of Congress and in the Senate Chamber; moral worth was scoffed at as though it were a thing to shun, unless its possessor had wealth along with it, and then the latter was the standard by which men were judged, not only by men of wealth, but by men of toil as well, for the shadow of that upas-tree, corruption, was over the heads of the workers, and each day grew darker for them.

To make moral worth the standard of individual and national greatness, the men of toil had to be roused to a sense of duty; they had to be taught what their rights and duties were. To do this the hollow pretenses of the political parties, which every year came before the country and on platforms of " glittering generalities " appealed for the suffrages of the people, had to be exposed and shown to the people in their true light.

Legislation for labor came through the halls of Congress and State Legislature as a bone comes through the fingers of a stingy master to a half-starved dog, with the meat picked from it. The bone was there, but it only served the hungry one as a reminder that there should be something else. When tested before a tribunal of any kind, nearly all of the legislation of that day would be declared unconstitutional. It was not, at that time, considered unconstitutional to grant a whole territory to a railroad company, or to grant a valuable franchise to a corporation, but the moment the well-picked bone that was bestowed upon the hungry dog—Labor—was taken to the Supreme Court, it was declared to be only a bone—nothing more. A knowledge of who his friends were in each Congress, in each session of the Legislature, was to be made the standpoint for action when the time rolled round to select new Legislators. Moral worth was to be established as the future standard; and why should not the laborer do his own legis-lating, instead of letting it out to a second party?

This was a question which was debated long and earnestly in the councils of the workingmen, and attempt after attempt was made, with little or no success at first, to elect workingmen to serve as representatives of the people. Those who represented, and those who were to be represented, were in need of education on the questions which concerned all alike; but it was evident that parties would never educate the people. They gave out their platforms each year, and before they were understood they were exchanged for something else, without accomplishing the reforms they aimed at.

Once every four years, in national contests, questions of political economy were brought before the people on public platform and in ward meeting; but with the sound of the candidate's voice went the thought of what he said, for it was understood that he talked for himself alone. A change had to come, and with it the placing of the Preamble of the Knights of Labor in every man's hand every day of the year, to be studied not one day in every four years, but every day in every year, so that those things that were pointed out in it would be carefully bedded in the mind of man or discarded as untrue, and therefore worthless.

Parties would never provide the means of diffusing such an educa-tion as was here sought for. Something else had to be found to serve mankind, and that something was presented to the American people when the Order of the Knights of Labor was instituted.

The electing of Legislators was attended with great difficulty at first, for the people still clung to the old idea of party preferment. Education was necessary in order to show the workingman his duty to himself. It was a dangerous undertaking to broach the subject of political economy in an Assembly for fear of arousing the ire of some old party adherent, whose fidelity to party was as strong as his love of home or his fealty to his religion.

In 1876-'77-'78 several elections were held in different parts of the country, and workingmen were elected to office; but they did not give satisfaction in every instance, for the reason that the enemies of the labor movement found too many willing ears to listen to tales of selling out, treachery and general depravity on the part of the newly elected ones. Those who were elected on new platforms, being new to politics, were sought by politicians of the old school, who generously took them under their wing and offered to show them how to legislate. Unaccustomed to duplicity and double-dealing, many of them fell victims to treachery, for they found that in associating with the old-school partisan they simply invited the contempt and scorn of those who elected them.

To elect men on a third ticket at that time was a reason why members of the existing parties should unite against the new members, and labor discovered that it was due to her to make use of the machinery already in existence before erecting new parties. The measures of reform were all-important, and the name of the party of no consideration. This was the doctrine to teach the workingman, and it was taught to him. It is being taught to him every day.

Parties are good only when they serve the best interests of the majority of the people. The majority of all parties is made up of toilers, and their interests should receive first consideration.

It was urged that inasmuch as the Preamble of the Knights of Labor dealt with such questions as called for legislation, the Order should at once be formed into a political party. Each of the old parties sought to convince the members of the Knights of Labor that there was no use for the Order; that the party to which they belonged would effect all reform legislation if allowed to do so in its own way; but the workingmen, who had carefully watched the history of the years which followed the close of the Civil War, felt certain that party leaders cared nothing for the people; and they were right in many instances. The party leader saw that the people cared nothing for themselves, and why should he care for the people? The people took no interest in politics except during campaigns, why should the office-holder take any interest in the people except to get their votes? Political leaders strongly urged the disbanding of the Knights of Labor. They asserted that the ordinary trade union was sufficient to take care of the interests of the wage-worker. On that subject the Grand Master Workman of the Knights of Labor, in reply to a letter published by a prominent Democrat, in which the latter urged that all labor organizations affiliate with the Democratic Party and give up their labor organizations, said in 1883:

" A great deal has been said of late concerning the dismemberment of the Knights of Labor and the forming of a federation of trades. The principal reason given for the proposed action, summed up in a few words, is that each trade or craft, in being organized for itself, can more easily and successfully engage in a strike. There are other arguments made use of to bolster up the ' federation ' idea, but that appears to be the principal one. At least it is the one to which the most prominence is given in the Eastern press. One thing is certain, the originator of that idea was neither a Knight of Labor nor a member of a trade union, for members of these associations know that the tendency of the times is to do away with strikes; that remedy has been proved by experience to be a very costly one for employer and employe.

"The trade union does not favor a strike; it is regarded as a *dernier ressort* by every labor association in the land; and as no good can come of the dismemberment of an association which, among other things, aims at the perfecting of a system by which disputes between the laborer and capitalist can be settled without resorting to so costly an experiment as the strike is acknowledged to be, why the Knights of Labor and the various labor associations of the country are in no great danger of being disbanded.

"I called the strike an experiment, and I would have every advocate of such a measure note these words. Strikes have been resorted to for centuries, and to-day, after hundreds of trials have been had, men cannot embark in a strike with any assurance of success based upon a former precedent. Every one must be decided upon its own merits. I will never advocate a strike unless it be a strike at the ballot-box, or such a one as was proclaimed to the world by the unmistakable sound of the strikers' guns on the field of Lexington. But the necessity for such a strike as the latter does not exist at present. The men who made the name of Lexington famous in the world's history were forced to adopt the bullet because they did not possess the ballot. We have the latter; and if the money of the monopolist can influence us to deposit our ballots in favor of our enemies—if we cannot be depended on to go quietly to the pooling booth and summon to our aid moral courage enough to deposit a little piece of paper in our own interest—how can it be expected of us to summon physical courage enough to do battle for our rights as did our fathers at Lexington? and if we do go to the tented field, will not the same agency that induced us to vote against ourselves induce us to thrust our bayonets into the hearts of our friends instead of our foes? I answer yes, for a faithless citizen never made a faithful soldier.

"What, then, is the duty of the hour? Men may argue from what I have said that I believe our cause to be hopeless; and did I not have faith in the Knights of Labor I would say, ' Yes, the cause is lost.' Other men entertain different opinions, and positively assert that the panacea for all the ills we suffer will come through the adoption of such advice as they have to offer. For instance, ' Democrat ' says in his letter of July 4 that in order to secure the blessings we seek we

' have only to merge ourselves into the great Democratic Party and help to swell the triumph of the plain people in 1884.' I must be pardoned for differing with him. I do not believe that it lies within the province of any party to protect the many against the unjust encroachments of the moneyed few, unless the many are properly instructed in the science of government.

" The party is the concrete man. If the individuals comprising the party are ignorant of their rights, and must trust to the wisdom or discretion of party leaders, they either follow in the wake of blind leaders or permit themselves to be blindly led along by their leaders. In either case it will not be the intelligence they display or the instructions they give that will urge their leaders forward in an honest groove, and under such circumstances as these the duty of the citizen ceases as soon as he casts his vote.

" Will ' Democrat' assure us that, if each of the associations he names (the Grangers, the Knights of Labor, the Amalgamated Association, and the various trade unions) should cease to work and ' merge into the Democratic Party,' they would not be obliged to reorganize again in a few years to protect themselves from the Democratic Party ? Will any Republican assure the members of these associations that a general reorganization will not be necessary should they merge into the Republican Party ? Remember, I am not assailing parties. The party is good or bad, as the majority of its members determine. Who is to blame for the misdeeds of a party ? The majority. Who comprise the majorities in the Democratic and Republican Parties ? Why, ' the plain people,' of course. I believe that there is no man so good that he will not bear watching.

" What is true of man is true of party, and in either case the watchers must be educated ; they must be actuated by one common impulse. In other words, they must be organized. That there are men who believe that political parties require both watching and teaching, I am positive. Let me quote the words of a man whose fidelity to the Democratic Party can not be questioned, but whose love of justice is stronger than his regard for party. In his letter to the Constitutional Club of New York, Judge Jeremiah S. Black says:

" ' What is the remedy ? No enforcement of the Constitution and laws, which command what is right and prohibit what is wrong, for that cannot be effected without officers who are faithful. As it is, our Governors do not govern, and Legislators laugh in your face when you tell them of their oaths. Shall we turn them out and fill their places with true men ? That is easier said than done. Monopoly has methods of debauching party leaders, cheating voters and deceiving the very elect, which perpetually defeat our hopes of honest government. If the power of the corporations increases a little more, they can put their worst rascal into the highest office, as easily as Caligula's horse was elected consul by the people of Rome.

" ' You will infer from this that I am somewhat discouraged, and it is true that very recent events here in Pennsylvania have much disappointed me. But that is no reason why you should despair. You have what we have not, an organization to make your grievances known, and I hope that from your meeting the truth will go forth to rescue and rouse up like the sound of a trumpet.'

" It may be inferred from the position I have taken in the foregoing lines that the mission of the Order of the Knights of Labor is to become a political party, and that it is intended to take precedence of the Democratic Party. The inference would be wrong. The Order of the Knights of Labor is higher and grander than party. There is a nobler future before it than that which clings to its existence amidst partisan rancor and strife. The Order of the Knights of Labor is a friend to men of all parties, and, believing that the moment it assumes the role of a political party its usefulness will be destroyed, it has refrained and will refrain from doing so. The moment we proclaim to the world that our Order is a political party, that moment the lines are drawn and we receive no more accessions to our ranks from the other existing parties, with the exception of here and there a member who becomes a convert through conviction that we are right.

" We have political parties enough. Every one of them in its early days was honest and gave promise of good results, but the moment that success perched upon its banners the vultures, who feed upon spoils, also perched upon its body, and to a certain extent frustrated the designs of its organizers.

" The same would be true of the Knights of Labor. If that Order is not to become a political party, what good can it accomplish ? This brings us to the root of the question, and gives the reason why there can be no dismemberment of the Knights of Labor. One reason why political parties degenerate is because the masses of the common people are not educated. We may be able to read and write, but we are not educated on the economic and social questions with which we are brought in contact every hour. If we were, we could more easily discern the difference between good and bad legislation, and we would not be clamoring so often for the repeal of bad laws. The chief aim of the Knights of Labor is to educate, not only men but parties; educate men first that they may educate parties and govern them intelligently and honestly. Ralph Waldo Emerson gave this advice before leaving us. He said :

" ' Let us make our education brave and preventive. Politics is an after-work, a poor patching. We are always a little late. The evil is done, the law is passed, and we begin the up-hill agitation for repeal of that which we ought to have prevented the enacting. We shall one day learn to supersede politics by education. What we call our root and branch reforms of slavery, war, gambling, intemperance, are only medicating the symptoms. We must begin higher—namely, in education.'

" ' To supersede politics by education,' it first becomes necessary to organize the masses into an association where they can be educated. Take fifty men of one calling and place them in a room organized under the laws of a distinct trade society, and they will discuss nothing but such matters as pertain to their trade. If they do not mingle among those of other trades they will grow indifferent to the wants of others ; they will remain in ignorance of their own rights through their ignorance of the rights of others. Selfishness will be the rule, and the ' up-hill agitation for a repeal of that which we ought to have prevented the enacting ' will stare us constantly in the face.

'' I am aware that the Knights of Labor meet with opposition from the leaders of some labor organizations. They anticipate that, in the event of their associations becoming a part of the Knights of Labor, their occupation, like Othello's, will be gone ; but they entertain groundless fears. We seek the co-operation of every labor society, the dissolution of none. We seek and intend to enlist the services of men of every society, of every party, of every religion and of every nation in the crusade which we have inaugurated against these twin monsters—tyranny and monopoly ; and in that crusade we have burned the bridges behind us ; we have stricken from our vocabulary that word fail ; we aim at establishing the complete rights of man throughout the world ; we take as our guide no precedent ever set by mortal man unless it be right ; we tolerate no dissensions, and will have no disbanding save as ordained by the Great Master Workman when He calls from our ranks each individual member and bids him join that silent majority, whose votes upon the questions of this world find voice only on the pages of the recorded past.''

That letter was written in August, 1883, and was incorporated in the annual address of the Grand Master Workman to the General Assembly of the Order, which assembled in Cincinnati in September of that year. The letter deals with other subjects than those which relate to politics, but that is the particular feature of the document to which the attention of the reader is now directed.

To cause the worker to understand that to bring about reforms which were political in their nature, without forming a new party, was a difficult undertaking. Politics meant party to a great many, and the thought of gaining control of the existing parties did not occur to them. There were honest men who insisted that a new party should be made up of Knights of Labor and industrial organizations. They failed to see that if men would be led by the nose by leaders, and would let their thinking out to others to do in the old parties, these men would allow others to lead them in the new political party. Consequently a profitable field would be opened up to a new set of politicians, who would naturally crowd to the front in a successful movement, no matter what its name might be. The duty of the Knights of Labor is to place citizenship above party.

The success of the abolition movement, and the formation of a party which eventually rode into power on that issue, was and is often given as an argument in favor of the formation of a new party of labor. A labor party is not likely to become a success for the reason that it is not in accord with the genius of American institutions to form a party of one class of citizens. American citizens vote not for party, not for a class, but for the whole community; and that party through which the most people can be benefited is the one for whose candidates the people should vote, even though they become guilty of political apostacy every year. Class distinctions have wrought almost irreparable injury to the people of the United States. The workingmen are making an honest endeavor to rid the country of them by purifying parties and purging them of the evil tendency to lay everything at the feet of monopoly.

When the anti-slavery agitation was in progress there was but one issue before the people, viz.: the abolition of human bondage. It was easily understood. It appealed to the love of justice, which finds an abiding place in every heart. Everybody would admit that it was not right to enslave a man. The distinction between the black and white man was one thing that kept the question so long in agitation before the final issue was reached. Again, the slave was in chains; he was helpless and weak; he was ignorant of his rights; he was powerless to speak out or lift a hand in his own behalf, and the chivalrous spirit of the American people was finally aroused. It was only necessary to secure the attention of the people. As soon as attention was directed to the attitude of the slave, as he crouched in dread of the lash, the victory was won; for a glaring wrong will not be tolerated on the soil of the United States after the eyes of the people are turned full upon it and it becomes the subject of thought and investigation.

The elements which combined to make the party that picked up the slave successful were few, but they appealed most eloquently to lovers of liberty in all parties. To concentrate the attention and thought of every workingman and every student on the various phases of the labor question of the present day, and have each issue find warm adherents in all parts of the country at the same time, is next to impossible. The interests of the different States are not always the same. That economic measures which would carry in a political campaign in one State would fall short of anything like a cordial support in another.

At different times and under various names labor parties have been formed by earnest men who were actuated by a desire to have the very best thing possible done for the worker, but one after another they have failed for want of support; and had any one of the labor parties which came before the people during the last twenty years been successful in the effort to secure control of affairs, it would be but a question of time when it would be open to the same objections that now find favor with those who oppose the political parties of the present day. The fault is not with the party, but rests entirely with the citizen. The party should be subservient to the will of the citizen, but the relations are changed in placing the party higher than citizenship.

The duty of the citizen does not begin on the morning of the day on which he is to vote, nor does it end with the going down of the sun on that day, yet this is the practice of the vast majority of citizens of the United States, who labor under the delusion that they are voting for the candidate, and that they confer a favor upon the office-seeker in going to the polls on election day.

As most of the measures advocated in the Preamble of the Knights of Labor must come through political action, and as the greater portion of the ills of which the industrial masses complain is the result of unwise or dishonest legislation, it is essential that the people be educated to know what is wrong and what is right in our methods of conducting public affairs. It was not the intention to place the Preamble before the members and the country and say: "In this document we ask for measures of relief for the people; you must at once form a party, and push them forward into law." It is the intent of those who understand that document to have each measure carefully studied and debated in the Assemblies of the Knights of Labor, with a view to securing the very best effort and thought of the membership upon these questions, so that they may be thoroughly and clearly understood by all. If the Preamble should be set forth as a political platform, and the people asked to vote for the candidate who advocated that platform, the interest would, in all probability, centre on the candidate, and die out with the sound of the last notes of the campaign.

The Preamble is set before the members for discussion and thought, so that every one will know what is required, so that each one will know whether the Preamble is the best that can be devised or whether a better one should take its place. It occasionally happens that when a labor party is formed, and a candidate put up on a distinctively labor platform, a failure to poll a respectable vote for the candidate is regarded as an indication that labor has no fault to find with the existing state of affairs, and matters become far worse than they were before.

Again, it is sometimes said that the Order of the Knights of Labor favors certain parties, and it is given in evidence that the chief officer of the Knights of Labor made political speeches while acting in the capacity of General Master Workman. The latter assumption is not correct; but it is true that the General Master Workman did make a speech in favor of the party which placed Henry George in nomination for Mayor of New York in the fall of 1886. Owing to the deliverance of that speech he was requested to again enter the political arena for the purpose of making a speech in behalf of a labor party, which was being formed in Philadelphia, during the month of December, 1886. As the reply which he sent to the committee explains the situation as it then existed, it is given in full, as follows:

" *To the Committee:*

" GENTLEMEN :—I have before me your invitation to address the convention of the United Labor Party this evening. While I am sensible of the honor conferred in selecting me to act as speaker of the evening, and while under ordinary circumstances I would be pleased to lend my services in aid of the movement in which you are engaged, yet there are good and valid reasons why I should not respond to the call thus made upon me. To refuse to attend your meeting without giving my reasons would, in my opinion, be unjust, in view of the fact that I recently addressed a mass-meeting in the city of New York in behalf of the Labor Party.

" When the laboring people of New York nominated Henry George for Mayor, they acted independent of party and without regard to the man whom they placed at the head of the ticket. The nomination was made, not as a compliment to Mr. George, nor was it made on the impulse of the hour; it was made after calm deliberation, and because it was necessary for the people of New York to show that they disapproved of the methods of public officials, who violated every principle of right and justice, instead of compelling those over whom they had control to demand a strict enforcement of the law. The nomination of Henry George by the laboring men of New York was a solemn protest against the manner in which the rights of the many were ruthlessly trampled under foot by the ringsters of the party in power.

" The law requires that the people assemble at the regular polling places and nominate the men to be voted for at the general election. The welfare of the nation and of the people demands that the people shall name the men to be voted for; but in this day and generation the people have as little to do with the making of nominations as the slaves of the South had to do with making nominations in ante-bellum days.

" I do not charge that the entire blame for this state of affairs rests entirely with the politicians, for if the politicians did not have willing subjects they could not operate upon them. The blame cannot properly be laid to any one class of people. All are responsible. The millionaire does not go to the polls to cast his vote; he simply awaits the result of the election. He does not attend the primaries, but takes good care to see that his most powerful ally is there and at work. It may have escaped the notice of a great many who attend the primaries, but it is there that voters are interfered with, insulted and shoved away from the polling places. Timid men stay away; decent men do not care to be treated in this manner; law-abiding men stay away rather than engage in quarrels. The consequences are that you will find men swaggering about and bullying those who have manhood enough to differ with them. Bribery is at work, and those who could not be reached by its influences in any other way are filled with rum.

" The ally of the monopolist, to whom I referred a moment ago, is strong drink. I know that what I say in regard to it and its influences is true and beyond the contradiction of any man. New York City is no exception to the rule. It is simply pre-eminent. The ' heeler ' of Gotham finds his counterpart in every city and village of the land. Had the men who threw the bombs in Chicago on the 4th of May aimed their missiles at the heads of these plague spots on our political system, I would have had no tears to shed.

" The work of the heeler was rated at the highest price by the leaders of all parties, and it was not so much a question with them whether the people favored the nomination of a certain man as it was to find out how the heeler would take it. The people were regarded in the light of a machine whose sole duty it was to carry forward the work on election day which had been mapped out for them by the manipulator at the primaries.

" While this state of affairs continued to exist without protest, the voice of labor could exert but little influence in the legislative halls of State or nation. When the people petitioned for anything they were either refused outright or given some slight recognition in the way of legislation that meant nothing beyond the mere words contained in the act that was passed.

" The vast majority of those who were elected to legislative positions were lawyers, who knew as well how to make a law that meant everything or nothing as they did to enact legislation that could be interpreted in the interest of the whole people. I do not say this by way of reflection on the lawyer; but it is unfortunately true that, when our government was founded, the fallacious idea took possession of the minds of the people of that day that none but lawyers could make laws. The consequences are that they have continued to make laws ever since, and the laws for the most part are made for lawyers only.

"If you doubt this statement attend one of the sessions of the nearest court, and you will hear lawyers disagreeing as to the meaning of the simplest term in law. After the trial is over the learned judge will render his decision in accordance with his view of the law, and the chances are that if you watch the matter carefully some lawyer will carry the case to a higher court for a different kind of a decision. I do not charge that the lawyer is responsible for this, but it is in the nature of the lawyer's profession to take a fee.

"The experience of other days is constantly staring him in the face while he holds his seat in the Legislature, and the chances are that what would seem to be a bribe to other men would only serve as a fee to him. Again, it is natural for men to legislate for themselves and that class to which they belong. A plain, straightforward law would require no lawyer's services to interpret, and, as a consequence, the more complicated and intricate the law the better for the lawyer. I speak of this to show the necessity for representation in the halls of legislation according to occupation or profession.

"I would not deny the lawyer the right to take his seat in Congress or in the State Legislature, but side by side with him should sit the representatives of other professions and callings according to the number of those who follow those callings and professions. If this is done and the people are properly represented by men of their own selection, we can have good laws enacted, and we will have only ourselves to blame if such is not the case. As it is, I claim that we are to blame for not attending more carefully to the work of enacting legislation. The work of enacting legislation begins at the primaries and among the people.

"This brings me back to the starting-point. Why did I speak in New York, and why will I not speak at any other political meetings? The people of New York made a nomination; every influence had been exerted to make the vote ridiculously small. Had Henry George received less than the thirty thousand votes that were pledged him, it would have been said by the enemies of labor that it was a defeat for labor; that labor did not keep its promise to its own agent. It would have been held that no matter what kind of treatment the working people received they would still continue to vote the ' regular ticket,' and, as a consequence, but little respect would be shown the representatives of labor when they applied for the enactment of just laws or the repeal of unjust ones.

"I have contended that inasmuch as we have a Department of War at the seat of our national government, we should have a Department of Labor as well. We already have a Bureau of Labor Statistics, but that is not sufficient. The President of the United

States does not confer with the Chief of that Bureau when about to take action on an important matter, and Congress never reads the report of the Bureau. What is wanted is to have established at Washington a Department of Labor, with the secretary of the department as one of the Presidential advisers, the same as the heads of the other departments now are.

"It may be asked, ' Why does labor ask so much ? ' and the answer is because we require so much labor to manage the country, for without it we would make but little headway ; everything depends on it. That being true, it is no more than right that the interests of labor should be considered before important action is taken by the President or his Cabinet.

"We have asked that a Department of Labor be established. We have been told that labor had no real grievances, and in support of that statement the labor vote of the country has been pointed to on many an occasion. I had all of these things in my mind's eye when I decided to go to New York to talk at the Henry George meeting. I wished to enter from a platform in the first city in the Union my protest against the influence of rum in our elections. I wished to ask the workers of New York not to allow a small vote to be cast. I wished to have the vote so large that the blindest of blind partisans could not fail to see that labor had a grievance. It was my desire to see that the vote would speak for itself when we again asked for legislation at Washington. It was my desire to make it possible for the Legislative Committee of the Knights of Labor at Washington to be able to answer the questions which were put to them last session : ' Who are you ? Whom do you represent ? and what will be the effect on our political fortunes if we vote as you require ? ' Had Henry George died the night before the election, I would have urged the men of New York to vote as they did on election day as a protest against ring rule, corruption and perjury.

"My name was used by partisans in New York to stem the tide. It was urged that I wrote a letter against Henry George, and that I opposed the movement generally. I knew of no better way of giving the lie to all of these false statements, and at the same time doing my part toward the establishing of a sentiment that would eventually tend to secure to labor some of the benefits that she asks for, than to go in person and refute the charges. I did it, and there my duty ended

"In going to New York on that occasion I made a departure from a rule that I have observed for some time, and which I do not intend to break again, viz., not to speak at a political meeting again while I hold the position of Chief Officer of the Knights of Labor. While it might be entirely proper for me to speak at such a meeting, yet it creates the impression that the Order of the Knights of Labor is being drawn into the contest, and it is my duty to do all that lies in my power to keep the Order, over which I have been chosen to preside, above the tide of partisan politics. At New York I spoke as an individual, voicing the sentiment of united labor, and not as General Master Workman of the Knights of Labor. While I am General Master Workman, I will never again occupy a place either as speaker or officer on a political platform.

" I would advise you not to take any action as a party. It seems to me that it becomes the duty of all interested to endeavor to educate the masses to free the ballot-box from the degrading influences of the bribe-giver and taker, as well as from that tool of monopoly—whisky. Put forth your every effort to discover what is wrong in the management of the municipal affairs of your city. Do not, as is too often the case, allow the interest to die out on the eve of election day, but continue until you have located the cause of the trouble. You will find that in order to remove the cause of the trouble you will have to begin at the bottom and work up, instead of beginning at the top and falling down. If your movement means what its name indicates, keep it up and enlist the services of all honest men, for all such are interested in honest government, regardless of their calling in life."

The appended decisions of the General Master Workman will serve to show what the attitude of the Order of the Knights of Labor is on the question of political parties as related to the organization :

237. The Order of the Knights of Labor is not a political party. It is more and higher, and must be kept so. It is the parent of principles. In it are born and crystallized sentiments and measures for the benefit of the whole people.

238. Our Order is above politics, and electioneering for any candidate in the sanctuary must not be practiced. Our Order teaches MAN his duty by educating him on the great question of labor. " Discuss labor in all its interests," but not the merits or demerits of any candidate.

240. It is not compulsory to vote for a brother for any public office, but in choosing members for the Assembly select none but men whom it would be an honor to vote for for any position.

241. Political economy, in a fraternal and candid spirit, may and should be freely and exhaustively discussed in Local Assemblies. In this way, and in this alone, can members become thoroughly informed as to their rights as citizens, both in the abstract, or higher laws of God, and legally, or in the present laws of the land. In this way the justice or injustice of their surroundings is made apparent, and they are enabled more intelligently to discharge the duties of citizenship, exercise the elective franchise, and realize exactly where they stand and where they consistently belong. But it should never be discussed in an angry, ungentlemanly or acrimonious manner. In that case the laws of Knighthood are imperative. The Master Workman must close the Assembly.

259. Political party action must not be taken in the Local Assembly, but must be done outside, in club or party organization, through which political sentiment may be crystallized into statute law.

While citizenship is rated so low and party methods so high, there will exist a necessity for a more general diffusion of knowledge concerning the duty which the citizen owes to his family and his country. That action should be taken is an absolute necessity, the welfare of the country demands it; but that action must be carefully planned: it must be for the good of the greatest number; and a knowledge of all that goes to make the many poor and the few rich must be the standpoint for the action of the future.

Soon after men began to study the Preamble to the Knights of Labor they began to act. Unfortunately for the movement, many of those whose perceptive faculties enabled them to comprehend the full scope of the Preamble in a short time thought that others, not so well equipped mentally, should realize the full necessity for action. Enthusiastic and earnest men sought to realize a benefit for mankind, by nominating candidates for office whose past record would be a guarantee that the principles of the Knights of Labor would be "crystallized into statute law." When candidates who entertained such views were nominated by either party, their election was always contested by the agents of corporate power through every system of terrorism imaginable—bribery, treachery, blacklisting, threats of dismissal from position, and, finally, the espionage of the corporation official at the polling place.

It is within the recollection of the writer that when contesting for a political position, in 1878, on a labor platform, in the city of Scranton, local superintendents and bosses employed by the coal companies were stationed at the several polling places, where the men over whom they had charge deposited their ballots. These mine superintendents took the precaution to place the ticket which they favored in the hand of every employe of the company who came forward to vote; not that alone, but they watched the man until he cast his ballot. In many instances men who refused to vote the ticket thus forced on them were discharged from the service of the coal corporations of Lackawanna Valley.

Numberless instances can be pointed out to show that those who possessed the wealth of the nation were determined to control the legislation of the same. Massachusetts was cursed with the political tyrant, who stood at the polling place in that State until the indignation of the masses forced him to abandon his post. New Jersey is still under the rule of corporate power so far as the freedom of the employes of corporations is concerned, for it is an established fact that, at the election held in that State in the fall of 1887, men employed on the coal docks at South Amboy were called into offices of the corporation and provided with tickets, which were numbered the same as the men are numbered in the service of the company. They were not told to vote the tickets, but they were watched by agents of their employers, and the man who refused was certain of dismissal from the service of the company at the first offense.

This system of compelling men to vote as the corporation willed has been so extensively practiced, and has been made the subject of so much discussion and publicity, that it is unnecessary to cite any more cases. The matter is simply referred to to show that, no matter how well qualified the citizen may be to perform his duty at the polls, he will not be likely to accomplish much good in that direction so long as the door of the polling booth is held in the grasp of corporate power. A plan must be devised and adopted throughout the nation which will allow the voter to go to the polls and deposit his ballot free from interference from the boss of corporation, saloon or political party. Many plans are being discussed and perfected which aim at throwing a safeguard around the ballot. That one which will succeed, and which will best serve the interests of the American people, will be the one which will keep all traders away from the polling place; and traders at the ballot-box are traitors to the State.

The expenses of elections should be borne by the nation, State, county or municipality, and not by the candidates for office. The nomination of candidates should not be kept within party lines, but should be done by citizens under some well-regulated law, such as the Australian system. The ballots should all be printed on the one slip; they should not be peddled about outside of the polling booth, but should be placed in charge of the election officers, to be handed to each registered voter as soon as he qualifies. There should be no contested elections; the election officers should be required to ascertain beyond the shadow of a doubt whether the citizen is entitled to vote; once the ballot enters the box there should be no question concerning its legality. If it develops that illegal votes are cast the election board should be held responsible, and not the city, county or State. The costs of rectifying the wrong should be borne by the offenders.

Every citizen should be permitted to take the printed tickets of all candidates in nomination to a small apartment and there select those for whom he wishes to vote without let or hindrance from a second party.

Elections for national and congressional officers should be conducted on a day set apart for that purpose; no other elections should be held on that day. At all elections the number of ballots cast should be publicly announced from the polling place every hour, and the votes so cast should be inclosed in a sealed packet. At the close of the polls in the evening the total result should be publicly announced by the election officers. An official notice of the total vote cast should be posted up in a conspicuous place at the polling booth within one hour after the closing of the same. Such written notice should be guarded by the election officers for at least one hour after being posted up, so that no interested party would interfere with it. Such a plan would enable all citizens to know the result at once, and the practice now in vogue of holding back the returns from one district, in order to hear from others, would be discontinued. An honest election would be the result.

To stop another villainous practice, election day should be made a national holiday by act of Congress and State Legislature.

The special session of the General Assembly of the Knights of Labor which met in Cleveland, Ohio, in May, 1886, adopted the following resolution, which is a request for the recognition of election day as a national holiday :

Resolved, That it is the sense of this General Assembly that the occupation of the bribe-giver and the bribe-taker should be destroyed. To do this it will be necessary to educate those who suffer most through bribery and corruption that it is as hurtful to the welfare of the nation to receive a bribe as to give one.

In order to deal with this question more effectually and intelligently, we should use every means within our power to secure for the toiler the right to protect himself upon that day which, of all days, is important to the American citizen— ELECTION DAY. That he may have an opportunity to protect his interests on that occasion, we should ask that election day be made a national holiday, on which no employer shall have the right to demand service at the hands of his employes.

That resolution passed by a unanimous vote, and met with the approval of the entire Order. The reason why that was passed was because employers of labor were, and are, in the habit of working their employes up to the very hour of closing the polls on election day. It is a common thing in the coal regions for the corporations to insist on their workmen staying in and around the mines until too late to vote on election day, even though the mines were worked but half-time during every other day in the week. Steel and rolling mills have been operated the same way, and the unfortunate workman who would leave off before the last horn would blow would be discharged from the service of the company. Such practices as these should not be tolerated, and there will be no system devised to check the evil until the day on which men register their will at the ballot-box is declared a national holiday ; until the citizen can exercise his will free and untrammeled at the polls ; until he can vote free from the scrutiny of political boss or corporation superintendent.

With these reforms in view, and with the Preamble of the Order being discussed at each meeting, the member of the Knights of Labor must become a better citizen than before he joined the organization. The knowledge which he gains by discussion and study of economic questions will constitute the standpoint for action which is suggested in the Preamble of the Knights of Labor.

THE LABOR BUREAU.

Every addition to true knowledge is an addition to human power.
—*Horace Mann.*

The third declaration of the Preamble of the Knights of Labor reads:

" III. To arrive at the true condition of the producing masses in their educational, moral and financial condition, by demanding from the various governments the establishment of Bureaus of Labor Statistics."

An examination of the Preamble of the Industrial Brotherhood will show that that body demanded " from the several States and from the national government the establishment of Bureaus of Labor Statistics." When the Industrial Brotherhood made the demand that body was composed of representatives from trade unions representing constituencies which existed within the United States, and the Preamble was intended for the inhabitants of the United States alone. When the Preamble was taken up by the General Assembly of the Knights of Labor at Reading, it was changed only in those parts that referred to action at the hands of government. As the Order was expected to be spread all over the globe, its declaration must be made to conform to the principles and aims of the association, and, instead of making a demand from any particular government, the intention was to make the demand " from the various governments."

At the time of the adoption of the Preamble at Reading there were but four Bureaus of Labor Statistics in existence. These were created by State Legislatures at the request of labor organizations in these States, and were the first fruits of the agitation begun on the question by the National Labor Union of 1866. Massachusetts established a Labor Bureau in 1869, Pennsylvania in 1872, Missouri in 1876, and Ohio in 1877. The Missouri Bureau was enlarged in 1883 in order to afford greater facilities for the transaction of the legitimate business of the institution.

It was the intention in organizing these Bureaus of Labor Statistics to procure from the toiler himself statements concerning his condition in life. It was expected of him to give full and accurate information on all questions relating to his welfare, and at the outset many men were victimized for speaking plainly when interrogated by the agents of the Bureaus. The agents of capital had access to the records of the

158

Bureaus, as the agents of labor could have had if they were as alert then as now.

When workingmen discovered that their identity would be disclosed to their employers if they gave a true statement of the impositions practiced on them they became very cautious, and for a number of years it was impossible to direct the attention of the laborers to the importance of making returns upon the blanks sent out by the Bureau. When it became known that the eyes of the workingmen were turned in the direction of these Bureaus, and that they desired to have them conducted in such a way that no man would be discharged for stating facts, more interest was shown in the work of gathering statistics.

Particular pains were taken by employers to effect the discharge of prominent men in the labor organizations because of the reports which they made to the Labor Bureaus of their States. They felt that in time employers would be required to make returns to the State of accounts of actual earnings, and by discharging workingmen whose names and business were divulged by the Labor Bureau they artfully threw a veil over their own affairs. They reasoned that if a workingman knows he will be discharged because of the publication of his name or statement of condition, he will want to have his Legislature protect him by keeping secret his name and business. If the workingman does not wish to have his own affairs exposed to public gaze, over his own signature, he will not be likely to ask for the passage of legislation which will require that the affairs of his employer be made the subject of scrutiny at the hands of the Bureau.

The idea was advanced that it was not in accord with the spirit of our free institutions that men should be compelled to make statements concerning conditions in life, earnings and expenditures. It was claimed that it was an infringement on the personal liberty of the individual to attempt, by act of Legislature, to pry into the affairs of workmen, corporation or individual employer. When laws were passed creating Bureaus of Labor Statistics they were shorn of the power to become of real value to the country at large, for the reason that it was left optional with the employer and employe to give or withhold information necessary to make a complete return of actual conditions, earnings, etc.

Intelligent, thinking laborers at once availed themselves of the opportunities afforded them by these Bureaus to place their real condition in life before the country. They determined to secure all of the advantages that were possible through these agencies. Other workingmen, who for years had suffered all manner of privations and indignities, and whose sensibilities were blunted by hard luck and ill treatment, attempted to create a sentiment in their favor by making extravagant, exaggerated and untruthful returns. 'This had a tendency to cast discredit on the institutions that were designed to benefit the toilers.

The legitimate aim of the Labor Bureau is to ascertain beyond the shadow of a doubt what the earnings of labor and capital are in order that justice may be done to both, in order that unscrupulous employers will not have it in their power to rob labor of its just dues and take all the profits of the combination of labor and capital for their own aggrandizement.

When blanks were sent out for the purpose of securing reliable information, it was discovered that in making returns the employer would invariably make a return of what he paid his workmen. He was disposed to be generous in the matter of stating what was paid to labor; what labor could live on; how much the workman spent for strong drink; what a fondness the workman had for canned goods; and such other information as could best be given by the workman himself. His own affairs were not considered proper subjects for public scrutiny, and not being obliged to state what his own profits were, or what he spent for strong drink, he made no mention of such insignificant trifles.

The Bureaus were established for the public good; and if it is for the public good that the affairs of an individual be made known, he should be compelled to state facts under oath. It is now well known to the public what the workingmen receive and what they can live on. In some instances the Labor Bureau has proved to be of advantage to the employer, for, if he learned through the aid of the Bureau that "his help" could subsist on a dollar a day less, he was always inclined to reduce wages to the lowest limit. It is because the proper sphere of the Labor Bureau has not yet been attained that it has not proven so advantageous as was expected. Laws must be passed which will make it compulsory on employe and employer to answer every question in relation to their business that the public is at all interested in. The public has a right to know what a corporation earns. It is granted valuable franchises by the public; it lives on the public; it is designed to benefit the public; and to the public it should render an account of its stewardship. The legitimate earnings of capital should become known to the people in order to put a stop to illegitimate profit-taking. The shield of the law should be thrown around the worker, in order that he may secure that to which he is justly entitled as a part of his investment (his labor) in the concern where he finds employment.

The means by which employers or moneyed men acquire wealth will one day be made the subject of the most rigid scrutiny through the medium of the Labor Bureau. The law will one day set a limit to the now boundless ambition of the money-getter, and he will be deprived of the power to get more than enough. He will not be permitted to get enough to place him in a position where he will stand as a menace to the State. The mode of living of the toiler must be improved; his condition while at work, his treatment by his employer, his moral standing, and the tendency to crime, which comes of his poverty, will all become known through the intervention of the Labor Bureau.

The agitation for the establishment of Labor Bureaus was begun in the States where the Knights of Labor were intrenched in 1878, immediately after the adjournment of the Reading Convention. The agitation for the establishment of a National Labor Bureau was begun after the special session, which was held in Philadelphia in June, 1878.

The New Jersey Legislature was petitioned during the winter of 1878 to establish a Labor Bureau. A bill was drawn up and presented to the House by a member of the Knights of Labor, who, although not a member of the Legislature, was deeply interested in the passage of measures of reform in the State. He had the bill drawn and given into the hands of the members of the Legislature. All the labor organizations of the State took an active interest in the work, and the following March saw the establishment of the " Bureau of Statistics of Labor and Industries of the State of New Jersey."

The " Bureau of Labor Statistics " of Illinois was established in 1879. In the Legislature of the State that year there were ten Greenback-Labor and seven Socialist members. Many of them were members of the Order of the Knights of Labor; and both Socialists and Knights being committed to the Labor Bureau question, they introduced the bill and worked so successfully as to pass it into law before the adjournment of the session of 1879.

A " Bureau of Statistics " was established in Indiana, but it deals with every question on which statistics are required. It makes no pretensions to being a Labor Bureau.

During the session of the New York State Legislature of 1883, Hon. David Healy of Rochester, a Knight of Labor, introduced a bill looking to the establishment of a Labor Bureau. The measure was successfully carried into law before the close of the session of that year.

California also established a " Bureau of Labor Statistics " in 1883. The influence of the Knights of Labor was the prime factor in the passage of the bill. The Knights had been agitating for years on the Pacific coast, and in 1883 made a strong effort to gain recognition for labor at the hands of the law-makers of the State. In the effort to establish the " Bureau of Labor Statistics " of California, while the agitation was begun and continued by the Knights of Labor, they had the hearty co-operation and assistance of trade unions and the Trade and Labor Assembly of the Pacific coast. Nearly all the members of these organizations were members of the Knights of Labor.

To the Knights of Labor of Michigan is due the credit of establishing the " Bureau of Labor and Industrial Statistics " of that State.
The bill was drawn and presented by a Knight of Labor, and its
passage through the Legislature was carefully watched by the members of that body, who were also members of the Knights of Labor.
The Order throughout the entire State was much interested in the
measure, and took energetic steps to make the passage of the bill
possible.   The Michigan Bureau was established in 1883.

In the same year Wisconsin fell into line by enacting a law creating
a " Bureau of Labor Statistics." The measure was favored by the
Knights of Labor of that State, and its passage through the Legislature was hastened by the active agitation which was kept up while
the bill was on its passage.   The bill originated with the Knights of
Labor.

In 1884, Iowa established a "Bureau of Labor Statistics," and Maryland passed a law creating a " Bureau of Statistics of Labor." In
both States the measures were presented at the request of Knights of
Labor, and everything that could be done to further the interests of
the bills was done by the Order in these States.

In 1885, Kansas, through the influence of the Knights of Labor,
established a " Bureau of Labor Statistics." The most active work
in the way of aiding legislation that could be done was performed by
the Order in Kansas. Every member in the State petitioned and
wrote to the Legislature requesting that the Bureau be established.

Connecticut established a " Bureau of Labor Statistics " in 1885.   It
is due to the Order of the Knights of Labor that Connecticut boasts
of a Bureau, for they were the originators of the measure, and were
untiring in their efforts to have it become the law of the State.

Five Bureaus were instituted in 1887 in the States of Colorado, Maine,
Minnesota, North Carolina and Rhode Island, and it is owing to the
untiring efforts of the Knights of Labor of these States that these
Bureaus were established. They were introduced, pressed by and at
the request of Knights of Labor.

In 1884, the measure which William H. Sylvis introduced to the
National Labor Union Convention of 1867, looking to the organization
of a National Labor Bureau, became a law, and the " Bureau of
Labor " was created at the seat of the United States government.
The bill was introduced in the House of Representatives by Hon. J.
H. Hopkins of Pennsylvania, who worked untiringly for its successful
passage.   The members of the Order of the Knights of Labor watched
the various turns and halts which the National Congress took in passing the bill into law.   The first concern of the politician found expression in the inquiry : " How will the passage of the bill help my party ?"

Labor need not feel flattered because of the passage of the bill creating a National Bureau of Labor, for it was love of party and fear of

losing votes that caused over two-thirds of the members of the House of Representatives to pass the bill. In the Senate the hostility to the bill was equally as great, and it was only when the members of Congress who belonged to the party in power felt that the interests of that party would not be likely to suffer that they allowed it to become a law. Before reaching its final reading the bill was so amended in the Senate that its passage, as amended, would be of no practical benefit to the workingmen of the nation. Those who labored for its passage in the House of Representatives insisted that the bill should not be shorn of its most important features, and asked for a Committee of Conference, which was granted. The committees of the House and Senate agreed upon a bill which, although not so favorable to the interests of the masses as that presented in the House, was far in advance of that which would have been adopted by the Senate. President Arthur signed the bill creating the National Bureau of Labor, June 27, 1884 :

AN ACT to establish a Bureau of Labor.

Be it enacted by the Senate and House of Representatives of the United States of America in Congress assembled, That there shall be established in the Department of the Interior a Bureau of Labor, which shall be under the charge of a Commissioner of Labor, who shall be appointed by the President, by and with the advice and consent of the Senate. The Commissioner of Labor shall hold his office for four years, and until his successor shall be appointed and qualified, unless sooner removed; and shall receive a salary of three thousand dollars a year. The Commissioner shall collect information upon the subject of labor, its relation to capital, the hours of labor and the earnings of laboring men and women, and the means of promoting their material, social, intellectual and moral prosperity. The Secretary of the Interior, upon the recommendation of said Commissioner, shall appoint a chief clerk, who shall receive a salary of two thousand dollars per annum, and such other employes as may be necessary for the said Bureau; *provided*, that the total expense shall not exceed twenty-five thousand dollars per annum. During the necessary absence of the Commissioner, or when the office shall become vacant, the chief clerk shall perform the duties of Commissioner. The Commissioner shall annually make a report in writing to the Secretary of the Interior of the information collected and collated by him, and containing such recommendations as he may deem calculated to promote the efficiency of the Bureau.

Approved June 27, 1884.

When the National Labor Bureau was established, the workingmen of the United States, feeling that the Commissioner of Labor, as the Chief of the Bureau was designated, should be in sympathy with them in their efforts to improve their condition, petitioned the President to appoint the chief officer of the Knights of Labor to the position. D. A. 66 of Washington began the agitation by asking the General Master Workman to become a candidate, and when he applied, in person, to President Arthur, he presented petitions from fifteen hundred and sixty-seven branches of different labor organizations asking for his appointment. In addition to the petitions, he also laid before the President editorial clippings favorable to his appointment from thirty-seven labor papers, and one hundred and fifteen from the daily press of the United States. The President informed him that he would consider his petition and claim to the position, but also said that a remonstrance had been handed to him from the manufacturers in which the following statement occurred :

It is feared by the employers of labor that if Mr. Powderly is appointed by your excellency he will exert his influence in opposition to the interests of employers. It is also feared that he is in sympathy with the communist element, and that he will be influenced and guided largely by that class.

Many influential citizens and workingmen's organizations petitioned the President to appoint John Jarrett to the position of Commissioner, and were successful in having his name sent in to the Senate for confirmation. In the meantime Mr. Jarrett's enemies were not idle, and produced evidence to show that, while making a political speech, he reflected severely upon the administration of President Arthur. This evidence was presented to the President, who withdrew the name of Mr. Jarrett from before the Senate, and, after some delay, he sent in for confirmation the name of Carroll D. Wright, who, at that time, occupied the position of Chief of the Bureau of Labor of Massachusetts. It is said to be due to the influence of Benjamin F. Butler that Mr. Wright was selected by the President.

For several years there has existed in the New England States a society having for its aim the reform of the divorce laws of the country. The United States Senate passed a resolution instructing the Commissioner of Labor to gather, during the year 1888, statistics concerning the number and causes of divorce. The Commissioner protested against this innovation, but in vain. It was not clear to his mind that the legitimate scope of the Bureau took in the gathering of statistics on the subject of divorce. The workingmen who took an interest in the gathering of labor statistics naturally felt indignant, and protested against further departures from the work of the Bureau. This interference on the part of the Divorce Reform Association had a good effect, for it directed attention to the Bureau and caused many to take an interest in it who had hitherto regarded it with indifference.

In his address to the General Assembly which met in Minneapolis, Minn., in October, 1887, the General Master Workman advised that an agitation be begun in the direction of establishing a National Department of Labor at Washington. He said :

" I believe the day has come for united labor to ask at the hands of Congress the passage of a law creating a Department of Labor at the seat of the national government. I would respectfully ask the Committee on Legislation to prepare a bill and introduce it to Congress at the next session. We have to-day a Department of War ; we do not need it at all in comparison to a Department of Labor. The Navy Department is not such an important one, for we do not require the use of a very extensive national navy. The prosperity of the whole country rests on the broad shoulders of labor, and there is nothing now so prominently before the nation and the world as the question of labor. Nearly every action taken now by the Executive or his Cabinet deals in one way or another with the question of labor; its ramifications extend everywhere, its power is felt everywhere, and its usefulness is now recognized everywhere.

"All this being true, it is no more than just that the President should have as a member of his Cabinet a man who represents more than war, more than a few vessels, more than a sentiment, more than a class. Labor cannot be called a class, for it is everywhere. To have a man in his Cabinet with whom to consult on the question of labor, the President would be in a better position to deal with the question of capital. Labor to-day is entitled to far more at the seat of government than a mere Bureau, but it will not receive any more unless it asks for it. I recommend that we ask for the establishment of a Department of Labor."

The recommendation met with favor, and was unanimously agreed to by the assembled representatives. The Legislative Committee appointed at the Minneapolis session, consisting of Ralph Beaumont, James Campbell and John J. McCartney, was instructed to work for the measure. No effort was spared to bring the matter before Congress. Local and District Assemblies appointed committees to wait upon their representatives in Congress and request their co-operation in aid of the measure.

The bill was presented to the National Legislature by Hon. John J. O'Neill of Missouri, who, after consultation with the Knights of Labor Legislative Committee, decided not to ask that the head of the department be made a Cabinet officer, for the reason that such offices are usually bestowed upon political favorites, whose claims to recognition are based upon partisan service, while the head of such a department, as that which would have to deal with the affairs of industry, should be selected because of his ability and not because of his partisanship. The measure passed both Houses of Congress, and on June 30, 1888, received the official signature of President Cleveland:

AN ACT to establish a Department of Labor.

Be it enacted by the Senate and House of Representatives of the United States of America in Congress assembled, That there shall be at the seat of government a Department of Labor, the general design and duties of which shall be to acquire and diffuse among the people of the United States useful information on subjects connected with labor, in the most general and comprehensive sense of that word, and especially upon its relation to capital, the hours of labor, the earnings of laboring men and women, and the means of promoting their material, social, intellectual and moral prosperity.

Sec. 2. That the Department of Labor shall be under the charge of a Commissioner of Labor, who shall be appointed by the President, by and with the advice and consent of the Senate. He shall hold his office for four years, unless sooner removed, and shall receive a salary of five thousand dollars per annum.

Sec. 3. That there shall be in the Department of Labor, to be appointed by the Commissioner of Labor: One chief clerk, at a salary of two thousand five hundred dollars per annum; four clerks of class four, all to be statistical experts; five clerks of class three, one of whom may be a stenographer; six clerks of class two, one of whom may be a translator, and one of whom may be a stenographer; eight clerks of class one; five clerks, at one thousand dollars per annum ; one disbursing clerk, who shall also have charge of accounts, at a salary of one thousand eight hundred dollars per annum; two copyists, at nine hundred dollars each per annum; two copyists, at seven hundred and twenty dollars each per annum; one messenger; one assistant messenger; one watchman; two assistant watchmen; two skilled laborers, at six hundred dollars each per annum; two charwomen, at two hundred and forty dollars each per annum; six special agents, at one thousand six hundred dollars each per annum ; ten special agents, at one thousand four hundred dollars each per annum; four special agents, at one thousand two hundred dollars each per annum, and an allowance to special agents for traveling expenses not to exceed three dollars per day while actually employed in the field and outside of the District of Columbia, exclusive of actual transportation, including sleeping-car fares; and such temporary experts, assistants and other employes as Congress may from time to time provide, with compensation corresponding to that of similar officers and employes in other departments of the government.

Sec. 4. That during the necessary absence of the Commissioner, or when the office shall become vacant, the chief clerk shall perform the duties of Commissioner.

Sec. 5. That the disbursing clerk shall, before entering upon his duties, give bond to the Treasurer of the United States in the sum of twenty thousand dollars, which bond shall be conditioned that the said officer shall render a true and faithful account to the Treasurer, quarter-yearly, of all moneys and properties which shall be by him received by virtue of his office, with sureties to be approved by the Solicitor of the Treasury. Such bond shall be filed in the office of the First Comptroller of the Treasury, to be by him put in suit upon any breach of the conditions thereof.

Sec. 6. That the Commissioner of Labor shall have charge, in the building or premises occupied by or appropriated to the Department of Labor, of the library, furniture, fixtures, records and other property pertaining to it, or hereafter acquired for use in its business; and he shall be allowed to expend for periodicals and the purposes of the library, and for the rental of appropriate quarters for the accommodation of the Department of Labor within the District of Columbia, and for all other incidental expenses, such sums as Congress may provide from time to time.

Sec. 7. That the Commissioner of Labor, in accordance with the general design and duties referred to in Section 1 of this act, is specially charged to ascertain, at as early a date as possible, and whenever industrial changes shall make it essential, the cost of producing articles at the time dutiable in the United States, in leading countries where such articles are produced, by fully-specified units of production, and under a classification showing the different elements of cost, or approximate cost, of such articles of production, including the wages paid in such industries per day, week, month or year, or by the piece; and hours employed per day ; and the profits of the manufacturers and producers of such articles; and the comparative cost of living, and the kind of living. " It shall be the duty of the Commissioner also to ascertain and report as to the effect of the customs laws, and the effect thereon of the state of the currency, in the

United States, on the agricultural industry, especially as to its effect on mort-gage indebtedness of farmers;" and what articles are controlled by trusts or other combinations of capital, business operations or labor, and what effect said trusts or other combinations of capital, business operations or labor have on production and prices. He shall also establish a system of reports by which, at intervals of not less than two years, he can report the general condition, so far as production is concerned, of the leading industries of the country. The Com-missioner of Labor is also specially charged to investigate the causes of, and facts relating to, all controversies and disputes between employers and employes as they may occur, and which may tend to interfere with the welfare of the people of the different States, and report thereon to Congress. The Commissioner of Labor shall also obtain such information upon the various subjects committed to him as he may deem desirable from different foreign nations, and what, if any, convict-made goods are imported into this country, and, if so, from whence.

Sec. 8. That the Commissioner of Labor shall annually make a report in writing to the President and Congress of the information collected and collated by him, and containing such recommendations as he may deem calculated to promote the efficiency of the department. He is also authorized to make special reports on particular subjects whenever required to do so by the President or either House of Congress, or when he shall think the subject in his charge requires it. He shall, on or before the fifteenth day of December in each year, make a report in detail to Congress of all moneys expended under his direction during the preceding fiscal year.

Sec. 9. That all laws and parts of laws relating to the Bureau of Labor created under the act of Congress approved June twenty-seventh, eighteen hundred and eighty-four, so far as the same are applicable and not in conflict with this act, and only so far, are continued in full force and effect; and the Commissioner of Labor appointed under said act approved June twenty-seventh, eighteen hun-dred and eighty-four, and all clerks and employes in the Bureau of Labor author-ized to be appointed by said act or subsequent acts, shall continue in office and employment as if appointed under the provisions of this act, and until a Com-missioner of Labor, other officer, clerks and employes are appointed and qualified as herein required and provided, and the Bureau of Labor, as now organized and existing, shall continue its work as the Department of Labor until the Depart-ment of Labor shall be organized in accordance with this act; and the library, records and all property now in the use by the said Bureau of Labor are hereby transferred to the custody of the Department of Labor hereby created, and on the organization of the Department of Labor on the basis of this act the functions of the Bureau of Labor shall cease.

Sec. 10. That on the passage of this act the Commissioner of Labor shall at once submit estimates for the expenses of the Department of Labor for the next fiscal year, giving in detail the number and salaries of officers and employes therein.

Approved June 13, 1888.

Up to the present time Bureaus of Labor and Industries have been established in twenty States. These, together with the National Bureau which recently became a Department, are doing a great deal for the advancement of the masses. The agitation and earnest work, which resulted in the establishment of these institutions, came largely from the members of the Knights of Labor, who, acting on the third declaration in the Preamble of the Order, have been untiring in their efforts to leave the impress of the organization on the statute books of State and nation. Wherever the power of the organization has been used to secure legislation, it has been successful, particularly where the legislation is calculated to aid the toiler in his search for better things.

It is hoped that through the aid of the Labor Bureau the laborer will in time know how much of that which he produces belongs to him as a reward for labor done. It is hoped that it will be known how immense fortunes are acquired by men who do not work. It is hoped that the future will see a system established which will prevent the accumulation of such vast sums of money in the hands of one individual or one corporation.

In the days of the old-time slavery a man brought in the market from six hundred to twelve hundred dollars. His master provided him with shelter, fuel, clothing, food and medical attendance. The overseer, while he might at times be cruel, would not overwork the slave, for fear that the master would lose on the investment should the poor creature become unfit for service. To-day slavery is said to be abolished. The capitalist does not have to buy his slaves; they come to him in threes where twos could perform the required duty; they receive less for their daily wage than would be required to supply the necessities of the old-time slave. The slave of ante-bellum days had no vote upon which his master could depend, but the slave of the present generation thinks he has a vote until election day comes, when his master tells him that he must cast it for the party, or man, who stands the highest in the estimation of the employer. The slave of former years had no debts hanging like a millstone around his neck, for his master paid for everything; the present-day slave is never out of debt. The slavery of the olden time never produced a millionaire; the new slavery has given us thousands of them to curse the nation with their baneful presence. Under the new dispensation it is hoped that the acquiring of immense fortunes will be impossible, so that moderate means may be afforded to every man who works with hand or brain. Capitalist and laborer should be compelled to make accurate returns when called on by the agent of the Labor Bureau.

There is an old proverb which says "there is always room at the top." That is no longer true, for the man of wealth has monopolized the seat at the top, and there is no room for any but those who come with hands already full. The top so anxiously looked to a few short years ago has passed into the hands of a trust, and no poor man need look in that direction again until conditions change. The top has been monopolized the same as the corner lot, and will continue to be so monopolized until the true condition of the producing masses in their educational, moral and financial status becomes known through the aid of Labor Bureaus and the other acquisitions to the store of knowledge which are being brought within reach of the workingmen of America.

LAND—TRANSPORTATION—TELEGRAPHY.

These millions of acres belong to man,
    And his claim is that he needs;
And his title is sealed by the hand of God—
    Our God, who the raven feeds;
And the starving soul of each famished man
    At the throne of Justice pleads.

Ye may not heed it, ye haughty men,
    Whose hearts as rocks are cold—
But the time will come when the fiat of God
    In thunder shall be told:
For the voice of the great I AM hath said
    That "the land shall not be sold."—*A. J. H. Duganne.*

The regulation of the public lands of the United States, in one form or another, has consumed much of the time of Congress and has been the subject of a large share of public agitation since the adoption of the Constitution of the United States. Various acts have been introduced and discussed having for their object the securing of the settler in the possession of his homestead. The first of these that became a law was the Pre-emption Act of March 3, 1801, which gave the right of pre-emption to certain persons for lands lying between the Miami Rivers, in what was then known as the territory of the United States northwest of the Ohio River. Under one act after another the benefits of pre-emption were extended until the law of June 30, 1880, which extends the right of settlement to unsurveyed as well as surveyed lands, with a credit of from twelve to thirty-three months, which is given the pre-emptor by residence. Pre-emption is a premium granted the settler on condition that he makes permanent settlement and a home on the land which he lays claim to. By act of application at a land office, and a payment of a fee for the registration of his claim to the land, the right is conferred to occupy a certain tract of land of not more than one hundred and sixty or less than forty acres for a limited period, with the stipulation that at the end of that period the claimant shall pay to the United States $1.25 per acre for the land in the tract entered upon or claimed, when a patent for the land will be issued. Actual settlement upon the tract claimed, for the exclusive use of the pre-emptor, and not for the purpose of speculation or sale, must be shown before the patent is granted.

The pre-emption question was before the people and Congress until the year 1841, when the Pre-emption Act which was passed appeared to have settled the question.   In 1852 the granting of free homes became a national issue with the political parties of that day.   On August 11, 1852, the Free-soil Democracy met in convention in Pittsburg, Pa., to nominate candidates for President and Vice-President, and, having done so, adopted the following as the twelfth plank in the platform on which they went before·the people:

That the public lands of the United States belong to the people and should not be sold to individuals nor granted to corporations, but should be held as a sacred trust for the benefit of the people, and should be granted in limited quantities, free of cost to landless settlers.

From the promulgation of that platform until 1862 the land question was a national issue with all parties.   It was discussed in primaries and at mass-meetings, the whole people were aroused, and Congress was obliged to take action as early as 1859.   The march of the Western settler had begun, and was sweeping across the prairies to the land of the setting sun.   The demand for homes on the Western lands became very great, and the pressure for the enactment of a law which would confine locators to small holdings, with actual occupancy, improvement and cultivation as requisites for possession, swept in upon Congress, and continued until the passage of the Homestead Law of 1862.

In January, 1859, there was a bill before Congress relating to pre-emption.   On the 20th of that month Hon. Galusha A. Grow of Pennsylvania moved the following amendment:

Be it further enacted, that from and after the passage of this act no public land shall be exposed for sale by proclamation of the President, unless the same shall have been surveyed, and the return of such survey duly filed in the Land Office, for ten years or more before such sale.

The amendment was adopted, but when the bill itself came up it was defeated.   On February 1, of the same year, the bill before Congress was "A bill to secure homesteads to actual settlers on the public domain."

The bill passed the House by a vote of 120 yeas to 76 nays, and went to the Senate, where it lay until the adjournment of Congress, although several attempts were made to bring it before the body for discussion.   The bill was introduced by Mr. Grow in the House. On March 6, 1860, Mr. Lovejoy of Illinois, from the Committee on Public Lands, reported the same bill to the House.   Again it received the approval of the House by a vote of 115 yeas to 65 nays, and was sent to the Senate, where it was referred to the Committee on Public Lands.   Andrew Johnson, Chairman of the Committee, reported a substitute for the bill, granting homesteads to settlers at 25 cents per acre.   When this bill came before the Senate, Mr. Wade of Ohio moved to substitute the House Bill, but the motion was lost.

The Senate passed Mr. Johnson's bill on May 10, 1860, and a Conference Committee of both Houses considered the two measures and finally accepted the Senate Bill, with a few amendments. Both Houses having adopted a Homestead Law, it went to the President, and on June 23 President Buchanan vetoed the bill, and returned it to Congress with his objections.

In the Thirty-seventh Congress, on July 8, 1861, Mr. Aldrich introduced a Homestead Bill, and after much deliberation and opposition it came before the House for discussion. On February 22, 1862, the Speaker of the House of Representatives announced that the regular order would be the consideration of the Homestead Bill. After a short debate, and the offering of a few amendments, the bill passed the House and went to the Senate, where it was again changed by amendment. The House at first refused to concur in the amendments, but on May 15 both Houses agreed upon a bill, and it went to the President for approval. On May 20, 1862, President Lincoln signed the Homestead Bill, and it became a law.

The act has been amended several times, but the amendments have been in the direction of extending its benefits.

The first act conferring a grant of land upon a railroad was passed in 1833, and authorized the State of Illinois to divert the canal grant of 1827, and construct a railroad with the proceeds of the sale of said lands. The act was not utilized by the State. The act of September 20, 1850, was the first railroad act of any real significance or importance. By it was initiated the system of granting lands to railroads, which prevailed until after July 1, 1862. On that date Congress incorporated, by a direct act, the Union Pacific Railroad. Under the provisions of this act they were to build a railroad and telegraph line from the Missouri River to the Pacific.

With the granting of lands to railroads began the raid of the speculator and the crowding of the settler from his homestead. Railroads began to push their serpentine routes through prairies, over mountains and across the plains. As they traveled westward the acres became scarcer for the settler, and he had to go further away from civilization to find land on which to erect his home. Millions of acres were granted to railroads, and they selected the best and most fertile portions of the public domain. Speculators, who could not gain possession of territory under the homestead laws, organized railroad companies in order to lay claim to lands in the hope that the government would never declare them forfeited if they were not tapped the whole length by the railroad to which the grant was made.

The Credit Mobilier scandal, the wholesale robberies perpetrated upon the government by land-grabbers, and the tendency to monopolize the best acres in the national domain for speculative purposes, called the attention of the workingmen to the land question, and we find the National Labor Union speaking out on the subject in its platform.   When the Industrial Brotherhood gave out its Preamble in 1874, the fifth resolution, or demand, was for

" The reserving of the public lands, the heritage of the people, for the actual settler—not another acre for railroads or speculators."

It was not that there was a dread of a scarcity of land that this demand was made. It had its birth in the unjust manner in which the public lands were being absorbed, and, although it was not as clear-cut a declaration as that which emanated from the convention of the Free-soil Democracy in 1852, it briefly expressed the sentiments of those who endeavored to attract the attention of the wage-workers to greater issues than the wage-question.

In the first General Assembly of the Knights of Labor at Reading the declaration of the Industrial Brotherhood on the land question was indorsed and adopted.   In the meantime those who had acquired lands through sharp practice or otherwise kept them in reserve, wait-ing for advanced prices, which always accompany a desire to occupy the land.   The steady flow of immigration drove mechanics from their homes in the cities, and many determined to till the soil in preference to working for reduced wages in the large trade centres.   With his face turned toward the land, the workingman saw standing between him and the most valuable acres the form of the speculator, and he determined to enter his protest against so unjust a system.   At first his voice was not heard, but with the growth of organization he began to make his power felt, and he began to ask for something more than to keep the land from the speculator; he wished to compel the specu-lator to make restitution.   When the General Assembly met in Pitts-burg, Pa., in September, 1880, the Grand Master Workman, referring to the land problem, said :

" Millions of acres have been stolen from the people, and, while we may think that that question is of no interest to us here to-day, I sincerely believe that for every acre of the land which God designed for man's use and benefit that is stolen another link is riveted to the chain with which the land and bond lords hope to finally encircle us.   A few short years ago, if the representatives of labor met in convention such as this is, the land question would not necessarily intrude itself upon them ; but during those few short years we have slept, and to-day, whether we will or not, it is thrust upon us."

He urged upon the General Assembly to express an opinion upon the question, but no action was taken at that session, and the fifth section of the Preamble remained unchanged.   No reference was made to the matter at the Detroit Convention in 1881, but at the New York session, which convened on September 5, 1882, at No. 8 Union Square, the address of the Grand Master Workman contained the following:

In my opinion, the main, all-absorbing question of the hour is the land question. And did I allow this opportunity of expressing that opinion to the Knights of Labor of America to pass by without taking advantage of it, I would prove myself false to my own convictions of right and justice. The eight-hour law, the prohibition of child-labor and the currency question are all of weighty moment to the toiler. But high up above them all stands the land question. Give me the land, and you may frame as many eight-hour laws as you please, yet I can baffle them all and render them null and void. Prohibit child labor if you will, but give me the land, and your children will be my slaves. Make your currency of what material you choose; but, if I own the land, you cannot base your currency upon the wealth of the nation, for that wealth is the LAND. You may make the laws and own the currency, but give me the land and I will absorb your wealth and render your legislation null and void.

Look over our Western fields to-day and note the rapid strides with which monopoly is seizing upon the fairest acres our country contains. The people of Ireland suffer from landlordism to-day; but a gleam of hope is ever before them, for if the worst comes they can go to America. Let the robbery of the people's heritage go on in the United States in the future as it has in the past, and the hope of the emigrant will die out in his bosom, and soon a sentence to the mines of Siberia will be preferable to a residence in the land of his birth.

The land is the heritage of God! He gave it to *all* his people. If He intended it for all His people, then no one man or set of men has a right to monopolize it. We cannot say that the whole people who now inhabit the earth can claim the land. That would imply absolute ownership; and if one man has no right to own the land, many men cannot own it. If all the people of the present day own the land we live on, what right will the millions yet unborn have to the earth to which their Creator will one day bring them? These are questions worth pondering over. There are men who fear the land question. There were men who feared the appearance of Banquo's ghost; but that ghost was an honest one, and no honest man had cause to fear it. So it is with the land question— no honest man need fear it.

If I am told that our National Legislature had a right to grant the lands to corporations, I ask the question from whom did they derive that right? The answer must be—*the people.* Yet I deny that right, for a people now living cannot give away what was ordained for the use of a people yet unborn. But granting that they had that right, than I challenge—nay, defy—any man to produce a petition, coming from the people to Congress, asking that body to give away the land. If, then, that body had no right to give away the land, it should be compelled to restore it. It may be said that such a proceeding would unsettle society. Very well, then, let society for the time be unsettled; for it were better that a momentary disturbance take place now than a greater one later on; for with a rapid concentration of the land in the grasp of the few and the rapid increase in population, the time is not far distant when men will rise in the morning, and, after eating their morning meal, they will turn away from the table not knowing where the next one is to come from. When that hour comes, the labor question will be harder of solution than it is at present. When that day comes it will take more than the sophistry now in use to convince these hungry men that one man has a right to own the land and all it contains, while they, the children of the same Father, have *nothing.* When that day comes the logic of a hungry stomach will settle the question which wise heads are now endeavoring to solve, and, knowing no law but that of want, they will obey that law, even at the risk of *unsettling society.* So it were better that we look to the welfare of future generations, and do justice while it can be done peaceably.

If I ever come to believe in individual, absolute ownership in land, I must, in order to be consistent, believe that the man who owns the land owns the people who live on it as well. If a man owns an island in the ocean, and he wishes to clear it of tenants for the purpose of turning it into a grazing field, the man who admits that he has a right to own the land in absolute title must also admit that he has the right to order these people off its surface. If he orders them off, there is no alternative but to obey. Suppose that through unjust exactions of rent the tenant has had no opportunity of saving money enough to pay his passage to a foreign land, a very pertinent question to ask would be, Where will the tenant go? The only answer the believer in absolute ownership of land can give will be—*into the ocean.* Does any sane man believe that God ordained that any man' should have such power? Such a doctrine is monstrous. It won't do to say that such a case is only a supposition, and that no danger of its ever occurring exists. The question to consider is—Would it be just or right for such a thing to take place? If not, then take steps to remove a system that would make such a thing possible. Give heed to this land question; be not afraid of the taunts or jeers of our enemies; do not quail at the name of communist, if it is applied to you, for it were better to be called a communist than be a party to the plundering of a people of the inheritance ordained for them by God.

> "The law condemns the man or woman
> Who steals the goose from off the common;
> But lets the greater felon loose
> Who steals the common from the goose."

God hasten the day when the "greater felon" will be brought to justice! And may our organization be brave enough to shoulder its portion of the responsibility, and share in the glory of achievement. If there exists such a thing on earth as a just title to the ownership of land, I have yet to learn of it; but in searching for it I found this in "Blackstone's Commentaries on the English Law:"

"Pleased as we are with the possession [of land], we seem afraid to look back to the means by which it was acquired, as if fearful of some defect in our title * * * * * we think it enough that our title is derived by the grant of the former proprietor by descent from our ancestors, or by the last will and testament of the dying owner. Not caring to reflect that accurately and strictly speaking there is *no foundation in nature, or in natural law,* why a set of words upon parchment should convey the dominion of land; why the son should have a right to exclude his fellow-creatures from a determinate spot of ground because his father had done so before him; or why the occupier of a particular field, when lying upon his death-bed, and no longer able to maintain possession, should be entitled to tell the rest of the world which of them should enjoy it after him."

With so highly respectable and eminent an authority as Blackstone to quote from, we ought not to fear to open up this question; and if the few words I have uttered in passing will cause others to think, then the discussion to follow must lead to good results.

The convention did not deem it prudent to take any action on the recommendation of the Grand Master Workman. The Order at that time was not known to many. Its influence was but limited, and the agitation of the land question was in its infancy. As a consequence, suggestions such as those made to the General Assembly attracted little or no notice. The only attention given to the subject at the time was to subject the writer to no small share of adverse criticism because of the extreme views he advanced. When the next convention was held at Cincinnati in 1883, the Grand Master Workman again presented the subject to the body for its consideration in the following language:

I deem it proper to again draw the attention of the General Assembly to the land question. I referred to it in my last annual address, and it is worthy of the most serious consideration that this body can bestow upon it. The public lands of this country are being filched from us, not slowly, but quickly and surely. What action will the toilers take to not only prevent any further stealing of the people's heritage, but to restore to the people every acre that has been stolen from them in the past? The people of Ireland are driven by enforced emigration from their native land; they flee from the landlord, who has gained the right to demand rent for the land of Ireland, only to face him in a still worse form on this continent. It is astonishing, but true, that alien landlords own millions of acres of American soil. We do not permit Americans to go abroad and accept titles from monarchists, but we do permit monarchists to come to this country, and without disowning their allegiance to monarchy they are permitted to buy up the best lands we have on the continent. Seven titled noblemen living in England and Ireland, living in an atmosphere where they cannot but hate everything that is American, own eight million nine hundred and fifteen thousand acres of American soil. These men are all landlords. In England they, by their influence, secure the passage by the British government of an " Enforced Emigration Act " for the purpose of driving their victims from their own land to this country, that these vultures may be enabled to face them again where they have absolute control of the soil, and can exact such terms as please them.

It is not because I was born in this land that I speak so strongly on this subject, but because I believe that this country was intended and should be held for the oppressed of the earth. I am opposed to allowing any man to possess our soil who will not do as we do; who will not do as the humble foreigner does; that is, swear allegiance to the flag that was born amid the struggle against tyranny and baptized in the blood of men who hated royalty and oppression. Monarchy could not retain its hold on this country one hundred years ago, the people were aroused; but what the steel of the tyrant could not conquer then, the gold of the descendant of that tyrant has since then succeeded in taking from us. I recognize no right on the part of the aristocracy of the old or new worlds to own our lands. We fought to hold them once, and if it is necessary I am willing to advocate the same measures again; but I will never cease this agitation while the foot of the alien oppressor has a resting place within our boundaries. This land question is the one great question of the hour; open your eyes to its enormity, my friends, and act. I will in other places deal more exhaustively with this question of the land for the people, but for the present leave it in your hands.

No notice was taken of the advice contained in the address, for the reason that the land question appeared to be a remote issue, and one not likely to intrude itself upon the workingmen of the present century. The records of that session show that a great deal of valuable time was spent in legislating upon strikes and lockouts. With these harassing details to attend to, the General Assembly was worn out before the time arrived when consideration could be given to such matters as were alluded to in the address of the Grand Master Workman.

In the meantime the Preamble remained unchanged. No alteration was made in it from the date of its adoption, and at the Philadelphia session of the General Assembly a change was recommended by the Grand Master Workman. In his address he said :

The fifth declaration made in our Preamble demands the reserving of the public lands—the heritage of the people—for the actual settler—not another acre for railroads or speculators. While I entertain very decided views on this question, still I have no desire to force them on the members of the Order, but I do hold that we should not stand still on a question of such magnitude as is this land question. On previous occasions I made recommendations, or at least called the attention of the Order to the land question. I now recommend that the section quoted above be changed to read :· " We demand the reserving of the lands of the nation for the people of the nation—not another acre for railroads, speculators or gamblers of any description, whether citizen or alien, resident or non-resident—and that all lands now held for the purposes of speculation by corporation or individual shall be restored to the care of the people."

While the convention did not adopt the suggestion of the Grand Master Workman, it made a radical change in the entire Preamble, and when it went out to the Order the fourth section referred to the land question, and read as follows:

That the public lands, the heritage of the people, be reserved for actual settlers —not another acre for railroads or speculators—and that all lands now held for speculative purposes be taxed to their full value.

Here and there throughout the Order Local Assemblies took up the subject for debate; others drew up resolutions expressive of their sentiments and forwarded them to their representatives in Congress. No small share of public attention was given to the restoration of misappropriated lands during the years 1884-'85-'86. The General Master Workman mailed to each member of Congress copies of his annual addresses from 1882 to 1885, or that portion of them which referred to national affairs. The address of 1885, delivered at Hamilton, Ontario, in October of that year, contains the following reference to the question of land legislation :

At the last session of the General Assembly I called the attention of that body to the rapidity with which the heritage of the American people was slipping from under their feet. Native and alien landlords are absorbing all of the fertile lands of the nation, and it can no longer be said :

> " To the West, to the West, to the land of the free,
> Where the mighty Missouri rolls down to the sea ;
> Where man is a man, if he is willing to toil,
> And shall have for his labor the fruit of the soil."

The man who goes to the West to-day, and is willing to toil, must toil for another, and the fruits of the soil which his labor produces must be given to the stranger. The man who takes up his claim of one hundred and sixty acres of land, provided he can find it unoccupied to take up, must compete in the market, in the sale of his products, with the men who hold farms of from fifty thousand to five hundred thousand acres each. It was thought that the introduction of bonanza farming would cheapen the products of the land when thrown upon the market. Such is not the case. The man who is wealthy enough to own and operate a large farm of from fifty to a hundred or five hundred thousand acres can afford to await an advance in prices, while the small farmer must sell his produce at once or lose. The bonanza farmer says to the small farmer: " I have a million bushels of wheat which I can throw upon the market now or wait an advance in prices. You must either sell to me at the price I now offer to you, or else I will glut the market with the wheat I have on hand, and you must sell for a still lower figure later on." The man who has never given this subject any consideration will say at once: "Such a step as that will have the result of cheapening food." The reverse of that is true, for no sooner has the small farmer's produce been absorbed by the large one than the latter corners the wheat, and, no longer in dread of competition from the man with the small farm, he demands a higher price for the wheat than before; and no matter how plenty the wheat may be, the large elevators of the country can hold it long enough to starve the people into paying the most exorbitant prices for it. It may be asked why do not the small farmers send their produce to market by rail? Because the owners of the large farms are, as a rule, directors or stockholders in the railways, and discriminate against all who do not comply with their demands. If they are neither directors nor stockholders, then the railroads will discriminate in their favor and against the owners of small farms.

The practice of permitting aliens to hold large tracts of land while living in foreign countries has been carried to such an extent that, as far as can be estimated, upward of twenty-one million acres of American lands are owned by men who have never set foot on American soil. At the last session of Congress a bill was introduced by Mr. Oates which reads as follows: "That no alien or foreigner, or persons other than citizens of the United States, and such as have legally declared their intention to become citizens thereof, shall acquire title to or own any lands anywhere within the United States of America and their jurisdiction; and any deeds or other conveyances acquired by such after the approval of this act shall be void."

We should insist on the passage of that law, and then have another one written upon the statute books of the nation which will forever prevent any person from acquiring title to or owning any more land than he can cultivate. The number of acres should not exceed one hundred. We must go still further than that, and demand that all lands now held for speculative purposes be restored to the public domain.

This question is a living one, and is of such a nature that we cannot shirk or avoid it. It may be intimated that I aim at disturbing "vested rights." I have all the respect in the world for vested rights, but have no respect at all for vested wrongs; and if the holding of such large tracts of land is not wrong, then never did a wrong exist. If it is the intention of a railway company to lay its tracks through a certain tract of territory, and if it happens that the route is surveyed through a piece of land owned by a poor man, can he retain possession of his land under the plea that it would be disturbing vested rights? By no means. If he does not accept the price offered to him by the company his land is appraised by disinterested parties, and a price fixed upon it which he must accept, and in the transaction no thought is given to the "disturbing of vested rights." Under what plea is he obliged to surrender his right to the land? That of ministering to the public good. It is for the public good that this railway should be put through; the welfare of the people demands it, and it must be done. It is under the same plea that the lands now held in such large tracts for speculative purposes should be restored to the people. I believe that the burglar who enters the house at night while the inmates are sleeping and carries off such money and valuables as he can lay his hands on has as just a title to these possessions as has many a man who now lays claim to American lands.

I have heard it said that if the land was offered to men who live in large cities they would not avail themselves of the opportunity to go upon it and make homes for themselves. I admit the truth of that assertion, and go a step further and say that it would do them no good to go upon it unless they had some assurance of succeeding. The majority of men who live in large cities are not adapted to the life which a farmer must lead, and the minority, no matter how well adapted they may be to such a life, may be lacking in the experience necessary to the successful operation of the farm. But whether experienced or not, if the most careful, thrifty man be placed on a farm, admitting that the land, dwelling, barn and out-houses are given to him free of charge, if he is lacking in the capital necessary to defray the cost of implements, seed and stock, he will fail unless help is extended to him in this direction also. This being true, it need not to be wondered at that men who have spent the greater part of their lives in cities and towns shrink from so important and hazardous an undertaking as settling upon land must naturally be.

The real facts in the case, plainly stated, are that very few men who have lived any length of time in the city or town have enough money laid by to even defray the expenses of themselves and families to the land. There are in all of our large cities and towns a number of men and families who would make excellent farmers if they were provided with sufficient means to give them a start in agricultural life; but they are deficient in means, and they must remain to compete with others in our crowded centres in the race of life. What is the duty of Congress in this matter? I believe that assistance should be given to all who wish to leave the cities and adopt agriculture as a calling. This can be done if the people demand it. In the older countries the evil effects of centuries of misrule are so firmly rooted that the people seem to be powerless to defend themselves. In this country it is different. But we have in the past been very generous to large corporations. Laws have been enacted with a view to developing the country. Our government has fostered private enterprises, created and granted exemptions, and in many ways encouraged the developing of corporate wealth. All this was done to build up the country. The object was a very good one, and it has been successful. But in building up the country immense private fortunes have been created, and through the possession of vast tracts of land and immense sums of money some of the creatures of the government are as powerful, if not more so, than their creator. In the future the duty of the government must be to build up and guard the interests of its people. The laboring element of this country, which includes the agricultural, mechanical and laboring classes, must be protected; they must become so strong that they can resist the extremes of poverty and wealth.

Some years ago Hon. Hendrick B. Wright presented a bill in Congress which sought to assist the poor man to secure a homestead for himself and family. The scheme was sneered at by Legislators and business men, but the remedy offered by Mr. Wright was a good one, and should be put in operation. I am not prepared to say that the plan of his bill was the best that could be offered, but it was in the right direction, and may be improved upon in the light of the experience gained since then. Let us formulate a plan by which the people may gain access to the land without the fear of being disinherited.

Following close upon the heels of the Hamilton session of the General Assembly came the agitations, disturbances and strikes of 1885 and 1886. Every moment of the lives of the General Officers was devoted to the troubles which sprung up in the labor world, and for three years the attention of the entire Order was diverted in a different direction from that which pointed to the vital question of land reform. In none of his later addresses to the General Assembly did the General Master Workman refer to the subject, and but little time was allowed him to even give a thought to the matter.

In his report to the special session of the General Assembly, which met at Cleveland in May, 1886, J. P. McGaughey, Secretary of the

General Co-operative Board, urged that the co-operative funds of the Order be devoted to the purchase of land for the relief of members who resided in large cities; but no action was taken on the report. Mr. McGaughey submitted a statement taken from the report of the Committee on Public Lands of the House of Representatives at Washington in relation to alien landlordism. It reads:

The country had a magnificent possession in the public domain of that time, and under proper management would have afforded grand results for generations to come. Areas of land, sufficiently large to make great States, were donated with reckless liberality to railroad and other corporations, and, by a lax, easy administration of injudicious laws, men of wealth have been illegally permitted to acquire other great areas of the public lands; and now this generation has seen the vast territory we had at its beginning so reduced that less than 5,000,000 acres of arable agricultural land remain for the settlers, and about 50,000,000 of acres only of lands susceptible of improvement by irrigation. These lands are becoming more and more valuable year by year; and tempted by the promise, sure to be realized, of immense profits, as well as the absolute security of the investment, these lands, by devious methods in many cases, have been secured in great areas and holdings by capitalists and corporations, foreign as well as domestic.

In the hands of many of these foreign owners and holders these lands are made subject to a system of landlordism and conditions totally un-American and kindred to that existing in the old world—systems and conditions which have spread ruin and misery wherever they have existed in Europe. Beside this, out of the heritage of the American people—the public lands—we are at present permitting the coining of immense private fortunes in the hands of the foreign nobility and gentry at the expense of our own people, and giving these foreigners the control of the homes and happiness of the thousands of citizens or those who have come here to identify themselves with us. As an illustration of this, a published statement showing that 20,747,000 acres of land are held by foreigners is appended. Among the large holders mentioned are the Marquis of Tweedale, Sir Edward Reed, the Holland Company and several foreign syndicates, the possessions of each numbering millions of acres.

It is unnecessary to enter into detail and give the facts and figures which prove that public lands were voted away by Congress in a most reckless manner. It is not required that statements be submitted concerning the extent to which bonanza farming has been carried in the United States. This information will be found in an interesting volume entitled "Land and Labor," by William Godwin Moody, and a repetition is entirely unnecessary, for those who care to inform themselves on these points will find the subject exhaustively discussed in the pages of that little book.

The demand of the Order of the Knights of Labor is "that all lands now held for speculative purposes be taxed to their full value." The great difficulty is to ascertain to what extent lands are now held for the purpose of speculation. While it is true that no greater evil exists than the holding of lands for such purposes, it is equally true that to properly estimate the number of acres thus held is almost impossible; and should a law be passed in compliance with the demand of the Knights of Labor, it would fall far short of the object intended, for the

holders of lands would claim that they were not holding them for
speculative purposes, and no one could prove that the contrary was
true until they were offered for sale. Even then it would be difficult
to prove that speculation had anything to do with the sale.

If the Knights demanded that "all lands held by parties, other
than the government, shall bear an equal proportion of the taxation
required for the maintenance of the government, and unimproved
lands shall be assessed at the same rate as the nearest improved land,"
they would come nearer to the establishment of a just rate of taxation ;
and whether lands were held for speculation or not, they would not
escape their just proportion of taxation. Through the operations of
the system of holding land for speculative purposes labor is drained of
its last dollar, and poverty abounds where comfort would be found if
we were living under a just and humane system of land ownership.
Every acre of land held for speculative purposes is a tax upon
industry ; it is more : it is a legalized theft, and does more to promote
discord and spread discontent than all other causes combined.

While the present system exists it will be impossible for any great
number of toilers to secure homes of their own. Those who do earn
enough to purchase homes are taxed for every act of labor that enriches
the soil, and the conditions under which workingmen have to live
after they purchase homes are such as to cause them to dread the idea
of investing in land. In industrial centres, particularly in the coal
regions, workingmen, as a rule, purchase lands on which to erect
homes from their employers, and through the possession of these
homes, and the fear of losing them, they are in many instances forced
to submit to impositions which they would not tolerate if the fear of
losing employment first, and the homes eventually, did not haunt
them. The black-list has often served to return to corporations the
building lots which employes contracted for.

A case is cited where five men purchased five hundred acres of coal
lands adjoining a large city at a cost of $50,000. Upon the land they
built a coal-breaker, sunk a shaft, and erected machinery at an extra
cost of $150,000, the total investment being $200,000. The surface of
the land was staked off into town lots and offered for sale to employes
and others who wished to buy. The prices of the lots run from $100
to $250, according to location. The centrally-located lots were kept
off the market and reserved for future sales, when a sufficient number
of the cheaper lots had been sold to enhance the value of those in
reserve. In less than three years a town of about three thousand
inhabitants had been built up in that neighborhood. Stores, churches,
schools and one or two small factories had been built, and the corporation had sold two hundred of the $100 lots and one hundred and
seventy-five of the others.

The sum realized on the sale of these lots was $45,000. The lots averaged five to the acre, and, after the sale of the three hundred and seventy-five lots, the company had remaining, including the spot on which the breaker and buildings were erected, twenty-one hundred and twenty-five lots. Those who purchased from them paid inside of three years within $5,000 of the total sum invested in the land. At the end of three years the price of the remaining lots advanced to $300 and $500, according to location.

The company invested in more real estate, and erected more tenements for the use of those of their employes who were unwilling or too poor to purchase homes. In disposing of the lots each deed contained a clause reserving the coal and mineral beneath the surface for the use of the company, and at the end of the fourth year those who purchased lots had paid back to the company the $50,000 it had invested in the entire tract, together with the interest on the money. The title to the coal still remained vested in the corporation. Through this operation the company had secured the coal beneath the surface of five hundred acres for nothing, except an exercise of good business qualifications.

The price of the second lot would never have been advanced had no purchaser appeared to take the first one. It was no act of the members of the corporation that raised the price of the lots to $300. It was the action of the community in locating in and around the centrally-located lots. The corporation did not speculate on the probable amount of labor each member would perform in the service of the company. It speculated on the probable number of lots that would be sold, and, when the demand became brisk, the necessities of those who desired homes were taken advantage of and the price of the remaining lots was almost doubled. The corporation paid taxes on their lands by the acre, while their purchasers paid by the lot, and, as nearly all of the lots were sold on contracts running from three to six years, the interest at six per cent. paid the taxes and insurance of the corporation.

The workmen not only paid their own taxes while improving their homes, but they also paid the taxes and insurance of the company, and for every spadeful of earth thrown up in the improvement of the homes of the workmen; the company rated the remaining lands at higher figures than before, because of the labor of other hands than their own. In this instance, and its parallel may be found in every community, the corporation not only speculated in the land, but in the labor of those who occupied it as well.

When the works were started the company paid a fair rate of wages, but after the first year the stock of the concern was watered to about double its original cost, and in order to draw interest on an honest investment of $200,000, and on a fictitious stock of an equal amount, the wages of the workmen were reduced ten per cent.

Those who had not invested in homes were at liberty to quit the service of the company and move elsewhere, but those who had purchased or contracted for the purchase of homes were obliged to remain, and there were enough of them to carry on operations, with the aid of a number of cheap imported workmen, who took the places of those who left the town to seek for more remunerative employment.

Other exactions than reductions of wages were imposed upon the men who had been induced to locate in that town, and, instead of the possession of a home proving a blessing, it turned out to be a hardship under the system in vogue at that point. This illustration will fit hundreds of cases to be met with in all parts of the country, and portrays the iniquity of the system which permits speculation in land to throttle the independence of the citizen.

From the window where I sit a view is had of a farm belonging to a large coal-mining and carrying company. Part of this land is used for grazing purposes; some of it is under grain and vegetables. It is leased to different parties by the year. Only the surface is leased, however, and the corporation will not sell the land for building purposes, it is said, until they can command $1,500 a lot, if they do then. This land is destined to become very valuable. It is situated within a mile of the heart of the city of Scranton, with its hundred thousand inhabitants, and is located on an eminence overlooking the business part of the city. The tract in question contains one hundred and forty-six acres of land. An examination of the tax duplicate of the city shows that it is assessed at a valuation of $52,740, and, at the tax rate of 20¼ mills on the dollar, pays in school and city taxes $1,318.50, or a fraction over $9 per acre. The lots on the opposite side of the street sold, or were offered for sale three years ago, at the rate of $900 for fifty feet front and rear, and one hundred and fifty feet in length. When the lot on which the house I occupy was contracted for I was obliged to pay a tax of $6 per annum for school and city purposes, while the land around it paid at the rate of $1.50 per annum, or $4 less than I paid for the same number of square feet. Up to this time nothing had been done to change the appearance, quality or nature of the lot— only the act of transferring it to me for building purposes caused the assessor to demand $6 from me, while asking but $1.50 from the corporation. To-day the land on either side of mine, on the same side of the street, sells for $1,200 per lot.

I have erected a house, and on that and the lot pay a tax of $50 per annum. On my labor and improvements I am required to pay at the rate of $50 a year, while a great corporation holds the surface of its one hundred and forty-six acres in reserve, waiting for others to locate in the neighborhood that it may demand $1,500 per lot. If for the crime of improving my lot I am fined $50 a year, why should not the corporation, which holds the adjoining lands for speculative purposes, be required to pay at least the same rate of taxation ? It is being enriched every time I plant a tree, a shrub or a flower. If I put a new coat of paint on my house I am required to pay a higher rate of taxation for the labor done, and because I have performed that labor the corporation across the street advances the price of its land. It charges whoever will buy for my labor, and contributes little or nothing, in comparison to its resources, to the tax rate of the city, while expecting to derive a large profit from those who reside therein.

The corporation will argue that it gives employment to thousands, thus enabling them to purchase homes, etc. The reverse is true, for it is the labor of the thousands which makes the corporation rich and great, while it, through exorbitant charges for building lots, prevents the poor from owning homes, thus retarding the growth of the city. That is a question which will not be discussed here.

In the one hundred and forty-six acres, lots the size of mine to the number of seven hundred and forty may be staked out and sold. If offered at reasonable prices to-day they would be sold, and dwellings would be erected on each one of them.

Seven hundred and forty additional property-owners would be contributing to the wealth of the city, but are held off by the avarice of those who have control of the land in question. These lands are now taxed as farm lands, although within a stone's throw of the city hall. If each lot were assessed as it should be, and required to pay its proportionate share of taxation, the taxes of every other resident of the city would be lowered in consequence, or the city would have that much more of a revenue with which to make improvements. At the rate at which I pay for improvement, these acres, if assessed, would pay $37,000 per year; if assessed as my lot was when I purchased it, and before I changed it a particle from its original state, this tract of one hundred and forty-six acres would pay $4,440 a year, instead of $1,318.50, as at present, and there is no just reason why that corporation and all others should not pay at the same rate as individuals do.

Every acre escaping its proportionate share of taxation is imposing a burden on some other person, and to that extent is robbing that other person as surely and as effectively as though the pockets of that person were picked on the public highway.

That the greater portion of the lands of the nation is held by individuals or corporations is true; that they do not pay their proportionate share of taxes under our present laws is true; that other persons residing in the nation must make up the deficiency and support the State is also true; that whoever contributes what these landholders should contribute is being wronged is as true as any of the other propositions, and it is certain that the laws which permit such violations of the rights of the people are radically wrong.

It is asserted that to prevent speculative land-holding would injure the farmers of the country. There is not a vestige of truth in that statement. Farmers do not cultivate their lands for the purpose of speculating in the price of the farm, nor do they sell their farms unless they intend to give up farming, or remove to another location. If they sell for the latter purpose, then speculation will work as injuriously to them as to all others, for speculators are no respecters of persons.

Large land-owners are a menace to the farmers as well as to others, and it is as much to their interest to stem the tide of land-grabbing as it is to the mechanic or laborer in the city. The resident of the large city labors under the delusion that the land question has nothing to do with him. He is far removed from " the country," and will never engage in farming; as a consequence, he regards with indifference the agitation going on in the direction of requiring land to pay its just share of what is now wrung from the aching back of the laborer. To bring the question squarely before the resident of the city, we will accompany him to Castle Garden and witness the process of "settling immigrants on land" when the steamer comes into port. A foreigner, who was a farmer at home, naturally wishes to become a farmer in America. The agent of the land-grant company meets him when he lands, or used to do so before the company established an agency in Europe to send men over, and offers him an opportunity to take up land in the West at interest ranging from six to twenty per cent. The immigrant accepts the offer, and with his wife and family goes to the land. He is poor and has to borrow money to buy tools, stock and seed. He pays interest on the money he borrows, as well as on the money he hopes to be able to pay the corporation. At the end of five years he has not succeeded in raising the mortgage on his farm, and has barely succeeded in raising a living on it. It may be that his farm is part of a tract held by an alien landlord, possibly the one who drove him from his home in Europe; but whether it is or not, the effect on him is the same, for the instinct of the landlord is the same the world over, and when the time expires the mortgage must be paid as well as the rent. Not being in a condition to meet his obligations, our farmer is forced to surrender to the sheriff, and gives to the land-owner every acre that he agreed to purchase from him, with all of his stock, tools and fixtures that the interest did not eat up before. Penniless as when he landed, loaded down with a debt which he did not bring to this country with him, older and as a consequence less able to earn a living for a family that has grown larger, he leaves the farm. He cannot take up land anywhere else, and his path lies in the direction of the city. On arriving there he goes to the factory to seek for employment among men who imagine that the land question does not concern them.

Standing at the door of the factory is another man who has just landed in America. Both men are strangers to each other, but they are actuated by one impulse; they want bread for themselves and families, and their mission to that factory door is to obtain employment that they may earn bread. The superintendent or foreman responds to the knock, and when he opens the door two men ask for work. The factory is running with a full complement of operatives, but here are two men seeking work. They are in distress and will work cheap rather than see their families starve. The third man at work on the inside is told that he must perform labor for a smaller remuneration or give way to one of the two who stand at the door, and he either quits work or agrees to remain at a reduction in wages. In either event the number of the unemployed is not reduced, and the farmer from the West, uniting with the immigrant from the East, assist in reducing the wages of the man in the middle, of the man in the city, who scoffs at the idea of farming, or land, having anything to do with him.

The trade unionist, basing all his hopes on a reduction of the hours of labor or an increase of ten per cent. in wages, does not realize that through our iniquitous land system men enough are turned away from the land every year to fill the factories should they strike for shorter hours or better pay. Blind to their own best interests, the trade unionists refuse to strike hands with the farmers, the Knights of Labor, and others in the work of land reform, while speculation in land, the unequal payment of taxes on land, and the operation of immense tracts of land on the bonanza-farm principle, drive hundreds of thousands away from the land who would never darken a factory door if they could till the soil and make a living at it.

All who cannot find work to do must live on the labor of those who are employed, and an advance of ten per cent., if it comes under such conditions, is soon lost again where thousands seek for work. The hours of labor will be reduced in vain where hundreds of thousands seek for employment as a result of unjust taxation and speculative land-holding. Our cities are increasing in population at an alarming rate. Men are swarming in from the country, claiming that it is no longer possible to make a living on the land. Syndicates, corporations and millionaires are engaging in agriculture on a magnificent scale; they claim that they are making bread cheap for the people of the cities. They are also increasing the population of the cities, and adding to the number of those who cannot earn the money with which to buy bread.

Under such a system as this the farmer and mechanic are at the mercy of the corporations who control the factories and the farms. With machinery in the hands of corporate power, turning men out of employment while it turns out riches for the owners; with large farms being tilled by hired men who hold no interest in the land, and who go to the cities in winter; with mortgages driving farmers into the cities at all seasons of the year; with the small landholder paying the taxes of the large one; with labor carrying the burdens which land should bear; with railroads squeezing out of the shipper "all that the traffic will bear;" with it possible to learn a trade, or a part of it, in five days in 1889 that required as many years thirty years ago, how is it possible for the mechanic or laborer in the city to maintain a respectable standard of wages or lessen his hours of toil ? It has become fashionable of late for the trade unionist to shout "hay-seed" at the man who belongs to an organization that would elevate all men of toil, but numskull is the epithet that should be applied to the resident of the city who imagines that the question of land reform is not as important to him as the securing of increased wages or shorter hours of toil.

It is demanded in the thirteenth resolution in the Preamble of the Knights of Labor "that a graduated income tax be levied." It is hoped by this operation to reach our wealthy men, and force them to pay a just proportion of the revenue necessary to conduct the affairs of State. The income tax may be levied, but who is to ascertain what a man's income is ? It is easy to learn what the income of the workingman is; but go beyond the domain of honest toil, and the chances of getting acquainted with the income of the wealthy are very few. Men's honor must be regarded as the standard by which to gauge the income of the wealthy, but the man who speculates in land will not tell the truth about his income if he can save money by telling a lie. Honor will not oblige him to state the truth, for speculation smothers honor. Perjury will be resorted to to retain the wealth which unfair dealing has won, and the greatest difficulty will be experienced in ascertaining what is a man's income.

In the city of Detroit there resides a wealthy man who owns hundreds of thousands of dollars' worth of property in the city. In his dwelling is a picture for which he paid $25,000. He admits that he paid $15,000 for it. His assessed valuation for all of the property owned by him in the city is but $25,000. He deceived the assessor, he wronged the city, he defrauded every other citizen in Detroit, and is as dishonest as though he were a forger or an embezzler. How could we trust to the honor of such a man to render a true account of what was his income ? His double may be found in every square in every town and hamlet in the United States; and in large cities it is an acknowledged fact that it is not possible to properly estimate the amount of property held by the wealthy. Take any of our great trunk lines of railway running through more than one State and attempt to estimate the income of one of the directors, and complete failure must attend the effort.

No law can be framed that will prove effective in collecting an income tax. Wherever such laws have been in force they have failed of their object, and have proved to be unsatisfactory. One resident of New York owns a house and lot in that city. He is assessed for the value of that property. He owns stock in a score of railroads and has a controlling interest in many of them. These lines of railway are interstate lines. How will it be possible to arrive at a correct knowledge of the income of that man for each railway in which he is interested? How can such a tax be collected, and who will compel that man to acknowledge that he is the possessor of stock in these railways when it is to his interest to deny ownership of it in order to escape the payment of taxes on it? If we trust to his honor to tell the truth, will it not be like leaning on a broken reed, when we know that that man has stopped at nothing short of murder to get possession of that stock? The average man will have to become much better than at present before the levying of a graduated income tax will so far touch his heart as to cause him to pay it.

The present method of assessing property is not equitable. Through its operations those who possess the most pay the least for the use of it. The greater part of the burden is heaped upon the shoulders of those who are least able to bear it. The cottage of the mechanic, the hovel of the laborer and the homestead of the farmer pay according to their full value, while the palace of the millionaire is assessed for a tenth or a twentieth part of what it is worth. The laborer, farmer and mechanic tell the truth when asked what the value of their possessions is, while the millionaire resorts to the same methods to avoid paying his taxes that won for him so much more of this world's effects than his neighbors are possessed of.

Take another view of the matter and we are forced to admit that the graduated income tax, if it could be collected, would prove unjust and burdensome, as well as a stumbling-block, in the way of enterprise. Two men owning adjoining farms might start in the field of agriculture on equal terms. The opportunities might be the same at the beginning, the soil the same, the amount of wealth possessed by each of equal value. In all things their chances at the start might be equal. One might be thrifty and industrious; the other, careless and lazy. The thrifty farmer might reap a rich reward for labor done in the way of enriching his farm, raising a large number of horses, cows and sheep. His buildings might be very valuable, and his farm at the end of a few years might be worth five times as much as at the start. With the lazy farmer the situation might be exactly the reverse; and if a graduated income tax were levied, the industrious farmer would have to pay for the other's laziness; the lazy man would have to pay no more than when he began farming, while the other would have to pay dearly for being enterprising and industrious. The premium would be on laziness in this instance. The income derived from the farm would be taxed. That income would represent the industry of the farmer, while the other man would not be required to pay anything for being lazy, and yet his farm might be equally as good as the other. The rule that would apply to the railroad king, the stock gambler or the bondholder would not apply to the industrious farmer. He would have to pay on the result of hard labor, while the others would not admit that they possessed a great amount of wealth as a result of sharp practice, stock gambling or railroad wrecking.

The advocates of a graduated income tax would tax all incomes above a certain figure, allowing those under it to escape. Here is another weak point. It is also a loop-hole through which to escape payment. Why should any one, or any income, avoid taxation if the opportunities of acquiring an income are the same for all. If they are not the same for all, then the principle on which the graduated tax is levied is wrong. If the opportunities under the law are the same, and men do not keep pace with each other in acquiring incomes, it is because men are differently constituted, and the difference, being in the men instead of the opportunities, renders it absolutely impossible to legislate in an equitable manner on the collecting of a tax upon incomes. In admitting that the tax should be graduated on incomes, we recognize the fact that they will differ with different men; that the conditions under which men labor are not equal, and as a consequence we should aim more particularly at equalizing the conditions than at graduating the incomes. To attempt to graduate the tax upon the incomes of the people of the present day would be vain, while we allow the conditions which make it so easy for man to cheat his neighbor to remain unchanged.

The laws now in force which regulate the methods of taxation should be amended in some instances, and in others repealed. It is the supposition that laws are founded on the necessities of the people, but such is not the rule of action in making laws of the nineteenth century. The necessities of the whole people are not so potent in shaping legislation as the shrewdness, the lack of conscience, the use of money and the influence of corporations. This statement every one believes to be true, and it is true, unless the press, the pulpit and the statesmen of the land have been deceiving the people for the last quarter of a century. The evidence to bear out their assertions is so conclusive that there need be no doubt of the truth of what they say.

The laws in force at this date were made as people understood them when made, and as people come to understand the necessity for a change they will change them. Agrarian agitator, communist, socialist, disturber and demagogue will be shouted at the man who advises a change in a law by which a certain class is benefited; but once the law is changed according to the will of the people instead of the interested few, it becomes the voice of the people, and must be obeyed by that class as well as all others.

Last year it would have been murder to take the life of a murderer by electricity in New York. The criminal would have to choke to death by hanging. To hang a murderer in New York for a crime committed since January 1, 1889, would be murder. The law has been changed, conditions are different. Hanging was law, and consequently recognized as right. Electricity is law now, and hanging is wrong. There were people who believed that hanging was wrong, but they had to tolerate it while the law upheld it. Ten years ago the advocate of death by electricity for murderers would be scoffed at, but the advocates of electricity persisted, and to-day they are right because the law says so. So will it be when changes are made in our land laws. They must be made. The people will understand the necessity for a change, and that point reached it is but a step to the change itself.

Fifty years ago the cry was to teach the people how to read; to-day it is to get them to read, for they know how, and to understand what they do read, so that the best possible use may be made of the learning. What is required most is a thorough education of the people on the subjects which relate to their well-being. Through the ignorance of the people, as a mass, the class was permitted to "get there," it mattered not how; and having accomplished that feat they were permitted to "stay there" by those who did not appreciate the value of a change of legislation.

A careful examination of the subject will prove that the levying of a graduated income tax will not accomplish the desired result. The assessing of property now practiced will not place the burden where it rightfully belongs, and there must be some other remedy, some other means by which equity may approach nearer to us in the management of our affairs. It is offered as a solution of the difficulty that the number of acres to be sold to each individual shall not exceed one hundred and sixty, and that a penalty be inflicted where violations of the law are discovered. I once entertained such a belief.

Such a law would be a dead letter from the beginning, and would inaugurate an era of fraud and perjury that would be lamentable to contemplate. Through one pretext or another men would procure the services of others, and under assumed names would purchase lands exceeding the limit of one hundred and sixty acres. Bogus ownership, holding in trust, fraudulent entries and a hundred other dishonest practices would be resorted to to evade the law, and it could not be enforced. On the other hand, even at the limit of one hundred and sixty acres, millions of people would be disinherited and deprived of their rights to the soil, or to the use of the same.

Pennsylvania contains about twenty-nine million acres of land.

She has a population of upward of five millions. Estimating the heads of families at one to five, there are one million people in the State who would be entitled to one hundred and sixty acres each should such a law be established. Divide the twenty-nine million acres into separate tracts of one hundred and sixty acres each, and we would have acres for less than two hundred thousand people. How would we provide for the remaining eight hundred thousand heads of families should they demand the right to purchase one hundred and sixty acres each? Each person living within the State, who has not attained majority, would, at no distant day, have a right to lay claim to one hundred and sixty acres of the soil of Pennsylvania, and it would be impossible to supply the demand. Such a law would from the start be worthless and inoperative.

We must admit that the natural right of each individual to the use of the soil is equal to that of every other individual; and should it come to pass, after the promulgation of such a law as is spoken of, that the required number of persons laid claim to the lands of the State and became possessed of them, it must also follow that the remaining millions would exist, if they existed at all, without political life, they would be deprived of all rights which were born with them, and unless a new distribution should take place they could lay claim to nothing within the State except that which was bestowed on them in charity by the fortunate possessors of the soil.

While such a law would prove disastrous, and while it is only a " supposed case," it is well for the people to consider it in order that they may arrive at correct conclusions concerning the distribution of land. Every one of those who would be entitled to the land would not want it. Some would not be content with one hundred and sixty acres; others would be content with less than an acre; while others would prefer living as tenants for life. So far as the actual desires or wants of the people are concerned, they can never be regulated by law, either in the distribution of land or anything else.

Not caring to enter upon the land for the purpose of cultivating it, and deprived of the opportunity to hold it for speculative purposes, the majority would take but little interest in the subject, and in a short time we would find other laws growing upon our statutes, and again, in another form, the rights of the people would be jeopardized through unjust enactments. Some want land for farming purposes, others require it for manufacturing purposes, others for stores and dwellings. The amount required by one would not compare, in proportion, with that which others would want, for we cannot erect a fixed standard by which to regulate the wants or necessities of mankind.

It is presumed that each person at birth is entitled to a place somewhere upon the earth's surface during existence. If the Creator intended that each one of His creatures should inhabit the earth, and have a right to stay upon its surface until He should call him to the future world, then it must follow that none of God's creatures should have the right to determine where his neighbor should stay while on earth. Every person has an equal right with every other person to the use of the earth, and, no matter what laws may be passed, the use of the soil is all that can be conferred.

If it were possible to imagine a condition of society with the population so dense that there would be a scramble for the use of the soil, we would see the laws that now find place upon the statute books swept away; the privileges, miscalled rights, which land-owners now possess, would be disregarded; and laws, such as would deal out the greatest measure of relief to the greatest number, would be passed in their stead. The wants of society would regulate the holding of the earth's surface by mankind. Each individual, then, has a natural right to the use of the earth, no more or less, and no law can vest in him the right to hold the soil in absolute ownership beyond a time when the rights of others demand that he surrender that right for the good of the greatest number.

What man may lawfully do to-day may be looked upon in a far different light when the necessities of the whole people have changed the conditions under which he exercised that right.

We may scoff at the idea of ignoring the right of man to absolute ownership of the earth, but want will set aside that right in the interest of a higher law. Those who now steadfastly hold to the opinion that man has a right to hold in absolute title as many acres of land as he pleases will not be willing to admit that other men have no right to purchase any part of the earth, even though they have the means wherewith to do so.

The believer in absolute ownership must also be a believer in no ownership. He believes in absolute ownership for himself and no ownership for others. Those who own the earth to-day are upheld in that ownership only because necessity has not driven the many to the point where they require the use of the land. When necessity drives men to that extremity, what is now called right will appear only as a privilege, and that privilege will have to give way to the requirements of the people.

It is plain, then, that the use of the earth is all that man can lay claim to, and it is but equity that he should pay for the privilege of using it for his own purposes. Some do not want to use their portion, and may allow others to do so. Those others should pay for that use, and pay for it in proportion as its possession benefits them, that the remainder may be recompensed for that which they surrendered to them. The advocates of a "single tax," the same to be levied upon the land, come the nearest to the remedy for the evils of the present system. Everything erected upon the earth's surface is the result of labor, but the industry displayed does not confer ownership on the workman. The land made more valuable as the result of man's industry escapes taxation, while he whose labor enriched it is taxed and receives no part of the wealth his labor creates, save enough to keep body and soul in union with each other. The result of labor is assessed, and as a consequence labor pays the assessment, while the land, which is made more valuable, escapes paying its due proportion of revenue to the State.

At first sight it may appear that land does pay the taxes, and that there is no necessity for a change in the operations of the tax collector. While it is true that it is from the earth the laborer extracts that which does pay the taxes, it is also true that it is the laborer who pays the taxes, and not the earth from which he produced the wealth. We have a multiplicity of taxes to-day. We have water taxes, gas taxes, street taxes, city taxes, school taxes, mercantile taxes; taxes for the maintenance of the Board of Health; the corpse is taxed before it can be buried, the undertaker is taxed for burying the corpse, the cemetery, which escapes taxation, taxes the corpse for occupying a portion of it; taxes for the payment of salaries of officers; State taxes, county taxes, bridge taxes, poll taxes, poor taxes, sewer taxes; taxes for keeping a horse, a dog, a cow, a pig, a watch. Every outhouse erected is taxed; a new fence adds to the taxation of the property-owner. If the citizen is satisfied with a certain kind of an indispensable outhouse, which does not come up to the requirements of the Board of Health, he is fined for maintaining a nuisance, and if he makes alterations and improvements upon it he is fined by the tax collector for doing so. The cartman is taxed for every hack, cab, omnibus, stage or animal he possesses, and if he does not keep them in a certain style he is fined for it.

In Pennsylvania we pay an occupation tax. The laborer is assessed at a valuation of $50, while the millionaire is assessed at but $200. There is a multiplicity of taxes to pay, and by the time the tax-payer goes the rounds and pays each one he is tired out and disgusted. It would be far easier to levy a " single tax," basing it upon land values, and have but one payment to make, at one place, instead of a score of different taxes at as many different places, each one rated at a different valuation, according to the intelligence or disposition of the assessor, each tax paying a commission to the tax collector.

As has been stated, the tax assessor cannot accurately estimate the value of the house, or its possible contents, by standing in front of it and taking an outside view of it. He cannot ascertain what the ravages of time have done to depreciate the property; he cannot examine the walls, cellar, garret or other parts of the house, and cannot, does not, do his duty as it should be done; he simply guesses at the value of the property, and then goes to the owner to find out if he has guessed aright, and he always finds that he has guessed too high, unless the owner happens to be a friend of his, and then there is no fault to find.

Taxes are not honestly levied at present, and under the law favoritism may be, and is, shown in every city and township. It is argued that it would not be fair or equitable to tax land values, and let the property erected on the land escape taxation. It is because the property, such as houses, barns, stores and factories, that now stand on the land, is not taxed as it should be, and because it cannot be properly or equitably assessed, that a single land-tax would prove to be the very essence of equity, that I advocate it. Everything is uncertain at the present time; but levy the tax on the value of land, and a tape-line, properly and judiciously handled, will enable the assessor to decide with accuracy the exact valuation of the property he measures and levy his assessment accordingly.

One man may be content to live in a hovel; he may accumulate money in speculation and hoard it away without adding to the wealth or beauty of the city or town he lives in by the addition of a coat of paint to his wretched home. His house may be situated in the heart of a city; if so, his land is certainly as valuable as that of his neighbor, who has erected a beautiful house, which is a comfort to the owner and an addition to the wealth and beauty of the town. If all of his neighbors adhered to the plan on which he worked, there would be no handsome residences or buildings in the place, business would shun the town and enterprise would die.

If the property nearest to his is worth $10,000, and the miser is asked to sell his land and hovel, he, too, will ask $10,000 for them, and give as a reason that "my next neighbor asks that price for his place, and mine is worth more, for it is unencumbered with much of anything in the shape of a house, and there will be no trouble in clearing it, so that the purchaser may build such a house as he pleases." If all his neighbors owned such places as he, they could not demand $10,000 for them.

All this time the owners of the beautiful houses and grounds have been paying high taxes, while the miser has continued to pay a nominal sum. All this time the community has been enriching this man and making his land more valuable; all this time the community has been paying the taxes on the miser's property, for through his greed he has escaped payment, since the improvements alone are taxed, and he, having made no improvements, does not contribute his just share to the support of the community, but when the time comes to sell his land he charges the purchaser for the labor of those around him who have not received any of the benefits of enriching his land.

Every resident of such a neighborhood is entitled to a share of the value of that property. They do not ask that the owner pay them a percentage of the proceeds of the sale, but they have a right to expect that he should contribute his share of taxation to assist in supporting the community.

What is true of the lot in the city is also true of the farm in the country. The miserly farmer who drains his land of the last dollar, and hoards that dollar away from sight, injures the neighborhood he lives in by obliging the other farmers to pay a higher rate of taxation. Under our present laws there is no encouragement to the farmer or property-owner to beautify or improve his place. He knows that he will be taxed for it, and he also knows that if he lives in a hovel he will escape taxation. The reward is not conferred for thrift, for improvement, for enterprise, but for niggardliness and improvidence.

What would be an equitable basis on which to levy a single tax ? is asked. Ascertain the rental value of the property, and assess it accordingly ; assess all around in the same ratio. The speculative value of land may be said to be fickle and unsatisfactory. The owner of a piece of property may ask a certain price for it when speculating in land, and the necessities of the seeker may not have pushed him to a point where he is willing to give that price. The speculative value of the land is not easy to ascertain, except on application to the owner, but the rental value of property is known to the whole community.

It has been advanced as an objection to rating taxation according to the rental value of the land that a city like Philadelphia would have to pay taxes enough to maintain the whole machinery of the State, cities, townships, and all. That argument may hold if we admit that the rents in Philadelphia are not too high, but there is no reason why rents should be so exorbitant. Here is the point at which I wish to introduce the landless man, the worker in the city and town, the tenant who exists under the delusion that he is not paying taxes because he owns no property. The rental value of the land is increased or diminished according to the necessities of the renters, the tenants. If tenants are scarce, and that is seldom the case, then rents are low, and it should be observed that taxes do not fall whether the property rents well or ill. It is not the real value of the property that the proprietor exacts a high rent for, it is the necessities of the tenant he taxes when leasing the place. It appears, then, that it is the tenant who pays the taxes of the man who owns the property; and if taxes were levied on the rental value of the land we may rest assured that exorbitant rents would not be charged as at present, and taxation would be more equitably levied and paid than under our present system.

But taxes would not increase under this plan of collecting a single tax, the same to be levied on the rental value of the land. They would be distributed over a larger area, take in more tax-payers, reach the owners of unoccupied lands now held for speculative purposes, and as a consequence a greater number of persons would be contributing to the support of the State. The greater the number of tax-payers the smaller will be the amount each one will have to pay; the lower the rate of taxation on property, the greater the stimulus to the workman to purchase a homestead of his own. But why should a large city pay so much more than the country? is asked. It will not pay more than the country under such a system of taxation, for every community will pay an equitable rate of taxation. It is the surrounding country that makes the land in the city valuable.

If no revenue came into Philadelphia from outside of the city limits; if the inhabitants of Pennsylvania should decide to divert trade to Pittsburg and not patronize Philadelphia again, the business of the latter city would naturally drift to Pittsburg. The surrounding country assists in paying the taxes of all our cities, and should receive some of the benefits from their investments. Rents are not so high in small towns as in large cities, and as a consequence the rate of taxation would not be so high; but if all lands, whether in city or country, are taxed according to their rental value, then no lands will escape. No one man or set of men will have to pay the taxes of any other man or set of men, and all unoccupied lands now held for speculative purposes will contribute their full share to the support of the State.

But the poor man who owns a lot along-side of the residence of a millionaire will have to pay as much for his lot as the millionaire, and that would not be fair, is another objection, one, too, that is often advanced. I know of no place where the millionaire and working-man own adjoining properties, and if there is such a case in the United States at the present day it will be only a question of time when, under our present system of taxation, the millionaire will own the two lots.

If land is worth anything to man in any part of the globe he should be willing to pay for the use of it; and if that land is situated in the heart of a city along-side of the land owned by a millionaire, then the owner should pay for its use the same as the millionaire. We have millionaires now by the thousand where we once had them by the dozen, and they have become millionaires because they have been permitted to hold vast tracts of land free from taxation. They have been permitted to absorb these lands while operating mines, factories, railroads and other industries, through the operation of which they have made life unbearable to some of their workmen that they might drive them to the land, and there take advantage of them again. With land paying its full share of taxation, and that is all that is required, the millionaire of the future will become such through his own ability, if at all, for he will not have the land to speculate in while amassing wealth.

The " single tax will ruin the farmers " is shouted across the prairies and over the plains. If lifting a part of the burden from the back of the farmer, and placing it on the shoulders of the man who holds more acres than the farmer without the payment of a hundredth part of the taxes which the farmer is obliged to pay, is ruin, then indeed will the farmers be ruined. The farm may be decreasing in value, yet the farmer may have to keep up the same rate of taxation. He may have to invest a great part of his income in fertilizer and improved machinery to make his farm pay; but so long as he does not tear down his house and barns and erect hovels and sheds, he will have to keep up payment at the same old rate to the tax gatherer. His yield of produce may not be as large as last year, but his yield to the tax collector will not be lessened in proportion. If there is a class of men on the soil of America who are directly interested in securing the passage of a single-tax law that class is to be found where farmers are numerous.

What troubles the farmer is that some one who knows nothing about the question has informed him that he will have to pay as much per square foot for his land as the resident of the large city will have to pay, and that taxes are to be levied the same on city land as on the farm. The rental value of the farm, according to the rate of the neighborhood in which it is situated, is all that he will have to pay, and at that same rate must the improvident farmer and the idle speculator also pay. The industrious farmer will not have to pay, as he does now, for the indolence, niggardliness or shrewdness of his neighbor.

Previous to the birth of the land speculator in the West, the farmer was not troubled with such an encumbrance as a mortgage on his land, now he has an abundance of them. It was not to fight off the single tax that the farmers of the United States met in national convention in Georgetown, D. C., in January, 1873, for the purpose of organizing the National Grange. They met because they were being gathered into the net of the mortgage-holder, because of excessive taxation, and because of discrimination in freights. It was not the grasshoppers or the drought that worried the farmers so much as the monopolist and speculator. They were being oppressed and are still oppressed. The formation of organizations such as the Farmers' Alliance, Patrons of Husbandry, Wheel and several local organizations suggests the idea that the market in which the farmer buys and sells may have something to do with the case. To-day the farmer buys in the dearest market in the world and is forced to sell in the cheapest. Until conditions change he has no say in the matter, for the means of transportation are beyond his control and are held by monopoly.

I do not believe, with many advocates of a single land tax, that it will prove a "cure-all" for every ill that industry is heir to; far from it. Neither would I have it take the place of a duty on imports from foreign countries. Several land reformers would have the single tax answer all purposes of taxation, and in that they are right, but there are many who do not regard a duty on imports as a tax. It is supposed to be a protection to American labor to have imports subject to a duty, and that question should be agitated, discussed and fought out on the line of protection until the end is made plain. It is not clear to many that a tariff is a protection, and until all doubts are dispelled that question should not be obscured or confounded with the single-tax discussion. If the day comes when men will realize the benefits to be derived from a single land tax they will also know whether the duties now levied in the name of protection serve the purposes for which they are levied.

The agitation on the subject of protection has been going on for years. It is one on which men differ in various localities, and is a question which should be judged on its own merits while the land question is being adjusted. There are protectionists among farmers as well as among mechanics. Free-traders are to be found among both. Neither will agree to abandon his pet theories until his pocket is touched, and it is a most difficult thing to teach either one that a tariff on imports is not what he thinks it is. Every man will realize the necessity for a change in our land system, and should not have other and lesser questions thrust upon him while discussing the taxation of land values.

If protection is the end in view then taxation has nothing to do with a tariff, but it should be first settled whether we are being protected. The fullest light should be had and the people properly educated on that question before it is allowed to merge into any other, and land reformers can very well afford to leave the question of protection outside the pale of discussion until the end is made plain in the matter of land taxation. If protection is really the end in view, when we levy a duty on imports, then absolute and unqualified prohibition of the landing of imports alone will settle the question. We can afford to allow the tariff agitation to proceed independently while we settle the land question. That once done we will find that the other problems are easily solved.

There are questions which deal directly with the land, and should be discussed by farmer and laborer. The veins through which the life-current of the country flows do not belong to the system to which they are indispensable. Fancy a man whose arteries do not belong to him, whose heart-beats are directed by another, by one over whom he has no control, and the reader will form an idea of the condition of this country, with the public highways in the hands of corporations, acting independent of and, in some instances, in defiance of the government.

The railroad and telegraph systems of the country are public highways. They take the place of the canals, water-ways and government roads of fifty years ago. They have made it possible for the large cities to absorb the mechanic and laboring population of the nation. All except tillers of the soil are being allured into the cities, and soon there will be no middle ground. It is the tendency of the times to build up cities, and I see no great harm to follow if the connection between city and country, between farm and factory, is steady, strong and satisfactory to both. It is not satisfactory to-day, and will not be until those for whom the railroads were built control them.

The Mississippi River is a great national highway, and every year Congress makes appropriations for its improvement. It belongs to no one, and is used by all. It is public property. The man owning land along its banks cannot levy a tax on all that passes his door in boat or shallop. No corporation would dare to absorb or control it, for the reason that it is the means whereby the common business of the country on either side of it for miles is carried. Why make an exception ? Why not turn the management of the great rivers of the nation over to private corporations ? It is, or will be, said that no corporation built the rivers or caused them to flow, and that they differ from the railroads and telegraphs. There is not a particle of difference in the uses to which both are put, but the railroad will tolerate no interference from the citizen or resident, will carry only what it pleases, and will not allow any person to run a train over its rails unless it be turned over entirely to the corporation owning the railroad.

How different with the water highways! Every person who wishes to may fit out a boat and act as a common carrier between points on the water front. The water is free to all, and is kept so by action of the government. The old government road was fitted out and kept in repair by the government. It was free to all. The canal was free to all until the railroads came into existence and took from the people the privilege of using them.

When the General Assembly of the Knights of Labor convened in Philadelphia in 1884, they made an important addition to the Preamble of the Order in demanding:

That the government shall obtain possession, by purchase, under the right of eminent domain, of all telegraphs, telephones and railroads; and that hereafter no charter or license be issued to any corporation for construction or operation of any means of transporting intelligence, passengers or freight.

At the sessions of 1885 and 1886 no reference was made to this section in the Preamble, but at the Minneapolis session the General Master Workman in his annual address said:

The XVIIIth Clause in the Declaration of Principles

Reads as follows:

"That the government shall obtain possession, by purchase, under the right of eminent domain, of all telegraphs, telephones and railroads; and that hereafter no charter or license be issued to any corporation for construction or operation of any means of transporting intelligence, passengers or freight."

I believe that the time lost in delaying action on that clause is time wasted, and most respectfully call the attention of the General Assembly to the matter with a view to having some action taken.

I believe that the government of the United States should operate its own lines of telegraph. I believe that it is absolutely necessary for the welfare and prosperity of the country that the government establish a telegraph system to be used in the interest of the people. The last Presidential election witnessed a scene which no patriot wishes to see again. The fate of the nation hung in the balance. The country was in doubt as to which of the candidates for the Presidency had been chosen. It was plainly stated in the metropolis of the United States that one man, whose name I will not mention here, was tampering with the election returns from certain parts of the country with a view to defeating the will of the people. It was not only stated that such was the case, but no one doubted it. It was only when threats of hanging him to a lamp-post were made that the announcements went forth that the returns would be given to the people as accurately as they came in.

At that time the telegraph company on whose wires the news came in had a powerful and growing rival. To-day it has absorbed that rival, and is reaching out for more power. At that time the telegraph system of this country was under the control of many men and different managements. To-day it is under the control of one management, if not of one man. The tendency of the present age is toward centralization, and it is not unreasonable to suppose that in the near future the railway lines of the nation will be under the control of one management, if not under the control of a single man. The history of the past decade, the tendency of the hour and the rapid march of events in every walk of life tend to show that the power of the corporation is giving way to the rule of the monopolist. Such being the case, is it not true that the individual who controls the telegraph and railway lines of the nation also controls the people of the nation? Men may say that it is socialism to talk of having the government assume control of the railways and telegraphs of the nation. Even so, is it not better to advocate such socialism than to witness a defeat of the people's will—a debauching of the servants of the people? Is it not better for the people to attend to their own affairs in such a way that no individual will have it in his power to defraud them of their inalienable right to life, liberty and the pursuit of happiness, than to allow a single man to manage that business, not for them, but for himself?

"Title by eminent domain" is the title by which the government acquires an estate in the real property of an individual when the same is necessary for public use. The right of eminent domain, or the right to take private property for public use, is inherent in every government. A government also has power to exercise this right in favor of individuals or corporations engaged in prosecuting works of a *quasi*-public nature, such as railroads, turnpike and canal companies. But when property is so taken full compensation must be made therefor to its owner, and that mode of taking it, which is prescribed by law, must be strictly followed.

The government having a right to take, either for itself or for corporation or individual, the private property of an individual, has also the right to own property of the same description. The rights of all the people are more sacred in the eyes of the government than the right of the individual. The right of the individual must not be trampled upon by the government. What the government should not do the monopolist must not do, and in order to prevent the monopolist from infringing upon the right of the people the government should interfere. I would not advocate the purchase of the property of the telegraph system now in use by the government. I believe that the government can easily erect, operate and control telegraph lines of its own, allowing those now in existence to remain in possession of the present owners. The government certainly can erect its own line much cheaper than it can purchase the vast amount of watered stock now loaded upon the original stock of the existing telegraph system.

We should have trunk lines of railways running North and South, East and West through the United States, under the control of the government. The government could then ascertain at what figures passengers and freight could be carried, and the rates fixed by the government would be the standard at which other lines would carry passengers and freight. There would be no injustice in this, and those who would not care to part with their railways and telegraphs could continue to operate them at a reasonable profit. It is absolutely necessary that the government should take steps to protect itself against the hand of the traitor at home.

We hear a great deal about our coast defenses being of little use. Suppose that our coast defenses were required, and it became necessary to transport troops from one part of the country to another; then imagine the railways of this country in the hands of one management, and that management opposed to the government, and you will see what a delay in transporting troops would cost the government. You may say there is no probability of such a thing ever happening. That makes no difference, a well-regulated government will never place itself in the power of an individual or a single corporation. With the rapid introduction of foreign airs and customs to this land, it is reasonable to suppose that not a few monarchial ideas are imported also. I know that the case of the government's connection with the Union Pacific Railway will be cited as a warning against the government having anything further to do with the management of railways. Because the dishonest transactions which characterized the management of the concern were allowed to go unwhipped of justice, and because the people allowed their own government to be swindled, is no reason why a like transaction should occur again. I believe the government should control our railways and telegraph.

The Legislative Committee was instructed to work for the passage of a bill to create a governmental system of telegraphs. The railroad question was not pushed for the reason that the convention deemed it best to take up but one subject at a time.

On November 23, 1887, the General Master Workman issued a circular letter to the Order asking their co-operation in securing names to petitions to Congress to establish a system of telegraphy to be managed in connection with the Postoffice Department. Blank forms of petitions were sent out with the circular. The request was made that they be returned to the General Office early in January, thus giving but a little over three weeks to act on the petition and circular. Promptly on time came the petitions signed by over 1,000,000 of people. They were intrusted to the care of Ralph Beaumont, Chairman of the Committee, who placed them in the hands of the various Congressmen, by whom they were introduced.

A bill was introduced and referred to a committee, but the agitation on the question of tariff *vs.* free trade overshadowed every other thing, and Congress adjourned without taking action. The National Legislative Committee prepared the bill that was introduced, and submitted statistics and arguments in its favor. The National Board of Trade favored the measure and worked for its passage, but the result was not satisfactory. Action is only delayed, for the agitation will continue and grow in strength as the people become educated to the necessity for managing their own business.

That the monopoly now controlling the telegraphs of the country realized the danger which menaced it, and recognized the justice of governmental control in at least some slight degree, is apparent to all who read the argument, or memorial, presented to Congress against the measure by Norvin Green, the President of the Western Union Telegraph Company. Said he :

> It may be worthy of suggestion, however, that if the government must go into this kind of business there are many articles of far more general use and consumption, which, if taken hold of and furnished at a cheap and uniform rate to the masses, would afford vastly more general relief to the public. Coal, a product of the earth, and unmined a part of the eminent domain, is essential to the preservation of life and an absolute necessity to twenty times as many people as ever need to use the telegraph.

The reason that so few use the telegraph at present is that it is beyond their reach, and they cannot get access to it on reasonable terms. The same is true of coal. Thousands would use it where hundreds do now if Norvin Green's suggestion were carried out. While the use of coal is essential to the comfort of the individual, the control of the telegraph is essential to the future life of the nation. Coal is no more a product of the earth than the material of which the telegraph system is composed, and both are essential to the welfare of the people. As well might Mr. Green have said that when the telegraph was invented the people who knew nothing about it, who did not use it then, who could not understand it or get access to it, would never use it because they had never done so before.

The sending of messages will one day supersede in a great measure the sending of letters. The sending of letters is under the control of the government, and is being managed much better and cheaper than it could, or would, be done by the corporations of the land. A letter weighing an ounce may be sent from Scranton to San Francisco for two cents. To send it under care of an express company would cost twenty-five cents, or twelve times more than the United States government charges for the same service.

There is no reason why the placing of the means of transportation under the control of the government will not cheapen the cost of transportation in all things as it did in the case of our mail service.

The government does transact part of the business of the country now, and leaves off where its honor is involved. A letter may be sent from New York to San Francisco, or to any other point, in which an order for a thousand dollars' worth of produce may be inclosed. The government obliges the corporations owning the railways to carry that order for material, and it will, at the point of destination, deliver the order to the man for whom it is intended, and there its functions end; but when the order is filled and the material is ready for shipment, and carted to the depot, the government will not undertake to oblige the railway to transport the goods to the man who ordered them through the medium of the government. If it is right for the government to transact a part of the public business of the nation, it certainly is right for it to control all of it, and do so in such a manner as to give satisfaction and relieve the strain which now oppresses business.

The passage of the Interstate Commerce Law was simply an experiment in angling for the truth, but the only remedy lies in the control of the railways and telegraphs of the nation by the people of the nation. There is no reason why the stamp of the government cannot be affixed to a bale of cotton, a barrel of oil, a car of wheat, a car of coal or a package of goods as well as to a letter which carries an order for these things. If the control of the railways and telegraphs is vested in the government, which confers the right upon these corporations to transact the business of the nation, then the produce of the farmer may be conveyed to market by the cheapest and safest route, and the man in the city will receive his food without paying tribute to monopoly, as at present. These questions of land and transportation go hand in hand, and are so closely allied that they become one when studied. Being one question, their proper solution will cement, in indissoluble bond, the interests of the workers in town, city and country, whether their names are written as farmers, mechanics or laborers.

THE CIRCULATING MEDIUM.

> The hope of the poor may perish,
> The workman's song be stilled,
> And ruin wide, the land betide,
> Till the Shylock's vaults are filled.—*Mrs. S. M. Smith.*

Take not usury of him, nor more than thou gavest: fear thy God that thy brother may live with thee.—*Leviticus* xxv: 36.

Those who read the platforms of the National Labor Union and the Industrial Brotherhood will find that the men who attended the conventions of these associations considered the currency question the most important of all that came up for consideration. Mr. Sylvis evidently believed it to be of vital importance. In a document issued by him in 1868 he said:

We must show them that when a just monetary system has been established there will no longer exist a necessity for trade unions.

When the General Assembly adopted the Preamble in 1878 it found the XVIIIth Section as follows:

To prevail upon the government to establish a just standard of distribution between capital and labor by providing a purely national circulating medium based upon the faith and resources of the nation, issued directly to the people, without the intervention of any system of banking corporations, which money shall be a legal tender in the payment of all debts, public or private, and interchangeable at the option of the holder for government bonds, bearing a rate of interest not to exceed three and sixty-five hundredths per cent., subject to future legislation of Congress.

When the convention adjourned the XVth Section of the Preamble of the Knights of Labor read as follows:

To prevail upon governments to establish a purely national circulating medium, based upon the faith and resources of the nation, and issued directly to the people, without the intervention of any system of banking corporations, which money shall be a legal tender in payment of all debts, public or private.

In drafting that resolution, originally, it was not the intention to legislate for the workmen of any country beyond the limits of the United States. The Knights of Labor intended to organize in all countries; hence the substitution of " governments " for " the government," as adopted by the Reading General Assembly. Those who assembled at that convention did not believe in bonds of any kind, and that part of the section referring to government bonds was abolished.

No other section of the Preamble has attracted less attention than that, and none other is of more importance to the people. Every Knight of Labor is in duty bound to labor with what ability he is possessed of to abolish the system by which so large a supply of the money of the country is placed under the control of banking institutions. Although the national bank is a creature of the United States government it affords no greater safeguard to depositors than any other banking concern. The gains are not shared in by the people, and that institution which flourishes beneath the protection of the government of the people is not in any way subordinate to the will of the people.

The fifth paragraph in Section 8, Article I, of the Constitution of the United States, says Congress shall have power "to coin money, regulate the value thereof, and of foreign coins, and fix the standard of weights and measures." Instead of issuing money, the government permits private institutions to do so. Instead of regulating the value of money within the boundaries of the United States, banking concerns are practically permitted to do so by controlling the volume. In one part of the country the money is worth two per cent., and in others it is as high as twelve, and in some places twenty per cent. The value of the money used by the people is not fixed or regular. It fluctuates at the will of those who have it to lend, or who are enabled, by reason of their control over a large portion of it, to withdraw it from circulation at their pleasure. The right to issue or coin money is a high sovereign prerogative, which should not be delegated to any lesser creature than the government itself. The standard of weights and measures is fixed by the government. It is the same everywhere; but sixteen ounces of sugar can be bought much cheaper in a State where the rate of interest is but six per cent. than it can be procured for in one where the rate of interest is twice six per cent. No State can fix the standard of weights and measures; no State can coin or issue money; but an institution, which is subordinate to no power beyond the extent of its circulation, is permitted to transact business beneath the great name of the national government, and regulate the value of the money it loans according to the necessities of the borrower. The credit of the bank is indorsed by the government, while it demands usury from the citizen.

The fact stands squarely before every man who reads that those who are engaged in speculation, in banking, in note-shaving, in managing corporations and trusts are growing wealthy with amazing rapidity, while those who use the money, those who do the work of the nation, the laborers of the farm, mine, railway and workshop, are growing desperately poor each day.

The present system is fostered by the government, and is iniquitously unjust. In June, 1888, the First National Bank of New York City published a statement that its circulation was $423,220. In December of the same year it issued another statement to the effect that its circulation was but $45,000, a contraction of the people's money of $378,220 in six months. The government did not authorize the contraction of its currency, although it was charged, and without contradiction, on the floor of Congress, during the late Presidential campaign, that $62,000,000 of "the surplus" in the United States Treasury was being loaned to banks free of interest. It is an indisputed fact that this policy was inaugurated years ago, and there is no reason to suppose that the administration which went out of office March 4, 1889, was any better in that respect than its predecessors.

In 1860 the population of the United States was 31,000,000; in 1889 the population was over 62,000,000, or double that of 1860. The population did not increase between 1860 and 1865 owing to the Civil War. In 1865 the circulating medium of the nation was about $1,900,000,000, divided as follows: State banks, $142,919,638; one and two year notes of 1863, $42,808,710; demand notes, $472,603; fractional currency, $25,005,828; compound interest notes, $193,756,080; national bank notes, $146,137,860 ; legal-tender notes, $431,066,428; coin, $400,000,000; temporary loan, redeemable on ten days' notice after thirty days, bearing four to six per cent. interest, and paid out by the Treasury on account and entering into circulation, $400,000,000 to $800,000,000. At that time the money was being used by the people of the loyal States only, those lately in rebellion were just beginning to again make use of the currency of the nation.

The country was prosperous, and the people, individually, were practically free from debt. If the money of the United States had been distributed among the people in 1865 each man, woman and child would have received about $61. Since 1865 the circulating medium of the nation has been contracted or reduced to less than $1,600,000,000. Our currency circulation is less by $300,000,000 to-day than it was in 1865, while our population is double what it was then. Then we had $61 per capita; to-day we have but $26 for every person in the nation should it be necessary to give to each one an equal share of the circulating medium.

It is the same with nations as with individuals. If the purchasing capacity is cut down one-half, the power to consume is curtailed to that extent. With every inducement offered to men to employ money to-day, it is absolutely necessary that it be provided for their use. If a man required $60 in 1865 in order to supply his wants, he certainly should have more than that amount to-day, and yet he is forced to do business on less than half of that sum. The cry of inflation has often scared men away from the currency question, but it should be borne in mind that those who demand of the government to issue a purely circulating medium do not ask that any man shall receive one cent of that circulating medium for which he does not render an equivalent. No man is to get what he does not earn. It is because a few absorb the earnings of others now that the demand goes up for new measures, new laws, and a sufficient supply of currency to carry on the business of the nation.

We will liken the nation to an individual who has surrendered his right to handle his own money. He employs ten men to perform labor in his fields. Through their efforts the fields are made to yield double. In a short time twenty men are necessary to do the required work. When he employed the first ten he could afford to pay them $60 a month, but, having surrendered the right to manage his purse, he finds on employing the additional ten men that, while he is richer, better able to carry on farming than before, and more in need of assistance than ever, he is not able to pay the men more than $25 a month. The inevitable result is that he will cramp his effort, try to do the work of twenty men with ten, and make a failure of it, the same as the United States government is now making of its attempt to do the work of 62,000,000 people on a capital which formerly enabled but 31,000,000 to carry on a very limited business, a business which did not bring to its aid the wonderful inventions of steam and electricity, which now call for more in effort and means than the world ever dreamed of before. It is not inflation that we need dread, but the grasping of more than man can honestly acquire. Only the nation itself was in debt at the close of the war. Now the people are in debt everywhere.

To contract the circulating medium of a nation to an amount which will not allow the full business capacity of its people to be put to the test is a gross injustice, the full extent of which cannot be estimated. Such a transaction operates solely in the interest of those who have money to lend. The system which permits it is such as will create a large borrowing class who must of necessity become the slaves of the money-changers. So long as national banks exist the volume of money in circulation will not equal the demand for its use.

When money is scarce the borrower will pay a greater price for its use than when it is plenty, and, as the chief aim of the banker is to loan money at a high price, it will always be to his interest to keep the volume of currency so low that the wants of the people cannot be supplied except through the payment of high rates of interest. The law which permits extortion of that kind is injurious to the welfare of the nation; it is a law which permits one portion of the people, and a mere fraction at that, to take advantage of the necessities of the other and greater portion. The chief aim of government in a republic is to do equity to all citizens and residents. In fostering such an institution as a national bank, the Congress of a republic shows itself indifferent to the welfare of its people.

The history of the legislation by the United States Congress on the currency question since 1862 is one record of partiality to a class that lives on the necessities of others. It is the history of favoritism to Wall Street, New York. Such legislation would not be enacted if industry were consulted as well as that favored class which reaps the greatest reward from its exercise.

When legislation bearing on the money question is presented to Congress, the ink is scarcely dry upon the printed proof before it is expressed to Wall Street for the opinion of its money-changers. Those who make the wealth of the country are never consulted. When a newly-elected President is making up his Cabinet, the farmers, laborers and merchants of the nation are not consulted, but Wall Street must give consent or the Secretary of the Treasury will not be chosen. The press of the United States, without regard to party, always takes it for granted, editorially, that Wall Street has the right to dictate who shall handle the purse-strings of a nation which owes everything in the way of prosperity and progress to those who till the soil, dig the coal, operate the railways and run our factories, while all of the misery, hard times, idleness and starvation that make the nation mourn can be laid to the door where our Presidents seek for men to manage the finances of the country.

There is, no doubt, a reason for all of this. Industry cannot afford to go further in the way of bestowing rewards than the giving of the majority of the votes by which the President is elected. Wall Street can afford to be more generous, and, if indications are worth anything, she is liberal enough to those who serve her interests. Nearly every prominent official of the government, who was connected with the Treasury Department for the past twenty years, has been favored with a good position beneath the drippings of Wall Street at the close of his term of office. Many of them did not wait to serve out their full terms, but took the first chance that was offered to them. This system of accepting reward, presumably for favors done, was not confined to one party. Under the recent administration the Secretary of the Treasury, the Treasurer of the United States and the Assistant Subtreasurer resigned to accept similar positions before the close of the first four years of those who " turned the rascals out."

It is high time that the vast territory embraced within the boundaries of the United States, and situated beyond the limits of Wall Street, New York, should enter its protest against a policy which has for years ignored the best interests of the people. The reader has only to pick up one of the daily papers containing the reports of the world's progress to realize that the United States is ahead of other nations in its annual average of production. Labor, it is estimated, produces more than in any other country. If this be true it should follow that the necessary amount of money ought to be forthcoming to pay for the labor performed. The demand for money certainly is greater, and the supply per capita ought to be much larger than it is. France, with less natural need for money, has a supply per capita far greater than the United States. Here we have a per capita of $26, while France enjoys and makes use of $50.75 per capita.

The Bland Act of February 28, 1879, directed the purchase of an adequate amount of silver each year to coin not less than $2,000,000, and not more than $4,000,000 annually. In the ten years which have passed since the passage of that act only $20,000,000 have been coined, the minimum fixed by law. This shows that the policy of each administration has been opposed to the full remonetization of silver as well as to affording the people an adequate supply of money. Many people labor under the impression that if silver is coined into money we will have to carry and handle a cumbersome, heavy currency. The phrase "cart-wheel currency" has been applied to the silver dollar.

It does not follow that because the silver is coined into money that it must be used in transacting business, for Congress has by law directed the issue of silver and gold certificates, the same to be made of paper, and with these in circulation we have a paper currency representing the silver and gold which have been deposited in the Treasury of the United States. These certificates now represent a material which lies idle in the vaults at Washington. A purely circulating medium is doing part of the work of the nation based only on silver and gold, which the government was forced to purchase from those who were fortunate enough to own gold and silver mines.

Knights of Labor believe that a circulating medium, in sufficient quantity, should be based on the faith and resources of the nation itself, instead of being founded on a gold or silver mine owned and operated by an individual in the United States. They believe, or they ought to believe, that the supply should equal the demand; and if silver dollars to the extent of $4,000,000 may be coined each year, the necessities of the people require that the full sum allowed by law should be coined instead of the minimum of $2,000,000, which has been issued each year since 1879. Congress believes that the country should have a larger circulating medium, but the money power of the country holds a majority of that body too tightly in its grasp to allow the passage of any laws which will relieve the strain upon the industries of the nation.

An attempt was made in January, 1888, to increase the circulation of the national banks ten per cent., but Representatives Weaver of Iowa, Bland of Missouri, Anderson of Kansas and Brumm of Pennsylvania took so decided a stand against it that the people of the nation heard the discussion which took place at Washington, and the measure was defeated. All legislation enacted in the interest of the banking fraternity has gone silently through Congress. If a noise is made it is not so likely to go through, and for that reason the existence of such institutions as the Order of the Knights of Labor, Farmers' Alliance and kindred organizations is a necessity. These associations, representing the people, must counteract the pernicious efforts of the Shylock element which rates six per cent. on money invested as of more consequence than the happiness of toiling humanity.

When the Philadelphia session of the General Assembly adjourned in 1884, the XIVth Section in the Preamble took the place of the XVth on the currency question. On motion of Ralph Beaumont, the following was adopted:

The establishment of a national monetary system, in which a circulating medium in necessary quantity shall issue directly to the people, without the intervention of banks; that all the national issue shall be full legal tender in payment of all debts, public and private; and that the government shall not guarantee or recognize any private banks or create any banking corporations.

That section speaks for itself. It does not call for any more than enough to do the business of the country. A "necessary quantity" is all that is demanded. It demands that the government of the people shall issue a people's money direct, and shall not delegate the authority to do so to any bank or other institution.

Every Knight of Labor, who has studied the principles of the Order, realizes that when the transportation facilities of the nation are managed by the chosen agents of the people under governmental control the land system of the country is properly regulated, and speculation in the earth prohibited, and a national circulating medium established and issued direct to the people without rendering a dividend to the middleman—banker—the prosperity of the whole people will be established, and that there will be less of poverty than now exists. Those who will be poor and destitute under such circumstances will be the improvident, intemperate and those afflicted by nature or accident.

To properly discuss the currency question would occupy more space than can be consumed in this brief chapter. Instead of quoting authorities I would recommend the reader to study a book called "Whither Are We Drifting," published by George C. Hackstaff, St. Louis, Mo. It contains the history of the legislation on the currency question since the breaking out of the Civil War, and should be studied by every one.

The history of the currency question of the United States is being made every day. The legislation proposed and discussed during the Fiftieth Congress on this important issue would, if recorded, occupy more pages than will be contained in this volume. The question is, apparently, very complex, and will continue to be so until it is solved by legislation, which will require that the circulating medium shall be issued direct to the people without let or hinderance from any other institution, foreign or domestic.

INTRODUCTION OF FOREIGN LABOR.

Of what avail the blood that's spilled,
Of what avail our wounds and pains,
To loose the fetters from the black,
And bind both black and white in chains?

If the importation of Europeans to take the places of American workmen had been practiced prior to 1858, it had no appreciable effect on the condition of the laborer of that day, and was not taken notice of by the workingmen of the United States. In that year three strikes in the moulding trade, all in progress at the one time, was the occasion for a meeting of "boss moulders" at Albany, N. Y., where a combination was formed of those engaged in the moulding business. From this meeting a circular was issued to the employers of labor throughout the country asking for the formation of a "league for the purpose of importing workmen from Europe to take the places of employes who, under the influence of the union agitation, had become so restless and dissatisfied with their employers as to strike against their interests." Such was the language of the circular which was circulated, and it is the first known record of an organized effort to import human beings to America to take the places of others who would not submit to reductions in wages, or agree to an increase in the number of apprentices in workshops. The largest and most determined strike of the three referred to was against increasing the number of apprentices in a moulding shop in Albany, N. Y.

The experiment which was made in 1858 must have encouraged the employers, for we find that in ten years the practice of importing cheap men had grown until it became recognized as a menace to the welfare of the American worker, so much so that the convention of the National Labor Union of 1869 saw fit to ingraft the following resolution in its platform of that year:

Resolved, That we are unalterably opposed to the importation of a servile race for the sole and only purpose of tampering with the labor of the American workingmen.

That resolution was aimed more particularly at the Chinese than at any other race. During the long strike of that year in the anthracite coal regions, the operators threatened to import Chinese to operate the mines, and, though the threat was never carried into execution in the coal regions, Chinese were brought over to other points in the United States.

During the month of May, 1869, C. F. Sampson, a shoe manufacturer doing business in North Adams, Mass., imported seventy Chinese, and employed them in his factory. The workmen whose places were taken by the Chinese received $3 a day; the Chinese contracted to work for $1. In July of that year Mr. Sampson brought over sixty more Chinese, and discharged more of his old workmen to make room for them. There could be no fault found with the Chinese because of their desire to secure larger wages, but they were not a success at shoemaking. The only thing accomplished by their importation was the cheapening of the labor of the white mechanics whose places were taken by the Mongolians. In 1880 the shoe factories of North Adams saw the last of the Chinese, and with the exception of a few who are engaged in the laundry business there are none in the place.

A firm engaged in the manufacture of cutlery at Beaver Falls, Pa., became dissatisfied with their workmen early in 1872, and on the 3d of July of that year seventy-five Chinese arrived in the town, were taken to the cutlery works and assigned to duty in place of the white workmen who were discharged. In the beginning of 1873 one hundred Chinese were employed in the cutlery works in addition to those brought over the preceding year. The white workmen were paid from $3 to $6 a day. They were all discharged, and Chinese to the number of three hundred finally monopolized the work of the factory. They were contracted for through an agent named Odd Chuck, who made an agreement that they were to receive pay according to their skill. Some earned $18 a month, while others commanded $1 a day. They were, according to the stipulations of the contract, to work ten, but were employed for eleven hours each day. The gates of the factory were kept closed all day to prevent the egress of the Chinese, or the ingress of the workmen who were displaced by them. When the contract expired Odd Chuck entered suit against the company for compensation for the extra hour worked each day by the Chinese. He recovered between $5,000 and $6,000, but the Chinese workmen never received any of it. In North Adams and Beaver Falls the Chinese subsisted on rice and pork. When a death occurred the corpse was, according to contract, shipped back to China. Their clothing and everything they required, except food, was imported from China. The cutlery firm lost, through the employment of the Chinese, over $42,000, which, at that day, was considered a large sum of money. Their business was ruined, and at the present time the residents of Beaver Falls know but little concerning the firm who did business in 1872, and who drove the white workmen away to make room for the Chinese. There are no Chinese employed in the manufacture of cutlery in Beaver Falls at this time. Those who reside there are engaged in the laundry business.

These attempts to introduce the Chinese to the workshops were watched with anxious eyes by the workmen of America. There is no doubt but that they would have been brought to the coal regions to take the places of dissatisfied miners were it not for the fear that the law would not be powerful enough to protect them while at work. The attempt would have been made, however, had the experiments made in North Adams and Beaver Falls proven successful. Enough had been done in the way of agitating the Chinese question to call the attention of the American workmen to the evils likely to be visited upon them should the importation of Chinese continue, and the subject was debated in the meetings of labor societies of that day with a view to adopting a remedy for the evil which threatened the mechanics in the shape of cheap foreign labor.

When the first convention of the Industrial Congress was held in Cleveland in 1873, it adopted and placed the following in the declaration of principles which emanated from that body :

We demand the prohibition of the importation of all servile races, the discontinuance of all subsidies granted to national vessels bringing them to our shores, and the abrogation of the Burlingame Treaty.

The ratifications of the additional articles of the Burlingame Treaty were exchanged at Pekin on the 23d of November, 1869, and the question of Chinese immigration occupied no small share of the attention of the people of the United States at that time.

Had the Burlingame Treaty been abrogated the immigration of the Chinese would have continued. The danger which menaced the laborer would not have been lessened a particle. The " Chinese question," as it is called, would come under a more appropriate heading if called the coolie trade, for only that class of Chinamen are imported or come into competition with American workmen. In China the third or lowest class of society is composed of chair-bearers and earth-diggers. These are called " coolies," or " low laborers."

When the Burlingame Treaty was being made, a great many coolies were being imported to South America and Cuba. The tide turned toward California about that time, and has continued ever since. There are in San Francisco six Chinese companies, or societies, for the protection(?) of Chinamen coming direct from China. Each company represents a different part of the Flowery Kingdom. Whenever a ship lands on which Chinese are passengers, an interpreter goes aboard and registers the number of Chinamen and the names of the places in China where they come from. These Chinese passengers, or coolies, are assigned to whichever of the six companies represents the part of China they were taken from. The companies are known to be traders in their fellow-countrymen. The Legislature of California appointed a committee to investigate the Chinese question in 1877, and ascertained that the six companies held ownership in 148,600 Chinamen, as follows:

Sam Yup Company	10,100
Yung Wo Company	10,200
Kong Chow Company	15,000
Ning Yeung Company	75,000
Yan Wo Company	4,300
Hop Wo Company	34,000
Total	148,600

The committee found that up to the time of the investigation one hundred and eighty millions of dollars had been sent to China by the people of that race who resided in California, and that not one dollar had found its way back again. What the one hundred and eighty millions of gold would have produced if earned in this country and expended here by American workmen is hard to imagine, but it would have eased the strain of the hard times which made 1877 and 1878 two of the worst years for labor that this country ever passed through. Nearly all of the Chinese women brought to California were brought over for the purpose of prostitution, and on their arrival were placed in " barracoons," or places where they were forced to remain until such time as they were taken by their masters. These women entered into contracts to sell their bodies for a term of years for the purpose of earning sufficient to enable them to live at their ease in China when the term of the contract expired, or for the purpose of supporting some relative, or paying some debt in China ; but of the proceeds of their immorality they received only enough to sustain life while under contract, and when set at liberty were fleeced of what was due to them.

During their stay in this country the Chinese never associate with other people, never adapt themselves to our habits, modes of dress or our educational system ; they carry their pagan idolatry into every walk in life ; never pay heed to the sanctity of an oath ; see no difference between right and wrong ; and live in the same fashion in California as their ancestors did in China twenty-five hundred years ago. The people of California, without regard to creed or political belief, deluged Congress with petitions to pass a law which would put a stop to the further immigration of the Chinese to this country. The agitation continued until 1882, when Congress passed a bill of which the following is the preamble and enacting clause :

WHEREAS, In the opinion of the government of the United States the coming of Chinese laborers to this country endangers the good order of certain localities within the territory thereof. Therefore, be it enacted by the Senate and House of Representatives of the United States of America in Congress assembled, that from and after the expiration of ninety days next after the passage of this act, and until the expiration of ten years next after the passage of this act, the coming of Chinese laborers to the United States be, and the same is hereby, suspended : and during such suspension it shall not be lawful for any Chinese laborer to come, or, having so come after the expiration of said ninety days, to remain within the United States.

The remainder of the law deals with the particular methods of preventing the landing of Chinese laborers, and affixing penalties for infractions of the law. It received the sanction of President Arthur, and was signed by him May 6, 1882.

Since the passage of that act Chinamen have landed on Canadian soil, and have entered the United States across the boundary line which separates the two countries. They have landed in American ports under assumed names, and in various other ways. The great difficulty in detecting the difference between Chinamen, owing to the resemblance they bear to each other, gives rise to no end of trouble in preventing the coming of this servile race to America, and the complaint of the people of the Western States and Territories that the law is constantly violated continues to be made.

In desperation the people of the Pacific coast have repeatedly petitioned Congress to do something to enforce the law, but the Chinese still continue to come. In various places along the Pacific coast and in the Territories the citizens of cities and towns have revolted against the presence of the Chinese, and in many instances violence has been resorted to. On September 2, 1885, the coal miners at Rock Springs, Wyoming Territory, massacred between thirty and forty Chinese, burned their dwellings, and drove many others from the place. That this act of inhumanity and butchery is inexcusable is true, but the precedent had been established that the law could be violated with impunity by the Chinese and those who desired to employ them. Exasperated at the success with which they had evaded the law and insinuated themselves into their places along the Pacific Railway, the white workmen became desperate and wreaked a terrible revenge upon the Chinese. Had steps been taken to observe the law, and had the Chinese been as rigidly excluded as they should have been, the workmen at Rock Springs would not have steeped their hands in the blood of a people whose very presence in this country is contamination, whose influence is wholly bad, and whose effect upon the morals of whatever community they inhabit tends to degrade and brutalize all with whom they come in contact.

In his address to the General Assembly at Hamilton, Ontario, October, 1885, the General Master Workman referred to the Chinese evil as follows:

THE CHINESE EVIL.

The law which was passed by Congress and approved on the sixth day of May, 1882, was intended as a check to the importation of Chinese into the United States and the Territories. The violations of that law were so numerous and glaring that Senators and Representatives from the Pacific coast brought the matter before Congress at its last session, and demanded further legislation on the subject. Nine-tenths of the people on the Pacific coast, and of the whole country in fact, are opposed to the importation of the Chinese under any conditions whatever. It is not necessary for me to speak of the numerous reasons given for the opposition to this particular race—their habits, religion, customs and practices have all been made the theme of newspaper comment and report for several years. Congress has been appealed to, but the necessity for speedy action was not apparent to that body—a false delicacy about offending a foreign power has caused much suffering among our own people.

The question of regulating the importation of Chinese and the proper guidance of those already here has been before the country so long that it no longer rests with the people of the Pacific coast, nor with the people of the Territories ; the whole people must act through their representatives, and put a stop to the further importation of the Chinese under any and all circumstances, for any purpose whatever, and for all time to come.

The recent assault upon the Chinese at Rock Springs is but the outcome of the feeling caused by the indifference of our law-makers to the just demands of the people for relief. No man can applaud the act by which these poor people were deprived of their lives and homes. They were not to blame. They were but the instruments in the hands of men who sought to degrade American free labor. Had those who made the attack upon the Chinese at Rock Springs but singled out the men who smuggled them into the country and offered them up as a sacrifice to their own greed, I would have had no tears to shed. But even then the evil would not be checked. The taking of the lives of the Chinese, or those who import them, will not effectually prevent others from pursuing the same course in the future.

I am pleased to state that no blame can be attached to organized labor for the outrage perpetrated at Rock Springs. If the voice of the men who are associated together for the purpose of educating and elevating the laboring people had been listened to some years ago, the historian would not be called upon to chronicle the fact that the men of Wyoming lost all respect for a law that was first broken by the power that created it; for if our Congress had fixed a just penalty for infractions of the law, if Congress had not winked at violations of the statute and refused to listen to the plaint of those who suffered because the laws were outraged, the men at Rock Springs would not have taken the law in their own hands as they did. But they only destroyed the instrument; the hand and brain by which it was guided still remain; and nothing short of the enactment of just laws and a full and impartial enforcement of the same will prevent other and far more terrible scenes of bloodshed and destruction than the one to which I have alluded. I believe that I am justified in saying that if the voice of free, dignified labor is not listened to, and that speedily, the hand of outraged, insulted labor will be raised, not only against the instrument itself, but against the hand that guides it as well.

The men of the West must not be allowed to fight the battle single-handed and alone. The evil they complain of is no longer confined to one section of this country. It is spreading, and its influences are being felt in all of our industrial centres ; and if a desire to assist our brothers in a righteous cause is not sufficient to animate us and spur us to action, then self-interest will soon prompt us to bestir ourselves. The entire Order must act as one man in this movement. I have copies of all bills submitted to Congress upon the question, and will place them in the hands of the special committee on legislation, if such a committee is appointed at this session of the General Assembly. Examine them carefully and draw up a bill and a demand for its passage, and let us approve of them ere we adjourn. Slave labor must die, and free labor must be its executioner.

When the General Assembly convened at Richmond in October, 1886, a document presented by D. A. 162 of California was considered favorably by the body. It sums up the situation so vividly and forcibly that I deem it worthy of a place in these pages :

The undersigned committee, appointed by D. A. 162, Knights of Labor, of the State of California, to present to the General Assembly a statement of the pressing necessity for action to aid in freeing our own race from the want and degradation being put upon it by the blighting effects of Chinese labor and the frightful results of Chinese presence, hereby presents the following:

The voting population of this State amounts to about 190,000, while the adult Chinese males amount to more than 100,000; in other words, more than one-third of our whole male population consists of Mongolians. More than 90 per cent. of all these are the slaves of what are here known as the Chinese Six Companies. They are coolie slaves. Their labor is slave labor. They live almost exclusively upon rice imported from China. They can work for twenty-five cents a day, board themselves, and save a profit. This kind of labor, under the direction of their masters—keen, shrewd business men who have imported it—comes directly into competition with the labor of our own people. It confronts them in every avenue of industry. In the workshop, in the field, in the mines—everywhere –the Chinaman, with his foul presence, stands as a menace to free labor and to free men. The Chinaman is ignorant, conscienceless and corrupt. He is crafty, he is criminal, he is depraved. His only virtue is his industry; and in this he acts with deadly results upon that of our own people. He consumes practically nothing springing from white labor. A thousand of them will occupy a building that would only accommodate fifty Americans. They huddle together like rats in a room. Their very presence drives white people from the locality they inhabit. They patronize nothing American. They hate and detest our people. They have no conception of our free institutions; they know nothing of our schools, our charities or our religion. They are a set of thieves, cut-throats and pagans. They exalt perjury to a fine art, and their language affords a perfect shield against its punishment. Their vices are hydra-headed. They crowd our men of families out of employment, and leave them to want and destitution. They make hoodlums and criminals of our boys, and drive our girls to worse than death by working for wages which to them means starvation. They establish among us courts of their own, secret tribunals, that to them supersede the courts of law. They have murderous highbinders, professional murderers, retained and paid for their work, who dog the steps of their victims until opportunity permits them to stab them to death, and perjury saves them from the penalty. They establish opium joints that afford the means of destroying the morals and lives of its victims. They make nearly all our cigars, clothing, boots and shoes, slippers, underwear, woolen goods, overalls, soap, matches, boxes; they can all the fruit and fish; they raise nearly all the vegetables; they pick nearly all the fruit, hops and grapes; they raise nearly all the potatoes; they make nearly all the salt; they catch nearly all the fish; they make our brooms, cordage, ropes, brushes, candles, chemicals, fringes, glue, linseed oils, matches and pickles; they make nearly all our shirts; they laundry nearly all our clothes; thousands of them are servants in kitchens, offices and banks; they act as chambermaids in hotels, boarding-houses and private residences; and they run most of the sewing machines in all branches of their use. In one word, wherever there is a demand for labor you will find the meek-eyed but malignant-hearted Chinaman.

It is no answer to all this to say that our people, who know all this, ought not to employ them. Greed and avarice are the same the world over; and Californians find the same excuses for their exercise here that the corporations and moneyed aristocracy elsewhere find for the enslavement of labor. This evil grew upon us before we were aware of its danger. It is so deeply rooted that it has driven white labor out of its way, and now many employers, who would be willing to make a change, find it difficult to obtain the white labor to supplant it. Their course has manufactured tramps and petty criminals in the ranks of men made homeless and penniless by lack of employment only.

It is the province of our noble Order to break this thing down. It seeks to elevate, not to strike down labor. Its mission is to lift up, to dignify, to disenthrall labor, and to compel the purse-proud to recognize the manhood labor typifies. To that end this committee, representing D. A. 162, Knights of Labor, especially, but the Pacific coast generally, prays the General Assembly to aid us in every way possible in tearing this evil up by the roots. We implore you to believe that the dark coloring herein given of the white-labor interests of this coast is but a feeble picture of the whole truth. Despair writes itself in haggard lines over the features of labor. Sullenly but certainly disaster and death stalk abroad, destroying our cause. The weak and irresolute long since surrendered at discretion. It is only the bold and courageous who stand up to give battle to the oppressor. To fail now is to surrender for all time the cause of Him whose right arm has builded, defended and maintained the heritage of our fathers, which a godless few would rob us of forever. This yellow cloud of ruin has overrun California. It has sent its poisonous flood over the Territories, and it is now rushing its streams throughout the East. A few years at most will see the white labor of the whole country stagger in delirium from its fatal touch.

The Chinese women on this coast are nearly every one to be found in houses of prostitution. Our courts furnish frequent evidence of the sale of Chinese women for purposes of prostitution. Home life, as we understand and honor it, is unknown to them. Among all the Chinese population of this coast there cannot be found a single Chinese family with the surroundings of an American home. And the testimony of all physicians will prove that thousands of boys have their physical systems destroyed by disease contracted in these infamous dens of vice, and that in nearly every case they were enticed into them by Chinese courtesans.

Hence we beseech you to gird on the armor which shall encourage the fainthearted and call them back to the faith that the giant, Labor, will battle on and battle ever for, until the hated Mongol shall be driven from our shores, and until the banner of requited labor shall proudly ride the breeze of emancipated America. This grand consummation will not be accomplished until the last Mongol has been sent from our shores.

In the furtherance of this result the remedy adopted by the true-hearted Americans who threw the British tea into Boston harbor—that of non-patronage and non-intercourse—seems to be the most effectual. Avarice and greed will induce men to employ these Mongol herds simply because they can employ them for less wages, and thereby aid in reducing our laboring classes to the condition of serfs. The application of the boycott becomes a necessity to them, and an act of mercy and humanity to those they would enslave. We, therefore, invoke it, not only as an act of justice to the poor, but as one of the highest patriotism to the Republic.

Meantime, we earnestly appeal for action by which the members of the Order everywhere be requested to ascertain the position of their respective candidates for Congress upon the matter of abrogating the treaty with China permitting the immigration of Chinese to the United States, and to vote for those who most fully pledge themselves to so vote.

Brothers, we turn to you in this hour of peril as the sheet-anchor which can and will accomplish this greatest victory of mankind. Evolve this in your councils, and you will merit the everlasting chaplets of gratitude a regenerated and grateful people will twine upon your brow.

Respectfully submitted,

F. J. CLARK,
J. P. DALTON,
A. G. READ,
        Committee.

At the Indianapolis session of the General Assembly, D. A. 49 of New York presented the following resolution :

That special efforts be made to organize the Chinese.

The committee to whom the resolution was referred reported unfavorably on it, and when it came properly before the convention a motion was made to concur in the report of the committee. A point of order was raised that there was nothing in the Constitution to prevent the organization of Chinese. The General Master Workman decided that the point of order was not well taken, as three previous sessions of the General Assembly had adopted resolutions unfavorable to the residence of the Chinese in America, and, not being considered worthy of residence in America, they could not be regarded as proper persons to become members of the Knights of Labor. The report of the committee was concurred in by a vote of 95 to 42.

Except on the Pacific coast the influence of the Chinese was not felt to any great extent. The eastward march of the Chinese immigrant began when the Pacific Railway was built, and ever since the proximity of that race to our shores has been a standing menace to the welfare of the American laborer.

The method by which immigration to the United States was stimulated by those who wished to take advantage of the ignorance of the immigrant was by means of advertising abroad for laborers. The practice began in 1869, and has been continued ever since. From a London paper, published in 1871, the following advertisement is taken :

Five hundred navvies wanted in New York and Pennsylvania to work on railroads. Wages from $1.75 to $2.50 a day. Single men preferred.

In the New York papers of that day advertisements were kept standing, in which inducements were offered to the newly-landed immigrant to proceed to the coal regions of Pennsylvania. Such announcements as the following were of daily occurrence :

Two hundred men wanted to take contracts in the coal fields of Pennsylvania. Good wages guaranteed and steady employment assured.

When the New York papers reached England and the continent of Europe, these announcements were copied by European journals in the hope of relieving the crowded centres of the old world of their overflowing populations.

When an advertisement for two hundred men appeared in a metropolitan paper, it usually turned out that there were no vacancies in the ranks of labor at the point to which the men were directed, and the sole object in inserting the advertisement was to send more laborers into the coal regions than were necessary, so that where two men were seeking for the same situation they would, in competing for employment, more readily consent to work for reduced wages.

Under the impression that the taking of "contracts" in the coal regions would afford an easy means of earning a livelihood, thousands of men flocked into the Schuylkill and Luzerne coal fields to find that the contract referred to only afforded the privilege of operating a chamber in a coal mine with an assistant, whose duty it was to load the coal for so much a ton, after the contractor cut or blasted it from its bed.

The immigration from Poland began to make itself felt in 1872, and, though the Poles were poor and ignorant of our laws, they were anxious to learn, and soon began to improve their condition. The tide began to set in from Hungary in 1877. The railroad strikes of that year created a desire on the part of railroad operators to secure the services of cheap, docile men, who would tamely submit to restrictions and impositions. Hungary was flooded with advertisements which set forth the great advantages to be gained by immigrating to America. The Italian immigration has been going on for several years, but no authentic record of the actual hiring of men abroad for service in the United States is obtainable beyond the year 1880.

When the first session of the General Assembly of the Knights of Labor was held in Reading in 1878, it was deemed advisable to omit the thirteenth section of the Preamble, the one which called for the prohibition of the importation of the servile races. The subject was discussed for some time, and it was because the Order recognized neither race, creed nor color that it was thought best not to insert anything in the Preamble which could be construed as opposing any portion of humanity. While it was a beautiful sentiment which actuated the men who gathered at the first General Assembly, and while it appealed to the best instincts of the membership at large, it was found to be in direct opposition to the best interests of the members of the Order. The basic principle on which the Order was founded was protection, not protection from the manufacturer or employer alone, but from our own avarice, our weaknesses, and from cheap workmen also. Theoretically, it sounded very well to extend a welcome to all to a share in the protection to be derived from organization, but it was discovered that to carry out the practice would load this country down with men to whom the American laborer could extend no aid, and who were too ignorant to help themselves.

With the growth of organization among workingmen began an investigation into the methods resorted to by employers in order to secure cheap workmen. This investigation developed the fact that land-grant companies, steamship companies and manufacturers had agents in all parts of Europe engaged in the business of advertising for workmen to go to America. In giving his testimony before the

New York Senate Committee on December 14, 1882, Jay Gould gave a partial insight into the methods by which immigration to the United States was stimulated. A portion of the testimony will explain how the agents of American corporations add to the population of the country:

QUESTION—You stated that speculation promoted immigration. How does it do this?

ANSWER BY MR. GOULD—It induces the construction of railroads into new territory, and that induces the roads to send abroad to get immigrants to settle upon the lands.

Q.—To what extent have you influenced immigration?

MR. GOULD—That's impossible to tell. We are advertising in all lands abroad. The immigrant comes and may go on our lands or elsewhere. When I was in Europe you couldn't go anywhere but you saw agents of American land-grant companies.

Q.—Do all the roads have these agents?

MR. GOULD—All the land-grant roads. The Union Pacific, Central Pacific, Atchison and Topeka, Kansas Pacific, Chicago and Burlington, Missouri and Nebraska, Rock Island, Missouri, Kansas and Texas, Texas Pacific, and St. Louis and Iron Mountain.

The greater the number of immigrants sent out from European countries to America, the greater the profits of the agents who infested nearly every large city in Europe. Voluntary immigration never proved detrimental to the interests of the American people, for under the old-time conditions men and women rarely left their homes abroad until they had a reasonable prospect of earning a livelihood in the new world. But, under the stimulus of "so much per capita," the agent took especial pains to earn his wages by sending as many as he could to the land of the free. Thousands upon landing in American ports found themselves penniless, and were forced to go "elsewhere" than to the points to which the agent directed them.

The agent of the land-grant railroad company was supposed to drum up customers for his company, and to send only those who could afford to at least make a pretense of purchasing farms adjoining the road in whose interest he was at work. The agent in many cases was also in the pay of a steamship company, and never allowed his conscience to prevent him from holding out inducements of the most alluring character to every man, woman or child who could rake, scrape or borrow the passage money. The presence of these agents in Europe was known to more than the land-grant steamship companies. Employers of labor in large establishments frequently held stock in many of the railway companies, or were intimately acquainted with those who did own stock, or were directors in the railway or steamship companies. Whenever the surface of labor affairs became ruffled in consequence of a strike, or through any other cause, the services of the foreign agent were invoked in the interest of the employer that he might procure cheap, docile labor; and the news of a strike, especially in the coal regions, was the signal for an influx of foreign workmen, who were hired to come to the United States under the impression that they were to receive good pay and steady employment, without a sacrifice of honor in the acquirement of either. It finally became an established fact that the retention of agents abroad was a part of the practice of large corporations, and workingmen began to question whether it was wise to support a policy which made it possible for the employer to flood the market, free of duty, with strong, able-bodied laborers from the old country, while the article which came in competition with that which was turned out of the factory of the American employer would not be permitted to pass a port of entry except on payment of a tariff which was said to have been levied for the " protection of American labor."

With thousands of Chinese landing on the Western coast, and hundreds of thousands of laborers being imported into the Eastern cities and towns, the struggle for existence began to grow fiercer for the American workingman. It caused him to think and to ask himself some questions, such as, Why does the United States Congress impose a tariff upon the manufactured article under the pretense of protecting the workman, when in reality he receives no better treatment under a high tariff than under no tariff, so far as his usage by his employer is concerned; why is it that that which I make in the shop can receive recognition at the hands of my government, while I am not taken into consideration at all; why is it that the article which the foreign workman fashions cannot land on our coast except on payment of a duty, while the foreigner himself can land and enter into competition with me free of tariff; why is it that my employer so assiduously demands that a protective tariff be imposed on these articles under pretense of protecting the American workmen from foreign competition; why is it that he presents to me the petition to sign against the reduction of the tariff, telling me, as he does it, that it is to my interest to sign it, so that foreign cheap labor will not kill our industries, and at the same time be engaged in making terms with the foreign agent for the shipment of alien workmen to enter into competition with me and my fellow-laborers; if foreign " pauper labor " is what we are opposing when we establish a tariff, why is it that we only keep out the product of the " pauper," while allowing the " pauper " himself to land free of duty?

These were the questions that troubled the minds of mechanics and laborers of America, and they have not ceased to do so at this writing, for it is an indisputed fact that many of those who cry the loudest for protection to American labor are in reality actuated by the most selfish of interests, and care nothing whatever for the welfare of the American workman so long as the article in which they are interested, as to its manufacture, is protected.

" Protection to American labor " is the watchword on which the American manufacturer enters the halls of Congress to ask for an increase of tariff on the articles manufactured in his workshops, and by his employes; but " every man for himself, and the devil take the hindmost," is the motto which would be emblazoned on his shield if he wrote the truth upon it.

This is the truth. Every man on American soil is at once a high-tariff man and a free-trader. Scratch a high-tariff man and blood is drawn from a free-trader, and *vice versa.* The manufacturer of steel rails will demand that the highest duty be imposed on the importation of steel rails, but when he is about to invest, either in articles for home consumption or for use in his mills, he will make an effort to get the cheapest article even if he has to import it. He, therefore, requires that a tariff be placed on steel rails only, letting all else in free of duty. The grower of wool clamors for a tariff on wool, but is heard protesting against a tariff on steel rails, so that it will not cost so much to construct the railway which will convey his wool to market. The glass manufacturer wants to have glass placed on the list of protected articles, but would clip off wool, steel rails, and everything else. The most rampant free-trader, while denouncing the tariff, will become a protectionist in order to keep up the price of some particular article in the manufacture of which he is interested. But high-tariff man and free-trader will both object to the payment of living wages to the American workman, and both will call in the services of the foreign agent when they require cheap help.

The following, which appeared in the JOURNAL OF UNITED LABOR in May, 1882, describes the situation as it existed at that time:

Immigration to America is becoming so large that an inquiry into the causes which prompt men, women and children to flee from their homes, friends, kindred and early associations and seek a home in this country is worthy of at least a hasty examination. In the year 1881 there came to this country 720,000 souls, a vast proportion remaining in the East, there being only 120,000 who sought homes in the West and Northwest. The causes which have led to this unusually large immigration can best be ascertained by a careful reading of speeches of State officers and documents presented to trade councils and other deliberative bodies of the old world.

In a paper recently presented to the Chamber of Commerce at Minden, Westphalia, the following alarming sentence occurs: " The immigration from this district is *lamentably* large, and it may be permitted us as patriots to put the question: *Has the German Empire been founded for the purpose of driving forth its citizens into exile.*" It has been admitted by close observers in Germany that the farmer is taxed from *ten to twelve per cent. of his income.* As though this was not enough for the honest toiler to bear alone, they have that unbearable military system to support, which, taken in connection with failure of crops, general depression of trade and ecclesiastical strifes, has proved sufficient to send to America in the year 1881 no less than 210,485 Germans. One day early in the year three steamers sailed from Bremen with nearly 5,000 of these exiles.

In the report of the American Consul for April, 1881, he says:

"The streets are crowded with these people to such an extent that they cannot find lodging at night; that the police authorities have frequently to care for them, not because they have no money, but that all lodging-houses are full. They cannot afford to wait here, and they crowd into the Lloyd Company's offices and *kneel* before and kiss the hands of the managers, praying, with streaming eyes, to be taken on board "

Again we are told that Germany, admitting a very lively immigration last year, has no hesitancy in pronouncing an exodus for this year. Men who by hard work have acquired a little property are throwing it upon the market at a great sacrifice, in order to raise funds with which to reach the inviting plains beyond the Mississippi. Her weavers and spinners, who have produced, at starving wages, the woolens which have clothed American citizens, are becoming American citizens themselves, and hope to spin and weave, at living wages, woolens for those left behind.

Again, another cause for the general distress prevailing in Germany is the American-raised wheat, which, owing to the low freight rates, both by water and rail, is causing the German agriculturist to either come down in his price or go out of the business, as the competition is too strong for them to hope to cope with us. In 1880 the poor found it cheaper to buy American wheat than to use German rye, although up to 1879 wheat was twenty-five per cent. higher. By this new competition German food producers are kept down to barely living prices, and a farmer on less than twenty-five or thirty acres of ground must have some other resources in order to exist; hence factory work is the main support of the present farmer.

But look at the result of this change of farming to factory work. In the corset manufactories women and children work ten hours per day for six dollars and fifty cents per month, and expert weavers, working eleven and twelve hours, are paid seventeen to eighteen dollars per month. In Bavaria and the Thuringian States the opposite is true, as many factory men have taken to farm work, although they receive but from twenty-five to thirty cents per day.

The German government is now casting itself about to remedy this matter of wheat importation, as they openly admit that German agriculture is threatened with danger from America. But America, furnished with technical science, capital and richness of soil, has entered the arena, a rival of superior force; and unless the German States place a protective tariff on American bread-stuffs, or discriminate by railway freight against us, it is only a question of a very short time until the agricultural classes of Germany must abandon their fatherland and come to America in order to live at all. Likewise the cattle-drovers of the plains of the great West will, through our improved means of transportation, render even stock-raising in Germany unprofitable.

In Austro-Hungary the bad harvests have worked a general feeling of alarm, and in many instances destitution of the deepest kind exists, although the level prairie lands of Hungary for a while can bid defiance to American competition. In the year 1880 the harvests were almost a total failure, and so generally destitute were the masses that the government was obliged to set her citizens to work on the public works, when men, women and children gladly toiled for the mere pittance of thirteen, nine and five cents per day. Laborers were, in some instances, so weakened by destitution as to be unable to lift a stone weighing ten pounds. In 1881, owing to the large immigration to this country, the Austro-Hungarian deficit amounted to $24,000,000; and when the proposition was made for placing additional taxes upon the people, the farmers and peasants began to petition the Emperor to spare them, and in some instances the presenters of the petitions have gone down on their knees and implored the Emperor to help them in their great distress.

But how can a reduction of taxes occur so long as the national safety requires the presence of large standing armies? And yet each nation realizes that to disband their army is entirely out of the question, unless they court utter destruction from their nearest neighbors.

Great Britain and Ireland.—The condition of the toiling millions is too well known to invite any notice at our hands at this time.

Italy.—While the average American is disposed to loathing and contempt of this class of people, who have not troubled us to any great extent in the past, it might be well to inquire what is the cause of so many coming just at this time? Again we find that American competition in corn is fast driving the small farmer to desperation. The quality of the American corn was equal to a measure and a half over that of the native production. This, in connection with the low price, has struck terror to the heart of the Italian corn-grower, and bids fair, in a very few years, to completely control this staple.

Again, the disease of the silk worms has been disastrous to the poor. During the six years from 1870–'75 the production of silk averaged 3,200,000 kilograms a year, which declined in the following four years, 1876–'79, to 1,640,000 kilograms. This enormous failure in this one branch of industry was to the Italian laborer what the suspension of the coal or iron products would be to England or America. This, in connection with the ruinous taxes imposed by the government, has been the leading cause in driving the sons of Italy from her shores.

An official statement declares "that while an average family of Italian laborers earn $130 per year, the tax exacted of them is $15.44." Carefully prepared statistics, submitted by Senator Pepoli to the Italian Senate in 1879, show that 19½ per cent. of the income of the government is derived from such prime necessities as bread-stuffs, meat and salt, and nearly one-quarter of the revenue was so levied as to be unduly oppressive to the poor. Yet King Humbert on New Year's Day, 1882, strongly advocated the necessity of completing the military organization.

From the foregoing it will be seen that we may expect as great an influx this coming year as we have just witnessed in the past twelve months. The same causes exist now as ever, and so long as they do exist immigration to America will continue. The main causes of social discontent that still inflict the poor of Europe may be summed up as follows: Deficient crops, old uneconomical methods, grinding poverty, over-taxation, military burdens, and, above all, American competition.

This new perplexity in the troubles of Europe cannot be offset by any advantageous change. As a power, it is young, vigorous and constantly growing; and there remains for Europe but this final, and perhaps fatal, course: reduce taxation. If this is done her vast armies must be dispersed. Will any nation of Europe consent to do this, in view of the fact that to-day it costs two billions of dollars every day to maintain an armed peace; and even if this be done, in the face of such formidable competition as that now threatening them from America, can they find a new market for their produce?

The common inference, then, is that since taxation cannot be reduced, or wages for labor increased, and American bread-stuffs and cattle selling in their own markets for less than they can produce them, that the poor must seek a home elsewhere. And who, when the case is fairly stated, can blame them?

In 1883 manufacturers of window glass entered into an agreement to import foreign workmen to take the places of American glassblowers. L. A. 300 of the Knights of Labor had reached a stage in organization which approached nearer to perfection than any other association of workingmen in America. They were enabled by means of a thorough and compact organization to meet with the employer on "equitable grounds," and so effectually resisted all attempts to reduce wages, when the market did not call for a reduction, that the manufacturers became desirous of overthrowing the power of L. A. 300, so that they might secure the assistance of cheaper workmen from abroad, and, through the presence in this country of more glass-blowers than could find employment, they hoped to render the reduction of wages a task which would be easy of accomplishment.

One glass manufacturer in Kent, Ohio, and another in Baltimore, Md., contracted abroad for the services of several workmen. They were brought over and set to work. In order that the members of the Knights of Labor would have no opportunity to acquaint the foreign workmen of the true condition of affairs, the new-comers were assigned to boarding-houses into which a member of L. A. 300 would not be permitted to enter.

The courts in both places were appealed to by manufacturers, and injunctions were served upon the members of the Knights of Labor restraining them from approaching, *talking* to, or in any way interfering with the alien workmen. Through its Executive Council L. A. 300 engaged the services of a lawyer for the purpose of ascertaining what was best to do under the law. The advice of the attorney was to have a bill passed by Congress forbidding the importation under contract of foreign workmen. The advice was acted on. The attorney was instructed to draft a bill such as would be likely to pass. The bill was prepared in August, 1883, and James Campbell, Master Workman of L. A. 300, presented it to the General Assembly of the Knights of Labor which met in Cincinnati, Ohio, in September following. It received the unanimous and hearty indorsement of that body, the officers of which were instructed by resolution to go to Washington during the session of Congress to urge the passage of the bill in the name of the organization at large. Petitions were circulated throughout the United States asking Congress to pass the bill into statute law. The returns, made of these petitions, proved that the entire membership of the Order was in sympathy with the measure.

The Congress which assembled in December, 1883, for the first time in the history of that body, appointed a Committee on Labor, made up of the following-named Representatives: James H. Hopkins of Pennsylvania, Chairman; John J. O'Neill of Missouri, Martin A. Foran of Ohio, Henry B. Lovering of Massachusetts, Edmund W. M. Mackey of South Carolina, Darwin R. James of New York, and Martin A. Haynes of New Hampshire.

On January 14, 1884, Hon. Thomas Ferrell of New Jersey introduced a bill in the House of Representatives having for its object the protection of American workmen from competition with foreign contract labor. This bill was referred to the Committee on Labor, but was not reported upon. The bill which was approved by the committee and reported to the House was introduced by Mr. Foran, but the clause which would have made it most effective was stricken out before its final passage. In fixing the penalty for violation of the law, Mr. Foran's bill provided that of the fine of one thousand dollars to be paid by the offending party: "The one-half, or moiety, of said sum to be paid to the person bringing suit to recover the same, and the remaining half, or moiety, into the treasury of the United States." This was the section which received the unanimous indorsement of the labor organizations of the country. Those against whom contract foreign labor militates are too poor to enter suit against offenders. Many who are misled and induced to leave their homes to take situations in the United States would enter suit if poverty did not stand in the way, and with that vital part taken from the bill it became, to a great extent, a dead letter so far as the laboring people were concerned.

On February 1, 1884, the General Officers of the Knights of Labor, the officers of the glass-workers' associations of the country and of the Amalgamated Association of Iron and Steel Workers appeared before the Committee on Labor at Washington and presented arguments in favor of the Foran Bill. Congress adjourned soon after, and while the bill was in the Senate, it having passed the House before its adjournment.

At the General Assembly of the Knights of Labor held in Philadelphia in September, 1884, the Foreign Contract Labor Bill received a great deal of attention, and the question of amending the Preamble to cover the case was debated for several hours. Before adjourning the following section was unanimously adopted and added to the Preamble:

That the importation of foreign labor under contract be prohibited.

That section still remains a part of the Preamble of the Order, and is regarded as one of the principles of organized labor throughout the United States. It does not say that a certain duty shall be paid by the importer when he brings the foreign workman to the United States under contract. It is emphatic and declares for the prohibition of the importation of such a class of immigrants in order that the fullest protection may be guaranteed. When Congress reassembled in December, 1884, it was expected that action would be taken on the bill in question; but nothing was done and workingmen began to grow impatient. There is no doubt but that there were men in the Senate who felt that enough had been done when workingmen were recognized by the introduction of a bill in which they were concerned. They thought that, as on previous occasions, the workingmen would forget the matter, let it drop and think no more of it. This view of the case was not sustained by the action of the workingmen. On January 14 the following letter was mailed to the President of the United States Senate:

SCRANTON, Pa., January 14, 1885.

HON. GEORGE EDMUNDS, *President United States Senate:*

MY DEAR SIR:—The National House of Representatives passed a bill "to pro-hibit the importation of foreign contract labor into the United States," and it went over to the United States Senate for conference. I do not now recall the date, but believe it was some time in June, 1884. Since that time nothing has been heard from it. You will, I trust, pardon the liberty I take in calling the attention of the Senate to this matter, but it is of importance to the laboring men, the business men and mechanics of the United States to know what the Senate intends doing with this bill. Promises were made, pledges were given, party platforms spoke in unmistakable terms on this question during the recent political campaign, and now nothing remains but to fulfill these promises, redeem these pledges and confirm the statements made in the platforms of 1884. While the Senate was engaged in transacting important business I did not wish to intrude, but, now that the important work of the session has been completed, it is certainly time to call your attention to this matter, so that action may be taken ere Congress adjourns.

I see in the "reported" proceedings that days of valuable time are being devoted to the discussion of questions that are of no consequence whatever to the general interests of the nation. "The defense of ex-Confederates," or the condemnation of ex-Confederates, is a matter which would serve the best inter-ests of the entire country to bury in oblivion. No good can come of reviving dead issues. While the honorable gentlemen are fighting over again in wordy combat the battles which the powder and steel of the soldier have long since decided, while the slavery of the past is being discussed in the Senate, a new and more powerful slavery is being established, a slavery which will not only grind four or five million black men, but fifty millions white and black. One of the links in the chain by which the millions are to be bound is the one which permits the importation, under contract, of men and women who come only to degrade American labor. That link can be severed by decisive action on the part of the United States Senate. Do not think that I call your attention to this matter upon my own responsibility. I but obey the request of the 700,000 work-ingmen who respectfully ask for the speedy passage of this bill.

Very truly yours,

T. V. POWDERLY.

The bill was brought out of committee, was reported to the Senate, and passed that body about the middle of February, 1885, and on the 26th of that month it was approved by and received the signature of President Arthur.

Several attempts were made in 1885 and 1886 to violate that law, but the demon of discord had not been made sufficiently well acquainted with labor organizations to turn their attention away from their own interests, and they were, as a consequence, on the alert. On each occasion the attempted infraction of the law was reported, and steps were taken to have the matter properly adjusted. Those who reported the cases were too poor to enter suit against the violators of the law, and many immigrants were smuggled through Castle Garden without detection, and their presence discovered only when it was too late to send them back again. Public officials took no steps to enforce the law, to scrutinize the character of the immi-grants who landed, or to make investigations when asked to do so.

The Legislative Committee of the Knights of Labor brought the matter before several Congressmen immediately after the appointment of the committee. The result was the introduction of a bill to amend the foreign contract labor law. When this bill was presented to Congress every effort of the committee, of which Ralph Beaumont was the efficient chairman, was directed toward securing the votes of a majority in favor of it. The amendment received the approval of the House and Senate, and on February 23, 1887, was signed by President Cleveland.

Under that amendment the Secretary of the Treasury was authorized to adopt and enforce regulations which would prevent the landing of improper persons. On March 24, 1887, Secretary Fairchild issued a circular to the " Collectors of Customs, Commissioners of Immigration and others " to see that all immigrants were examined on arrival in order to ascertain who were entitled to land, and to make out a tabulated statement of the alien immigrants forbidden to land. He also required that extra caution should be observed in preventing the landing of those who came under the provisions of the law, and that all such persons should be returned to the countries from whence they came.

Congress made no provision for the payment of a part of the fine to the person who gave the information. As a consequence, there were but few who felt called upon to give information, and those who were most interested could not get the information to give. In the Deficiency Bill which passed Congress and was approved October 19, 1888, the Act of February 26, 1885, was amended as follows:

That the act approved February twenty-six, eighteen hundred and eighty-five, entitled "An act to prohibit the importation and migration of foreigners and aliens under contract or agreement to perform labor in the United States, its Territories and the District of Columbia" be, and the same is hereby, amended so as to authorize the Secretary of the Treasury to pay to an informer who furnishes original information that the law has been violated such a share of the penalties recovered as he may deem reasonable and just, not exceeding fifty per centum, where it appears that the recovery was had in consequence of the information thus furnished.

On November 20, 1888, the Secretary of the Treasury issued another circular to the "Collectors of Customs, Commissioners of Immigration and others " to enforce that law, and it is hoped that under its provisions the chances of escaping penalty will be materially lessened. During the year 1888, a political campaign being in progress, Congress appointed a committee to examine into and report on the violations of that law, and to inquire into the manner in which immigration was being carried on. Many startling facts were disclosed, and reported to Congress. A volume of several hundred pages contains the report of the committee, and in its pages will be found many exposures of the actions by which employers of labor attempt to win large rewards for themselves at the expense of the workmen of the United States and the good name of the nation.

The question of immigration has been before the people for some time. The laws relating to imported labor are strict, and, if the workingmen do not yield to the clamor of their enemies and abandon their organizations, they will one day make it impossible for an employer to bring aliens to this land to take the places of those who are unwilling to work for the mere pittance doled out to the laborer of Europe.

As the first half of the year 1889 draws to a close the monopolist of America is watching with an anxious eye to note the tendency of workingmen in the direction of organization. If they heed the advice of their enemies they will retire from their associations in disgust. Every device known to cunning and wealth is being used to drive workingmen away from the Knights of Labor, for no other organization has ever grappled with such weighty problems. As a consequence no other organization is so deserving of the opposition that the greed of the wealth-owners of America has aroused, and which will, if not checked, throttle the independence of the workman and make him a more willing subject for discipline than he is at present.

CO-OPERATION UNDER DIFFICULTIES.

Man upraised above his fellows,
Oft forgets his fellows then ;
Masters, rulers, lords, remember
That your meanest kinds are men !
Men of labor, men of feeling,
Men of thought and men of fame,
Claiming equal rights to sunshine
In a man's ennobling name.

The fourth plank in the Preamble of the Industrial Brotherhood called for "the establishment of co-operative institutions, productive and distributive." When the Preamble was adopted by the Knights of Labor in 1878 that declaration was allowed to stand in the same language as Section 4 of the preface to the Constitution of the old Order. No changes were made until the General Assembly met in Philadelphia in 1884, when the section referred to was given a new number, and, instead of demanding the "establishment of co-operative institutions," it was agreed that all Knights of Labor " endeavor to associate our own labors to establish co-operative institutions, such as will tend to supersede the wage-system, by the introduction of a co-operative industrial system."

While most of the reforms called for in the Preamble of the Knights of Labor require that political action be taken in one way or another, it was felt that everything should not be left to the State or the nation. That the worker should bestir himself in another way, while seeking for a reform in legislation, was required by the principles of the Knights of Labor.

The social changes that passed over the face of the industrial world so rapidly since the breaking out of the Civil War were so numerous, so unexpected and unparalleled in the experience of wage-workers, that they became perplexed and looked to old remedies in vain. Doctors sprung up on every hand who offered to cure the ills of the nation if their prescriptions were adopted. A panacea for every ill was proposed, and insane projects of every description were advocated by specialists who dreamt that they had discovered the secret of perpetual prosperity for the people. All, or nearly all, of them turned toward the government for the relief which they hoped to secure through the plans which they brought out of their hiding places; with the aid of the government, and a little of their own ingenuity, it was hoped to overcome all the evil tendencies of the times; " at all

230

events let the government do something to help us in this hour of distress." It was expected by many that the remedies so eagerly expected could be brought about in a very short time. They forgot that reforms to be lasting and beneficial must be of slow growth and inaugurated after plans are fully matured and well understood, and that, while they could be planned and led up to by a careful system of training, they could not be forced or hurried.

For the last thirty years the tendency has been to crystallize trade by consolidation of interests and wealth; combinations of many systems and plants under one head sprung up on every hand, and small traders went down by the hundred to make room for the millionaire manufacturer, dry-goods or provision house. The late A. T. Stewart led the few who engaged in the warfare on the small dealers, and in a short time others followed his example in other fields of industry and trade. Poverty was forced across the door-sill of many a merchant who was not lacking in push or enterprise to carry on his business. People applauded the man who could build a palace of trade which would compel small dealers to sell more cheaply. They were called enterprising and thrifty who ruined thousands in their greed for large profits and sudden wealth.

This craze for wealth has entered every avenue of trade. It has devotees in railroad circles, in banking houses, in manufacturing establishments and in every known calling, industry or occupation.

Railroad competition, once healthy, has gone, and in its place we find the railroad pool. Farmers by the thousand have handed over their farms for little or nothing to the syndicate; operators who mine coal have pooled their issues against the interests of the people, until we pay as much to transport a barrel of flour or a ton of coal to market as the article itself is worth when it is landed at its destination. In the matter of coal, three times the original cost is sometimes added. To what does all of this tend? Is there not a lesson for the wage-worker in all that he witnesses passing on around him to-day? Does it not show that men of means have learned what he has been so slow to pick up, and that they are making every cent a dollar through co-operation?

I asked a man for a situation a few years ago, and was on the point of being engaged when I inquired what price would be paid for my labor. The answer was not encouraging, and on making my disappointment known to the old gentleman he seemed very much surprised, and said: "When I was a young man I hired out to a farmer for twenty-five cents a day and board. I saved my money. Soon after that I came to this city and was able to buy a corner lot and several other pieces of valuable property. To-day I am rich as you see by my own industry and effort. I don't see why others cannot do as I did."' He was told that others could do exactly as he did if the conditions were the same. He stated that he paid fifty dollars for the corner lot when he bought it. I offered him fifty dollars for the same lot, but he would not part with it for less than $25,000. I asked him to point out a corner lot anywhere as near to a town as his was when he first invested that I could procure for fifty dollars, but he did not do it. He told me, however, that he had several hundred lots which he would sell at prices ranging from six to ten hundred dollars a piece on the outskirts of the city. He would be very reasonable, he said, in allowing me to make my payments, and would charge only the legal interest allowed by the State.

Following out his own idea of making a living or getting on in the world, if working for twenty-five cents a day and board would enable a man to buy a corner lot for fifty dollars, and the march of improvement, genius, invention and industry had so increased the value of the corner lot until it is rated as being worth $25,000, why should not that which had more to do with enhancing the value of his lot than anything else—labor—be entitled to compensation in the same ratio? Had the price of labor kept pace with the price of corner lots, he would have had to pay for my services at the rate of $125 a day instead of the twenty-five cents a day, to which he referred. But the land is all absorbed, and, no matter how high the price of labor may be, the workman cannot secure the corner lot as his predecessor did. True, the corner lot is still there, but the man who was fortunate enough to be born first got his chance to grab it before his less fortunate neighbor was ushered into the world. The corner lots are all taken, but new labor is coming to the world every day. A co-operation of economy, money and chance has given to a few men corners in everything, as well as lots, on the soil of America to-day.

What is to be done? who is to do it? when is it to be done? are the questions asked on every hand. It will not do to ask the man of wealth to let go his hold on the corner lot just yet. If he did so it would be gobbled up at once by some other man who served out a "twenty-five-cent" apprenticeship when a boy. People will persist in being born into a world that no longer holds out the inducements which were offered to the man who took possession of the corner lot, but there are no more corner or any other kind of lots being made. All the lots are here and spoken for, with few exceptions. Must the people stop coming? must they forego being born? or will it answer every purpose to let the greed for gain continue at the same rate that it is progressing to-day? What is to be done? Money will not stop accumulating; talking from stump and rostrum will not check the aggressions of capital, no matter how eloquently or forcibly a man may plead for the recognition of the just claims of labor. Those who hold labor by the throat will not let go for a single instant unless it be to catch a fresh hold. No argument will persuade the suckling to let go until the fount runs dry. Must we wait until that time comes? Will we look for relief to him who gets all the meat from labor's bone? How long will it take to educate the people to a true sense of duty? Will it take as long as it did to free the black slaves, and must history be repeated in the doing of it? The anti-slavery agitation might have gone on yet, and no one would have stirred hand or foot to remove the fetters. John Brown might have died, returned to life and died again, and yet no chain would break; but when Sumter's gun was fired, then the nation spoke, action was taken, and we know the result.

The action necessary to free the twenty-five million wage-slaves which this nation holds within her boundaries will be taken when the competitive system of labor shall give way to the true co-operative system. The results of the past thirty years have demonstrated that the present competitive system is rotten to the core, that it is crumbling of its own weight; it is unhealthy, it is baneful, and through its operations a few men have rushed on to a point which other men could not reach. A few have grasped all, and in their greed they have struck down trade after trade, industry after industry, factory after factory. Workmen alone complained thirty years ago—yes, ten years ago; to-day merchants who have been crowded out, manufacturers who have been ruined, and farmers who have been ground beneath the juggernaut of competition are arraying themselves alongside of the starving ones who have never stepped out of the ranks of labor. What will they do? Ask the men of wealth, "What will ye do?" and the answer comes: "We will get, get, get, until there is no more to get; no matter who starves, we will get; it is our mission, and we will fulfill it." Such is the answer, if we judge by the actions of the past ten years.

It is a matter for congratulation that those who have accumulated all that is worth accumulating are so few and the dissatisfied ones so many, for in that fact rests the solution of the problem. The many must act, and they must act together in a system of co-operation that will stop the grinding process.

Under the competitive system labor has no share in what it develops. It has to take what the master deals out to it; but once it receives a share in what it creates, industry will become a part of him who produces, and the secret of content is found.

It is intended by the Knights of Labor to supersede the wage-system by a system of industrial co-operation, productive and distributive.

The Order has embarked in a number of co-operative enterprises. Some of them have been successful, and none of them have proven entirely fruitless.

In the winter of 1883 the coal miners at Cannelburg, Ind., were forced out of employment by the Buckeye Coal Company of that place, and were denied the right to toil in the mines of that company. The miners set to work to lease an adjoining property, sunk a shaft and equipped it. The General Executive Board of the Knights of Labor was asked to assist the men, and the aid was granted. Machinery and tools were supplied. The General Executive Board advanced the funds, took charge of the concern, and made it the property of the Order at large. The mines were to be run on the co-operative plan. When everything was ready to ship coal, the Ohio and Mississippi Railway Company was asked to lay a switch to the mine. They promised to do it, but failed in keeping the promise for nearly a year, or until they felt that they had exhausted the patience and funds of the rival to the Buckeye Coal Company. It was then discovered that the work of combination had extended so far as to pool the issues of the coal and railway companies. The stockholders or directors of the railway company were the owners of the Buckeye mine. Every stumbling-block that could reasonably be procured was placed in the way of the new enterprise, and it was at last suggested that the two companies consolidate and send their coal together to the same market.

Long and painful were the days that passed over the heads of those who had spoken in favor of co-operation. Here was a chance to combine the two kinds of co-operation, productive and distributive. Produce the coal and distribute it among the customers. Surely nothing could be easier; but when it came to transporting the coal from the producer to the consumer, the railway company pursued a policy of obstruction, until the last straw was about to be placed on the back of the labor camel.

The mines had to be leased to a company which entered into an agreement with the old coal company. Although the Knights of Labor still own the mine, yet they are prevented from demonstrating that the co-operative system is the best by reason of the power that monopoly has secured over the legislation and transportation of the country. This was a lesson for the Knights. It taught them that distributive co-operation will not, cannot, be a success while the power rests with the railways to do as they please, regardless of the interests or welfare of the people. It taught them that a co-operative system of railways must be established in the United States, or something so nearly akin to it as to satisfy the want which is being made known to-day.

We may boast of the individual enterprise of the American people as much as we please, but it has no chance when thrown into competition with the combination and the pool. The individual or the number of individuals who attempt to embark in an enterprise anywhere within the boundaries of the United States will do so, not at the will of the government, but at the order or dictation of the combination or trust. Once it was deemed a healthy sign to have different lines of railway running through a town. Cheap freight rates and easy transportation could be expected then; but to-day that hope is dead, and combination of interests will stand between the town and prosperity if the railways will it so. Labor, co-operating with the enterprising man who bought the fifty-dollar lot, increased the price of his land until he pompously asserts to-day that his own habits of thrift have won for him such large gains. His thrift was but an insignificant factor in the enterprise; it was co-operation that made him rich, but all the co-operators did not share in the profits of the labor done. The system that is coming to the front to take the place of the present one will give to every man who toils that to which he is justly entitled, and no system of juggling will prevent it. Its coming is inevitable, and they are wise who take the pains to read the handwriting on the wall and prepare the way for the dawn of the new era in industrial life.

While many of the attempts to establish co-operative institutions have been abandoned, and while many of them have apparently failed, the truth is that none of them, even those which ended the most disastrously, have entirely failed. Experience alone will teach men how to co-operate, and wherever a co-operative enterprise has failed its failure may be attributed to the same causes as combined to reduce other concerns to the same condition. Lack of business qualifications, lack of confidence in each other, hostility of those engaged in a similar line of business, the boycotting of the wares of co-operative institutions, and a lack of the necessary funds have been among the causes of failure of co-operative institutions. While these causes combined to bring about failure, they also served as educators, and taught workingmen that education on the question of co-operation must precede action.

The basic principle of the Order of the Knights of Labor is co-operation, but the first recommendation to the General Assembly on the subject was made when that body met in Pittsburg, Pa., in September, 1880. In the address of the Grand Master Workman of that year the following appears:

Organization once perfected, what must we do? I answer, study the best means of putting your organization to some practical use by embarking in a system of co-operation, which will eventually make every man his own master —every man his own employer; a system which will give the laborer a fair proportion of the products of his toil. It is to co-operation, then, as the lever of labor's emancipation that the eyes of the workingmen and women of the world are directed, upon co-operation their hopes are centered, and to it do I now direct your attention. I am deeply sensible of the importance, of the magnitude, of the undertaking in which I invite you to engage. I know that it is human nature to grow cold, apathetic and finally indifferent, when engaged in that which requires deep study and persistent effort, unattended by excitement. Men are apt to believe that physical force is the better way of redressing grievances, being the shorter remedy; but even that requires patience and fortitude, as well as strength. I need but point out to you the war of the Revolution, which took nearly eight years of hard fighting and persistent effort upon the part of men who fought for a principle. Had these men fallen into the same error which labor has so often fallen into, there would be no independence; had they gone to their homes after the battle of Bunker Hill, there would be no Bunker Hill monument erected, even though the result of that battle was encouraging. To the subject of co-operation, then, do I invite your attention, and I liken it unto the Revolutionary War. If you decide upon carrying it out at this convention, it will be the Bunker Hill of Industrial Independence; but you must also bear in mind, though the longest term allotted to man be yours to live, you will not see during that term the complete triumph of your hopes. The war for American Independence had its Bunker Hills and its Washingtons, but it also had its Valley Forges and its Benedict Arnolds. The enthusiasm of the hour will avail us nothing, and co-operation requires every Washington of labor to be up and doing. The laboring man needs education in this great social question, and the best minds of the Order must give their precious thought to this system. There is no good reason why labor cannot, through co-operation, own and operate mines, factories and railroads. By co-operation alone can a system of colonization be established in which men may band together for the purpose of securing the greatest good to the greatest number, and place the man who is willing to toil upon his own homestead.

There was no official action taken at that convention. At the session held the following year, in Detroit, Mich., A. M. Owens, who was there elected General Treasurer, offered a resolution which had for its object the establishment of a co-operative fund. Henry A. Fecker of Indiana presented an essay on co-operation to that session of the General Assembly. The number of resolutions and amendments presented at that meeting was so large that they could not be acted on, and the General Executive Board was authorized to compile and prepare the Constitution. In doing so the first law looking to the establishment of a co-operative department was prepared and inserted by Gilbert Rockwood, who had the compiling of the Constitution in hand. The law is given in full as follows:

ARTICLE VIII.
CO-OPERATIVE FUND.

Section 1. Every male member of the Order shall, on and after July 1, 1882, pay to the Financial Secretary of his Local a sum equal to ten cents per month as a co-operative fund of the Order, which fund shall remain with the Local, to be used solely as provided for under the provisions of Article XXV of this Constitution. Women shall in like manner pay a sum equal to five cents per month.

Sec. 2. Every member shall receive from the Financial Secretary a certificate of stock in the Co-operative Association of the Knights of Labor of North America for every thirty cents so paid, which certificates shall always be exchangeable at par, with the Grand Secretary, in amounts of not less than three dollars, or any multiple of three, for the three-dollar working capital certificates of the Order.

Sec. 3. All certificates of stock, of whatever value, shall be the personal property of the member to whom the same is issued, their heirs, executors and assigns; and every holder of any three-dollar certificates of stock shall be entitled to an equal share, for every such certificate, of all profits arising from the investment of the funds, as hereafter provided for.

Sec. 4. All certificates of stock must be registered by the Financial Secretary, and a strict account of the co-operative fund kept in a separate book.

At the New York session of the General Assembly the first Co-operative Board was elected, and the disposition of affairs relating to co-operation was intrusted to it.

When the General Assembly met the following year in Cincinnati, Ohio, the Co-operative Board had little or nothing to report, and made no recommendations upon the subject. Changes were made in the laws, and a new Board was elected to take charge of the department.

At the Philadelphia session the General Co-operative Board, in concluding its report, said:

As our Order will in all probability soon enter upon the task of establishing co-operative institutions, it is very important that the lessons here taught be carefully studied. The conclusions reached by the Board are:

1. That in establishing our co-operative institutions we must not forget that men reared under the conditions of wage-service cannot jump at once to the much higher level of co-operation. The man who has acted for a lifetime under outside pressure, when that pressure is suddenly removed becomes listless, apathetic, incapable of exertion. He is much as the locomotive is when the fireman neglects to pile on the fuel—the locomotive does not make steam and cannot do its work. Therefore, it seems that in our institutions we must preserve that feature of the wage-system which calls upon the man to put forth his best exertions, and to put them forth harmoniously, or be stricken from the pay-roll.

2. That individual incentive must be provided. It seems that although the desire for social honor may be a motive force with many, yet, after all, the material benefits are the most generally desired, and that, therefore, gradations of wages must be retained.

3. That the executive officers must be endowed with ample power to discipline refractory members—of course always subject to appeal.

4. That the executive officers be amply endowed with authority to select the men best adapted to the work in hand.

The first part of the report detailed the routine of the Board in conducting its correspondence. It related nothing of a practical nature.

When the General Assembly met in Hamilton, Ontario, in October, 1885, the General Master Workman, in his address, thus referred to

CO-OPERATION.

A great deal of the time of the last General Assembly was devoted to the discussion of co-operation in its varied forms, and fully as much of the time of this meeting should be devoted to the same end. We cannot discuss this question too much, nor can we too heartily encourage the growth of a sentiment favorable to co-operation. But many of our members grow impatient and unreasonable because every avenue of the Order does not lead to co-operation. This is a wrong impression, and is calculated to do injury to the very movement they advocate. We cannot make men; we must take them as we find them; and after a member has been educated in the principles of co-operation, he is wrong in supposing that every other man is as well informed on the subject as he is. The great fault with a great many co-operators is that they advocate the establishment of co-operative institutions on too large a scale. It frequently happens that no thought of co-operation is entertained until men are on strike or locked out. Then they get together, talk the matter up and decide to embark in co-operation. This is the wrong time to take so important a step, for at such a time no preparations have been made, no funds laid by, and one of the first things the members do is to borrow money on heavy interest; either that, or they go to some outside party who has plenty of money and get him interested so far as to take a mortgage on the entire plant of the concern. They hang a millstone around their necks in the beginning, and it eventually pulls them down until the interest on the mortgage swallows them up, confidence in co-operation is destroyed, and the men who went into it in that way are among the worst enemies of it afterward. I believe that one of the first things to be done is to get the members of the Assembly to make terms with some particular dealer in the start, purchase their goods from him, note the profits they make, and at the same time lay by a small sum each month for the purpose of buying a stock of goods in the future. They should make it a special study, and, when they select any person to do business for them, they should choose a person who has a knowledge of the business he is to transact. I have seen co-operative ventures fail because of a lack of business qualifications, and nothing can remove the idea that the persons having the matter in charge were dishonest. Workingmen are not business men by any means; and as long as we continue the question of getting a few cents more in the day for labor done, and neglect to look after the matter of investing the money we do get to the best advantage, and in a way that will bring back the best results and the largest returns, we will continue to be ignorant of the laws by which business is governed.

The Co-operative Board at that session reported having conducted a large correspondence with the Order on the subject, but could not speak very encouragingly of the results attained. The hesitancy in investing money in such institutions no doubt caused the Board to make use of these words in concluding its report:

As one of the first necessities in instituting co-operative industries is ready money, the Co-operative Board would suggest that the General Assembly empower the Co-operative Board to issue redeemable scrip in such amounts as the Board may deem necessary for successfully carrying on the enterprise for which such scrip may be issued. We recommend that Local Assemblies and District Assemblies use every effort to establish co-operative stores, when deemed practicable by the Co-operative Board, as the readiest means for accumulating capital; for the improvement of their social and domestic condition; to buy or build their own cottages or dwelling-houses, or for any other purpose conducive to their welfare.

The Co-operative Board made no report to the Richmond General Assembly, nor did the General Master Workman have anything to say on the subject. Since that time a number of hasty attempts have been made to establish co-operative institutions, but they were not thought of until the parties interested were locked out of employment or were on strike. Every dollar invested under such circumstances is a dollar lost, as far as testing the value of co-operation is concerned, for those who are directly engaged look for exactly the same results from the co-operative concern that they formerly expected from the railway company, the factory or the mine. If they do not realize the full extent of their expectations they are as ready to strike against the co-operative institution as the other; and while education on the question is so limited, the success of co-operation will not be made apparent. Education on this subject is required. The odds will be against co-operation as long as the avenues of distribution are in the hands of monopoly, for it is to the interest of the upholders of the present system to discourage every attempt at co-operation, so that the workman will abandon the idea of becoming his own employer.

A number of co-operative stores, bakeries and manufactories are being successfully managed by Knights of Labor in the United States and Canada, but they were instituted after careful planning and much deliberation. All others have proved to be failures. Until industrialists learn to co-operate in the affairs of government, co-operation in any other channel or business will be attended with many risks, doubts and fears.

THE EIGHT-HOUR PROBLEM.

More hours for manhood, none for greed ;
More for the mind's supremest need ;
More for the poor all good to speed,
Less hours of toil for bread.—*E. R. Place.*

Although the demand for a reduction of the hours of labor to eight
per day was made by the National Labor Union in 1866, and still
later by the Industrial Brotherhood, the agitation did not assume
very great proportions until the Knights of Labor took up the question by the adoption of the Preamble of the last-named society in
1878. Before entering upon the task of placing before the public the
history of the movement since 1878, a brief survey of the field of
operations previous to that date will prove instructive.

In 1825 the question of reducing the hours of labor to ten per day
was begun, and it was continued by the organizations of that day
until it was recognized by the United States government. In 1837
Martin Van Buren entered upon the discharge of his duties as President of the United States, and one of the most important acts of his
administration was to issue an order making ten hours a day's work
in all government workshops, although the employers of other
establishments doing similar work obliged the men to work eleven
and twelve hours a day as before. The employes of the government
worked but ten, and suffered no reduction in wages.

Those who take pains to study the question of machinery and its
effect on labor will at once admit that it is absolutely necessary to
reduce the hours of labor. The contrast between the hand labor of
thirty years ago and the machine labor of to-day furnishes a sufficient argument for those who take the side for shorter hours for the
mechanic.

I will not attempt to detail the efforts of Congress to give to labor
a recognition of its ability to perform a sufficient amount of labor in
eight hours each day, but a few of the acts of legislation will be cited
to show that the movement has received the sanction of the government—and, indeed, that is all the early pioneers hoped for—and
having attained that end they were content to keep up the agitation
on the line of shorter hours among the members of labor organizations in the hope that those directly interested would ultimately see
the necessity for exerting themselves, and for making sacrifices, if
required, in order to establish the short-hour system.

240

By Act of Congress, passed December 21, 1861, and amended July 16, 1862, the wages of government employes were to be regulated according to rates paid in other establishments. The act is as follows:

That the hours of labor and the rate of wages of employes in the navy yard shall conform, as nearly as is consistent with the public interests, with those of private establishments in the immediate vicinity of the respective yards, to be determined by the commandants of navy yards, subject to the approval and revision of the Secretary of the Navy.

When the agitation was begun by the National Labor Union in 1866, William H. Sylvis threw himself into the work with all of his splendid ability, and through his efforts more than those of any other one man we owe most of the results accomplished during the years intervening between 1866 and 1872. In a circular sent out by Mr. Sylvis to the Iron Moulders' Union, in the early part of 1868, he said:

The agitation of the eight-hour question was very great during the greater part of 1867, and several organizations became involved in strikes to enforce it. Some of our unions were unfortunately drawn into these troubles. The strikes to enforce the eight-hour rule, whether in our own unions or others, were entered into against my earnest protest. While I am in favor of the eight-hour system, I have always held it to be unwise and eminently foolish to attempt to enforce the system by strikes. What we want is agitation, education and legislation. Convince the people that it is right, and then demand the necessary legislation. If our representatives refuse to give it to us, turn them out and put somebody in who will. The universal adoption of the eight-hour system is only a question of time. If we want it we can get it.

The demands of the National Labor Union and the trade unions of the United States were made with such vigor in 1867 that Congress took up the question, and in 1868 passed the following law, which received the approval of President Johnson on June 25 of that year:

That eight hours shall constitute a day's work for all laborers, workingmen and mechanics now employed, or who may hereafter be employed, by or on behalf of the government of the United States. And all acts and parts of acts inconsistent with this act be, and the same are hereby, repealed.

The Secretary of the Navy, Adolph E. Borie, rendered a decision in interpreting that law by which the wages of the government employes were reduced one-fifth, and when the matter was brought to the attention of the Attorney-General, E. R. Hoar, he coincided with the views entertained by the Secretary of the Navy. Mr. Sylvis at once took up the question and wrote to Mr. Hoar, requesting that a different construction be placed upon the law. He cited the petitions which had been sent in to Congress asking for the passage of the act, also the speeches of Congressmen and Senators on the measure, but all to no avail, and he finally turned to President Grant for redress. The President began at once to examine into the matter, and after investigation wrote Mr. Sylvis that he would make an order directly the reverse of the decision which had been rendered, and on May 19, 1869, he issued a proclamation directing that no reduction of wages should follow a reduction of the hours of labor in government workshops. No attention was paid to the proclamation by those whose duty it was to enforce the law, and again Mr. Sylvis appealed to the President—this time in person—but before action was taken the body of William H. Sylvis was laid to rest in Laurel Hill Cemetery, on the banks of the Schuylkill, in Philadelphia. He died on the 22d of July, 1869.

Richard F. Trevellick continued the agitation, and corresponded with the President on the subject until the 11th of May, 1872, when President Grant issued another proclamation directing the heads of departments having the payment of employes in charge to make no reduction in the wages of those whose hours of labor had been reduced to eight per day. This order also failed of effect, and Congress was appealed to. On May 18, 1872, Congress passed a resolution directing that all mechanics, laborers and workmen employed by the government between June 25, 1868, and May 19, 1869, should receive compensation at the rate of ten hours' pay for eight hours' work.

Evasions and obstructions have from time to time been thrown in the way of the accomplishment of the designs of those who worked for this important measure, but the principle had been recognized by the government that eight hours were sufficient for men to toil, and with that indorsement the agitation has continued ever since, and it will continue until the establishment of the eight-hour workday is an accomplished fact. That which now retards the movement is the lack of unity and education among workingmen and manufacturers on the exact method of establishing the system.

In his address to the General Assembly at Chicago in 1879, Grand Master Workman Stephens, referring to the hours of labor, said :

THE HOURS OF LABOR.

It might seem to some almost superfluous to present anything for your consideration upon the subject of the hours of labor; nevertheless, I deem it highly necessary to call your attention to the ominous frequency of the attempts being made all over the country to break down the ten-hour standard and enforce longer hours. Whether these movements are preconcerted and form a part of an organized effort to offset and obstruct the eight-hour movement, time will tell. They are sufficient to warrant us in using all reasonable means to prevent any growth in that direction. An open warfare in manufacturing districts in England against short hours and a plain demand upon employes for an increase of hours of labor show what may be expected in this country; and they give us timely warning of the struggle and fierce opposition to be encountered before eight hours can be firmly established by statute law in the various States, backed as such laws will have to be by penal enactments for infringments in order to make them efficient. And, furthermore, they must be classed in the criminal code instead of the civil list. Active exertion and agitation will be necessary to bring public sentiment up to a point that will successfully carry the principle through the ballot-box. Until that is done absolutely nothing valuable has been gained.

Beyond a generally expressed desire to push the agitation in favor of shorter hours no action was taken, and the matter went over for another year.

During the following year R. F. Trevellick, A. R. Parsons, Chas. H. Litchman, Samuel C. Hunt and Dyer D. Lum, acting in the capacity of an eight-hour delegation, worked for the proper recognition of the eight-hour principle before Congress. Mr. Litchman, then Grand Secretary of the Knights of Labor, placed the matter before the Grand Master Workman, who, on his suggestion, issued a proclamation to the Order asking that nothing be left undone to strengthen the hands of this committee. Notwithstanding their zealous efforts in behalf of the measure they succeeded in accomplishing but little, and weary of spending their time and means, for they received no compensation for their services as members of the committee, they were forced to give up the struggle.

When the General Assembly met in Pittsburg, Pa., in 1880, the address of the Grand Master Workman contained an expression on the subject. Said he:

THE EIGHT-HOUR LAW

must also claim a share of your attention. During the past year, acting upon the advice of several prominent members of the Order, I issued a proclamation asking that an effort be made to aid this project, but it met with little success. And why? Because there was no law up.n our statute book which obliged members to take action thereon.

A reduction in the hours of labor is a necessity to which we can no longer close our eyes. To the inventive genius of the mechanic and laborer are due the new and varied improvements in machinery of all kinds. The man who sits comfortably clipping the coupons from his bonds never invents anything, unless it be a new way to squeeze more labor out of the toiler for less money. He must depend upon the man who labors for everything, including the wonderful inventions in the way of improved machinery. Does the improvement of any of the machines in use, or the invention of a new one, add to his labors? No. On the contrary, he is enabled thereby to reap a greater profit, for, if an employer, he discharges the man who invents the machine and hires a boy to run it for less money.

The wonderful machinery of to-day renders it possible for man to perform tenfold more labor than a century ago. Have the hours of labor been reduced accordingly? On the contrary men are obliged to work longer in proportion to-day than they did in the past.

If to the workman's brain is due these wonderful inventions, then to his body should come the rest made necessary by such drains upon his mental system; the only way to give that rest is to reduce the hours of labor, and every opportunity looking to that end should be improved; but a mere request to lend assistance in reducing the hours of labor will not avail. Men *must be compelled to help themselves,* and a law should be passed at this General Assembly requiring each member to assist by voice and pen, by petition and means, every honest effort looking toward the amelioration of the condition of the wage-slave, by reducing his hours of labor. I shall in future avail myself of the opportunities afforded by the publication of the JOURNAL to give my views at length upon this question.

Grand Secretary Litchman, in his report to the same convention, said:

One of the cardinal principles of the Preamble of our Constitution is the reduction of the hours of labor to eight. The Grand Officers have felt it their duty to aid in every way possible any movement for the accomplishment of legislation in that direction. Having been requested to serve as one of a committee to urge upon Congress the enforcement of the present national eight-hour law, the Grand Secretary felt it his duty to accept the invitation and do all in his power to induce members of the Order to second the efforts of the committee by petitions to Congress and personal appeals to Congressmen. Circulars have been issued from time to time giving to the Order full reports of the progress made. As a result of the labors of the eight-hour delegation, resolutions passed the House calling for a strict enforcement of the eight-hour law according to the spirit and intent of those by whose labors the law was originally adopted. These resolutions, passed the House by an overwhelming vote, were laid over in the Senate by the objection of a single man, Senator Withers of Virginia. The delegation has the assurance from prominent members and friends of the measure that it shall be called up and pressed to a vote early in the session when Congress convenes in December. It will be necessary that there should be some one there to look after and remind Senators of the former promises. I would strongly urge upon the General Assembly the necessity of having some one in Washington at the opening of the Senate to take such measures in the name of the united labor of America as shall convince the Senators that workingmen are in earnest in this matter. The expense could not be very great, and the amount necessary would be well expended, as it would show to the members of the Order that some practical good had resulted from the contributions they had made to the treasury of the General Assembly. The importance of favorable action by Congress can at once be seen when we reflect that, once the United States government declares in favor of an eight-hour law honestly interpreted and faithfully executed, it is only a question of a very short time when each individual State will follow, and private enterprise from force of public sentiment be compelled to yield to labor less hours of employment as some compensation for the introduction of labor-saving machinery.

Notwithstanding the earnest appeal of Mr. Litchman the convention decided to take no action on the question; in fact, it could not do otherwise, for there were no available funds in the treasury to meet the expenses of the Order, and no appropriation could be made to defray the expenses of the representative to Washington. Mr. Litchman and the other gentlemen associated with him on the committee continued their efforts until 1881, when they retired from the field fully impressed with the belief that to have any influence with Congress it must be made apparent that voters, intelligent and resolute, stand behind whoever acts as the spokesman of industry.

No reference was made to the short-hour workday in the reports of the Grand Officers at the Detroit or New York session. At the Cincinnati General Assembly the Grand Master Workman offered the following recommendation, and it was adopted:

As an organization we advocate the establishment of the eight-hour system, but we are silent on that question where we can put it into practical operation ourselves. Let us pass a law limiting the hours of labor of employes of the General Assembly to eight per day, and thus establish some claim to the right to say that we practice what we preach, and remove any doubts from the minds of those who are skeptical as to the sincerity of our professions when we say we advocate the establishment of the eight-hour system.

Immediately upon the adoption of that recommendation the employes of the Order, except the General Officers, were instructed that their hours of labor for the future would be but eight per day, and for the same they would receive the same rate of compensation as they received for ten hours' work in the past. Since that session clerks employed in the General Office have worked but eight hours. D. A. 41 of Baltimore introduced the following resolution at the Cincinnati session :

That the General Assembly be requested to proclaim to the Order eight hours as a day's work, and name May 1, 1884, as the time when it shall be carried into effect by all District Assemblies and Local Assemblies under its jurisdiction.

Beyond the discussion which ensued no action was taken. At the Philadelphia session the year following, the General Statistician, Francis B. Egan, in his report on the statistics gathered by him during the year, said :

By the following table it is seen that seven-ninths of our members work ten hours a day, one-ninth work less than ten hours, and one-ninth over ten hours. These figures are for the first five working days in the week. On Saturdays four-ninths work ten hours, three-ninths work nine hours, one-ninth work eight hours and under, one-ninth eleven hours and over. This plainly shows that we are a long way from the time when eight hours will be recognized as a day's work. Nevertheless, let us not cease our efforts in endeavoring to attain so desirable a result. It is not many years ago since twelve hours was considered a day's work, but through agitation it was reduced to ten, and through still further agitation it will be reduced to eight.

No action was taken on the report of the General Statistician, but a radical change was made in the Preamble. The XIVth resolution referred to the question of shorter hours, and up to that session remained as it was handed down to the General Assembly at Reading in 1878. When the Philadelphia session adjourned the XXIst resolution in the Preamble stood as follows :

To shorten the hours of labor by a general refusal to work for more than eight hours.

In the hurry to get through with the business that important subject escaped the scrutiny it deserved. It was drawn up hurriedly, read but once to the convention, and passed along with the rest of the Preamble. Many believed that the Preamble was only intended to be a list of "glittering generalities," and that it mattered but little what it contained. The "general refusal" was interpreted by workingmen outside of the Order to mean quite another thing than that which was intended by those who adopted it, and attempts were made to draw the Order into strikes to enforce the "refusal."

On December 15, 1884, in the same circular in which he referred to the actions of those who paraded the streets waving the red and black flags, the General Master Workman, in speaking of the eight-hour agitation, said:

Notwithstanding all this, I wish to see a revolution; I wish to see some killing done; I wish to see the systems by which the worker is oppressed killed off; and I long to see a revolution in the working time of those who toil. With that object in view I request that all Local and District Assemblies take up for discussion Section XXI of the Preamble; discuss it thoroughly during the winter, first in the privacy of the Assembly, then in the public press and before the people. In your discussions remember this fact: that if legislation be piled up mountains high in defense of workingmen, the simple, inanimate thing called legislation will do no good of itself unless backed up by the will of the workingmen themselves. It must be enforced, and those to whose interest it is to have it enforced are the workers. If the workers are too ignorant to see the necessity for giving effect to legislation, they will need light; if they are too indolent to enforce it, they will require constant agitation; and if they are too cowardly to take what is already theirs, then they will require light, agitation, the example of others and manhood. We have all three classes in the Knights of Labor, and we must get rid of them by educating them. Manufacturers everywhere are beginning to concede that shorter hours are necessary, but they cannot compete with those who work their establishments ten and fifteen hours. Our Preamble now says: "To shorten the hours of labor by a general refusal to work for more than eight hours." The general refusal must be preceded by a general agitation, and that agitation must be begun by this Order. I ask that every Assembly take up this question at once. Let each one have its members write short essays on the eight-hour question. From the number let the Assembly select the best for publication in the public press of the land, in the local papers, but do not publish them indiscriminately and at different times. When they are written withhold them until a day when they all can be published together. Washington's Birthday, the 22d of February, will be a day of public interest. The eyes of the nation will be turned toward the papers. I, therefore, name that day as the one upon which to have all these articles appear. If in your locality no paper appears on that day, then endeavor to have it in the one next issued after that date. Make no public announcement of your intention to do this thing until it is done. To have them appear simultaneously all over the United States and Canada will in itself be very significant, and will cause men to stop and think. A feeble effort in that direction will be made by me in the February number of the *North American Review*. Let it be but the forerunner of more effective ones. Go outside of your Assemblies and get other societies to take up the agitation. Have it preached from pulpit and rostrum. After the ball has been opened, the agitation once begun, never let it die out until men and women, seeing the necessity for shorter hours, will regard it as a crime to work more than eight hours a day. Be still as death until the time named, then let the fire open up along the line from Maine to California.

The circular contains other matter which does not relate to the subject of shorter hours, but the concluding words in it were: "Do not forget Washington's Birthday and the eight-hour movement."

The article in the *North American Review* did not appear in the February number of that publication, but was withheld until the April number, and appeared under the title of:

THE ARMY OF THE DISCONTENTED.

In January, 1884, the following paragraph appeared in one of the daily papers:

"It is estimated that at the present time one million and a half of men are out of employment in the United States; it is safe to predict that, if opportunities were offered to these men to drop into useful occupations, a large majority would not avail themselves of them."

Since then the number of the unemployed must have increased, for nearly every day we read such items as this :

"The worsted mill connected with the Bigelow Carpet Mills, which employs about three hundred hands, shut down this morning for three weeks. This, with the five per cent. cut down at the Lancaster Gingham Mills, where two thousand five hundred hands are employed, which also went into effect this morning, makes Clinton's business outlook decidedly poor."

In the two years ending December 1, 1884, those employed in and around the coal mines worked but little over half-time, and for the length of time that they were not at work they must be counted in with the unemployed. If the figures above quoted were correct in January, it is safe to assume that at present the number will not fall short of 2,000,000. The census of 1880 shows that the number of persons engaged in gainful occupations was 17,392,099. Of this number 3,837,112 were engaged in manufacturing, mechanical and mining pursuits, while 5,183,099 gained a livelihood as laborers (agricultural and otherwise). Thus in 1880 we had in the United States, between laborers, mechanics, miners and those engaged in manufacturing establishments, 9,020,211 persons.

From a personal experience, I am led to believe that the greater portion of those who are now out of employment comes from occupations that go to make up the 9,020,211. It is safe to assume that the 2,000,000 unemployed persons are discontented with their lot; and not only are they discontented, but those who labor at the same occupations that they previously followed have every reason to be dissatisfied also. With so many men and women seeking employment, the tendency of wages must be downward. It does not follow, because men are out of employment, that such articles as their fellow-workmen produce should decrease in value, or that the profit on the manufactured article, accruing to the owners of the establishments in which they work, should be any less; on the contrary, the expectation is that diminished production will increase the price of the manufactured article, or at least prevent its depreciation when thrown on the market. Notwithstanding the reduction in the expenses of the mining company, we pay the same price for coal that we paid a year ago. It matters not that the carpet mills "suspend three hundred hands," the price of carpeting remains unchanged. The gingham mills and the cotton and woolen mills may reduce the wages of employes five and ten per cent., yet the price of gingham and calico continues as before. Whether the manufactured article commands the same price in the market or not, the employer, knowing that he can secure an abundance of help, reduces the wages of his employes. Those who are out of employment are no longer producers, and they certainly are not consumers to any increased extent. The wages of those employed having been reduced, their powers of consumption are limited. The merchant whose shelves are stocked with goods becomes discontented when he views the rows of men and women that stand in front of his store, peering with hungry-looking eyes through his windows at the goods so temptingly held to view, willing and anxious to buy these goods, but deprived of the means through enforced idleness or inadequate compensation for services rendered. Ask the business man what the cause of the depression is, and he, parrot-like, will say, "It is all regulated by the law of supply and demand." A moment's reflection would show him that the law of supply and demand, like all other laws, is open to different constructions. On his shelves is a supply of goods; outside of his window is a demand for these goods—a demand that is at all times equal to the supply. Why is it that the demand does not reach forth and secure the supply? The answer comes, "Because the medium of exchange is lacking; because labor is too cheap and plenty, and money too dear and scarce." That a deep-rooted feeling of discontent pervades the masses, none can deny; that there is a just cause for it, must be admitted. The old cry, "These agitators are stirring up a feeling of dissatisfaction among workingmen, and they should be suppressed," will not avail now. Every thinking person knows that the agitator did not throw two millions of men out of employment. The man who reads such paragraphs as this will not lay the blame of it at the door of the agitator.

"Mrs. Sarah Jane Geary, an Englishwoman, residing in this city, committed suicide a few days since. Her husband is a miner, and owing to the frequent suspensions of business in the mines during the past winter his meagre earnings were insufficient to support the family. The fact preyed on Mrs. Geary's mind, and she resolved to end her life that her children might receive her share of the food, otherwise they would go hungry."

The Cincinnati riots, that occurred less than one year ago, were not brought about through the agitation of the labor leader. If the demand for "the removal of unjust technicalities, delays and discriminations in the administration of justice" had been listened to when first made by the Knights of Labor, Cincinnati would have been spared sorrow and disgrace, and her "prominent citizens" would not have had to lead a mob in order to open the eyes of the country to the manner in which her courts were throttled and virtue and truth were trampled upon in her temples of justice. That the army of the discontented is gathering fresh recruits day by day is true and if this army should become so large that, driven to desperation, it should one day arise in its wrath and grapple with its real or fancied enemy the responsibility for that act must fall upon the heads of those who could have averted the blow, but who turned a deaf ear to the supplication of suffering humanity and gave the screw of oppression an extra turn because they had the power. Workingmen's organizations are doing all they can to avert the blow; but if that day dawns upon us, it will be chargeable directly to men who taunt others with unequal earnings and distort the truth, as was done in an interview recently had with Mr. William H. Vanderbilt:

"One of the troubles in this country just now is the relation of wages to the cost of production. A skilled workman in almost every branch of business gets every day money enough to buy a barrel of flour. I don't refer to ordinary laborers, but to men skilled at their trades. The man who makes the article receives as much wages in many instances as the article is worth when it is finished. This is not exactly fair, in my opinion, and must be adjusted. Until wages bear a truer relation to production there can be no real prosperity in the country."

I have seen no denial of the above, and take it for granted that it is a correct report. Mr. Vanderbilt starts out well enough, but he is in error when he says "that a skilled workman in almost every branch of business gets money enough every day to buy a barrel of flour." I know of no business in the United States in which a skilled mechanic, working regularly at his trade day by day, gets money enough for his day's labor to buy a barrel of flour. That they earn the price of a barrel of flour, I do not deny; but that they get it is not true. It may be that Mr. Vanderbilt refers to superintendents, foremen or contractors, for they are the only ones that receive such wages. The average wage paid to the skilled mechanic will not exceed $2.50 a day. I know of but few branches of business in which men can command that price. The wages of skilled mechanics are on the decline, while the price of flour remains unchanged, from $5.75 to $8.50 a barrel. If Mr. Vanderbilt will demonstrate how one can purchase a six-dollar barrel of flour for two dollars and a half, he will have solved a very difficult problem for the workingman. It is not the labor of the skilled mechanic alone that must be taken into account in computing the cost of the manufactured article; the average price paid to labor in the establishment should be the standard, if a standard of wages is required. An examination of the last census report shows that the number of manufacturing establishments in the United States was 253,852, and the amount of capital invested was $2,790,272,606; the average number of hands employed was 2,732,595; the value of the raw material was $3,396,823,549;

while the product of the manufactured articles was $5,369,579,191. Deduct the sum paid for the raw material from the product of the manufactured article and we have $1,972,745,642. This sum represents the difference between the price paid for the article when in a raw state and that received for it when manufactured. It is evident that something more than interest on money invested was required to give this additional value to the material. That something was the labor of the hands referred to. The total amount paid in wages to the employes of these establishments was $947,953,795. Deducting this amount from the $1,972,745,642, we have left $1,024,791,847. This sum goes to the manufacturer. It is estimated by some that the amount paid for raw material includes taxes, insurance, salaries and repairs; but, in the absence of reliable statistics, I am not prepared to prove that such is the case. By adding the sum paid for raw material to the amount of capital invested, we have $6,187,096,155, the total investment of the manufacturer. From this sum we have, pitted against every one of the 2,732,595 employes, a fraction over $2,264. While the average yearly earnings of each employe were $720, he received in wages but a fraction over $346, or a trifle over one dollar a day for every working day in the year. Subtract the wages of the employe from his earnings and we have left $374. The employe receives an average of $346 a year for his labor, while his employer receives $374 on an investment of $2,264. Instead of basing the cost of the manufactured article on the wages given to the highest-priced skilled mechanic, it should be based on the average wage paid to the men in these establishments. It thus appears that a barrel of flour costs several days' labor.

It may be said that many of the employes of the manufacturing establishments are minors, and consequently cannot perform as great an amount of labor as a corresponding number of adults. That argument might have had some weight years ago, but now it is fruitless. The age and strength of the workman are no longer regarded as factors in the field of production; it is the skill of the operator in managing a labor-saving machine that is held to be the most essential. It is true that a child can operate a machine as successfully as a man, and that muscle is no longer a requisite in accomplishing results. It is also true that less time is required to perform a given amount of labor than heretofore. This being the case, the plea for shorter hours is not unreasonable. Benjamin Franklin said, one hundred years ago, that "if the workers of the world would labor but four hours each day they could produce enough in that length of time to supply the wants of mankind." While it is true that the means of supplying the wants of man have increased as if by magic, yet man has acquired no new wants; he is merely enabled to gratify his needs more fully. If it were true in Franklin's time that four hours of toil each day would prove sufficient to minister to the necessities of the world's inhabitants, the argument certainly has lost none of its force since then. At that time it took the sailing-vessel three months to cross the ocean; the stage-coach made its thirty or forty miles a day; the electric wire was not dreamt of; and the letter that traveled but little faster than the stage-coach was the quickest medium of communication.

It required six days' labor at the hands of the machinist, with hammer, chisel and file, to perfect a certain piece of machinery at the beginning of this century. The machinist of the present day can finish a better job in six hours with the aid of a labor-saving machine. In a yarn mill in Philadelphia the proprietor says that improved machinery has caused a displacement of fifty per cent. of the former employes within five years, and that one person, with the aid of improved machinery, can perform the work that it took upward of one hundred carders and spinners to do with the tools and implements in use at the beginning of this century. In Massachusetts it has been estimated that 318,768 men, women and children do, with improved machinery, the work that it would require 1,912,468 men to perform if improved machinery were not in use. To insure safety on a passenger train, it is no longer necessary to have a brakeman at each end of the car; the automatic air-brake does the work, while one brakeman can shout "All right here!" for the whole train. The employe who has had a limb cut off in a collision must beg for bread or turn the crank of a hand-organ and gather his pennies under the legend, "Please assist a poor soldier who lost his leg at Gettysburg." He is no longer stationed, flag in hand, at the switch; the automatic lever directs the course of the train and renders the one-legged switchman unnecessary. It is said that the iron-moulder recently invented is capable of performing as much work as three skilled workmen; while the following dispatch to a Philadelphia paper, from Mahanoy City, shows what is being done in the mines:

"For the past three years the reduction in wages has been systematic and steady. When one of the officials of one of the great companies was interviewed on the matter, he replied that the advance in labor-saving machinery had lightened the labor of the men. A miner at one of the Reading collieries says that some months ago he expended a large sum for a patent drill, which enabled him to do five times the usual amount of work. He was employed in driving a gangway, the price paid being $10 a yard; but at the end of the week, when the officials saw the amount of work he had done, the rate was reduced to $4.50 a yard."

Take the iron-moulder as an illustration. Three flesh-and-blood men, who require shelter, clothing, recreation and social intercourse, who must eat or starve, who must pay taxes to support the State, and whose bodies can be taken to defend the State in case of invasion or rebellion; one iron-man, who does not feel, sleep, eat or drink, who never tires and never rests. Three flesh-and-blood men, who have children depending upon them for bread; one iron-man, who has no family to support; and the three men whom he has displaced must continue to support families or enlist in that ever-increasing army of tramps. Heat, steam, electricity and labor-saving machines pay no taxes, municipal or national; the men thrown out of employment through the introduction of these agents are deprived of the means of contributing to the support of the State, and an extra burden is shifted to the shoulders of those who continue to work. The existence of such a state of affairs gives evidence that the introduction of machinery, from which the many should derive an advantage, is being used for the benefit of a few, who already feel the blow given to trade through the displacement of so many consumers.

A great many remedies are recommended for the ills that I speak of. Let me deal with what seems to be the most important—the reduction of the hours of labor to eight a day. Men, women and children are working from ten to eighteen hours a day, and two million men have nothing to do. If four men, following a given occupation, at which they work ten hours a day, would rest from their labors two hours each day, the two hours taken from the labor of each, if added together, would give the tramp who stands looking on an opportunity of stepping into a position at eight hours a day. It is said that a vast majority of those who are idle would not work if they had work to do. That statement is untrue; but let us admit that five hundred thousand of the two million idle men would not work, we still have a million and a half who are anxious and willing to work. If but six million of the seventeen million producers will abstain from working ten, fifteen and eighteen hours a day and work but eight, the one million and a half of idle men who are willing to work can again take their places in the ranks of the world's producers. Need it be said that a million and a half of new hats will be needed; that a corresponding number of pairs of shoes, suits of clothing and a hundred other things will be required; that the wants of these men and their families will be supplied; that shelves will be emptied of their goods, and that the money expended will again go into circulation? It would entail hardship on some branches of business to require men employed in them to work eight hours a day. Miners and those working by contract could not very well adopt the eight-hour plan without lengthening their hours of labor. Before giving the matter a second thought, many of these men look upon the eight-hour agitation as of no consequence to them. If a mechanic is thrown out of employment and cannot find anything to do at his trade, he turns toward the first place where an opportunity for work is presented. If he is re-enforced by two million idle men, the number that apply at the mouth of the mine, or seek to secure contracts at lower figures, becomes quite large, and the miner and contract man grumble because so many men are crowding in upon them in quest of work. Every new applicant for work in the mine makes it possible for the boss to let his contract to a lower bidder; therefore it is clearly to the interest of the miner to assist in reducing the hours of labor in shop, mill and factory, to the end that the idle millions may be gathered in from the streets to self-sustaining positions.

The eight-hour system, to be of value to the masses, must be put in operation all over the country, for the manufacturers of one State cannot successfully compete with those of other States if they run their establishments but eight hours while others operate theirs ten or twelve hours a day. The movement should be national, and should have the hearty co-operation of all men.

A Scottish clergyman, Dr. Donald Macleod, in a sermon on "The Sin of Cheapness," says that "the craving for cheapness and hunting after bargains is not only economically false, but a cause of great suffering to thousands of men, women and children." If men worked shorter hours, they would learn that when a man begins to look for cheap bargains he strikes a blow at trade everywhere. The employer looks for a better bargain in labor, and reduces his force or hires cheaper men. His employe must practice enforced economy, which is no saving; he drives sharper bargains for articles manufactured by others; he cannot purchase as good an article, or in such quantities, as before; and the effect is felt where these articles are made, taking the shape of a reduction either in the working force or in the wages. When the President of the United States issued his Thanksgiving proclamation in 1884, there were millions of men and women in want of bread, notwithstanding "the abundant harvests and continued prosperity which God hath vouchsafed to this nation," and the cry, not of thanksgiving, went up from millions of farmers of "Too much wheat!" Doubting as to the exact meaning of the Creator in growing so much wheat, they invoked the aid of such institutions as the Chicago Board of Trade, in the hope of thwarting the will of God by cornering wheat. These men invoked blessings on their Thanksgiving dinners and thanked God for the turkey, while they hoarded the wheat away from those who asked for bread.

Give men shorter hours in which to labor, and you give them more time to study and learn why bread is so scarce while wheat is so plenty. You give them more time in which to learn that millions of acres of American soil are controlled by alien landlords who have no interest in America but to draw a revenue from it. You give them time to learn that America belongs to Americans, native and naturalized, and that the landlord who drives his tenant from the old world must not be permitted to exact tribute from him when he settles in our country.

On Washington's Birthday, 1885, a number of papers throughout the country contained communications on the short-hour subject, and the fact that so many papers had opened up their columns to the discussion of the question brought out a number of very able editorials from several leading papers on the necessity for shorter hours of toil for the laborer and mechanic. The agitation was continued during the spring and summer of 1885, and interest in the movement was not centered in the workingmen alone. Manufacturers began to discuss the question and study its possibilities. A " healthy public opinion " was being created and the tendency toward a reduction of hours was becoming quite rapid when the annual conventions of the labor organizations of the country were held. The Federation of Trades, at its annual session in 1885, named May 1, 1886, as the day on which to put the eight-hour system into operation, but the convention made no provision for the enforcement of the order. It was left to the discretion of each subordinate union to adopt its own plan of operations. Those who passed the resolution did but little to secure its enforcement, and from the very first the movement, so far as its operations on May 1, 1886, were concerned, was doomed to defeat.

When the General Assembly of the Knights of Labor met in Hamilton, Ontario, in October, 1885, the General Master Workman touched upon the subject in his address in the following words:

When the secret circular was issued on the 15th of last December, fixing Washington's Birthday as the date on which to begin an agitation on the eight-hour question, which is a political one, the answer which came from all parts of the country was astonishing. In the Dominion of Canada, and in every State of the Union, the papers gave special prominence to the question, and the agitation has continued unabated since that time. The short-hour movement has received more attention since the 1st of last January than it did in the ten years preceding that date. While speaking on the eight-hour question, let me say that the proposition to inaugurate a general strike for the establishment of the short-hour plan on the 1st of May, 1886, should be discountenanced by this body. The people most interested in the project are not as yet educated in the movement, and a strike under such conditions must prove abortive. The date fixed is not a suitable one; the plan suggested to establish the system is not the proper one.

The convention took no action on the matter. There was no discussion on the subject. That part of the address was not considered, and the convention adjourned without action. Soon after the adjournment of the General Assembly the street-car strike of St. Louis, Mo., attracted the attention of the country toward the Order, and inquiring minds began to investigate the aims and methods of the organization. Public attention once fastened upon the society, the press devoted much space to reports of labor meetings, and reporters were instructed to gather "labor news" wherever they could get it.

A reporter of the New York *Sun* was delegated to get up a story of the strength and purposes of the Knights of Labor, and he performed his mission in sending forth one of the most sensational and wonderful narratives that ever appeared concerning the Order. The article started out with a falsehood and in so misleading a manner that much harm was done, not only to the organization, but to the whole country. The introduction to the *Sun* article was in the following language:

Five men in this country control the chief interests of five hundred thousand workingmen, and can at any moment take the means of livelihood from two and a half millions of souls. These men compose the Executive Board of the noble Order of the Knights of Labor of America. The ability of the President and Cabinet to turn out all the men in the civil service, and to shift from one post or ship to another the duties of the men in the army and navy, is a petty authority compared with that of these five Knights. The authority of the late Cardinal was, and that of the Bishops of the Methodist Church is, narrow and prescribed, so far as material affairs are concerned, in comparison with that of these five rulers. They can stay the nimble touch of almost every telegraph operator, can shut up most of the mills and factories, and can disable the railroads. They can issue an edict against any manufactured goods so as to make their subjects cease buying them, and the tradesmen stop selling them. They can array labor against capital, putting labor on the offensive or the defensive, for quiet and stubborn self-protection, or for angry, organized assault, as they will.

The publication of that introduction did incalculable mischief. The correspondent for the *Sun* never obtained his information from a reliable source. He gathered it from those who felt that to tell a wonderful story was the best means of booming the organization. The organization began to boom, but those who sought its shelter were led to believe that they could secure the co-operation of the "500,000 workingmen," referred to in the *Sun* article, in the shutting off of the railroads and in stopping the "nimble touch" of the telegraph operators of America.

When that story was written the Order of the Knights of Labor was scarcely one hundred thousand strong, but in a few months, after the labor journals, the Western press and papers generally had copied the sensational romance of the *Sun*, the number doubled, and the majority of the new-comers was not of the quality the Order had sought for in the past.

In the early part of 1886 many of the new Local Assemblies began to pass resolutions favoring the "action of the General Assembly in fixing the 1st of May, 1886, as the day on which to strike for eight hours." They sent them to the General Master Workman, who saw at once that a grave danger threatened the Order through the ignorance of the members who had been so hurriedly gathered into the Assemblies. They were induced to come in by a false statement. Many Organizers assisted in keeping up the delusion for the purpose of making "big returns" to the General Office. In order to avert the danger which threatened the Order, and to place facts before the membership, the General Master Workman issued a secret circular on March 13, 1886, in which the following occurs:

It is evident that our members are not properly instructed, else we would not find them passing resolutions "approving of the action of our executive officers in fixing the 1st of May as the day to strike for eight hours." The executive officers of the Knights of Labor have never fixed upon the 1st of May for a strike of any kind, and they will not do so until the proper time arrives and the word goes forth from the General Assembly. No Assembly of the Knights of Labor must strike for the eight-hour system on May 1 under the impression that they are obeying orders from headquarters, for such an order was not and will not be given. Neither employer nor employe are educated to the needs and necessities for the short-hour plan. If one branch of trade or one Assembly is in such a condition, remember that there are many who are in total ignorance of the movement. Out of the sixty millions of people in the United States and Canada, our Order has possibly three hundred thousand. Can we mould the sentiment of the millions in favor of the short-hour plan before May 1? It is nonsense to think of it. Let us learn why our hours of labor should be reduced, and then teach others.

Many persons who blindly believed every statement made through the press or by interested parties that it was the aim of the Knights of Labor to strike for eight hours on May 1 grew indignant to think that the General Master Workman should issue such an order, since the General Assembly had resolved to act on May 1. In the discussion of the proposed movement no prominence was given to any other organization, and the greater part of the reading public believed that the Federation of Trades was but a part of the Knights of Labor. Many members of the last-named society were impressed with the same belief, and the General Master Workman felt that those who were so blind to their surroundings as not to know the name of the organization they belonged to, or the difference between it and other societies, could not be trusted to go very far or act intelligently in an undertaking of such magnitude as the establishment of the eight-hour system must necessarily be. There never was a time when the Knights of Labor were so flagrantly misrepresented or the aims and purposes of the Order so misunderstood. Designing and unscrupulous persons flocked into the Order in all parts of the country. The time-serving politician, the trader in votes, the seeker for office, the spoils-hunter, who sought for a following that he might appear to have influence, and the sharp, shrewd shop-keeper, with an eye to business, all thronged into the Assemblies during the spasmodic growth of the Order. Each one, anxious to further his own interests and to stand well in the favor of those who surrounded him, encouraged the belief that it was the Order of the Knights of Labor which issued the eight-hour order for May 1.

The silence and indifference of the organization which did issue the order gave rise to the impression that the whole affair must have been appropriated by the Knights of Labor. The anarchist element, ever busy in meddling with the affairs of the organization, and particularly interested at that time in the attempt to gain control of the machinery of the labor movement, availed themselves of every opportunity to spread discord and distrust because of the alleged lack of support of the General Master Workman of the Knights of Labor. That officer wished to see the eight-hour movement succeed. It was due to his efforts, as much as to those of any other one man, that the agitation of 1885 was begun and continued. While he sincerely wished to have the system established, he regarded the plan of operations to be inaugurated May 1 as being rash, short-sighted and lacking in system. He could not conscientiously lend his sanction to the scheme, and felt it to be his duty to warn those whose interests he had in his keeping against entering into the struggle under a disadvantage, and while laboring under a false impression that it was the Order of the Knights of Labor that named May 1, 1886, as the day on which to establish the eight-hour system.

The officers of the Federation of Trades did not hold any communication with those of the Knights of Labor. They imparted to them no part of their plans, nor did they in any way seek the co-operation of the Order of the Knights of Labor. As a consequence the General Officers of the Knights of Labor knew absolutely nothing of the strength, wishes or intentions of the other society until they were demonstrated in the strike for eight hours on May 1, 1886.

When the convention of the Federation of Trades met in Washington, D. C., in December, 1885, the Furniture Workers' International Union introduced a series of resolutions bearing on the question of inaugurating the eight-hour system on May 1. They appear in the proceedings of that session as follows :

WHEREAS, The last annual congress of the Federation approved of the opinion expressed by Secretary Frank K. Foster, in his annual report, that it would be in vain to expect the introduction of the eight-hour rule through legislative measures, and that a united demand to reduce the hours of labor, supported by a firmly-established and determined organization, would be far more effective than a thousand laws, whose execution depends upon the good-will of aspiring politicians or sycophantic department officials.

WHEREAS, The congress has adopted the following:

Resolved, By the Federation of Organized Trades and Labor Unions of the United States and Canada, that eight hours shall constitute a legal day's labor from and after May 1, 1886, and that we recommend to labor organizations throughout this jurisdiction that they so direct their laws as to conform to this resolution by the time named

WHEREAS, This resolution and the views upon which it is based, namely, that the workmen in their endeavor to reform the prevailing economic conditions must rely upon themselves and their own power exclusively, have found an echo in the hearts of all those organized workmen of this country who are fighting for a principle and are willing to make sacrifices in order to secure an improvement of the condition of themselves and their fellow-workers, and as there is in many parts of this country a strong movement going on for the purpose of carrying out this resolution.

WHEREAS, It is a well-known truism that the success of workmen contending against capitalistic oppression is due to their policy of concentrating their forces whenever they desire to gain a point.

WHEREAS, The workmen of this country interested in the reduction of the hours of labor are considering the Federation of Trades and Labor Unions as a medium through which that concentration of forces can be accomplished and to which belongs the leadership in this movement; and

WHEREAS, The Federation has taken upon itself a great responsibility in regard to the movement inaugurated by this organization, as a failure of the same would be detrimental to all organizations and would throw back the movement for the reduction of the hours of labor for many years to come. Therefore be it

Resolved, That the Legislative Committee be hereby instructed to again appeal to the workmen of this country for the purpose of pointing out to them the necessity of acting on their own account, and to call upon them to unite the different trades in their respective cities that they may be able to more thoroughly assist each other, morally and financially.

Resolved, That all organizations under the jurisdiction of the Federation be called upon to report to the Legislative Committee on or before March 1, 1886, whether or not they have resolved to introduce the eight-hour workday; and, if so, what steps they have taken in that respect, how they are organized throughout the country, etc.; whereupon the Legislative Committee shall request all of those organizations having not yet determined to join in introducing the reduction of the hours of labor to assist such organizations with all the power at their command; *provided, that together with the reduction of the hours of labor they do not ask for an increase of wages.*

Resolved, That all organizations intending to reduce the hours of labor on May 1 shall give an opportunity to the respective manufacturers and employers to give their consent by submitting a document to be signed by them to that effect, the contents of the said document to be prepared by the Legislative Committee, and the same to be forwarded to all organizations.

To these resolutions two amendments were added, one by Mr. Edmonston and the other by Mr. Gompers. That offered by the former stands upon the record in the following words:

We recommend to all labor organizations a thorough canvass in their respective trades for the purpose of securing the co-operation of as many as possible to effect this object.

The amendment of Mr. Gompers was:

Resolved, That the trades and labor unions be and they are hereby requested to forward to the Secretary of the Legislative Committee on the evening of May 1, 1886, or as soon thereafter as possible, what results have been attained in the establishment of the eight-hour law.

The resolutions and amendments were referred to the Committee on Resolutions. The result was the presentation of the following recommendation by that committee:

Your committee recommends the adoption of the eight-hour resolution presented by the furniture workers' delegation, with the amendments of Messrs. Edmonston and Gompers.

The report of the committee was adopted by the convention, and no further action was taken at that session. That organization, as such, never again held a convention. When the trade unions met in annual congress in December, 1886, they met under the name of the "American Federation of Labor," and have been known by that name ever since. It was not generally known that the Federation did not advocate the retention of the same rate of wages for eight as that which prevailed under the ten-hour system, and manufacturers universally regarded the movement as having for its object a strike for ten hours' pay for eight hours' work. The mistake of the Federation was to assume that the workmen of the country regarded it as the only medium through which the eight-hour system would be brought into effect, and that the leadership in the movement belonged to the Federation. Had the resolutions been published to the world, and presented to other labor organizations for approval, a far better feeling would have prevailed, for the impression which pervaded the masses was that the resolutions of the Federation counseled a strike as the means by which to bring about the desired result. Why the Federation allowed this erroneous impression to prevail has never been explained.

The strikes of May 1, 1886, have been made a matter of record in other histories. They are still fresh in the minds of the many who watched the course of events at that time, and but a passing glance will be sufficient.

When the 1st of May came around the movement to establish the eight-hour workday was confined to a few of the large cities. Whether the recommendation of the Federation to "give an opportunity to the respective manufacturers and employers to give their consent by submitting a document," etc., was carried out is not certain. The organizations to which the resolutions were sent, and on which they were supposed to be binding, could not, no doubt, reconcile the recommendation to give employers an opportunity to "give their consent" with the resolution which declared "that the workmen in their endeavor to reform the prevailing economic conditions must rely upon themselves and their own power exclusively."

If they were to depend upon their own power exclusively they should not be required to gain the consent of the employers by any means, and it was upon that interpretation of the resolution that many acted. The strikes in the large cities afforded the anarchist element an opportunity which it could not create or bring about itself. Being destructive in everything, these men could not construct an opportunity, but on May 1 they found one ready-made. They availed themselves of it in Chicago, and sought to turn a peaceful, law-abiding strike into a revolution, which they, in their short-sighted view of the case, supposed would spread throughout the whole country. The strike for eight hours would not have succeeded had the whole power of the Federation and the Knights of Labor been directed toward that end.

The conditions under which labor operated were not favorable; the education among workingmen had not passed its A, B, C; manufacturers, in dread of the result, were shutting down, and no hours of labor for a time seemed more probable than eight or ten hours. Until men are made to understand the question, and know its full bearing upon their interests, they will work ten, twelve and fifteen hours a day whenever the opportunity is offered to them. One has only to witness the avidity with which the chance to work overtime is taken advantage of in our large cities to know that poverty is a far more powerful factor in shaping the actions of men than principle. A few callings succeeded in establishing the eight-hour plan at certain points, but the same line of work in other cities continued to operate on the ten-hour plan, and the inevitable result could not be otherwise than a return to the long-hour workday in all of the establishments throughout the country.

Owing to the phenomenal increase in membership, and the consequent accumulation of business at the headquarters of the Knights of Labor, the General Master Workman found it necessary to issue a call for a special session of the General Assembly. The delegates assembled in Cleveland, Ohio, on May 25, 1886, and remained in session until June 3. The chief business before the convention was to discuss and take action on the question of strikes and boycotts into which the Order had been plunged during the few months intervening between the closing of the Hamilton session and the 1st of May. On motion of Robert Schilling of Milwaukee, Wis., a series of resolutions were presented to the body and adopted, in which the actions of the General Executive Board and the General Master Workman, since the Hamilton session, were approved and indorsed.

Not a dissenting vote was cast against the resolutions. The vote was all the more significant from the fact that the delegates to the special session at Cleveland were the same as those who had attended the regular session the previous October. Frank K. Foster, whose name appears in the resolutions adopted by the Federation of Trades, was a representative to the Hamilton and Cleveland sessions, and it is presumed that, if he were dissatisfied with the action of the General Master Workman on the eight-hour movement of May 1, he would have recorded his vote in opposition to the resolutions by which the course of that officer was officially indorsed.

While the convention was in session at Cleveland, a Chicago manufacturer, Edwin Norton, was present at the invitation of the General Master Workman and read a paper on the eight-hour movement, in which he outlined a plan for the gradual introduction of the system. His remarks were well received and left a strong impression on the minds of the representatives, but the exciting scenes enacted at that session in the controversy with the trade unions of the country took up the time and attention of the members of the convention and left them but little time for thought on such an important issue as was there presented to them. The recent fiasco at Chicago and the ill-feeling which existed throughout the country between employers and employes created the impression that no immediate steps should be taken in the direction of securing a reduction in the hours of labor, and the convention adjourned without taking action on the plan proposed by Mr. Norton.

When the next regular session of the General Assembly convened at Richmond, Va., in October, 1886, the body was so large and unwieldy that it could not transact, in a satisfactory manner, all the business which was presented to it by the assembled representatives of the Order throughout the country. Six hundred and fifty-eight men and women assembled to legislate for a half-million members. Many of them had not been initiated into the Order six weeks, and knew absolutely nothing about its principles. They could not take action on everything that was presented, and, although they were as intelligent, respectable and progressive an assemblage of men and women as ever met on the American continent, their lack of knowledge of the routine work of the Order placed them at a disadvantage in legislating for its future.

The General Master Workman in his address, referring to the eight-hour question, used the following words:

The eight-hour strike, which took place May 1, was not successful except in cases where employers and employes were acting in harmony, or where employers were willing to adopt the plan. In many cases the old system of working long hours has been revived. The Federation of Trades recommended May 1, but adopted or suggested no definite plan by which the short-hour system could be inaugurated. I cautioned our members against rushing into this movement. I had the right to do it, and am firm in the belief that had I not done so great loss would have been entailed upon vast numbers of our Assemblies. What I said in my secret circular of March 13 has been severely criticised, and I have been accused of opposing the eight-hour movement. No statement ever was further from the truth. I opposed the strike on May 1 because I knew that neither workmen nor employers were ready for it, because the education which must always precede intelligent action had not been given to those most in need of it, because no definite, business-like plan for the inauguration of the eight-hour-movement had been mapped out. In fact, no preparations had been made to put the plan, if it can be called a plan, into execution. These are the reasons why I opposed the movement in May, and for the same reasons do I still oppose it.

A reduction of the hours of labor is a necessity, and sooner or later must be had; but we must not forget that in many places the ten-hour plan has not yet been adopted. It may do very well for an organization which looks after the interests of but one craft or calling to neglect those who stand most in need of help, but a Knight of Labor must never close his eyes to the wants of the humblest of his fellow-creatures.

The very discussion of the sudden introduction of the eight-hour plan injured business, so much so that in many places men were reduced to half-time or thrown out of employment altogether. Millions of dollars' worth of work was left undone because of the uncertainty in regard to taking contracts or in making engagements to perform work. Never was it more clearly demonstrated that "An injury to one is the concern of all" than in the movement I am speaking of. The house-builder, through uncertainty as to how many hours of labor his employes would work for him, made no contracts to erect buildings, and the carpenter was thrown out of employment; the man who made the window-glass, the man who made the nails—in fact, every man or woman engaged in the manufacture of articles which go to build or furnish a house—suffered through the attempt to enforce the eight-hour system on May 1. The move was in the right direction, but the time and circumstances were not suitable.

Before the eight-hour plan is adopted the Knights of Labor and the trade unions of America must lay aside their jealousies and differences, come together, name a day on which to put the plan into execution, adopt the plan of action, which must be gradual and such as will not inflict injury upon either employer or workman. The plan presented by Mr. Norton of Chicago to the special session of the General Assembly at Cleveland is a good one in nearly every particular, and, if the workingmen's organizations and the manufacturers' associations agree upon putting such a plan into practice, it can be done without a jar or friction. No workingman need strike, nor need business be unsettled. Why should it not be done? Either adopt a plan for the perfection of this idea or else place it in the hands of the incoming General Executive Board, with instructions to perform the duty. If we do neither, let us strike the twenty-first declaration from our Preamble, and no longer proclaim to the world that we are in favor of eight hours for a day's labor.

No action was taken on the address of the General Master Workman except to approve of it and place it in the hands of appropriate committees for action. The Order of the Knights of Labor could not, through its General Officers, take any action on the eight-hour movement on May 1, 1886. At the time when they should be preparing, had they been so instructed, they were kept busy day and night in managing and settling the numerous strikes which followed the publication of the false statements concerning the strength, aims and objects of the Order. The Southwest strike was in progress during the two months preceding the eight-hour strike; the officers were taken up in the vain attempt to assimilate and educate the incoming tide of humanity which looked to the organization for relief rather than to their own efforts in the organization in behalf of all. That the course of the General Master Workman on the eight-hour movement was approved by the General Assembly was made apparent when his re-election came to him without opposition.

With the exception of keeping the eight-hour question prominently before the members in the Preamble of the Order, the Knights of Labor have done but little during the last two years. On April 7, 1888, the General Master Workman again directed the attention of the organization to the question, and recommended that municipalities, towns, cities, etc., take up the question and introduce the short-hour system on streets, roadways, bridges and other public works. He said that inasmuch as the majority of citizens in each municipality was made up of workers, it followed that the employers of labor on streets and public works generally were workers, and, if they did not take interest enough in the matter to establish the eight-hour system among their own employes, they could not consistently ask their employers to reduce the hours of toil in workshops and factories. The concluding lines of that article were:

The workingmen and the common people generally are the rulers in our cities and towns, and they should at once begin to make their power felt in the matter of shortening the hours of labor of the employes of these cities and towns. The Order need not be made a political machine to do this. Do not be deterred from making the attempt by having it said that you have no right as an Order to mix in politics. The Order must not be dragged into partisan politics, but our members should take an active part as CITIZENS in the discharge of their duty at the polls, and afterward by voting for men who favor shortening the hours of labor of employes in municipalities. Begin at once to perfect a practical plan of operation looking to the inauguration of the eight-hour day. Pass no resolutions declaring that you will do it on such a day ; pass no resolutions of any kind ; but work on the plan, and when the time comes to put it in operation it can be done without resolutions. Consult employers, get their views, arrange with them for meetings to perfect plans, and make an attempt to bring about a better feeling between workingmen and employers than has existed for some time back. It is true that many employers will not condescend to meet with or talk to their employes. Purse-proud worms, who are to be classed among the "ignorant rich," will live to stand in their own and the community's light for ages to come; but the world does not move around them. The day is coming in this land when the employer who has the manhood, the patriotism and the sense to talk in a straight-forward way to his employes will be entitled to, and will receive, more of honor and wealth than the selfish fellow upon whom fortune has showered riches and nothing else, except it be an ill-nature.

Up to the present time the work among Knights of Labor has been purely educational. The rapid accumulation of products of all kinds and the consequent suspensions of workmen until the accumulated products are consumed tend to show that the machine is fast taking the place of the man, and that, if the community is to reap any benefits from the introduction of machinery, the man must be protected and permitted to earn his livelihood by honest toil instead of spending one-half of his time in idleness. Idleness never consumes the product of toil. The greater the number of persons employed the greater will be the amount of currency which will circulate in the community, and the greater the extent of the circulating medium the greater will be the consumption of that which man produces. The question is an important one, and, while the writer believes that to introduce the short-hour plan among the mechanics of the land would be but to medicate the symptoms without touching the seat of the disease, he favors it strongly in order to give men more time to study how to eradicate the disease, root and branch.

At its last convention, held in St. Louis, Mo., December, 1888, the American Federation of Labor took action on the subject. The following, taken from the report of the meeting, shows what was done:

REPORT OF THE SPECIAL COMMITTEE ON THE EIGHT-HOUR WORKDAY.

ST. LOUIS, Mo., December 14, 1888.

To the President and Representatives of the American Federation of Labor:

We, your committee appointed to draft a plan for the accomplishment of the eight-hour law, respectfully state that we have very carefully considered the question, and will say that we heartily indorse the sentiment expressed and recognize the great necessity of securing a reduction in the hours of labor, and believe it within the possibilities of accomplishment.

WHEREAS, The advancement of science, the development of machinery and the ever-increasing sway of man over the forces of nature have enormously increased the productive capacity of society and made it possible to supply all material wants with a greatly decreased expenditure of the labor forces; and

WHEREAS, The length of the working day of the toiler has not been decreased in a just proportion to the effectiveness of labor.

Resolved, That the American Federation of Labor, in convention assembled, does hereby assert the right of the wage-workers of America to a larger control of their time and greater leisure for the enjoyment of the benefits of this nineteenth century of civilization.

Resolved, That we call on organized labor throughout the country to exert their every effort for the accomplishment of a reduction in the number of hours for the laboring class. Hence your committee most respectfully makes the following recommendation: That the incoming Executive Council shall arrange upon Washington's Birthday, 1889, simultaneous mass-meetings in all cities of the country, such meetings to be addressed by speakers appointed by authority of the Executive Council; that on Independence Day, July 4, the same action under the control of the Executive Council shall be pursued; and that on Labor Day, 1889, a like action be again taken, to be followed upon the succeeding Washington's Birthday, 1890, by another series of grand simultaneous mass-meetings upon that question. This is to conclude the period of agitation. The Executive Council shall also gather statistics from all the organizations in order to ascertain what hours prevail among such organizations, how many members will be affected, the condition of their finances, and approximately what financial support would be required. The Executive Council shall also prepare printed circulars, which are to be issued to all manufacturing firms in the country, requesting them to meet representatives of this organization in conference, so that a friendly arrangement of a reduction in the working hours may, if possible, be effected.

In addition to the agitation afforded by means of the mass-meetings above suggested, we also enjoin upon the Executive Council the propriety of issuing a pamphlet giving a thorough exposition of the question of reducing the hours of labor.

Your committee was unable to agree upon selecting a fixed date for the practical enforcement of a general demand for eight hours, thinking that the setting of a certain date for such an extraordinary effort for a practical demand can be best agreed upon by the convention rather than by this committee.

Respectfully submitted,

J. S. KIRCHNER, *Chairman.*
F. K. FOSTER.
WM. H. KLIVER.
(Signed)   WILLIAM MARTIN.
ALEX. JOHNSON.
HENRY EMRICH.
WM. J. DILLON, *Secretary.*

It was ordered that the report be acted on section by section.

All the sections were unanimously adopted as reported by the committee, excepting the last clause fixing the date for inaugurating the eight-hour system.

Delegate Blackmore moved the date be fixed at June 1, 1890.

Delegate Perry offered to amend as follows:

That the matter of fixing the date be referred to the incoming Executive Council, with the following instructions:

The question be referred to affiliated unions for a vote and returns be submitted not later than six months, and the effort be confined to a union of those industries whose interests and methods of work are similar which shall cast the largest percentage of majorities on their membership in favor of an eight-hour workday , and the unions, or associated interests so designated, shall receive the support of all unions in affiliation with the American Federation of Labor, and the same rule to apply to the next in majority of votes cast when the first union, or associated interests, shall have met the issue and established the eight-hour workday.

Delegate La Vine offered an amendment to the amendment that the eight-hour movement be confined to the building trades exclusively.

Delegate Applehagen offered a substitute to fix the date at May 1, 1890.

After an exhaustive and well-tempered discussion, participated in by the bulk of the delegates, as to the ways and means to carry on the movement, the previous question was ordered.

The vote was first taken on the proposition to fix the date at June 1, 1890, which was lost.

The amendment offered by Delegate Perry was next voted on, and was defeated.

Amendment offered by Delegate La Vine, to confine the movement to the building trades, was next in order, and was not sustained.

The substitute offered by Delegate Applehagen, to fix the date at May 1, 1890, prevailed by a large majority.

The question recurred on the report of the committee as amended, and on this the ayes and nays were ordered.

Ayes—Ackerman, Appel, Applehagen, Anderson, Bechtold, Blackmore, Cain, Daley, Dillon, Donnelly, Delabar, Evans, Fildew, Fitzpatrick, Foster, Forsberg, Goldwater, Gompers, Haller, Hasson, Hill, Holland, Johnson, Kliver, Kirchner, La Vine, McGregor, McLaughlin, Mahoney, Martin, Nutt, Ogg, Penna, Shields, Volz, Weihe, Werdes and Weaver. Total, 38 ayes.

Nays—Archie, Bower, Emrich, Ives, Lake, Perry, Taylor and Reinhardt. Total, 8 nays.

Excused—Miller.

Amid tumultuous cheers and enthusiastic applause, the motion to adopt the committee's report and fix the date for the inauguration of the eight-hour workday at May 1, 1890, was declared adopted by a vote of 38 ayes to 8 nays.

An agitation is now going on in trade-union circles looking to the establishment of the eight-hour workday on May 1, 1890. Whether it is the intention to inaugurate a general strike on that day is not stated either in the resolutions adopted by the Federation or by any of the speakers who address meetings on the subject. The plan of action to be pursued is not outlined as yet, and beyond the lines of educational work nothing has been settled upon.

The reason why men are forced to work long hours to-day is because machinery controls mankind. It guides our destinies, and its wonderful achievements make it possible for the man who owns machinery to control those who manage it as effectually as though the slave ship had dumped its load of human chattels on the floor of the factory. To talk of reducing the hours of labor without reducing the power of machinery to oppress instead of benefit is a waste of energy. What men gain through a reduction of hours will be taken from them in another way while the age of iron continues. It is certain that eight hours each day are sufficient for man to labor. He should not be required to toil longer than that; but when the absolute ownership of machinery and the unlimited control of land are allowed to continue for the aggrandizement of the individual instead of for the welfare of the people, it will always be in the power of those who control to render the lot of the workman so burdensome that he will consent to violate the laws of the land and the laws of organizations in order to earn sufficient bread to sustain life. The advocates of the eight-hour system must go beyond a reduction of the number of hours a man must work and labor for the establishment of a just and humane system of land ownership, control of machinery, railroads and telegraphs, as well as an equitable currency system, before he will be able to retain the vantage-ground gained when the hours of labor are reduced to eight per day, as called for in the twenty-first resolution of the Preamble of the Knights of Labor.

PAPER READ BEFORE THE CLEVELAND CONVENTION

By EDWIN NORTON, Esq.

General Master Workman and Members of the General Assembly Knights of Labor:

GENTLEMEN:—Through the kindness and upon the invitation of your General Master Workman, Mr. Powderly, I have the pleasure of addressing you briefly at this time upon a subject which is of vital importance to us all.

The question of shorter hours for a working day is one that has been before this nation for a number of years, and which is constantly increasing in public interest. It has received the careful study of many of the greatest thinkers among the ranks of our workingmen, employers and political leaders.

The politicians have, to all appearances, thus far had the best of it, for they have succeeded in enacting laws by which the legal number of hours for a working day have been reduced to eight, both in the United States government and in several of our States. This they have done with but little trouble or expense apparently to either themselves or their constituents.

But how has it been when those most directly interested in this important question have undertaken to bring about the change? As long ago as the year 1867 united effort was made to reduce the number of working hours per day, but, so far as we are informed, without permanent success.

Meanwhile various labor organizations have taken up the subject, and it has grown with their growth until the present year, which was fixed upon to again make the attempt to introduce the new order of things.

The result thus far is already a matter of history, and to-day the eyes of the entire nation are turned toward this city, watching with great interest to see what action will be taken upon this subject by this honorable Assembly gathered here as representatives of the largest body of organized workmen known in the history of the world.

The events of the past month in this country have, I think, clearly demonstrated that the only practicable solution of this important problem lies in the direction of peace and harmony. Appeals to violence can but end in opposition and delay, and it is apparent that the published principles of your Order, if faithfully lived up to by all its members, have in them the elements which will finally lead to a settlement of existing differences, upon a sure and lasting basis.

The losses by reason of the strikes which have taken place during the past few weeks are estimated by *Bradstreet's* to be in wages to employes alone upward of three millions of dollars, while the losses to the general business of the country aggregate the enormous sum of thirty millions of dollars, and it is questionable if even this large amount will cover the entire loss from all causes attributable to the strikes. These figures would indicate beyond doubt that the establishment of shorter hours, which is partially the cause of these strikes and lockouts mentioned, can only be found through a system in which strife and disturbance to the business of the country shall have no part; but rather where thoughtful, conservative and level-headed men, from among both employers and employed, shall take counsel together and act in harmony to eliminate, if possible, all sources of trouble between labor and capital, and by mutual concessions save that which is otherwise lost in strife, and aim to bring about a more perfect understanding of the conditions and relation which they bear to one another.

I think it will be admitted by all present that from the standpoint of the employer of labor, as well as that of capital invested in manufacturing industry, this question of fewer hours is one of the greatest importance in that it affects a vital point—the cost of production. This in very many cases has been reduced to a minimum by many years of patient work on the part of the employer, by thorough organization and subdivision of the labor employed, by the use of the most perfect mechanical appliances that thorough knowledge of his wants and ample capital will buy. Possibly he has seen from small beginnings his business expand into a large establishment, employing at fair wages more and more men each year, finding them steady employment, but being obliged to watch carefully every source of loss in order to guard against failure; the line drawn between success and failure being in many cases extremely fine. Such an employer, when confronted with a demand for a sudden change of all his business methods, such as is involved in a reduction of the hours of labor from ten to eight at one sweep, can see but one end to it, and that end is failure. Most men who are conducting manufacturing industries are busy men, who cannot take the time necessary to a careful study into matters of general public welfare without the risk of neglecting their own affairs; and therefore they do not, as a rule, pay as much attention as they should to matters that concern them very closely, and are suspicious of any change, being fearful that the result may prove disastrous.

If the question of shorter hours were simply one of sentiment, or one in which the employer could take sides in favor of without fear of endangering the very existence of his business through competition of those unwilling to adopt the plan, there is but little doubt that almost without exception they would vote in favor of it. If this is true, then it follows that, providing some safe plan can be devised for bringing about the change, it would not meet with very strong opposition even at first; and that, as it became more familiar to employers, it would receive their active support and co-operation.

It is now generally conceded that American labor-saving machinery has within the past few years revolutionized the processes of manufacture in most lines, and so increased the capacity of our country to manufacture goods of superior quality at much less cost than that of any other nation. It is also claimed that the extended use of this machinery has made it more difficult for good and competent mechanics and workmen to obtain employment, and that there are now a great number of skilled workers throughout the country quite unable to get work at any price. This may be true; but I do not attribute this fact to the use of machinery, for, so far as my own experience goes (being engaged in the use as well as the manufacture of labor-saving machinery), there is, and has been for some time past, a scarcity of skilled mechanics who can understand and speak the English language; but that the source of trouble lies in the fact that we are overcrowded with men from all foreign countries, who, many of them, have learned mechanical trades at home, where the practice is quite different from ours, and, having heard of this wonderful "free country" across the water, have determined to come here and get a portion of the wealth and prosperity that they are led to believe are to be had here for the asking. They arrive, and being usually out of money, and frequently without friends, are in no condition to dictate to employers what wages shall be paid them; and being unfamiliar with our language and customs, as well as with our machines and mechanical appliances to a great extent, they accept whatever wages may be offered, and thus enter into active competition with our American workmen; and to-day this element has grown to enormous proportions, and is constantly increasing from year to year, and stands squarely across the pathway of any change which looks forward to the betterment of the condition of the laboring classes of our people.

This has indeed been a "free country" in every sense of the word, and we have been overstocked with foreign labor of almost every nationality, who have come here much faster than they could be assimilated, even in our rapidly-growing country.

Many employers have encouraged this state of things in the past. Having some difficulty or misunderstanding with their workmen, they have concluded to employ "foreign help," and have filled their establishments with men of the class described above, to the exclusion of our own citizens; and in many cases they have found out their error when it was too late to recede. Again, in this too rapid immigration to our country, we have received from Europe a class of men, who, bred under the iron rule of monarchical forms of government, have developed into apostles and teachers of anarchy and socialism; and coming here with no care for our free institutions and a bitter hatred of all forms of established government, they are spreading among our people the ethics of destruction, and seizing upon every opportunity to destroy what all the world is trying build up, and thus create anarchy and ruin in our land in the name of "labor troubles." They have no interest whatever in "labor." They are the enemies of all—both employers and employed—and should be given a wide berth by organized workmen, as they are by all organized governments.

I am of the opinion that we can make no real and substantial progress toward the introduction of shorter hours without the active co-operation of your organization with that of other labor and trade unions, acting in unison with a national organization of employers of labor, to bring about the change gradually, step by step, with ample time between each change to enable business to become adjusted upon the new basis.

The plan which will be submitted for your consideration includes the gradual but fixed reduction of the hours of labor without a corresponding reduction of present wages, to take effect as soon as the proper organization can be effected and a sufficient number of members enrolled to insure success.

Workmen to be protected by the union of employers by an agreement on their part, among themselves, to give the preference, for a certain specified time during which this change is being brought about and firmly established, to workmen who were residents of the United States at the time the new rule is adopted, unless meanwhile the surplus of unemployed labor in this country is exhausted.

In this plan it would appear that a fair and equitable basis of compromise would be reached, which ought to lead to a permanent settlement of all the differences of opinion regarding shorter hours which now exist between employer and employe, and lead to a much better condition of affairs for our American workmen. I propose also that we go one step further and refuse to employ for the same length of time any foreigner who, having lived in this country for two years (the time prescribed by law), does not declare his intention to become an American citizen and make proper application for papers of naturalization. Employers have in the past without doubt, as a rule, taken too little care to impress upon their employes, by force of example and otherwise, the importance and value of a knowledge of our country and its institutions, such as can only be obtained by a performance of the duties of citizenship. Those who come to our country with no expectation of becoming citizens should not, under existing circumstances, have all the privileges and consideration extended to those who do. And thus aiding our workmen by protecting them from this foreign competition during the few years required to bring about shorter hours, other benefits would naturally result in the nature of an increased interest in the welfare of our country, which would be taken by all, and a consequent better government than can possibly exist under other circumstances.

We should not discriminate against any nationality nor individual who would accept the conditions offered. All should be made heartily welcome who intend to become citizens of this great and good country. From present indications it would appear that we have room for no others here upon any terms whatsoever; and, upon the theory that "self-preservation is the first law of nature," there can be no question that we are justified in this course of action. I firmly believe that, unless the employers of labor in this country unitedly take up this subject, it never can be otherwise brought about. The politicians dare not ; but a national union of employers, aided by organized labor, who would be quite as much interested as employers in the enforcement of the rule, could without doubt make a success of the undertaking.

A movement of this kind, having a national scope, would remove all the objections that naturally arise against an attempt to bring about a change in one locality, for the reason that our country is so united by railway and other means of communication that one section cannot be affected without a corresponding loss or a corresponding gain in other sections. We are no longer limited in our competition to any one locality. Manufacturers in one section are closely watching those in others, and are ever ready to take advantage of any industrial disturbance to improve their condition. The only means of regulating this question would be to have them all united in one organization, working for a common cause. Their interests would lie in the same direction, and, therefore, a national union might accomplish with perfect ease what otherwise would doubtless end in failure and loss to all if attempted.

A national union of manufacturers, working in harmony·with your organization to bring about this change of hours, would naturally do much to create and maintain a friendly spirit between employer and employed throughout the country, which in itself would be an end worth seeking, as it would be of great benefit to all, tending to a better understanding of all questions of public interest that might arise affecting either employer or workman. All such matters would be more easily adjusted than at present, and thus a peaceful way be opened up for the introduction of whatever would be of general public benefit.

We hear it said by some employers, as an argument against shorter hours of labor, that it would be an injury to the workingman to have them, for the reason that he would, "if afforded more leisure time, only spend it in the saloons," and not with his family nor in improving his condition, and that thus what was thought to be a benefit would prove a curse to him. I do not believe that this, as a rule, is true. I do not believe that any greater proportion of workmen spend their time in saloons than of employers. There is, without doubt, far too much time of both classes spent in this manner, but I believe, and so far as my own experience goes I know, that this statement is not true. It is the excuse of selfishness, and not worthy of consideration. Because evil exists, those who have no interest in it should not be made to suffer. Far better take some united action for wiping out the evil. A little more friendly interest in this direction shown by employers for the general welfare of their workmen will, in my judgment, reduce materially the profits of the saloons.

The fact that all the manufacturing industries of our country are now based upon the ten-hour day, and that this system has prevailed for many years, should cause us to fully realize that a sudden and radical change would so upset values as to bring about a demoralization which would be terrible in its consequences; while the same result may be eventually brought about in a gradual manner, so that each change will be slight in its consequences, and that there will be no reaction nor cause to regret having undertaken it; for in no case is the motto of your noble Order more true than in this: "That an injury to one (employer) is an injury to all (his employes)." This fact should be more forcibly impressed upon the minds of all.

If, as we are informed by the various labor unions, workmen are willing to accept reduced wages in order to bring about a shorter working day, and in order that their fellow-workmen now unemployed may find work, it would appear as if they would still more readily indorse and support a plan which would check the supply from foreign lands from coming to our shores until such time in the future as our present surplus of unemployed workmen now here could find work at profitable wages.

There have been propositions made looking to the imposition of a tax upon all foreigners who come to this country, in hopes that this will stop the present ruinous competition from that source. But we have no laws at present which sanction such a course, and before they can be enacted we must of necessity educate public opinion up to that point where they will ask Legislators to pass some laws which will fit the case. This we know to be a slow and tedious process. And even if a reasonable tax were by law imposed upon these people, it could only serve to slightly retard the stream of arrivals, and as soon as shorter hours obtained a foothold here, with a virtual increase of wages, they would be likely to come in spite of any reasonable tax which might be imposed as a restriction, and thus our army of unemployed would be increased, and any benefits arising from the shorter hours or increased pay for our workmen be lost by reason of the presence and competition of these foreign workmen.

The more practical plan would appear to be the one suggested. Let employers unite and organize, and publish to the world that "We have for many years taken in all the workmen they have sent us, and made them welcome; but that for a few coming years we cannot continue to do so, for the reason that we have already here large numbers of unemployed, and we think it fair to state to them that we cannot employ any more new-comers for the present until our surplus of unemployed have been provided with places at paying wages." We need not restrict those who cultivate the land, for we have ample room for all these in building up the wonderful broad and fertile acres of the West.

Such action, if generally adopted, when it became known abroad, could not fail to have the desired effect, and put a check upon the coming here of these workmen, who, if contemplating immigration, would hesitate to take the risk of earning a living in a strange land when they had been informed in advance they would not be welcome. In any case it would be better than to first tax them to the limit of their capacity to pay, and then bring them here without means of self-support, which would simply be making bad matters worse.

The opponents of shorter hours argue that a less number of hours for work would be impracticable, and cause great loss, from the fact that expensive plants of machinery would lie idle a portion of each present working day, and that this would work to the detriment of business. My answer to this would be that if at certain seasons there should be a demand for more goods than could possibly be manufactured in the regular working day, there would be no law against a reasonable amount of overtime. Workmen are generally reasonable in such matters; and I believe, when operating under a mutual agreement to make a reduced number of hours the standard for a day's work, that for such overtime as it was found necessary to run they would be willing to accept the regular per diem wages, and not insist upon a higher rate for such overtime, as frequently prevails in the present ten-hour day. The reason for this lies in the fact that the shorter hours without reduced pay are an equivalent to quite an advance above present rates; and were it understood that labor would be willing to perform such over-work as was necessary at regular current wages, it would go far to reconcile employers to adopt the change. The idea of having to increase the wages for overtime is one that looks unreasonable from the employer's standpoint, and I would suggest that at least up to ten hours no overcharge be made beyond the regular daily rate of pay.

Another argument against shorter hours is this: that if the rate of wages should remain the same as at present workmen would not be practically benefited by reason of the increased cost of living, caused by higher prices which would neces-sarily be charged for food, clothing, rents and all other living expenses.

To this I would reply that, if a gradual and not a sudden reduction of the hours is accepted by labor, values would be but slightly affected at any one time, and all branches of trade would have ample time to prepare for each change, and so adjust their business as to avoid the losses that must ensue from sudden and sweeping changes; while at the same time, wages remaining as now, workmen and their families would not be cut down in their ability to buy and consume goods. A reduction of one-half hour per day would add to the cost of manufact-ured goods five per cent. on account of labor, and probably not more than two and one-half per cent. in addition for interest on idle plant, rent, insurance, taxes and other expenses, which would be the same for a short as for a long day. It may be fairly considered, then, that seven and one-half per cent. would be added to the cost of living for each half-hour of reduced work, providing the capacity to produce goods cheaply is not changed in the least.

Now any person at all familiar with the inventive skill of the American nation will find it hard to believe that we have reached our limit in this respect. There is no doubt that each year a large portion of this increased cost would be met by improved methods, which would ultimately enable the amount of work formerly performed in ten hours to be turned out in the shorter day; and if this is true, then the laws of supply and demand would see that consumers did not pay more for goods than they are worth.

I am aware that reduced cost of production would not apply in all cases, and we must therefore concede that somewhat higher prices would have to be paid for the necessaries of life as a condition of shorter hours. But it is true that the present purchasing power of money is much greater than at any previous time in the history of the country, and the advance would not be felt so much on that account; while dividing the change into yearly installments would make it bearable by all. And if shorter hours are to be the rule in this country, this plan would seem to point out a safe means for bringing it about.

As having an important bearing on this question, it should not be forgotten that all alike, employers and workmen, cannot fail to be greatly benefited, should this plan under consideration be adopted, from the fact that there would be no further cause for strikes and lockouts to obtain this end, with their attend-ant losses, which fall upon all classes alike; that a business policy would be marked out for several years to come, which would give confidence to capital to invest in new enterprises; that differences of opinion between employers and workmen would be more readily adjusted than at present; and, finally, that no possible harm could arise from a trial of shorter hours, under the conditions named, even though it should fail to possess all the good points herein set forth.

I will not occupy more of your valuable time to-day in further explanation, but, with your kind permission, will read a rough draft for an organization of employers, which has for its object the purposes which I have described as fully as possible in the limited time which I have occupied.

Should these suggestions meet with approval by your honorable Assembly, that fact would, no doubt, go far to place the matter favorably before the Ameri-can people; and with an earnest wish for the betterment of the condition of all the workmen of our land, and thanking you for your kind attention, I will now read the circular mentioned, and respectfully submit the same for your further consideration :

TO AMERICAN MANUFACTURERS.

Believing that a permanent settlement of the existing disturbed condition of business in our country can only be reached by a reasonable understanding between employers and employes, and that a gradual reduction of the present hours of labor under proper protection and restrictions will not be detrimental to the best interests of all; and that during the gradual scaling down of the working hours, which would mean a corresponding increase of pay, our workmen should be protected by the united action of their employers from an influx of labor from foreign lands ; also, that a premium should be placed upon American citizenship in our workshops as well as in places of trust; and, also, that a basis should be found for ultimately reducing the working day to eight hours without disturbance to our manufacturers, and one which will meet with the co-operation of all labor organizations ; and in the belief that this course of action will meet with the approval of those who have the best interests of all our people at heart. Therefore, this union is formed for the perfecting and carrying out of the above purposes in the following manner :

Section 1. This organization shall be known as the "American Manufacturers' Union," and all manufacturers of any article throughout the United States shall be eligible to membership by signing the Constitution and such By-laws as may be adopted.

Sec. 2. The purposes of this organization shall be, first, united action on the part of manufacturers throughout the United States, looking to a gradual and fixed reduction of the present hours of labor, until eight hours for a working day (which is now the legal standard of the United States and of several States) have become the recognized rule throughout the country ; second, the protection of our workmen from the competition of foreigners, anxious to reap the benefit of their improved condition, by a refusal to employ during this period of change any persons who were not residents of the United States on the first day of January, 1887, unless, meanwhile we have exhausted the resources of our own country to furnish a supply of labor and, third, a refusal to employ after January 1, 1887, any persons whatsoever who, having lived long enough in this country to become citizens, do not willingly take steps to become such.

Sec. 3. This organization shall adopt the plan herein set forth on the first day of January, A. D. 1887, and it shall remain in force for five years, or until the thirty-first day of December, A. D. 1891, and as much longer as a majority of its members shall desire.

Sec. 4. All members of this union shall agree that during the year 1887 nine and one-half hours shall constitute a day's work; and that during the year 1888 nine hours shall constitute a day's work; and that during the year 1889 eight and one-half hours shall constitute a day's work; and that during and after the year 1890 the present United States standard of eight hours shall be recognized by all members of this union throughout the country as a legal day's work.

Sec. 5. Members of this union shall exact from all persons in their employment an agreement to accept the conditions herein set forth during the above period of time, and it shall be understood that no corresponding reduction of present wages shall be made on account of the reduced hours of work.

Sec. 6. This action shall not affect farm laborers, but relates to mechanics and skilled laborers of every kind.

ANARCHY AND THE KNIGHTS.

Deep as I felt, and stern and strong,
In words which Prudence smothered long,
My soul spoke out against the wrong.—*Whittier.*

The feeling of discontent which became apparent among the working people of the United States in 1886 presented an opportunity to a class of men, who affected to be "leaders of thought and action," to come to the front and take part in directing the current of industrial affairs into a course which they hoped would bring about a revolution, destroy the governmental structure and reduce the political affairs of the nation to a condition bordering on chaos. For years prior to 1886, whenever a labor meeting was called in any large city, a number of men, calling themselves socialists, would flock to the gathering, and either attempt to officer it or cause it to break up in disorder. To do either one was considered a victory by the "radical element," as they were pleased to term themselves. Socialism, as defined by Webster, is:

A theory of society which advocates a more precise, orderly and more harmonious arrangement of the social relations of mankind than that which has hitherto prevailed.

The definition of Webster and the practice of many who call themselves socialists diverge at every point. It is true that many men became identified with the socialist movement with a view to perfecting the arrangement of a more harmonious condition of society; but there are socialists who are not in harmony with the Websterian interpretation, and soon dispel the doubts of those who join them for the purpose of advocating such methods. The greater part of those who profess to be socialists, and who became prominent in the industrial affairs of late years, were anarchists, and when the time came to make public their real intentions they cast odium on the name of socialism and misconstrued its very nature by advocating anarchy as a means of settling the disputes between labor and capital. Many people believe that there is no difference between anarchy and socialism, but there is a wider line of demarcation between these two schools than now exists, or ever has existed, between the Democratic and Republican Parties. Socialism would improve the arrangement of social affairs; anarchy would destroy every vestige of order and effect the opposite of socialism. It is true that many who professed to speak for socialism knew absolutely nothing about it in its higher sense, and in advocating the extreme measures which they did drove thousands away from them. Anarchy is susceptible of two definitions. The one given it by Webster is:

Want of government; the state of society where there is no law or supreme power, or where the laws are not efficient, and individuals do what they please with impunity; political confusion.

That definition is more in harmony with the views of the extreme socialist than the definition given of socialism, and is practiced by them on all occasions, and in doing so they distort the aims and motives of the real socialist. Anarchy, as described by its apostles, is a state of society in which the people will be good enough to live without the restraining influences of law. It is contemplated that rules and restrictions for the government of mankind may be dispensed with as useless. Each member of society will have so high a regard for the welfare and happiness of his fellow-man as not to do anything that will intrude upon or injure his neighbor. In a word, no rule, no law, is the dream of the ideal anarchist. Society, as it now exists, is to be dissolved. Those whose tastes are congenial will form themselves into groups, small at first but increasing in numbers as the acquaintanceship extends. The groups are to be governed by the decrees of nature, and, being expected to live in strict accord with the rules which nature prescribes, no violence or injustice will be done to any portion of humanity.

Such is anarchy in the abstract, at least that is anarchy as described by its advanced teachers; but it is not the kind that is practiced by their disciples. It may be thought that what I say of anarchism is too harsh, but it will be borne in mind that I am dealing with it as I found it, and not in the abstract. With its theories I have nothing to do, but of its doings I have had some knowledge, and speak of it only so far as that knowledge extends. Those who doubt the destructive tendencies of the anarchists will have their doubts dispelled on reading the following from John Most's "Beast of Property," a pamphlet published by the New Haven Group of the International Workingmen's Association:

Everything, therefore, is ripe for communism. It is only necessary to remove its interested inveterate enemies, the capitalists and their abettors. During this crisis the people will become sufficiently prepared for the struggle. Everything will then depend on the presence of a well-trained revolutionary nucleus at all points which is fit and able to crystallize around itself the masses of the people, driven to rebellion by misery and want of work, and which can then apply the mighty forces so formed to the destruction of all existing hostile institutions.

Therefore organize and enlarge everywhere the socialistic revolutionary party before it is too late. The victory of the people over its tyrants and vampires will then be certain.

Instead of here developing a *program*, it is, under present conditions, of far greater importance to sketch what the proletariat must probably do immediately after the victorious battle to maintain its supremacy.

Most likely the following must be done : In every local community where the people have gained a victory, revolutionary committees must be constituted. These execute the decrees of the revolutionary army, which, re-enforced by the armed workingmen, now rule like a new conqueror of the world.

The former (present) system will be abolished in the most rapid and thorough manner if its supports—the *beasts of property* and horde of adherents—are annihilated. The case standing thus : If the people do not crush them they will crush the people, drown the revolution in the blood of the best, and rivet the chains of slavery more firmly than ever. Kill or be killed is the alternative. Therefore, massacres of the people's enemies must be instituted. All free communities enter into an offensive and defensive alliance during the continuance of the combat. Revolutionary communes must incite rebellion in the adjacent districts. The war cannot terminate until the enemy (the *beast of property*) has been pursued to its last lurking place and totally destroyed.

In order to proceed thoroughly in the economic sense all lands and so-called real estate, with everything upon it, as well as all movable capital, will be declared to be the property of the respective communes. Until the thorough harmonious reorganization of society can be effected, the proclamation of the following principles and measures might render satisfaction :

Every pending debt is liquidated. Objects of personal use which were pawned or mortgaged will be returned free. No rents will be paid. District committees on habitation, which will sit in permanence, allot shelter to those who are homeless, or who have inadequate or unhealthy quarters. After the great purification there will be no want for desirable homes.

Until every one can obtain suitable employment, the commune must guarantee to all the necessities of life. Committees on supplies will regulate the distribution of confiscated goods. Should there be lack of anything, which might be the case in respect to articles of food, these must be obtained by proper agents. Taking such things from neighboring great estates by armed columns of foragers would be a most expeditious way of furnishing them. * * * * * * All law books, court and police records, register of mortgage, deeds, bonds and all so-called *valuable documents* must be burned. * * * * * * Forced or procured marriages are unknown. Mankind has returned to the natural state, and love rules unconstrained.

Like all anarchists, Most shirks the responsibility of " developing a program." A program is distasteful to an anarchist, for the reason that it has the appearance of order. To develop a program would be to construct something, and as destruction is the chief aim of the anarchist, if not of anarchism, he will not do anything that is not in harmony with his tendency to destroy everything in the shape of law, rule and government, except such things as are prescribed by his own narrow, vindictive mind.

The anarchist in America is no more to be considered a part of the labor movement than the man who sits up nights to work his way into a bank vault that he may enrich himself from the earnings of others. The anarchist may consider that he works hard when preaching his doctrine of destruction. The bank robber must also work hard in order to succeed, but such exertions do not come under the head of " honest toil." Both are parallels.

The average anarchist is cowardly and deceitful. When he is asked to explain the principles of anarchy, he will give the definition which is advanced by the apostles of that school of thought. This he will do if those who surround him are not anarchists, but free him from such surroundings and he at once begins to rave in an incoherent manner of what will be done if anarchy once prevails. If he is confronted by the definition given by Webster of anarchy, he will charge Webster with being " an aristocrat, one of the bourgeoise; one who hates the proletariat." Take this same man to task on some other occasion with being a socialist, for he will claim that he is also a socialist, even though his every utterance gives the lie to his claim, and he will refer you to the definition given of socialism by Webster, and then defy you to show that there is anything wrong in it as he defines it.

It would be wrong to charge all socialists with being anarchists, or all anarchists with being in favor of the rule laid down by Webster; but those who come to the front as the mouth-pieces of socialism and anarchy advocate the use of force oftener than anything else, and as a consequence the country has learned to distrust the man who admits that he is a socialist, no matter how pure his intentions may be. This is the truth, no matter how much we may deplore it.

A cardinal principle with the rampant socialist and anarchist is to propagandize on every occasion that presents itself. If a new society of laboring men is established these extremists become members of it and attempt to force their ideas to the front. In canting phrase and with mock humility they will insinuate themselves into the good graces of men who would scorn them were they to disclose their real feelings, and, once they gain the good-will of such, they have inserted a wedge between the members of that society that sooner or later will drive them apart. The smooth-tongued advocate of anarchy seldom does anything himself toward furthering the ends of the movement he is a part and parcel of. He secures the services of dupes who do his bidding, either through loyalty to principle or ignorance. That they will play on the ignorance of workingmen is but too true; that they despise every effort to lift the pall of ignorance that is lowered over the fortunes of the toilers is also true. If the people become educated they will have no use for either anarchy or monopoly, and every step in that direction is fought down by both extremes.

In concluding a chapter on socialism, written September 1, 1884, Burnette G. Haskell said :

When the rising—which will be one of blind, wrathful, ignorant producers— comes, then must the socialists of America be prepared to unfurl the scarlet flag, and, with it in hand, head the assault as the leaders of the people, pointing out to them not only their wrongs, but their only salvation: " Free land, free tools and free money !"

Mr. Haskell should know how to voice the views of that school of anarchy that has shown its head in this country, for he was at that time one of the foremost men in that movement.

Writing for the ignorant and pandering to ignorance, that statement is capable of two interpretations, but its real meaning was that "the rising" was to be an armed rebellion against the establishment of law. It was to be composed of ignorant men, and as a consequence anything that would dispel ignorance would not meet with favor in the eyes of the leaders of anarchy. The "pernicious activity" of the anarchists made itself visible at every meeting of labor societies, and as an illustration I cannot do better than to quote from a letter written by Uriah S. Stephens on the subject. The letter was written August 19, 1879, while he was Grand Master Workman, and to a member of the Knights of Labor who had communicated with him on the subject of the interference of socialists. It reads:

> You must not allow the socialists to get control of your Assembly. They are simply disturbers, and only gain entrance to labor societies that they may be in better position to break them up. You cannot fathom them, for they are crafty, cunning and unscrupulous. I detest the name of socialism on account of the actions of the men who profess to believe in it. They rush to every gathering and attempt to man or officer it. Having done that, and having driven all decent men away, they are supremely happy in the delusion that they have spread their ideas still further. I have had an experience with them that you could not possibly have had, and I warn you against having anything to do with them either individually or as a body. They tear down and very seldom ever attempt to build up. They do nothing for the cause of labor, save to do it harm. If the socialists ever gain control of the * * * * * they will kill off the work of years. If they were sincere they would build up their own societies.

For the most part the meetings of anarchists are held under the roofs and influences of saloons, and it is only when exhilarated that they ever accomplish anything. There is no instance on record where they have ever done anything in the interest of reform, but in many places they have destroyed the hopes of men who were sorely tried, and who had almost gained what they were contending for when the incendiary speech of some anarchist turned public opinion, often very fickle, in an opposite direction.

During the telegraphers' strike in 1883 the leader of the International Workingmen's Association of the Pacific coast submitted to the group of which he was a member a proposition to destroy the property of the Western Union Company. A member of that organization, under date of August 18, 1887, writes the following:

> He informed certain members of the group that he had been requested by the telegraphers to furnish volunteers from the International Workingmen's Association for the purpose of destroying such property of the Western Union Telegraph Company as would be pointed out to them by a committee of strikers. After procuring the required number of strikers and they were ready at mid-

night to do the work assigned to them, they proceeded to his house and were informed that he was in bed, and that the order was countermanded. Each member began to see that had they proceeded without him, as he expected, they would doubtless have been arrested, as they believed it a trap for them.

This charge is made against the leader of that movement by men who were associated with him. It was not the International Work-ingmen's Association that would have suffered through such trans-actions, for these things could not be done without the knowledge of the police of San Francisco, and the odium would not attach to the anarchist society had the property been destroyed. The telegraphers would have been the victims. Such interference as that whenever a disturbance occurred had the effect of causing men, who were not connected with the labor movement in any way, to believe that it was the *bona-fide* labor societies that were responsible for the outrages that took place.

A man may advocate a "more precise, orderly and more harmoni-ous arrangement of the social relations of mankind" and be regarded with favor by all classes, but let such a person say that he is a social-ist, and what is known as the "better element" will raise its hands in horror and forever after shun him as they would a plague. I can conceive of no other subject concerning which so much ignorance is displayed as that of socialism, and those who display that ignorance do not do so because of a lack of education; they are willfully blind; they will not study it, but take their inspiration from the garbled reports of "socialist meetings," as they appear in the press. They judge of the aims and objects of socialism by those who, unfortunately for socialism, avow themselves to be advocates of that theory while belying their every utterance in their actions. Those who assert that socialism is destructive of law and order do not know what socialism is, for through its operations simpler, better, fewer and more humane laws than now exist would be in force, government would not disap-pear, but a more equitable form of government would prevail. The aim of socialism, in a word, is to make the world better.

In 1880 Osborne Ward, a socialist, lectured in Scranton to an out-door audience, and I presided at the meeting. Although not con-nected with the Socialistic Labor Party, I wished to hear all sides, and, therefore, presented Mr. Ward to his audience, and was well pleased with his exposition of the principles of the party he repre-sented. I did not in any way affiliate with the socialistic movement, but there were members of that organization who mistook my action in presiding at that meeting for approval of their doctrines, and it was published in their papers that I was a socialist.

In 1882 a member of the socialistic organization of New York City wrote to me asking that, as Mayor of Scranton and Grand Master Workman of the Knights of Labor, I issue a manifesto "declaring that all property is robbery." I gave a negative reply, and took occasion in doing so to state my position on the question of the kind of socialism that bubbled to the surface from the depths of the beer saloon. From that day began the obstruction of the anarchist element to the progress of the Knights of Labor. On every occasion they paraded themselves as the mouth-pieces of socialism and of the Knights of Labor.

On December 15, 1884, during the prevalence of very hard times throughout the country, I issued a secret circular to the Order in which I advised that a discussion be opened up on the eight-hour question, and, among other things, said :

The change is slowly but surely coming over the whole country. The workers, though for a time oppressed, must in the end profit by it. The discussion of the labor question takes up more of the time and attention of men in all walks of life at the present time than it ever did before. Men who have no sympathy with the toiler are being forced into the discussion, and converts to the cause of humanity are being made more rapidly than at any time in the world's history. Notwithstanding all this the number of the unemployed at the present time is very great and constantly increasing. Reduction in wages, suspension of men, stoppage of factories and furnaces are of daily occurrence. With such a state of affairs staring us in the face, a word of warning cannot be amiss. Indulge in no hasty or ill-advised action, no matter how great the provocation to strike against an injustice or a grievance of any kind. Count well the costs before taking action. Remember that the winter is upon us, the dull season of the year is at hand, the number of unemployed so great that the chances of filling the places of strikers are very numerous.

Under such circumstances as I have pointed out it is but natural for men to grow desperate and restive. The demonstrations in some of our large cities testify to that fact; but when men parade the streets waving the black flag and the red one, threatening the destruction of property and the lives of other men, it in no way advances the cause we are engaged in. Such outbursts do no good. If it were possible to get all the workingmen out in martial array, and fit them out for battle, would it not be possible to array them in a calm, rational manner on the side of justice devoid of violence? I would like to see the men who talk of destroying life and property take a practical view of the matter. Suppose that we have a repetition of 1877 on a larger scale. Who will do the fighting? Who will do the killing, and who will be counted among the killed? *Only the workingmen.* Workingmen will be hired to fight workingmen, and the men against whom the blow is directed will make a tour of some foreign country, and study the best means of suppressing mobs while the unpleasantness lasts, and come back in time to saddle the costs, in the shape of taxes, on the backs of the workingmen who are unfortunate enough to escape being killed. It will do no good to hold up the reflection of the French Revolution as a beacon to light us onward. Those who preach such a revolution have never done duty as soldiers, or they would not talk so lightly of warfare. They should remember that the men who led the French Revolution in its incipient stages, and who led the people in their assault on tyranny, were themselves led to the guillotine before the revolution ended, and their efforts brought to the front a dictator, who crowned himself emperor amid the plaudits of the same people who beheaded a king and overthrew the preceding empire. If we are to judge of revolutions by the example set before us in the French uprising, when we study its benefits, we must pronounce them failures. The tendency of the present day in France is toward monopoly in land and money, while the number of small farmers is growing smaller every year.

There were anarchists in the Order, and the reading of that circular had the effect of intensifying their animosity toward one whom they had hitherto endeavored to make a convert to their theories. They began a system of destructive tactics that well-nigh drove the Order out of existence. Their agents became members with the avowed purpose of sowing the seeds of discord, and in many places Assemblies lapsed rather than follow the lead of anarchists.

Not only have anarchists of their own volition entered the Order for the purpose of tearing it down, but they have been hired by monopolists to become members for the purpose of giving an anarchistic turn to the doings of Assemblies, so that public opinion might be turned against the Order. This is no stretch of fancy, for a lawyer, an official of Utica, New York, while sitting by my side in a car coming from Washington in the early part of 1887, made this statement to me:

We have succeeded in heading off your Order, Mr. Powderly. We do not fear it any longer, for its power is killed through the foolish actions of its members. You may preach to them to be guided by wise counsels, but we have paid anarchists to become members of your Assemblies that they might stir up the devil and bring discredit upon your whole movement.

That no misconstruction might be placed upon his language, I requested Mr. H—— to repeat his words. He did so, and I noted them down for future reference. He was slightly intoxicated, just enough to loosen his tongue, but not enough to benumb his faculties. He stated that he was an attorney for a manufacturers' association.

Through the actions of the anarchists the Knights of Labor were well-nigh destroyed on the Pacific coast. They lost no opportunity to introduce some new element of discord at every meeting, until the members who were not connected with the International Workingmen's Association withdrew in disgust, and severed all connection with the Knights of Labor. An ex-officer of one of the anarchist groups made this statement to me over his own signature:

I and many others know as a fact that it was the intention of the heads of the International Workingmen's Association to capture the Knights of Labor, as it was a powerful organization, ready-made to their hand, and would save them considerable labor in organizing if they could achieve their desire. Anyhow it could be and was used as a recruiting ground for their purposes.

While professing to be opposed to the continuance of the United States government, the anarchists, at their convention in 1886, decided that "each member should prepare himself to occupy some high office in the government (of the people) when the International Workingmen's Association should have gained control. Various high positions were then parceled out to those present in the meeting with the understanding that they would prepare themselves. Those filling the various offices were to remain unknown to the people at large after the nation was captured, the heads of all departments meeting and transacting their business in secret. The same principle to be maintained in conducting the affairs of government as in conducting the routine of the International Workingmen's Association, the secret five issuing all orders and exacting perfect obedience, though they were to remain unknown and consequently irresponsible.''

The above is in the language of one who still resides on the Pacific coast, and who knows the inside workings of the organization he writes about. The resolutions which were passed to capture the Order of the Knights of Labor were forwarded to me previous to the session of the General Assembly at Richmond, and in an address to that body, while a debate on the admission of certain delegates was in progress, I intimated that it was the intention of that body, known as the International Workingmen's Association, to capture the Order of the Knights of Labor.

That declaration inspired the most virulent and uncalled-for attacks from every quarter of the United States where there was a group of anarchists, but they did not publish them to the world as coming from groups of the International Workingmen's Association. They resorted to a most effectual means of doing injury. Having secured control in certain Assemblies of the Knights of Labor, they would decide in the anarchist group what should be done, and then have a Local Assembly of the Order, of which I was the executive officer, pass resolutions against my administration.

In this way the public and members of the Knights of Labor were deceived. The leaders of these groups were, for the most part, cunning and educated. Many of them were professional men, and knew well how to mould public opinion. Having the *entree* to the daily press, they lost no opportunity of spreading broadcast all manner of rumors concerning the autocracy of the officers of the Knights of Labor, while they themselves were under pledges to capture the United States government and manage it in secret through a committee of five, whose power would exceed that of the Emperor of Russia.

When the movement in favor of the establishment of the eight-hour workday took place on May 1, 1886, the places where the greatest show of strength was developed were Chicago, Ill., Milwaukee, Wis., Baltimore, Md., Boston, Mass., and St. Louis, Mo. At Chicago the sound of a bomb did more injury to the good name of labor than all the strikes of that year, and turned public sentiment against labor organizations so strong that it required the most strenuous efforts on the part of the officers of labor societies to keep their charges from being dragged down into the mire of anarchy.

The events of that year have been written, and such a short time ago that it is not necessary to reproduce them here, but there are matters in connection with the explosion of the bomb that did so much harm that should be known.

Passing over for the present the events which transpired on and succeeding the 1st of May, 1886, we find the General Assembly of the Knights of Labor in session at Richmond, Va. On page 240 of the Proceedings of that convention will be found the record of the election of the General Master Workman. This occurred on October 13. On the 19th of that month his salary was fixed by vote of the General Assembly. The record is on page 285, and on the day after the fixing of the salary—page 288—the following resolution was offered by a representative from New York City, James E. Quinn :

That this General Assembly regards with sorrow the intended execution of seven workingmen in Chicago, and appeals for mercy in behalf of the condemned.

The General Master Workman left the chair, and, when an opportunity presented itself, said :

I do not approve of the resolution in its present form, and would ask the General Assembly to give the most careful consideration to this question. I object to the word " workingmen " in that resolution. The societies which favored the measures which were put into practice on May 4 are not made up of workingmen, nor do they pretend to be such. Even though they were, this convention should object to the work done in the name of labor by these misguided men, instead of countenancing it, or any part of it, by showing a morbid sympathy for them as workingmen. The world regards all labor societies in the same light since May 1 ; and had it not been for the imbecile act which afforded the anarchists the opportunity to do an evil deed while the eyes of the world were upon the men of labor, we would not be regarded with suspicion by all who are beyond our sanctuaries.

If the word workingmen is stricken out of the resolution, and a condemnation of the methods which brought these unfortunates to their present condition inserted, I shall vote for it, but not otherwise. Under no circumstances should we do anything that can, even by implication, be interpreted as identification with the anarchist element. Their blind, unlawful act has cast a stain upon the name of labor which will take years to wipe out. Instead of owing them sympathy we owe them a debt of hatred for their unwarrantable interference at a time when labor had all it could do to weather the storm which had been precipitated upon it by men who apparently did not look very far into the future when naming the 1st of May as the date on which to put in operation a plan which, from its very nature, must revolutionize the industrial affairs of the country. We are apt to give too little thought to important measures, and to view them from the standpoint of our immediate surroundings, rather than from the standpoint of common-sense, and this is such a case. We see men in trouble and rush to their assistance without considering that our action may bring trouble to thousands. Think well over this before you vote, and then vote on such a resolution as will not commit the Order to any wild or visionary scheme which men, whom I believe to be its enemies, would like to see it become involved in.

After the views of the General Master Workman were stated, a representative from Missouri offered a resolution in accord with the sentiments expressed. It reads as follows :

> *Resolved,* That while asking for mercy for the condemned men, we are not in sympathy with the acts of the anarchists, nor with any attempts of individuals or associated bodies that teach or practice violent infractions of the law, believing that peaceful methods are the surest and best means to secure necessary reforms.

That resolution passed unanimously and met with the approval of nearly all who were present. The few who favored anarchy did not relish it because it lacked that indorsement of their ideas which they had hoped to carry away with them.

In response to the address of welcome of Governor Lee, the General Master Workman, in comparing monopoly and anarchy, said:

> To remedy the evils we complain of is a difficult and dangerous undertaking. The need of strong hearts and active brains was never so great as at the present time. The slavery that died twenty-two years ago was terrible, but, bad as it was, it never developed a millionaire, while the new slavery, which now reaches out with a far stronger hand than the old, has developed hundreds of them. The lash in the hands of the old-time slave-owner could strike but one back at a time, and but one of God's poor children felt the stroke. The lash of gold in the hands of the new slave-owner falls not upon one slave alone, but upon the backs of millions, and among the writhing, tortured victims, side by side with the poor and the ignorant, are to be found the well-to-do and the educated. The power of the new slave-owner does not end when the ordinary day laborer bends beneath his rule. It reaches out still further and controls the mechanic, the farmer, the merchant and the manufacturer. It dictates not alone what the price of labor shall be, but regulates the price of money as well. This new slavery counts among its victims servants of the State who have been chosen by the people to execute a people's will. Not alone does it control the Legislator at the State Capitol, but in the halls of our National Congress will you find its most willing, cringing slave. It reaches out even further, and holds in its iron grasp the judge upon the bench; not that alone, but it has the power and does confer the judicial ermine upon its most subservient creatures. Do I overestimate its power? Have I made a single misstatement? If my word is not sufficient, turn to the pages of the history of to-day—the public press—and you will find the testimony to prove that what I have said is true. Evidence in abundance can be adduced to corroborate every statement made by the press.
>
> The lash was stricken from the hand of the slave-owner of twenty-five years ago, and it must be taken from the hand of the new slave-owner as well.
>
> The monopolist of to-day is more dangerous than the slave-owner of the past. Monopoly takes the land from the people in million-acre lots; it sends agents abroad and brings hordes of uneducated, desperate men to this country; it imports ignorance and scatters it broadcast throughout the land,
>
> It, and it alone, is responsible for every manifestation of anarchy that our country has witnessed. All men may not be willing to admit that the statement is true, but when monopoly dies no more anarchists will be born unto this country, for anarchy is the legitimate child of monopoly. While I condemn and denounce the deeds of violence committed in the name of labor during the present year, I am proud to say that the Knights of Labor, as an organization, are not in any way responsible for such conduct. He is the true Knight of Labor who with one hand clutches anarchy by the throat and with the other strangles monopoly!
>
> We are told that it is because of the importation of so many ignorant foreigners that anarchy has shown its head in our country. Rather is it true that because

of the importation of foreign airs, manners and graces by the wealthy we have forgotten what it is that constitutes a true citizen of the Republic. The man who still believes in the "little red school-house on the hill" should take one holiday and visit the mine, the factory, the coal breaker and the mill. There, doing the work of men, will he find the future citizens of the Republic, breathing an atmosphere of dust, ignorance and vice. The history of our country is not taught within these walls. The struggle for independence and the causes leading to that struggle are not spoken of there; the name of Washington is unknown; and the words that rang out trumpet-tongued from the lips of Patrick Henry are never mentioned. Our country, her history, her laws and her institutions are unknown to these poor children. How, then, can the child of the foreigner learn to appreciate the freedom which they have never been told about, much less experienced?

The little red school-house must fail to do its work properly, since the children of the poor must pass it by on the road to the workshop. How can they appreciate the duties of citizenship when we do not take the trouble to teach them that to be an American citizen is greater than to be a king, and that he upon whom the mantle of citizenship is bestowed should part with his life before surrendering one jot or tittle of the rights and liberties which belong to him?

Turn away from these hives of industry, stand for a moment on a street corner, and you will see gaily-caparisoned horses driven by a coachman in livery; a footman occupying his place at the rear of the coach is also dressed in the garb of the serf. On the coach door you will find the crest or coat of arms of the illustrious family to whom it belongs. If you speak to the occupant of the coach concerning our country, her institutions or her flag, you will be told that they do not compare with those of foreign countries. The child who graduates from the workshop dons the livery of a slave, covers his manhood and climbs to the footman's place on the outside of the coach. The man who apes the manners and customs of foreign noblemen occupies the inside. The one who with strong heart and willing hands would defend the rights and liberties of his country has never learned what these rights or liberties are. The other does know, but has learned to love the atmosphere of monarchy better than that which he breathes in this land. Between these two our freedom is in danger, anarchism is fostered, and that is why we, as Knights of Labor, most emphatically protest against the introduction of the child to the workshop until he has attained his fifteenth year, so that he may be enabled to secure for himself the benefits of an education that will enable him to understand and appreciate the blessings of our free institutions, and, if necessary, defend them with his life.

During the year which followed no effort was spared to give out the impression that the condemned men were Knights of Labor, and that they had the indorsement of their Local Assemblies in acting with the anarchists. It is true that it was not stated that any of the condemned were Knights except Albert R. Parsons, but the idea was conveyed that they were entitled to the sympathy of the Order.

In his address to the General Assembly at Minneapolis, Minn., October, 1887, the General Master Workman detailed the experiences of the year so far as his connection with anarchy was concerned, and asked that the convention speak out in the name of the Order at large against the practices of the violent element which had gained admission to the organization. During the progress of the convention, on October 10, James E. Quinn presented the following resolution to the body:

WHEREAS, Considering that the development of the human mind in the nineteenth century has reached a point expressed almost universally against capital punishment, or the taking of human life by judicial process, as a relic of barbarism. Therefore be it

Resolved, That this convention express sorrow that the men in Chicago were doomed to death, and that it use every endeavor to secure the commutation of the sentence of death passed upon them.

When that resolution was read the General Master Workmen ruled it out of order. He had previously stated to those who said that such a resolution would be offered that he would do so. In ruling on the resolution he said that if necessary he would give his reasons for the action taken. Joseph L. Evans of Pittsburg took an appeal from the decision of the chair, giving as his reason that he wished to give the General Master Workman an opportunity to state why he made the ruling. The vote was put on the appeal, and the chair was sustained by a vote of 121 to 53. On a motion to reconsider the vote which sustained the decision of the General Master Workman, 14 representatives spoke against the decision of the chair and 10 in favor of it. The question on the vote to reconsider was called, when the General Master Workman was asked to state his reasons for ruling the motion out of order. He spoke as follows:

I know that it may seem to be an arbitrary act on my part to rule a motion out of order, and did I not have excellent reasons for doing so I never would have availed myself of the privilege conferred upon me by virtue of the office I hold. To properly explain my reasons it will be necessary for me to take you back to the 1st of May, 1886, when the trade unions of the United States were in a struggle for the establishment of the eight-hour system. On that day was stricken to the dust every hope that existed for the success of the strike then in progress, and those who inflicted the blow claim to be representatives of labor. I deny their claim to that position, even though they may be workingmen. They represented no legitimate labor society, and obeyed the counsels of the worst foe this Order has upon the face of the earth to-day.

We claim to be striving for the elevation of the human race through peaceful methods, and yet are asked to sue for mercy for men who scorn us and our methods—men who were not on the street at the Chicago Haymarket in obedience to any law, rule, resolution or command of any part of this Order; men who did not in any way represent the sentiment of this Order in placing themselves in the attitude of opposing the officers of the law, and who sneer at our every effort to accomplish results. Had these men been there on that day in obedience to the laws of this society, and had they been involved in a difficulty through their obedience to our laws, I would feel it to be my duty to defend them to the best of my ability under the law of the land, but in this case they were there to counsel methods that we do not approve of; and no matter though they have lost no opportunity to identify this Order with anarchy, it stands as a truth that there does not exist the slightest resemblance between the two.

I warned those who proposed to introduce that resolution that I would rule it out of order, and that it would do harm to the condemned men to have it go out that this body had refused to pass such a resolution. I stated to them that I knew the sentiment of the men who came here, the sentiment of the order that sent them, and, knowing what that sentiment was, a resolution that in any way would identify this Order with anarchy could not properly represent that sentiment. You are not here in your individual capacity to act as individuals, and you cannot take upon yourselves to express your own opinion and then ask the Order at large to indorse it, for you are stepping aside from the path that your constituents instructed you to walk in.

This organization, among other things, is endeavoring to create a healthy public opinion on the subject of labor. Each member is pledged to do that very thing. How can you go back to your homes and say that you have elevated the Order in the eyes of the public by catering to an element that defies public opinion and attempts to dragoon us into doing the same thing? The eyes of the world are turned toward this convention. For evil or good will the vote you are to cast on this question affect the entire Order, and extreme caution must characterize your action. The Richmond session passed a vote in favor of clemency, but in such a way that the Order could not be identified with the society to which these men belong, and yet thousands have gone from the Order because of it. I tell you the day has come for us to stamp anarchy out of the Order, root and branch. It has no abiding place among us, and we may as well face the issue here and now as later on and at another place. Every device known to the devil and his imps has been resorted to to throttle this Order in the hope that on its ruins would rise the strength of anarchy.

During the year that has passed I have learned what it means to occupy a position which is in opposition to anarchy. Slander, vilification, calumny and malice of the vilest kind have been the weapons of the anarchists of America because I would not admit that Albert R. Parsons was a true and loyal member of the Knights of Labor. That he was a member is true, but we have had many members who were not in sympathy with the aims and objects of the Order, and who would subordinate the Order to the rule of some other society. We have members, too, who could leave the Order for the Order's good at any moment. Albert R. Parsons never yet counseled violence in obedience to the laws of Knighthood. I am told that it is my duty to defend the reputation of Mr. Parsons because he is a member of the Order. Why was not the obligation as binding on him? I have never lisped a word to his detriment either in public or private before. This is the first time that I have spoken about him in connection with the Haymarket riot, and yet the adherents of that damnable doctrine were not content to have it so; they accused me of attacking him, that I might, in denying it, say something in his favor. Why did Powderly not defend Parsons through the press since he is a Knight, and an innocent one? is asked. It is not my business to defend every member who does not know enough to take care of himself, and if Parsons is such a man he deserves no defense at my hands; but Parsons is not an ignorant man, and knows what he is doing. When men violate the laws and precepts of Knighthood, then no member is required to defend them. When Knights of Labor break the laws of the land in which they live, they must stand before the law the same as other men stand and be tried for their offenses, and not for being Knights.

This resolution does not come over the seal of either Local or District Assembly It does not bear the seal of approval of any recognized body of the Order, and represents merely the sentiment of a member of this body, and should not be adopted in such a way as to give it the appearance of having the approval of those who are not here to defend themselves and the Order against that hell-infected association that stands as a foe of the most malignant stamp to the honest laborer of this land. I hate the name of anarchy. Through its encroachments it has tarnished the name of socialism and caused men to believe that socialism and anarchy are one. They are striving to do the same by the Knights of Labor. This they did intentionally and with malice aforethought in pushing their infernal propaganda to the front.

Pretending to be advanced thinkers, they drive men from the labor movement by their wild and foolish mouthings whenever they congregate, and they usually congregate where beer flows freely. They shout for the blood of the aristocracy, but will turn from blood to beer in a twinkling. I have no use for any of the brood, but am satisfied to leave them alone if they will attend to their own business and let this Order alone. They have aimed to capture this Order, and I can submit the proofs [here the documents were presented and read]. I have here also the expose of the various groups of anarchists of this country, and from them will read something of the aims of these mighty men of progress who would bring the greatest good to the greatest number by exterminating two-thirds of humanity to begin with. Possibly that is their method of conferring good.

No act of the anarchists ever laid a stone upon a stone in the building of this Order. Their every effort was against it, and those who have stood in the front, and have taken the sneers, insults and ridicule of press, pulpit and orator in defense of our principles, always have had the opposition of these devils to contend with also. I cannot talk coolly when I contemplate the damage they have done us, and then reflect that we are asked to identify ourselves with them even in this slight degree. Had the anarchists their way this body would not be in existence to-day to ask assistance from. How do you know that the condemned men want your sympathy? Have they asked you to go on your knees in supplication in seeking executive clemency for them? I think not, and, if they are made of the stuff that I think they are, they will fling back in your teeth the resolution you would pass. I give the men who are in the prison cell at Chicago credit for being sincere in believing that they did right. They feel that they have struggled for a principle, and feeling that way they should be, and no doubt are, willing to die for that principle.

Why, if I had done as they did, and stood in their place, I would die before I would sue for mercy. I would never cringe before a governor, or any other man, in a whine for clemency. I would take the consequences, let them be what they would. We may sympathize with them as much as we please, but our sympathies are due first to the Order that sent us here, and it were better that seven times seven men hang than to hang the millstone of odium around the standard of this Order in affiliating in any way with this element of destruction. If these men hang you may charge it to the actions of their friends, for, while pretending to be friends of theirs, the disciples of Most have lost no opportunity to strengthen the strands of the rope by their insane mouthings that it may do its work well.

Be consistent and disband as soon as you pass this resolution, for you will have no further use of any kind for another General Assembly. You have imposed upon your General Master Workman the task of defending the Order from the attacks of its enemies, and he feels that he is entitled to at least a small share of the credit for giving the Order its present standing. He has to the best of his ability defended the Order, but its friends will place in the hands of its enemies the strongest weapon that was ever raised against it if they pass this resolution. Of what avail for me to go before the public and assert that we are a law-abiding set of men and women? What will it avail for me to strive to make public opinion for the Order when, with one short resolution, you sweep away every vestige of the good that has been done, for, mark it, the press stands ready to denounce us far and wide the moment we do this thing?

This resolution is artfully worded. Its sinister motive is to place us in the attitude of supporters of anarchy rather than sympathizers with men in distress, and it should be defeated by a tremendous majority. It is asserted that this does not amount to anything, and that it is not the intention to identify the Order at large with these men. No more barefaced lie was ever told. That resolution would never be offered if we did not represent so large a constituency, and if it passes twenty-four hours won't roll over your heads until you see anarchists all over the land shouting that if these men are hanged the Knights of Labor will take revenge at the polls and elsewhere. In passing that resolution you place the collar of anarchy around your necks, and no future act of ours can take it off. If you sympathize with these unfortunate men, why do you lack the manhood to sign a petition for the commutation of their sentence, as individuals, and stand upon your own manhood, instead of sneaking behind the reputation and character of this great Order, which owes everything it has gained to having nothing to do with the anarchists? Pass this vote if you will, but I swear that I will not be bound by any resolution that is contrary to the best interests of the Order. You cannot pass a resolution to muzzle me, and I will not remain silent after the adjournment of this convention if it becomes necessary to defend the Order from unjust assaults as a result of the action taken.

As an Order we are striving for the establishment of justice for industry. We are attempting to remove unjust laws from the statutes, and are doing what we can to better the condition of humanity. At every step we have to fight the opposition of capital, which of itself is sufficient to tax our energies to the utmost; but at every step we are handicapped by the unwarrantable and impertinent interference of these blatant, shallow-pated men, who affect to believe that they know all that is worth knowing about the conditions of labor, and who arrogate to themselves the right to speak for labor at all times and under all circumstances. That they are mouth-pieces is true, but they only speak for themselves, and do that in such a way as to alarm the community and arouse it to such a pitch of excitement that it insists upon the passage of restrictive legislation, which, unfortunately, does not reach the men whose rash language calls for its passage. Its effects are visited upon innocent ones who had no hand, act or part in fomenting the discord which preceded the passage of the unjust laws.

Our greatest trouble has always been caused by extremists who, without shadow of authority, attempted to voice the sentiments of this Order; and from this day forward I am determined that no sniveling anarchist will speak for me, and if he attempts it under shadow of this organization, then he or I must leave the Order, for I will not attempt to guide the affairs of a society that is so lacking in manhood as to allow the very worst element of the community to make use of the prestige it has gained to promote the vilest of schemes against society. I have never known a day when these creatures were not ready to stab us to the heart when our faces were turned toward the enemy of labor.

It is high time for us to assert our manhood before these men throttle it. For Parsons and the other condemned men let there be mercy. I have no grudge against them. In fact, I would never trouble my head about them were it not for the welfare of this Order. Let us as individuals express our sorrow for their unhappy plight, if we will; but as an Order we have no right to do so. It is not the individuals who are in prison at Chicago that I speak against. It is the hellish doctrine which found vent on the streets of Chicago, and which, unfortunately for themselves, they have been identified with. No, I do not hate these men, I pity them; but for anarchy I have nothing but hatred, and if I could I would forever wipe from the face of the earth the last vestige of its double-damned presence, and in doing so would feel that the best act of my life, in the interest of labor, had been performed.

At the conclusion of that speech, which is for the first time given verbatim, a vote was taken on the motion to reconsider, and was lost. The reason that speech is reproduced is because the sympathizers with anarchy, who listened to it, have malignantly garbled it to suit their own purposes ever since. For two reasons it is best that it should be known, that there may be no mistake as to what was said, and that it shall find a place in history where it will be accessible to those who would know the truth.

George A. Schilling, in a "Short History of the Labor Movement in Chicago," bends the truth past the breaking point when he says:

> Powderly ruled it [the resolution favoring the anarchists] out of order. On the appeal from the decision of the chair by Representative Evans of D. A. 3 of Pittsburg, the entire subject became a matter for discussion. Powderly, as usual, spoke last and made a bitter attack on the condemned men. * * * * * * * * * * * On roll-call, fifty-two members voted against the decision of the chair, he being sustained by a large majority.

The chair did not even attempt to speak during the discussion on the appeal from his decision. That vote was decided without interference from him, and it was only when he was asked to do so on the motion to reconsider that he did speak. The same historian of anarchy, in writing of the Richmond session, asks:

> Why did Powderly not rule the subject out of order at Richmond? Was it because he was looking for the increase of salary to $5,000 per annum, and could not afford to oppose D. A. 49, with its sixty-two delegates, who championed the resolution for clemency?

Those who take the trouble to do so will find the record as I have given it in the Proceedings of the Richmond session, and they will learn that the General Master Workman was elected and his salary fixed long before the resolution came up. That he did speak on the motion is not questioned by those who were present; those who were not may read his remarks in these pages.

It has been said by anarchist sympathizers that the Minneapolis speech had the effect of causing the Governor of Illinois to refuse to commute the sentences of all the prisoners. Nothing can be further from the truth. The Governor knew nothing of it, neither did he ever hear of a public expression concerning the condemned men from the General Master Workman.

If George Schilling desired to be fair, he would have quoted from a paper called the *Knights of Labor*, published by George E. Detwiler of Chicago, a more scathing denunciation of the anarchists than anything that was said at the Minneapolis Convention. In its issue of May 8, 1886, four days after the Haymarket explosion, and *before* the anarchist trials, the paper in question said in a leading editorial:

> Let it be understood by all the world that the Knights of Labor have no affiliation, association, sympathy or respect for the band of cowardly murderers, cutthroats and robbers known as anarchists, who sneak through the country like midnight assassins, stirring up the passions of ignorant foreigners, unfurling the red flag of anarchy, and causing riot and bloodshed. Parsons, Spies, Fielding, Most, and all their followers, sympathizers, aiders and abettors should be summarily dealt with. They are entitled to no more consideration than wild beasts. The leaders are cowards, and their followers are fools. Knights of Labor, boycott them. If one of the gang of scoundrels should by any mistake get access to our organization, expel him at once—brand them as outlawed monsters. Do not even permit yourselves to hold conversation with one of them; treat them as

they deserve to be treated, as human monstrosities not entitled to the sympathy or consideration of any person in the world. * * * * * We hope the whole gang of outlaws will be blotted from the surface of the earth.

Those who still believe that the anarchists of Chicago and the socialists of America were one should read a pamphlet issued by the Socialistic Labor Party on June 1, 1886, in refutation of the charge that socialism and anarchism were one. It is entitled "Socialism and Anarchism, antagonistic opposites." Its first paragraph is:

In reading the newspapers we find the two names mentioned above frequently put side by side. Nay, we find them also associated with the terms communism and nihilism, as though these four "isms" had the closest relation to each other. This is a mistake. Socialism and anarchism are opposites which have nothing in common but their appurtenance to social science. Socialists and anarchists as such are enemies. They pursue contrary aims, and the success of the former will destroy forever the fanatical hopes of the latter.

In the Chicago *Star* of April 25, 1887, appeared an expose of the aims and purposes of the various groups of anarchists of America. The truth of the statements made in that article was vouched for by those who were in position to know whereof they spoke. It was from that document that I read the extracts which explained to the Minneapolis session the real aims of those who sought to cover up their diabolical schemes, first, under the name of socialism, and, later on, by appropriating the machinery of the Knights of Labor to do it under. From the close of the Minneapolis session to the opening of the Indianapolis Convention an open and persistent assault on the Order was continued by the anarchists and their sympathizers. Unfortunately for the Order it had on its Executive Board ardent sympathizers with anarchy, and it was not until they, together with others, were deprived of the power to do harm to the Order that it was rid of an element that aimed solely at prostituting its highest, purest principles and rendering them subservient to that element which at all times advised violence as the only weapon to be used in destroying the evil tendencies of the times. The Order can with a united front make headway against the assaults of monopoly, for its principles are pure, and under no guise can monopoly attempt to become a part of the Order for the purpose of carrying forward its plans of spoliaticn; but weighed down by a festering, putrid sore, which irritated most when the necessity for clear-sighted, conservative action was most apparent, with such an active enemy working to overthrow the Order from within, through agents introduced to the organization for that purpose, the officers and members who worked for the elevation of the toiler in endeavoring to put the principles of the Order into practical operation could do little else than give their attention to these destroyers, an attention which should have been undivided and centered wholly upon the aggressive, grasping monopolist and speculator.

IMPROVEMENTS(?).

They build their Babel in His sight,
From founding unto coping-stone;
Their pride is monstrous; in a night
They lie beneath it, overthrown.—*Boker.*

The abolition of the oath of secrecy in the obligation of Knight-hood by the Detroit session of the General Assembly, in 1881, occa-sioned no little dissatisfaction among those who believed that the veil of mystery was more potent for good than the education of the masses in an open organization. Under the rule of an organization, the name of which no member could speak above a whisper, the aims of which no one could explain, it was as easy to assert that the aim of the association was the overthrow of government and society as to admit that its real object was to purify government and reconstruct society. The extreme secrecy afforded an excellent opportunity for scheming brains to plot, plan and execute evil as well as good. The Grand Master Workman recommended the abolition of the oath in his address to the convention. After alluding to the opposition shown the Order by the church in many places, he said:

Many of our members are not possessed of sufficient intelligence to comprehend the nature of an oath, and ofttimes violate their vows without actually intending it; others, more intelligent and at the same time less scrupulous, break their obligations for a *consideration*. I maintain that a word of honor will bind a man of honor as securely as the most iron-clad oath, while a *being* devoid of honor will be bound by no obligation or law, either human or divine. I, therefore, advise that a man's regard for his honor in this world be made the test, instead of his fear of punishment in the next.

Members of the Order in New York objected to the abolition of the oath, and requested the Grand Master Workman to grant a dispensa-tion to use the old form. That officer was not at that time vested with authority to issue dispensations, and refused to allow the reten-tion of the old forms beyond the time allowed by law. From this refusal grew an opposition to him which was bitterly prolonged for many years. When the General Assembly met in New York the year following, the address of the Grand Master Workman contained these words:

The changes made in the secret work of the Order at the Detroit General Assembly have been misunderstood by a few. Shortly after the changes went into effect I was written to for dispensation to allow certain localities to work under the old A. K. This I had no power to grant, and of course refused. A revolt was contemplated but was not resorted to, the good sense of the members prevailing. Yet those who were active in exciting members to insubordination have lost no opportunity to blacken me whenever an opportunity presented itself. I care but little for this, but it can do an organization no good to find unnecessary fault with its officers. I can only say, watch your officers with a jealous eye. Breathe not one word against them until you are certain they deserve it, then let your punishment be swift and sure.

When an impartial person reviews the reason given for opposing the new work he fails to find a single convincing argument. Men who coincided with our views had no opportunity of knowing the position we held, but now that we can go before the world and explain and define our position we have no difficulty in securing the active co-operation of labor reformers everywhere. The result is most gratifying. I need but refer you to the report of the Grand Secretary, which shows the increase in members, to prove that the changes made at Detroit have had no injurious effect. If our cause is just, what need have we to fear the opposition of the whole world? I grant that members may be discharged and victimized for being members of the Order, but there is no good reason why the names or identity of members in any locality need be made more public than in the day when we practiced the utmost secrecy. A few Locals favor a return to the original secrecy of the Order, and would again bind men, under the penalty of becoming perjurers, to do their duty. The Order is powerless to punish perjury—that must come beyond the grave. I am opposed to an oath. I believe as Brutus did when he said :

> No, not an oath. If not the face of men
> The sufferance of our souls, the time's abuse—
> If these be motives weak, break off betimes,
> And every man hence to his idle bed ;
> So let high-sighted tyranny range on
> Till each man drop by lottery. But if these,
> As I am sure they do, bear fire enough
> To kindle cowards and to steel with valor
> The melting spirits of women, then, countrymen,
> What need we any spur but our own cause
> To prick us to redress? what other bond
> Than secret Romans, that have spoke the word,
> And will not falter? and what other oath
> Than honesty to honesty engaged
> That this shall be or we will fall for it?
> *   *   *   *   *   *   *   *   *
> *   *   *   *   * unto bad causes swear
> Such creatures as men doubt; but do not stain
> The even virtue of our enterprise
> Nor the insuppressive mettle of our spirits,
> To think that, or our cause, or our performance,
> Did need an oath; when every drop of blood
> That every Roman bears, and nobly bears,
> Is guilty of a several bastardy,
> If he do break the smallest particle
> Of any promise that hath passed from him.

Among the representatives was one from Baltimore, who felt slighted because of something that happened during the session. What occasioned his displeasure was never disclosed, and, being under the influence of liquor during the greater part of his stay in New York, it is not likely that he knew what it was at which he took offense.

On his return to Baltimore he became insubordinate, and attempted to form another organization within the Order of the Knights of Labor. About this time a number of Congressmen, hearing of the existence of the Order, sought admission to its ranks. Some of them were lawyers and could not be received as members. Others were of that character which did not find favor among members of the Order in the localities where they resided, and were rejected in the Local Assemblies there. These men formed an organization and called it the "Improved Order of Advanced Knights of Labor." It never attained any strength, neither did it exist outside of the city of Washington, D. C., until it was instituted in Baltimore. The principal cause for complaint against the old Order of the Knights of Labor was that no saloon-keepers, lawyers or old-line politicians would be admitted, and it was thought that the time had come to start one more political party. To make a party a success it was necessary to have men of experience at the helm, and who so capable of manipulating affairs as the saloon-keeper or the political lawyer, who earned more through bribes as an office-holder than fees as an attorney? The first circular sent out by the reformers of Baltimore was mailed in June, 1883. It is appended:

IMPROVED ORDER OF KNIGHTS OF LABOR.

The true labor movement must be so fixed with proper checks and balances that designing men cannot use it for their own personal gain; the humblest member in the movement must have a voice and vote for or against all important measures, thus rendering it impossible on the part of any to perpetrate and cover up fraud.

The power of levying taxes, expending money at will, abolishing, altering or creating laws, and granting dispensation is a power that cannot safely be intrusted to individual officers or committees. An organization in which the membership is at the mercy of a few ring-leaders or officers, with no power to investigate them, can never amount to other than a tax-paying body for the support and maintenance of those who in the end generally succeed in selling their supposed influence to political buyers or others.

In these statements we believe that all fair-minded men will agree with us. The cry is coming up from all quarters for an honest and defined system of organization, a system that will allow subordinate branches of the movement to live, without impoverishing them by inordinate taxation to support foolish and excessive expenditures and the payment of large salaries to a host of unnecessary and idle officers.

No one should be introduced into a labor organization without being fully informed of its aims and objects and the plan upon which it is organized to work, and if he cannot subscribe to the same let him remain outside. Within the order all must be in harmony as to plans and purposes.

The I. O. K. of L. is founded with a view to honest and economical management, and urges upon all workingmen, who have faith in the accomplishment of labor emancipation peaceably, by means of the workingman's ballot, to unite with us in the work.

Address   JNO. B. ROHLEDER, *General Secretary,*
128 Scott Street, Baltimore, Md.

The Secretary of D. A. 41 of Baltimore communicated with the Grand Master Workman on the subject, and asked what should be done with members who had attached themselves to the " Improved Order." The reply is given in full as follows:

OFFICE OF GRAND MASTER WORKMAN. }
SCRANTON, Pa., July 11, 1883 }

Conrad J. Kraft, Esq., Baltimore, Md.:

DEAR SIR AND BROTHER:—The " Improved Order of the Knights of Labor " is a *fraud.* It is based upon *nothing* except a desire to destroy the usefulness of the Order of the Knights of Labor. Its preamble assails all labor organizations because they have no " regularly defined course of action," and it utterly fails to point out the course it intends pursuing itself. The only idea one can get is that the originators intend starting one more political party, and hope to win power on the prestige of the Knights of Labor by adopting its name.

There is room in this country for but one Order of the Knights of Labor, and all improvements necessary can be made in that body, through the regularly accredited representatives of the Order at large in the General Assembly which meets each year.

The machinery of the Knights of Labor is in the hands of its members, to be retained in its present form, to be altered and amended as the majority shall decide. If any additional "checks or balances" are required, they can be adjusted much more satisfactorily by the membership at large than by any self-constituted "Provisional General Executive Committee."

The men who started the "Improved Order of the Knights of Labor " in the latter part of last January were members of the Congress then in session in Washington. They wrote to several men, whom they supposed were not members, asking their co-operation. The names of four of these men are standing on the record books of the Assemblies in the cities in which they live, and they are recorded as being black-balled because they were men "who stole the widow's house and the orphan's bread," and knowing that they could not gain admission to the Knights of Labor, or secure a re-election to Congress, they decided to start a new order to deceive members of our organization. They first called it the "Improved Order of Advanced Knights of Labor," but they met with no encouragement.

The Knight of Labor who is not willing to help improve our Order, and who starts a rival order, thus dividing the workers and attempting to destroy confidence in the officers of the organization, is a traitor and merits expulsion.

No officer of the Knights of Labor has ever been proved dishonest or unworthy of the position he held. There is room for improvement in every society, but the way to improve it is to correct what is evil in its laws and tendencies. If men want to start a new order they may do so, but they cannot start one in opposition, use the name of our Order, and at the same time remain members of the Order of the Knights of Labor that they may carry our secrets and doings over to the other. Such a man is an enemy, and our Order would be improved by his expulsion. He must leave one or the other. See that charges are preferred against every member who belongs to the Improved Order.

Fraternally yours,

T. V. POWDERLY,
Grand Master Workman.

The " Improved Order " prepared and published a ritual from which the following is taken:

THE PLEDGE.

I, —— ——, in the presence of these witnesses, understanding the object and purpose of this order, do solemnly pledge myself to labor with what zeal I possess for the promotion of its principles and the accomplishment of its objects; that from henceforth I stand severed from all party ties, and declare myself only in the movement of United Labor. I further promise to observe the forms and usages as laid down in the written and unwritten work of the order; and that I will never reveal to any one outside of the order the name of any of its officers or members or the numerical strength of its organization, and when I resign or leave the order I will give due notice thereof.

I moreover bind myself to labor for the good and welfare of all true Knights of the order, and to at all times work for the interest of a brother Knight in all necessary administrations. Failing to be true to this obligation, and becoming false to the principles of the order, I hereby authorize myself by all its discipline to become an outlaw to its members, subject to all penalties due a perjurer and traitor.

In the instructions given to new members we find the following:

In introducing the names of candidates for membership you will be strictly governed by the Constitution of the order, which excludes bankers, brokers, stock and other gamblers and professional politicians; otherwise there is no bar to membership except a known lack of honor and integrity in the applicant.

"The power to alter or create laws or grant dispensations" was not conferred upon the officers of the Knights of Labor, and there was nothing contained in the whole Preamble or ritual of the new which could not be accomplished through the old Order; but it was necessary to have a rallying-cry, and what so popular as to hint at dishonesty and autocracy on the part of officers? More of rascality and dishonesty have been practiced by so-called reformers while outwardly denouncing these vices than by those whom they charged with the offenses. The Order of the Knights of Labor had closed the door and locked it in the face of the liquor-seller, and this new order was to so far reform the old one as to allow the dispenser of sudden wealth and happiness to become a member and practice his calling under the protection, and as a member, of the order.

D. A. 41 did not countenance the new move, and presented a series of resolutions against it at the Cincinnati session of the General Assembly, which convened in September, 1883. The Grand Master Workman briefly referred to the existence of the "Improved Order" in his address, and said:

Within the last few months a few discontented men, who were under the impression that men could be forced to vote as they were advised if they could only be brought into an organization in which they were sworn to vote for certain principles or men, have formed an association and called it the Improved Order of Knights of Labor. I have no objection to the formation of as many societies as can find work to do for humanity, but I am of the opinion that there should be originality enough in the organizers of the movement to inspire them to choose a name of their own. The men who started the order referred to unblushingly proclaim that they adopted the name of the Knights of Labor in order to catch the votes of our members. If men will not vote for principles, then names are powerless.

The representative from D. A. 41 offered a series of resolutions, which were adopted and ordered sent out to the Order. They are as follows:

WHEREAS, It is the duty of this General Assembly and all true members of the Order of the Knights of Labor of North America to uphold the integrity and principles of the Order ; and

WHEREAS, There has been organized an association styling itself the "Improved Order of the Knights of Labor of North America," under auspices of men who still claim membership in the Order of the Knights of Labor; and

WHEREAS, The self-styled "Improved Order of the Knights of Labor" admits to its membership liquor dealers and others debarred by our Constitution and laws from membership in our Order; and

WHEREAS, By their actions they strike a blow at this organization and its principles. Therefore, be it

Resolved, By the General Assembly of the Knights of Labor, that all persons who are members of this self-styled "Improved Order of the Knights of Labor" are hereby declared to be no longer members of the Knights of Labor, unless they sever their membership in the said Improved Order, and District Assemblies and Local Assemblies under its jurisdiction are instructed to drop from the rolls of membership all persons who are members of the self-styled "Improved Order of the Knights of Labor."

Resolved, That all persons who are members of the "Improved Order of the Knights of Labor" are not eligible to membership in this Order.

Resolved, That this General Assembly repudiate all connection with the so-called "Improved Order of the Knights of Labor," and that this repudiation be published in the public press.

The promulgation of these resolutions above quoted sealed the fate of the Improved Order, and it was heard of no more.

Shortly after the adjournment of the Cincinnati Convention a disturbance took place in L. A. 2186 of Binghamton, N. Y. The Organizer at that place selected a number of business men who were averse to joining the Assembly already organized. When he sent the application for a charter to the General Secretary many members of L. A. 2186 protested and caused the Assembly to voice their sentiments in sending notice under seal, as required by law. The Organizer was expelled by his Assembly. The protest was presented to the General Executive Board, and that body refused to allow the organization to proceed.

This action on the part of the Board, although strictly in line with the Constitution, incensed the men who had applied for the new charter. They had never been members and knew nothing of the organization ; but three or four members of the parent Assembly who favored their admission left the Order because they were not admitted. These with the expelled Organizer, not over five in all, assisted in organizing a new society, which, all told, consisted of thirty-five members.

The General Master Workman was not a member of the Executive Board that year, and with the exception of advising harmony was not, officially, concerned in the difficulty at Binghamton. When the new society was established the following press dispatch was flashed over the wires from Binghamton:

THE KNIGHTS OF LABOR DIVIDED.

BINGHAMTON, N. Y., November 26, 1883.

There has been a break in the ranks of the Knights of Labor. It is determined by many members that it shall no longer be directed by one man. The cause of the dissolution is the arbitrary course pursued by Powderly of Scranton, who has tried to ride two horses at once. He has been brought to a halt. The leaders in the revolt are William Secor, James Tozer, William Crosby and James Barnes. Three hundred and fourteen persons have signed the roll of a new order, and applications for thirty-seven charters have been received. Over two hundred associations of the Knights of Labor refuse to sustain the glass-blowers in their strike, which was entirely uncalled for. The Independent Order of Knights of Labor will help the sick, the orphan and the widow, but will not give one cent to Pennsylvania demagogues. It is intended that it shall be a benefit association.

The action referred to as being arbitrary on Powderly's part was when he refused to set aside the action of the General Executive Board and issue a charter to the new Assembly. The Constitution gave him no such authority, and for obeying the law he was called arbitrary. When the new association was established it styled itself "Excelsior Assembly No. 1, Independent Order of Knights of Labor." A Constitution and set of By-laws were adopted. The requirements for membership are summed up in Section 1 of Order 4, which reads:

Any male citizen of the United States, twenty-one years of age, of unimpeachable moral character, of sound health, who actually earns a livelihood by honest industry, and who is a resident of the State within the precinct of an Assembly, is eligible to membership in such Assembly, and may join another by consent of the one.

One of the alleged causes for complaint against the Order of the Knights of Labor, and the principal one, aside from the case of "sour grapes," which caused the organization of the "Independent" movement, was that there was not charity enough displayed in the Knights of Labor. In drawing up the By-laws the following was inserted:

The funeral benefit is fixed at the sum of $100, to be strictly on the co-operative plan.

A beneficiary must be in good standing, of six months' record, and square on the books.

No premium is required other than the regular entrance fees, dues and assessments.

On the death of a beneficiary an equal assessment for the $100 shall be made.

No assessment is necessary when the funds are sufficient to pay a benefit.

The chief officer was never called on to render a decision as to what constituted "honest industry." He was relieved of that responsibility by the death of a member which occurred January 6, 1884, and, although six months had not elapsed, an assessment was levied on the members. Many refused to pay it, claiming that the Constitution had been violated; that the officers had acted arbitrarily in levying it. A necessity for a new society became apparent at once. Those who took such a decided stand against the officers of the Knights of Labor for not violating the Constitution in their interest were obliged to make good the $100 voted to the widow of the deceased. That assessment dampened the enthusiasm of the remaining members, and they left the organization one by one. The spring of 1884 saw the last of the " Independent Order " of Binghamton.

The dispatch which went over the wires, and reproduced in the foregoing, is much the same as has gone from every town and hamlet wherever a trifling disturbance has occurred ever since. Only five members of the new organization had ever been Knights; but thirty-five men in all signed the roll of the Excelsior Assembly, yet the glowing and robust imagination of the reporter saw " three hundred and fourteen persons " sign the roll. He saw applications received for thirty-seven charters, and had two hundred associations of the Knights of Labor refusing to sustain a strike which really had no existence as such, in which they were not concerned, and to the support of which they were not required to contribute.

The " Improved Order " and the " Independent Order " having disbanded, there was a lull in improvements for several years. When the minority could not control the sessions of the General Assembly which met in Minneapolis, Minn., October, 1887, a few men resolved to organize a " Provisional Committee " to purify the Order. The Secretary of the committee, Charles F. Sieb of Chicago, sent out a circular setting forth that the General Officers of the Knights of Labor were dishonest, extravagant and untrue. In issuing the same circular to the Assemblies of Cook County, Ill., after it had been mailed to other parts of the country, it was accompanied by the following:

At a mass convention of the Knights of Labor, held in the city of Chicago, Monday, November 21, it was decided to issue a circular letter requesting the Local Assemblies of Cook County to co-operate in the work of reorganizing the Order of the Knights of Labor on an honest and substantial basis. A convention has been called to meet on Wednesday evening, December 7, at 116 Fifth Avenue, upper hall, Mail building. All Local Assemblies interested in this movement are requested to send delegates. Basis of representation, three delegates to each Local Assembly.

While asking Assemblies to co-operate in reorganizing the Order on an " honest basis," the Secretary of the " Provisional Committee " was charged with failing to make an " honest " return of money which had been intrusted to his keeping by D. A. 24 of Chicago. The meeting was held, as per call, on December 7, and officers were elected to conduct the affairs of the Provisional Committee. Joseph

R. Buchanan was elected Master Workman, E. A. Stephens, Worthy Foreman, and William Holmes, Secretary. The chief cause of complaint against the General Officers of the Knights of Labor was that they had spent hundreds of thousands of dollars of the funds of the Order. In order not to leave themselves open to so great a charge, and possibly to remove temptation from the path of their officers, it was not deemed expedient to elect a Treasurer. The Provisional Committee was expected to steer clear of the errors of other organizations, and as a consequence no funds were to be raised for any purpose.

The " press dispatches " announced that large additions were made to the new order at this session, and that whole Districts of the Knights of Labor were turning over to their management.

On January 14, 1888, a meeting was held in New York. It consisted of the dissatisfied element of that city and vicinity. Such dissatisfaction existed at the meeting that those who were present were not satisfied with each other, and the only thing accomplished was the issuing of another manifesto. A general convention of all attached to the " Provisional Committee " was held in New York City, April 21, 1888, but there was nothing done except to dispute over methods of reform, and adjourn. Since that time the strength of the " Provisional " movement has been confined to the press dispatches and newspaper interviews, which have been manufactured by interested persons. Attempts were made to turn several numerically weak Assemblies over to the care of the " Provisional Committee," but without success. Only such persons or Assemblies identified themselves with the movement as were at heart opposed to the Order of the Knights of Labor from the time they became connected with it. Other movements in opposition to the Knights of Labor did not have the sympathy of any of the General Officers. With the " Provisional Committee " the case was different, for two members of the General Executive Board were not only in sympathy with that committee, but they provided it with information concerning the affairs of the Order, and assisted to weaken it wherever an opportunity presented. There is no doubt but that Thomas B. Barry and William H. Bailey kept the " Provisionals " informed of all that transpired, for they were in the confidence of the leaders of that movement.

In 1887 an Assembly ceased to work in Jackson, Tenn. A member of the International Workingmen's Association applied to Mr. Buchanan for information which would lead to the obtaining of the property of the Assembly by the International Workingmen's Association or the " Provisionals." That there was an understanding between Messrs. Bailey and Barry of the General Executive Board and Mr. Buchanan is shown by the following extract from a letter received by Mr. Bailey, and by him left among the papers of the General Executive Board in Philadelphia :

LIBERTY.   EQUALITY.   FRATERNITY.

OFFICE OF THE TENNESSEE CENTRAL COMMITTEE,
INTERNATIONAL WORKINGMEN'S ASSOCIATION.

JOSEPH E. VOSS, *Secretary,*   *North American Section,*
    P. O. Box 197.   *Southeastern Division.*

                                                JACKSON, Tenn., September 24, 1888.
W. H. Bailey, Ohio :

    DEAR SIR :—On the 3d of September I organized a Local Assembly under the Provisional Committee. There is a man here by the name of —— —— who has the charter, seal, * * * * * * and books. In my correspondence with Joseph R. Buchanan he said that perhaps you and Barry would give me an order for the articles, as they belonged to lapsed Local No. 4270, and we could have the charter renewed. If you send an order be sure and have the seal of the General Executive Board affixed, or it will not be recognized. * * * * * * * * * * * * * * * * * * Now, if you can possibly send me an order for the things that —— —— has, Buchanan will vouch for me. So will George F. Murray.
    Awaiting your answer, I remain fraternally yours,

                                       JOSEPH E. VOSS.

    When the Indianapolis session of the General Assembly of the Knights of Labor was called to order, the " Provisional Committee " was powerless for good or evil. Mr. Barry had been expelled from the Knights of Labor because of his intrigues against the welfare of the Order, and was refused a seat in the General Assembly. On the adjournment of the convention he, in retaliation, announced his intention to organize a new labor society to take the place of the Knights of Labor. The new society is being carried on outside and independent of the Knights. Its aims are not identical with those of the Knights of Labor. It is intended to be a purely trade society, if we are to judge by the questions which every candidate is asked on applying for admission. They are as follows :

    Is your trade organized locally or nationally ? Are you a member in good standing ? Have you ever been a member of your trade society ? If not, why ?

It is stated in the ritual that

    If the candidate seeking admission ever went foul on his trade, that act disqualifies him from membership in the Brotherhood of United Labor until he settles with his trade.

    The remainder of the ritual is a garbled copy of that used in another labor society. It displays no originality or merit, and is no improvement on that of other industrial organizations. A number of curiosity-seekers gained admission to the Brotherhood of United Labor in its infancy, and when they withdrew the majority of its members had retired, leaving less than enough to conduct the business of the " branches," which were established in a few of the large cities.
    At the Indianapolis Convention it became necessary, for the protection of the Order, that the General Master Workman should express

his sentiments concerning the election of a General Secretary-Treasurer. In doing so he gave offense to the incumbent of the Treasurer's office, who was a candidate for the position, by advocating the election of the then General Secretary, John W. Hayes. Frederick Turner, the General Treasurer, was defeated, and, smarting over his failure to secure an election, he, with others, determined to start a rival organization. In January, 1889, Victor Drury, Frederick Turner, Henry G. Taylor and four of the founders of the Order, James L. Wright, R. N. Keen, R. C. McCauley and Joseph N. Kennedy, agreed to institute a reform movement within the Knights of Labor by a return to the oath-bound secrecy of early days. Only one of the founders was in good standing at the time, James L. Wright. The others were either suspended or dropped from the rolls. What good purpose the founders' movement had in view is not discernible; in fact, there existed no reasonable excuse for its continuance after the adoption of the following, which occurs in the ritual adopted by them:

Are you prepared to bind yourself to use your own judgment, and act according to the same, uncontrolled by any outside power, and absolutely independent of the dictation of any church, prince, potentate or authority whatsoever, subject only to the rightful law of the land?

Every citizen is expected to use his own judgment and obey the "rightful law" of the land, and there existed no necessity for the propounding of such a question by the founders when a curiosity-seeker presented himself for admission. The founders' movement made no headway, and in less than six months from the date of its organization it had ceased to operate. But six charters were issued, four of these were procured by inquisitive persons, who organized for the purpose of knowing what was going on around them.

Movements having their origin in personal malice, ambition or revenge are not calculated to advance the interests of the masses, and such associations are naturely short-lived. The Baltimore movement was the result of disappointment, coupled with a desire to have something in the shape of an organization to trade upon in dealing with the bribe-giving politician. The Binghamton movement was originated in the hope that the Order of the Knights of Labor would relent and admit to membership those who were objectionable to the Assembly already existing at that point. Spite had something to do with it also. The Provisional Committee of 1887 was instigated by designing members of the International Workingmen's Association, who seized upon every pretext that would afford them an opportunity to cry "fraud, autocracy," etc. Disappointed ambition also actuated the movers in the reform agitation of that year. The Brotherhood of United Labor, or the "Barry Movement," as it is known, is not an honest attempt to reform existing evils, for its founder made no effort to reform while drawing his salary from the Order of the Knights of

Labor.   Not gifted with ability to manage a part of an organization, it cannot be expected of him to carry on the affairs of an entire society, unless it be a very small one.   Personal vanity and anger at his expulsion from the Knights of Labor actuated Mr. Barry, and afforded a stimulus in the early days of his effort to establish the Brotherhood of United Labor.   The advice of seeming friends, who, knowing that he was susceptible to flattery, made it appear to him that he would rise to fame on a tidal-wave of organization.   The founders' movement would never have had a beginning had Frederick Turner been elected General Secretary-Treasurer of the Knights of Labor at Indianapolis.   Each movement discovered at the outset that the very things which they condemned in the Knights of Labor— viz.: autocracy, expenditure of funds for the maintenance of various parts of the Order and centralization of power—were things with which they would have to deal in the new movements.   Not knowing how to deal with these matters in the old society, it could not be expected of them in the new.

To steer the course of the Knights of Labor clear of designing political managers, on the one hand, and the rule of incompetent one-idea leaders, on the other hand, has been no easy task.   The great mass of the Order has always been in active sympathy with the executive head, and to that fact must be attributed the success which the Order has met with in vanquishing its foes within and without.

TEMPERANCE.

Oh! that man should put an enemy in his mouth to steal away his brains.
—Shakespeare.

The avarice and greed of the employer, his disregard for the feelings of his workmen and the indifference to their welfare, shown in the frequent and unnecessary reductions in their wages, are very discouraging to the man of toil. The cruel blow inflicted when the superintendent informs the workman on Saturday evening that he is discharged makes it doubly hard for him to face his family with the dreadful news. None but those who have experienced the feeling can ever tell how hard it is for the mechanic to enter his home and appear cheerful and happy after being dismissed from his employment. At such a time the capitalist may appear to be an enemy, and so far as his interest in the workman is concerned he really is his enemy when the line is drawn between the man and the dollar; but as bad as such an employer is and as disheartening,as such treatment may appear, there is still another foe before whom the hard-hearted man of wealth appears almost as a friend—a foe who inflicts more of sorrow and of agony than lays in the power of the employer to mete out to his workmen.

When a man is discharged he can impart the news to his wife and family in such a way as to rob the dread intelligence of a part of its terrors; he can hold out a hope of securing another situation in a short time, and thus soften the blow as it falls upon the hope of securing enough of the comforts of life to keep the family in decent raiment and sufficient food. But when the poor unfortunate stops before going home after his dismissal and tarries for awhile in the grog-shop to drown his sorrow in drink, he forms an alliance with a foe who is far more terrible than the man who discharged him. The latter only dismissed him; he did not deprive him of his reason. The employer only deprived him of the right to work for a certain man, but drink deprived him of the power to look for other employment. The presence of the man who robbed him of his employment would not intrude itself within the portals of the workman's home, but the foe whom he met on the way home not only crossed the threshold with him, but it remained and went to bed with him; it deprived him of the power to keep up a cheerful appearance of good nature; it added to the misery and pain which the news of his discharge brought to his wife and children.

It may be said that we should not begrudge the poor fellow the brief moments of oblivion to his suffering and misfortune which came to him while under the influence of strong drink. What right has a man to become oblivious to danger while it stands so near to him? What right has he to drown his own sorrow by adding sorrow to the unhappy lot of those whom he loves? Is it not cowardly in a man to shut out the misery from his own sight, and by his own act magnify it in the sight of his family? Unless a man can remain drunk as a means of happiness, why should he for a moment become happy at the expense of his manhood?

Such questions as these would not be asked of the workman a dozen years ago by his most intimate acquaintance, but to-day every workman will ask himself whether it is wise, honorable or manly to do as he would have done a few years back. What has brought about the change? We see workingmen who belong to labor societies selling strong drink, and we are apt to say that it was not the influence of the labor society which wrought the change. We find men who work at a trade all day standing behind the bar in the evening dealing out strong drink to their shop-mates, who felt that it was a duty which they owed to them to give them a call of an evening just to show that they wished them well.

The effects of this practice were demoralizing in the extreme. It robbed the frequenters of such places of their independence, and gave to the rum-seller an influence over them in the society to which they all belonged. Had the workingmen of twenty years ago kept the rum-seller out of their societies it would have redounded to the good name of labor, and innocent men would not have perished on the scaffold for the crimes of others. Had not strong drink, in the name of friendship, allured men into the rum-shops of their fellow-workmen, a McParlan would not have exercised the power which he wielded in the coal regions of Pennsylvania. No murders were ever deliberately planned in the dread days of what the world was pleased to call " Molly Maguireism," but men who sold liquor were allowed to become members of societies where workingmen found admission, and after the meetings adjourned it was a common thing for the rum-seller to invite a half-dozen or more into his den and keep them there until brain, reason and common-sense were drowned in drink. I had it from the lips of one of the men who expiated his crime on the scaffold that he never entered into a conspiracy to injure any of God's creatures, but the crime of which he was accused must have been committed after he left a grog-shanty and was on his way home in company with two or three others who had stayed in the place until liquor became the master of their senses. They saw the boss, and instantly the cruel treatment which he inflicted on them in the mine flashed before their frenzied brains, and his death was the result.

Who was to blame ? Certainly the unfortunate wretch who drew his last breath on the scaffold was not alone implicated in that murder. The saloon-keeper was a party to it; the society to which both belonged was a party to it; and a false public opinion, which, in not daring to speak out against the rum hells of the region, lent its sanction to the practice which is here described, was also responsible for that murder.

There were clergymen in the coal regions who, without investigation, denounced labor societies, and applied the vilest of epithets to those who belonged to them, one of them going so far as to say from the altar of God : "Once we had Molly Maguires; now we have Biddy Maguires," referring to a Local Assembly of the Knights of Labor which admitted women to membership. This man of God(?) did not dare to speak out against that which was the legitimate parent of the Molly Maguireism of a score of years ago. He remained silent and shut his eyes to the yawning gates of hell, which were opened up to swallow the souls of his flock every day in the week before his eyes. During the dread days of Molly Maguireism he was silent, and, to his eternal shame be it said, condemned the poor unfortunates who were misled by the saloon-keeper, but never opened his lips in denunciation of the real author of a part of the crime which fastened a stigma on the fair name of the State of Pennsylvania. Press, pulpit, politician, merchant and professional man were alike responsible for the crimes of the workingmen of the coal region, for they kept their lips sealed and never spoke against the accomplice of the monopolist in driving men to deeds of madness and crime. These terrible lessons were not taught in vain, for, when the Order of the Knights of Labor entered the field as a champion of the rights of man, it took up the gauntlet against the intrusion of the agent of rum and forbade his entrance to an Assembly of the Order.

The organization, having groped forward in secrecy from the institution of the first Assembly until the General Assembly voted to make the name of the Order public in 1881, was not threatened very often by the invasion of the rum-seller; but it often happened that a member of the Order who had a friend in the saloon business would bring his name before the Assembly for admission. Such men seldom gained entrance; but when they were admitted there was no law to exclude them from the meetings, and as a consequence they remained as long as it was to their advantage to stay.

After the first session of the General Assembly at Reading in 1878, the organization began to gain some publicity and strength ; members with an eye to business saw an opportunity to reap a harvest, and they embarked in the rum business with a view to securing the patronage of their fellow-members.

Mr. Stephens, who was opposed to the admission of liquor dealers, was also opposed to the retention of those who entered upon the sale of liquor after joining the Order. He was called on to make a decision in the case of a member who opened up a saloon, and the following is what was intended to keep members from embarking in the rum traffic:

Members going into the liquor-dealing business shall apply for and be granted a final card, which is an honorable discharge, as with it they could renew their membership should they ever cease following that business.

But in the goodness of his heart Mr. Stephens made another decision, which was intended to cover the case of a man who lived away from a thickly-settled locality and kept a roadside tavern. The influence of the proprietor of a country hotel was not bad, and such a man would not do injury to the Order by becoming a member; in consequence thereof the following decision was made and promulgated:

Men of good report, respectable and honorable keepers of roadside inns, for the *bona-fide* entertainment of travelers and their animals, with bed and board for the same, connected with the real interests of the locality in which they live, do not come under the classification of saloon-keeper and liquor dealer, and may be admitted to membership under the "law of the ballot."

The Constitution of 1878 said: "No person who either sells or makes his living by the sale of intoxicating drink can be admitted." The respectable keeper of a roadside inn was not supposed to make his living by the sale of drink, and, as he only kept liquor for the accommodation of his guests, he was permitted under the decision of the Grand Master Workman to remain a member while making part of his living from the sale of drink. While the Constitution and the first decision of the Grand Master Workman were not favorable to the rum-seller, a decision subsequently made afforded the rum-seller and his friends a chance to raise objections to his ejection; the decision was in the following language:

Initiation of improper persons must stand as a fixed fact, and cannot be annulled. They can only be expelled for cause or crime afterward committed, and by due process and trial of Court, the same as other members.

Those who sell liquor will not admit that they are improper persons; but here was a chance to make money by assuming that position, and under the wording of that decision the liquor dealer remained in the Order. On the other hand, no one who sold liquor could be induced to admit that he was not respectable; and when the question was asked, "Do you keep a roadside inn?" the answer invariably was, "Yes." The keeper of the country grog-shop was a "respectable, honorable keeper of a roadside inn;" the man who run the worst rum-hole on the Bowery in New York would assert that he kept an inn on the roadside, and no one dared to say that he was not "respectable and honorable."

In a short time the liquor dealers began to learn of the existence of the Order; they had facilities for finding out which others did not possess. Where men congregated of an evening and entered a hall in large numbers the curiosity of the saloon-keeper was at once aroused. Having an eye to business, he naturally wished to know why they assembled there, and lost no time in inducing one of the members with whom he was acquainted to drop into his place of an evening, and he usually selected one who was fond enough of drink to lose his senses by imbibing too freely.

Once rum loosened the tongue of such a man it wagged on until the saloon-keeper learned the name of the society, the names of its members, and the aims, objects and numerical strength of the society. Once in the power of the saloon-keeper, such a man would be obliged to do what he could to bring trade to the door of his betrayer; not that alone, but the basest of means would be resorted to to bring the rum-seller into the Order. Many a hard, bitter fight was carried on for the purpose of adding the dispenser of liquor to the eligibles to the Knights of Labor.

Grand Secretary Litchman, in his report to the General Assembly at St. Louis in January, 1879, referring to the law which debarred the liquor-seller, said:

Some misunderstanding exists as to the amount of rum a man has to sell to become a rum-seller. My idea is that no grander principle was ever ingrafted upon the laws of a labor organization than that law of ours which denies membership to the rum traffic. The two deadliest foes of labor are rum and ignorance. We should show no quarter to rum and its damning, blighting influence; but should rigidly prohibit membership to any one who sells *even a single glass.* Thus will this foe be conquered or made powerless.

This is the first reference to the liquor problem made by a General Officer to the General Assembly, and stands to the credit of Mr. Litchman upon the records of the association.

The St. Louis and Chicago sessions of the General Assembly left the Constitution as adopted at Reading, so far as that part of it which related to the admission of liquor-sellers was concerned. The first decision made by the new Grand Master Workmen, after his election at Chicago, was one which virtually repealed those of his predecessor, so far as they related to the rum-seller. It reads:

Rum-sellers CANNOT be admitted to membership, and any member engaging in the business of rum-selling, directly or indirectly, whether by the barrel, gallon, quart, pint or gill, who sells either by himself in person or by proxy, must apply for and be granted a withdrawal card; and if he neglects to make application therefor at once, the Recording Secretary of the Local Assembly shall notify him of his neglect, and at the next meeting a withdrawal card shall be issued to the brother.

It was thought that that would effectually debar the rum dealer; but he was persistent and untiring, and soon invented a scheme by which he could draw custom through the instrumentality of the Knights of Labor. Agents of wholesale liquor houses gained admission and recommended certain retail houses to the members as being above reproach, and suitable places wherein an evening might be spent with far greater profit than at home. It was also impressed on the mind of each member that to patronize certain saloons would help a brother member in gaining a livelihood, and, unfortunately, there were some who required no great amount of coaxing to assist in placing a " shingle on the roof" of the agent of the liquor establishment. A new decision was required, and it was made in the winter of 1879. It is annexed:

An agent for any liquor establishment (be that establishment wholesale or retail, or be he the agent, manufacturer or dealer) is not eligible to membership.

It was natural to expect that the friends of whisky would cease in their efforts to make it a member of the Knights of Labor, but they still persevered. When a man was about to become a rum-seller he would endeavor to have his name proposed in an Assembly of the Knights of Labor. When the Investigating Committee called on him and questioned him as to whether he sold liquor or not, he promptly replied in the negative, as though it were something to be ashamed of. After his election, and before his initiation, he would engage in the liquor business, and thus evade the law, as he thought. Another decision was necessary, and it was accordingly made to cover the last point raised, as follows:

If during the interval between the election and the initiation of a candidate he engages in the liquor traffic, either for his own profit or that of another, he is disqualified and cannot be covered with our shield.

Having failed in obtaining admission to the Order, the dealer in spirits still persevered, in the hope that in some way the organization of the Knights of Labor could be made of benefit to him. He could not get into the Order, that was certain, and it was equally as certain that he would have to go out should he by any means run the gauntlet of the ballot-box and be discovered in the act of selling liquor. A new plan was resorted to, and one after another the money-makers began to embark in the sale of strong drink by proxy. It was reported to the Grand Master Workman that the wife of a member of the Order was engaged in the saloon business. He was asked for a decision, and made the following:

No person can be a member of the Order whose wife sells liquor. *He must* either obtain a divorce from his wife or from this organization. The latter can be granted in the shape of an honorable withdrawal card.

When the General Assembly met in Pittsburg in 1880 the decisions of the Grand Master Workman were approved by a unanimous vote and became the law of the Order, although they were not given a place in the Constitution until the following year, when the Detroit session of the General Assembly amended the Constitution to read:

> No person who either sells or makes his living, or any part of it, by the sale of intoxicating drink, either as manufacturer, dealer or agent, or through any member of his family, can be admitted to membership in this Order.

At the Detroit Convention it was voted to make the name of the Order public and allow members, Local Assemblies and District Assemblies to declare that they were Knights of Labor. The publicity given to the organization and the exaggerated reports circulated concerning the numerical strength of the Assemblies attracted the attention of saloon-keepers everywhere. They saw a vast field opening up before them, and they determined to gather in the harvest by resorting to such means as would draw customers to their places of business.

During the year intervening between the Detroit and New York sessions of the General Assembly more attempts were made to reduce the Order to a rum-consuming machine than were resorted to before or since. The law so effectually shut the rum-seller out that applications were frequently sent in to the Grand Master Workman to grant dispensations to allow the initiation of those who sold liquor. The applications were all refused, and the Grand Master Workman in his annual address to the convention of 1882 said:

THE TEMPERANCE QUESTION

Is a most important one, and I sometimes think it is the main issue. The number of applications from Locals during the past year to grant dispensation to allow the initiation of rum-sellers was alarming. I have persistently refused, and will enjoin my successor, if he values the future welfare of the Order, to shut its doors with triple bars against the admission of the liquor dealer. His path and that of the honest, industrious workingman lie in opposite directions. The rum-seller who seeks admission to a labor society does so that he may entice its members into his saloon after the meeting closes. No question of interest to labor has ever been satisfactorily settled over a bar in a rum-hole. No labor society ever admitted a rum-seller that did not die a drunkard's death. No workingman ever drank a glass of rum who did not rob his wife and children of the price of it, and in doing so committed a double crime—murder and theft. He murders the intellect with which his Maker hath endowed him. He steals from his family the means of sustenance he has earned for them. Turn to the annals of every dead labor society, and you will see whole pages blurred and destroyed by the accursed foot-prints of rum. Scan the records of a meeting at which a disturbance took place, and you will hear echoing through the hall the maudlin, fiendish grunt of the drunken brute who disturbed the harmony of the meeting. In the whole English language I can find no word that strikes more terror to my soul than that one word rum! It was born in hell ere the fiat of " No redemption " had gone forth. Its life on earth has been one of ruin to the bright hopes of youth and the peace of old age. It has robbed childhood of its delights. It has stolen the laugh from the lips of innocence, the bloom from the cheek of manhood. It has touched the heart of old age like the tip of a poisoned arrow. Its sound as it gurgles from the neck of a bottle echoes through many a desolate household as the hissing of a thousand serpents. You may deem me too radical on this point. Yet I never interfere with the right of a man to drink if he so elects. I hold that I have a right to, and do, shun rum as I would an enraged tiger, neither meddling with nor allowing it to meddle with me. So long as it keeps its distance, I am content to let it alone; but the moment it seeks to interfere with my rights by coming into the Knights of Labor, than my soul arises in arms against it, and I can find no words too bitter, no denunciation too scathing, to hurl against it.

At the first session of the General Assembly held in Reading a member of the Order from a town in Ohio came on in the expectation of being admitted to the floor of the convention, and, although not a delegate, he would have been allowed to sit with the representatives were it not for the fact that he became drunk and disgraced himself before the intelligence reached him that the convention had voted to admit him. His conduct was considered so reprehensible that an account of it was ordered sent to his Assembly, with instructions to punish him for his misdemeanor. With that one exception none of those who attended the first convention indulged in strong drink.

At the New York session of the General Assembly the representative from Baltimore indulged so freely in liquor that he became unfitted for duty before the convention opened, and remained in that condition until the adjournment was reached. The New York session made no change in the law which related to the exclusion of liquor-sellers, and during the year a most vigilant watch was kept over all parts of the Order to see that no inroads were made from that quarter. When the General Assembly met in Cincinnati in 1883, the Grand Master Workman in his opening address said:

I wish to say to the representatives that no drunken or disgraceful conduct will be tolerated at this session. At the first session of the General Assembly a member disgraced himself and was published in the Proceedings. The lesson was a good one. But at the last session a representative got drunk and disgraced himself and his constituents on the floor of the General Assembly; the General Assembly condoned his offense, and refused to do him justice by publishing him in the Proceedings. On his return to his District he made the report to that body that the whole General Assembly was drunk; that the Grand Master Workman made an excuse that some of his friends were dead and left the General Assembly in disgust, only to return when he heard that he was re-elected. I desire to say that a resolution to screen any member from the consequences of his wrong-doing here will be of no avail, for I will see to it that his constituents are made aware of his doings if he does not represent them properly. The actions of the man I refer to had a most damaging effect on the District he represented, and in future the fullest light must shine on the actions of each and all of us.

The caution was unnecessary, for every man who attended the session was a temperate man, and as such was capable of so conducting himself that no disgrace would attach to the Order by reason of his actions.

In the interim between the closing of the Cincinnati session and the opening of the Philadelphia session in 1884, the Order experienced a great deal of trouble from liquor. At that time it was a common practice with the proprietors of company stores to keep liquor for sale. Many a company store kept liquor and sold it without obtaining a license. It is on record where a certain company sold liquor to the employes, and entered the sales upon the pass books of the workmen as " sundries."

It was a fact which could not be concealed that workingmen spent altogether too much money for liquor ; they spent too much valuable time in saloons and groggeries when they should have been at home or at the meeting of an Assembly of the Knights of Labor.

The laws of the Order required that five cents a month be set apart from the dues of each member, the same to be used in case of necessity when a strike or a lockout would occur. Commenting on the unwillingness of the members to pay this fund, and the tendency to indulge in strong drink, the General Master Workman said to the convention which assembled in Philadelphia in 1884:

I was asked to relieve one Assembly of the payment of this fund on the ground that the members were too poor to pay it. I attended a meeting of the Assembly, and at the close of the same saw ten members go to a saloon. I accepted the invitation to go with them for the purpose of witnessing how men make fools, lunatics and paupers of themselves. In my presence six dollars ($6), the result of hours of honest toil, went to uphold a system that damns the efforts of those who advocate the rights of the many to a share in the patrimony of the Heavenly Father. The membership of that Assembly was but thirty-three, the Assistance Fund due from that number would amount to four dollars and ninety-five cents ($4.95) for the quarter, but they were too poor to pay it. I will venture the assertion now " that the amount spent by members of this Order for strong drink, since the fund was established, will double the amount paid into the hands of the Secretary of the Executive Board and the Districts of the Order." The old motto of " millions for defense, but not one cent for tribute," has by some been changed to " millions for the devil, but not one cent for assistance." This is a humiliating confession to make, but no one can deny that it is a truthful one. I would not have it so, yet I cannot alter the existing state of affairs. We talk of reforming the world, why, we cannot reform ourselves ! Do not look upon me as a fanatic or a radical upon this question of temperance, for I am not ; I only ask that the men who are in the vanguard of reform, men who would accomplish something of benefit for the race, to stop for one moment *now* and ask whether we should not go a step further than others are willing to go in this direction. Is it enough to say that we are opposed to the introduction of the rum-seller? Should we in organizing an Assembly say to the new members, "Admit no men who sell strong drink," and say nothing about patronizing the men who sell it? If it is wrong to sell it, it is wrong to drink it. For years I have been accustomed to look upon crime in all its hideous deformity. I have had men and women brought before me for almost every crime ; they have acknowledged being guilty of drunkenness, and from that all the way down to murder, and the crime which inspired me with more of sadness, more of horror and more of regret was the crime committed by the man who stood before me charged with being drunk for the first time. To all the others I could say, " You are near the end ;" to him I felt that it was only the beginning, only the entrance to that life of debauchery, degradation and misery which falls to the lot of the confirmed drunkard. Intemperance degrades man and unsexes woman, while it damns both past hope of earthly redemption. When I meet a man whose reason has been drowned in drink, and look upon his face, I feel that I am looking upon a murderer, I am looking upon a person who has no regard for virtue or morality, for that which upholds virtue and sustains morality is lacking, the God-like gift of reason; incapable of judging whether his next step will be for good or evil, he plunges madly ahead and takes the dagger with a willing hand from his worst enemy only to plunge it to the heart of his most cherished friend. The man who drinks to excess will sell his own honor and his wife's virtue, and for what? that his wife and children may wear rags; that they may curse the light by which they were ushered into the world; that they may say of him when he dies: "Though hell has claimed its own, 'tis only the body that has gone, the remembrance of his blighting touch still remains to curse us with its presence."

To the session of the General Assembly which convened in Hamilton, Ontario, in 1885, the General Master Workman said in opening the session:

DRUNKENNESS.

If there is a time when men should conduct themselves with manly dignity and decorum, it is when they are in trouble. I have observed that when a strike is in progress there are some men who insist on making exhibitions of themselves at the price of their good name, and of the good name of the Order that is held responsible for their actions. It should be made an offense, punishable with expulsion from the Order, for any member to become intoxicated while the good name of the Order is hanging in the balance. It is a criminal offense, and the severest penalty known to the laws of the Order should be visited upon the head of the offender.

We legislate against the admission of the man who sells rum, and make a member of the man who supports him; this does not seem just or fair. The character of the society is judged by the character of its members. If a member is seen upon the streets in a state of intoxication, the society of which he is a member is blamed for his conduct. We must, therefore, look after the character of our members with a jealous eye. If a traveling member is discovered to be drunk while carrying a traveling card of the Knights of Labor, it should be made a punishable offense. We have been altogether too lenient with offenders of this character, and we must adopt suitable legislation for the regulation of the evil I have pointed out. If a man given to the use of strong drink and a serpent applied for admission to the Order I would vote for the serpent in preference to the drunkard; for, if the viper transgressed the laws by disgracing us, we could crush the life out of his worthless carcass by stepping on its head; but we must let the other and worse transgressor live to continue his villainous work.

I do not ask those who join us to be saints, but I have a right to expect, and I do ask them, to be *men*. We cannot shut our eyes to this matter any longer; the crime must be punished, and a law for the government of the offense must be framed at this General Assembly.

At the same session, while speaking on the subject of electing officers, the General Master Workman, again referring to the subject, said:

We should make inquiry of the men who aspire to places whether they are in the habit of using strong drink. We cannot be too careful in this matter, for sometimes a good man does some very bad things when his wits create a vacuum in his head to be filled by the fumes of rum. In our dealings with the men who control capital we are pitted against the most intelligent men in the nation, and we cannot afford to lay aside any portion of our intelligence or cunning in dealing with them.

The Hamilton session made no changes in the laws bearing on the admission of men connected with the liquor traffic; indeed, there existed no necessity for a change in the legislation bearing on the subject, for the Order did not suffer from the influence of the rum-seller during the year. In the beginning of the following year the Order began to increase in numbers so rapidly that it became an impossibility to give that careful scrutiny to each applicant which the law required. The strikes of that period, particularly the great Southwest strike, caused such a rush to the Order of all classes of workingmen that many a man, who would at other times be rejected because of his intemperate habits, slipped into the Order, and by reason of his membership attracted the attention of the public to his misdeeds, many of which were charged to the organization which his very presence disgraced. New Assemblies, being organized at the rate of seven hundred a month, gathered in the good with the bad. Whole Assemblies were formed of men who, through curiosity, sought admission to the Knights of Labor. On the 3d of May, 1886, the General Master Workman issued a secret circular, in which he took occasion, among other things, to say:

We have had some trouble from drinking members and from men who talk about buying guns and dynamite. If the men who possess money enough to buy guns and dynamite would invest it in the purchase of some well-selected work on labor, they would put the money to good use. * * * * * * * * * * To our drinking member I extend the hand of kindness. I hate the uses to which rum has been put, but it is my duty to reach down and lift up the man who has fallen a victim to the use of liquor. If there is such a man within the sound of the Secretary's voice when this is read, I ask him to stand erect on the floor of his Assembly, raise his hand to heaven, and repeat with me these words:

"I am a Knight of Labor. I believe that every man should be free from the curse of slavery, whether that slavery appears in the shape of monopoly, usury or intemperance. The firmest link in the chain of oppression is the one I forge when I drown manhood and reason in drink. No man can rob me of the brain my God has given me unless I am a party to the theft. If I drink to drown grief, I bring grief to wife, child and sorrowing friends. I add not one iota to the sum of human happiness when I invite oblivion over the rim of a glass. If one moment's forgetfulness or inattention to duty while drunk brings defeat to the least of labor's plans, a lifetime of attention to duty alone can repair the loss. I promise never again to put myself in such a position."

If every member of the Knights of Labor would only pass a resolution to boycott strong drink, so far as he is concerned, for five years, and would pledge his word to study the labor question from its different standpoints, we would then have an invincible host arrayed on the side of justice.

The promulgation of that circular did much good in two ways. It had the effect of causing men who were known to be wedded to the use of liquor to leave the Order, and it was the means of causing upward of one hundred thousand members to take what they were pleased to call the "Powderly Pledge." Of this there can be no doubt, for the proofs are in the possession of the writer that at least one hundred thousand members took that pledge between the issuing of the circular and the convening of the regular session of the General Assembly in October.

At the special session of the General Assembly of the Order held in Cleveland in May, 1886, the evils which follow the admission of drunkards into the organization became the subject of debate. The injury done the Order in allowing an intemperate man to hold a commission as Organizer and represent the association was also debated, and as a result the following was adopted:

> Any Organizer who shall attempt to perform his duty while under the influence of liquor shall have his commission revoked.

At the Cleveland session the doors of the General Assembly were thrown open for the first time to admit a representative of another organization, and Mrs. Mary A. Woodbridge, representing the Woman's Christian Temperance Union, was admitted to the floor of the convention for the purpose of delivering an address of welcome to the assembled representatives. The courtesy shown to the Woman's Christian Temperance Union was never accorded before or since to any other organization.

Up to that time Organizers were not required by law to be temperance men, but the General Master Workman insisted upon each applicant certifying to his habits in that respect before a commission would be issued. It was a fact which could not be denied by the most ardent friend of the rum-drinker that the Order was cursed by a number of Organizers who frequently and openly violated the laws of the organization in instituting Assemblies while under the influence of liquor. When a commission was applied for, the blank on which the application was made bore the following notice:

> Assemblies recommending Organizers will be held responsible for their conduct. The officers of the Assembly will certify below whether the applicant is addicted to the use of strong drink. If he is, no commission will be issued. If a false statement is made, charges will be preferred against the officers who signed the application.

When the General Assembly met in Richmond in October, 1886, the law in relation to the commissioning of Organizers was ordered changed, and each applicant obliged to certify as to whether he indulged in strong drink. Of the eight hundred and fifteen Organizers appointed for the year ending November 1, 1887, over five hundred were total abstainers, and the remainder pledged themselves not to drink to excess while serving in the capacity of Organizers. Of the total number commissioned only seven were required to return their commissions because of drunkenness. At the Richmond session the law was amended to read :

No person who either sells or makes a living, or any part of it, by the sale of intoxicating drink, either as manufacturer, dealer or agent, or through any member of the family, or who tends bar permanently or temporarily, can be admitted into or remain in membership in this Order.

No Local or other Assembly or member shall, directly or indirectly, give, sell or have any ale, beer or intoxicating liquors of any kind at any meeting, party, sociable, ball, picnic or entertainment whatever appertaining to the Order. Any member found guilty of violating this law shall be suspended for not less than six months, or expelled. No fine shall be imposed for this offense. Any Local or other Assembly so offending shall be suspended during the pleasure of the General Executive Board, or shall have its charter revoked by said Board.

This law was not promulgated until June, 1887, and was the occasion of a storm of abuse and ridicule from those who favored absolute liberty on the part of an Organizer to drink if he so willed. It was because of this agitation that the General Master Workman took so strong a stand, not only against the use of liquor by Organizers of the Order, but members as well.

In a speech delivered in the old Mechanics' Hall, Boston, June 11, 1887, he said :

Let me say a few words concerning a cause which some years ago was not so popular as it is to-day. You who are going out will carry these words home with you. Tell them to every person you meet, whether Knight of Labor or not, that the greatest curse that labor has to contend with to-day it finds in its own home, in its own grasp; and the worst weapon that is wielded against labor to-day is held by the strong right hand of labor itself; and when that weapon is raised to strike the blow it is raised in the shape of a glass, that carries with it the rum which drowns man's reason. If I could put words in the mouth of every one leaving here to-night, I would have them say to every man, woman and child who labors throughout the length of the world, cast strong drink aside as you would an ounce of liquid hell. It damns; it blights; it sears conscience, body and soul; it destroys everything it touches. It reaches across the threshold of the home and ruins the family circle, takes the wife you have sworn to protect and cherish and drags her down from the pinnacle of purity and love which is her rightful station and tramples her in the mire, and then turns her into that house from which no decent, respectable woman ever comes alive. It takes her child from her grasp. It strangles innocence, purity; aye, even life itself at times. It takes the chair, table, furniture, the dishes, and the mirror from the wall, and it takes the little pictures your pennies bought and carries them all to the pawnbroker shop, and coins them into pennies again to be taken to the grog-shop, where your manhood is drowned in oblivion. I have seen men going from the door of the saloon, one in that direction, one in another, and another taking a different course; each one a thing for the finger of scorn to be pointed at; each one a thing for all strong, honest, decent men and women to shun; each one a thing to despise as you would a serpent; each one reeling through the streets in rags, with a face on which no intelligence is shown; each one with every feature of man obliterated, and only that of the beast to be seen. I have seen these things rap on the doors of their homes ; I have seen the women come to open the door; I have seen the smile vanish from the face; I have heard the cry of the child where the laugh should be heard; I have seen them at early morn and at close of day; I have seen them in my own city, have seen them in your city and State, have seen them in New York and in every city east of the Mississippi, and I know that if there is a damning blight and curse to labor it is that which gurgles from the throat of the bottle at the command of the rum-drinker. I have no hesitation in saying that the most powerful assistance we could have is a pledge from every man and woman: a pledge from every man to abstain from drink, and a pledge from every woman to help him on to success; for I know the women do not drink, and, from what they are doing in the Knights of Labor, I know that with their aid we can uphold the true and the good in our organization. If I could have the pledge of every man in our Order to-day, let it dwindle down to one hundred thousand or fifty thousand if it will, but give me one hundred thousand or fifty thousand sober, honest, earnest men, and I will wage the battle of labor more successfully than if you gave me twelve million of men who drink either moderately or drink to excess.

On the following day, in the city of Lynn, the General Master Workman delivered another speech, in the course of which he said:

Shoemakers drink whisky, so do machinists, so do hatters, and so does every other class of laborers drink whisky and beer. In one county in the State of Pennsylvania, I am told that in one year seventeen million dollars went over the counters of the whisky-sellers, eleven million dollars of which came from the pockets of the workingmen. Last October an assessment was levied for the support of our locked-out members, and among those who refused to pay it were the Assemblies located in that county to which I refer. They paid the assessment to the devil cheerfully enough, but when the men they were sworn to protect asked for assistance they hesitated, questioned and spent an additional dollar in the rum saloon. Every dollar, every cent, every dime paid by the workingmen in a saloon is a paving-stone for hell. No man has a right to spend one dime in a saloon. You have a right to personal liberty so long as you don't interfere with mine; but every member of the Knights of Labor who disturbs an Assembly meeting with his drunken, maudlin talk encroaches on the rights of others through the vaunted exercise of his personal liberty. Where, then, shall we draw the line? I would draw it right before the nose and in front of the whisky glass as the man would lift it to his lips. There may be some here who do not like what I am saying. Permit me to say that I do not mind that, for what I say is God's truth and has to be spoken. One of the reasons why labor organizations have failed in the past is because the leaders did not have the manhood to denounce liquor as a curse. Stop it, men, stop it! Not for a day or a week, but until God stops your life. It does no man any good. It does every one injury.

For making these two speeches the speaker was subjected to a severe criticism from those outside of the organization, as well as from many members. Few had the manhood to attack the position taken by the General Master Workman as being wrong, but they feared its consequences. Some of the members of the General Executive Board were not in sympathy with the views of the General Master Workman, and when an old and valued friend of his wrote him as to the policy of his attack on rum, he wrote an article for the JOURNAL OF UNITED LABOR, in which he defined his position as follows:

THE JUSTICE OF MY POSITION.

Among the letters that came to me to-day I find one from an old friend who takes me to task for my words on the temperance question, spoken some ten or twelve days ago in Boston and Lynn. He says:

"In the main you are right; even the rum-seller himself will not deny the justice of your position ; but remember that in the very organization of which you are the head there are many good men who drink; there are thousands who will not agree with you ; and, after all, why do you so bitterly arraign the poor drunkard? It is not required of you by the Constitution or laws of the Knights of Labor. You could well afford to remain silent, or at least neutral, preferring to teach rather by example than precept, etc. * * * * * * I very much fear that you will be misunderstood, etc."

My friend makes the candid admission, in starting out, that in the main I am right, that even the rum-seller will not deny the justice of my position. Having said as much he should have stopped—even then he told me nothing new. I know that I am right; I know that in refusing to even touch a drop of strong drink I was, and am, right. In refusing to treat another to that which I do not believe to be good for myself to drink, I know I am right. In refusing to associate with men who get drunk, I know I am right. In not allowing a rum-seller to gain admittance into the Order of the Knights of Labor, I know I am right. In advising our Assemblies not to rent halls or meeting-rooms over drinking places, I know I am right. I have done this from the day my voice was first heard in the council halls of our Order. My position on the question of temperance is right—I am determined to maintain it, and will not alter it one jot or tittle. If "in the main" I am right, why should I alter my course? If the man who sells liquor will "not deny the justice" of my position, why should I deviate to the right or left? If he will not deny, why should he not admit that I am right? I know that in the organization of which I am the head there are many good men who drink, but they would be better men if they did not drink. I know that there are thousands in our Order who will not agree with me on the question of temperance, but that is their misfortune, for they are wrong, radically wrong.

Ten years ago I was hissed because I advised men to let strong drink alone. They threatened to rotten-egg me. I have continued to advise men to be temperate, and though I have had no experience that would qualify me to render an opinion on the efficacy of a rotten egg as an ally of the rum-drinker, yet I would prefer to have my exterior decorated from summit to base with the rankest kind of rotten eggs rather then allow one drop of liquid villainy to pass my lips, or have the end of my nose illumined by the blossom that follows a planting of the seeds of hatred, envy, malice and damnation, all of which are represented in a solitary glass of gin.

Ten years ago the cause of temperance was not so respectable as it is to-day, because there were not so many respectable men and women advocating it. It has gained ground, it is gaining ground, and all because men and women who believe in it could not be browbeaten or frightened. Neither the hissing of geese or serpents nor the throwing of rotten eggs has stopped or even delayed the march of temperance among the workers.

"Why do I so bitterly arraign the *poor* drunkard?" For the reason that he is a drunkard, and because he has made himself poor through his love of drink. Did I, or any other man, rob him of the money he has squandered in drink, did I make him poor, the vilest names that tongue can frame would he apply to me. Must I stand idly by and remain silent while he robs himself? Did he rob only himself it would not make so much difference. He robs parents, wife and children. He robs his aged father and mother through love of drink. He gives for rum what should go for their support. When they murmur he turns them from his door, and points his contaminated drunken finger toward the poor-house. He next turns toward his wife and robs her of what should be devoted to the keeping of her home in comfort and plenty. He robs her of her wedding ring and pawns it for drink. He turns his daughter from his door in a fit of drunken anger and drives her to the house of prostitution, and then accepts from her hand the proceeds of her shame. To satisfy his love of drink he takes the price of his child's virtue and innocence from her sin-stained, lust-bejeweled fingers, and with it totters to the bar to pay it to the man who "does not deny the justice of my position." I do not arraign the man who drinks because he is poor, but because through being a slave to drink he has made himself and family poor. I do not hate the man who drinks, for I have carried drunken men to their homes on my back rather then to allow them to remain exposed to inclement weather. I do not hate the drunkard—he is what drink has effected; and while I do not hate the effect, I abhor and loathe the cause.

Take the list of labor societies of America, and the total sum paid into their treasuries from all sources from their organization to the present time will not exceed $5,000,000. The Order of the Knights of Labor is the largest and most influential of them all; and though so much has been said concerning the vast amount of money that has been collected from the members, yet the total sum levied and collected for all purposes—per capita tax, JOURNAL, assistance fund, appeals, assessments, insurance and co-operation—up to the present time will not exceed $800,000.

The total sum collected for the first nine years of the existence of the General Assembly was but $500,725.14. In nine years less than $600,000 were collected to uplift humanity to a higher plane, and to bring the workers to a realizing sense of their actual condition in life. It took less than $600,000 to teach the civilized world that workingmen could build up an organization that could shed such light upon the doings of landlords, bondlords, monopolists and other trespassers on the domain of popular rights that they were forced to halt for a time and stand up to explain. Less than $600,000 (not a dollar unaccounted for), and on the statute books of the nation you will find the impress of the workman's hand. On the law book of every State can be traced the doings of labor's representatives. Less than $600,000 to turn the batteries of greed and avarice against the Order of the Knights of Labor. Less than $600,000 to create a revolution greater, further reaching in its consequences and more lasting in its benefits than the revolution which caused the streets of the towns and cities of France to run red with human blood less than a century ago. Less than $600,000 to make men feel and believe that woman's work should equal that of the man. Less than $600,000 to educate men and women to believe that "moral worth and not wealth is the true standard of individual and national greatness." Less than $600,000 to cause every newspaper in the land to speak of the work being done by the Knights of Labor—some of them speaking in abusive terms, others speaking words of praise, according to the interests represented by the papers, or according as the work done harmonized with the principles of the Order. For paying less than $600,000 the members of the Knights of Labor have been told that they were being robbed. In one day an employers' association organizes and pledges itself to contribute $5,000,000 to fight labor. The next day the papers are almost silent on that point, but are filled to the brim with lurid accounts of the reckless, autocratic manner in which the officers of the Knights of Labor levy a twenty-five-cent assessment to keep over one hundred thousand locked-out men and women from starvation. Putting two and two together, it is not hard to guess why papers that applauded the action of the employers in one column should in another column advise the workers not to pay the twenty-five-cent assessment. $600,000 for sober men to use in education and self-improvement.

Now let us turn to the other side. In the city of New York alone it is estimated that not less than $250,000 a day are spent for drink, $1,500,000 in one week, $75,000,000 in one year. Who will dispute it when I say that one-half of the policemen of New York City are employed to watch the beings who squander $75,000,000 a year? Who will dispute it when I say that the money spent in paying the salaries and expenses of one-half of the police of New York could be saved to the tax-payers if $75,000,000 were not devoted to making drunkards, thieves, prostitutes and other subjects for the policeman's net to gather in? If $250,000 go over the counters of the rum-seller in one day in New York City alone, who will dare to assert that workingmen do not pay one-fifth, or $50,000 of that sum? If workingmen in New York City spend $50,000 a day for drink, they spend $300,000 a week, leaving Sunday out. In four weeks they spend $1,200,000—over twice as much money as was paid into the General Assembly of the Knights of Labor in nine years. In six weeks they spend $1,800,000—nearly three times as much money as that army of organized workers, the Knights of Labor, have spent from the day the General Assembly was first called to order up to the present day; and in one year the workingmen of New York City alone will have spent for beer and rum $15,600,000, or enough to purchase and equip a first-class telegraph line of their own; $15,600,000—enough money to invest in such co-operative enterprises as would forever end the strike and lockout as a means of settling disputes in labor circles.

A single county in Pennsylvania, so I am informed, spent in one year $17,000,000 for drink. That county contains the largest industrial population, comparatively, of any in the State. $11,000,000 of the $17,000,000 came from the pockets of workingmen. New York City, in one year, contributes $15,600,000 to keep men and women in poverty, hunger and cold, while one county in Pennsylvania adds $11,000,000, making a total of $26,600,000. Twenty-six million six hundred thousand dollars! I have a conundrum to ask you, Mr. Purdy: If the General Officers of the Knights of Labor are thieves because they levy an assessment which brings in less than a dollar a piece for each man, woman and child who needs it, what would you call the men who collect as a voluntary gift from foolish workingmen the sum of $26,600,000 in one year?

The press, and not a few indignant workingmen, raved because the twenty-five-cent assessment was levied; but both press and indignant workingmen remained silent while that damnable robbery of $26,600,000 was going on. Who arraigns the poor drunkard now? Does he not arraign himself before the bar of condemnation every time he ranges himself before the bar in a rum-hole?

The Richmond session of the General Assembly voted $50,000 to purchase headquarters for the Order. $45,000 went to buy the building on Broad Street, Philadelphia. For complying with the order of the General Assembly the General Officers have been abused and slandered most villainously, principally by men who never contributed a cent toward the purchase of the building. The enemies of the Order, or of the officers of the Order, have styled the headquarters "The Palace." On another street in the city of Philadelphia there is a saloon called "The Palace." I inquired of the proprietor what it cost him, and he said $20,000. Nine years ago he began business, selling rum, on a capital of $73, and in that time he has acquired the money with which to purchase the building and the lot on which it stands. He also owns $50,000 in railroad securities—all on an original cash capital of $73. His patrons are chiefly workingmen. Why do we not hear a protest go up against the means by which that palace was erected?

"It is not required of you by the Constitution or laws of the Knights of Labor." I know it. Neither is it stated in the Constitution of the Order that I shall not stand on the public highway and rob the passer-by, yet I know that I should not do such a thing. If I saw a man about to hang himself, the Constitution does not specify that I should not cut the rope.

"You could well afford to remain silent or at least neutral, preferring to teach by example rather than precept." If I cared more for the praise and approbation of labor's enemies than I do for the interest of labor I would remain silent. The man who remains neutral while his friend is in the grasp of the enemy, or while his friend is in danger, is a coward at heart and does not deserve the name of man or friend. Remain silent and neutral while the house is on fire and you have nothing left but blackened, defaced walls and—ashes.

Teach by example! I cannot in so large a country as this. If my example is good, then my words should proclaim it to the world. I am no better than other men, but the virtue of temperence is good, even in a bad man, and that is what I wish to hold up before our members and workingmen outside of our Order.

"I very much fear that you will be misunderstood." Do not fear; I will not be misunderstood when this letter is read. I am not a fanatic. I do not damn the man who sells liquor. I have nothing against him. Many men who now sell liquor were once workingmen, and were victimized through a strike or lockout. I would not injure a hair of their heads, but I would so educate workingmen that they would never enter a saloon. Then the money saved from rum and rum-holes would go to purchase necessaries, and such an increased stimulus would be given to trade that the rum-seller could return to an honest way of making a living.

I may be taken to task for being severe on the workingmen. It may even be said that I slander them. If to tell the truth is to be severe, then on this one question I hope some day to be severity itself; but I speak to workingmen because it is in their welfare that I am interested. I have not been delegated to watch or guard the fortunes of millionaires, and in no way can I hope to accomplish anything until I state my policy freely and frankly to those I represent. We are seeking to reform existing evils. We must first reform ourselves.

Some mischievous urchins once found a man sleeping by the roadside. They procured some soot and blackened his face. When he awoke and went into the crowded street every man he met laughed at him. He did not learn the cause of the merriment until a friend held a mirror up before him. He became very mad, and for a time felt angry toward the man who held the mirror; but he soon came to his senses, laid the blame where it properly belonged, and thanked the man who showed him why others ridiculed him. I am holding the mirror up to human nature. True, it exposes folly and vice. I may and do receive condemnation, but if I can only show the men I speak to who it is that is blackening their faces, characters and hearts; if I can only show them how to remove the stains and become sober men again, I will be content to put up with their anger, for I know that they will one day thank me or bless my memory for the words I have spoken and written in the cause of temperance.

No more cogent reason exists for the exclusion of the rum-seller from the ranks of the Knights of Labor than because of the influence exercised by the saloon-keeper on the politics of the day. It is a recognized fact that nominations for the offices of Congressmen, State Senators and Representatives, Mayors of cities, Aldermen and lesser positions are dictated by the men who sell strong drink.

The organization of the Knights of Labor while not pretending to be a political association, while it does not presume to dictate nominations or elections, is a political organization in the highest sense of the word. It is not a partisan organization, and seeks for measures through men and parties instead of for men for the sake of party. Its members have cause to know that many a good law has been defeated through the carelessness and indifference of men who had been enslaved by the rum-seller.

Knights of Labor know that good legislation has been frustrated by the drunkenness and debauchery of Legislators, who fell victims to the use of rum, and gave their allegiance to the dispenser of that article rather than to the people to whom they owed their election.

Unwise, pernicious laws have been passed, by enemies of the people, by steeping in the fumes of liquor the brains of men who were sent to enact legislation for the masses.

Rum and its influences had on many an occasion dominated who should be nominated, who should be elected, and what laws should be passed. It was recognized by the officers of the Knights of Labor that the men who sold liquor sold it not for the good of the masses but for their own aggrandizement, and that he who yielded to the rum element went over to the enemy of labor. As a consequence, it would never do to send men to represent the people in any capacity when it was morally certain that liquor had more of an influence over them than those who cast the votes that elected them to office.

Knights of Labor seeking for just, equitable legislation and the repeal of pernicious laws could not depend on those who were under the influence of that which made restrictive laws a necessity, and, therefore, they must in every way discountenance the slaves to rum by discountenancing the use of it. No better way could be devised to discountenance the use of rum than to forbid the seller to cross the door-sill of the Assembly as a member.

As the rum dealer of past decades was supposed to control more or less of the " labor vote," it was a practice among politicians to leave a sum of money at each saloon where the keeper claimed to exercise an influence over the workingmen. Where a workingman for any cause was engaged in the sale of rum, it was imagined that he had an influence over his former associates, and his saloon·was the resort of politicians of all parties before election.

To remove the stigma cast on the name of labor, it was deemed best to so separate the rum-seller from the workingman as to cause politicians to hesitate before seeking for the votes of the toilers through the grog-shop. As far as a labor organization could do such a thing, it has been done by the Knights of Labor. The member of the Order who votes at the dictation of rum is not obliged to do so because of any influence which can be brought to bear on him through his organization, which in no way stands as an ally to liquor or its devotees.

Soon after the adoption of the Constitution, in 1887, one or two Assemblies of brewery employes threatened to withdraw from the Order if the temperance feature was not altered or stricken out. The law which prohibited the sale of liquor at picnics, balls, etc., was objectionable to a great many who took the ground that it interfered with the personal liberty of the member. It was claimed that the organization was drifting into the Prohibition Party, and would eventually go to pieces because of its temperance principles. The principal reason why the use of beer was prohibited at picnics and other gatherings of the Order was because of the tendency to degrade the member under the auspices of an Assembly of the Knights of Labor. Men who would not drink on any other occasion would flock to a Knight of Labor picnic, and, under the impression that they were not doing anything wrong, would lose sight of reason and common-sense while imbibing beer. The organization could not consistently afford to forbid the beer-seller from entering the Order because his mode of making a living was objectionable, and allow an Assembly to make money or build up its treasury by selling the same article. If it was wrong in an individual to sell drink, surely the offense was not lessened when an assemblage of individuals engaged in the sale of it.

The Order of the Knights of Labor held from the beginning that the sale of drink was wrong. It required no written statement to be made to certify to that, for the fact that the man who sold could not be initiated was in itself a condemnation of the practice of selling liquor. It was hoped that by keeping the man who sold rum out of the Order it would serve as a means of teaching members that what was not good enough to come into the Knights of Labor was not good enough to associate with in places where strong drink was sold.

Another reason why the sale of beer was prohibited at picnics was because enemies of the Order seldom failed to take advantage of the weakness of some of the members on such occasions and ply them with liquor until they became drunk. Men who never were members of the Knights of Labor were frequently seen reeling from picnics held under the auspices of an Assembly of the Knights of Labor. Agents for liquor establishments, who had been refused admission to the Order, have been known to pay men of dissolute habits to attend picnics and get drunk with the express purpose in view of raising a disturbance in order to cast discredit on the name of the organization. Members of the Order were frequently taunted with such remarks as: "Your Order will not allow me to join because I sell liquor, but you will allow it to be sold at your picnics and gatherings when your association can make money out of it. We sell it only because we make money from the sale of it, and for the same reason your organization sells it when it can do so in such a way that no member can individually be held responsible." It was a cowardly way of dealing with the question, and there was nothing else to do than to throw open the doors of the Order to the rum-seller, or else close them against the sale of liquor in any form by the organization or any part of it at any time or place or under any circumstances.

The argument used that it interfered with the personal liberty of the member to prohibit the sale of liquor at picnics was not tenable, for the reason that the personal liberty question had been settled the day the liquor-seller was forced to leave the Order. The liberty of the member to sell drink was interfered with when the law was passed which forbade the seller of drink to cross the threshold of the Assembly-room. The personal liberty of the member was not interfered with when the sale of liquor was prohibited at picnics, for the picnic was not a personal affair; it was a Knight of Labor gathering, and was held under the auspices, not of the individual, but the Assembly. The member was not forbidden to drink, but the Order refused to give him drink. He could procure it elsewhere, but the good name of the Order would not be tarnished; and if he went elsewhere and became intoxicated, and then returned to the K. of L. picnic, it would be known that he took such a step, since he could not possibly get drunk at the picnic where no liquor was sold. The personal liberty cry is not worthy of consideration for a moment. There is nothing, I am sorry to say, in the laws of the Knights of Labor which will prevent a man from drinking as freely as he pleases; his personal liberty is not assailed by the Order, but the personal liberty of every other man is assailed by the man who drinks. No sober man would be allowed the liberty accorded to a drunken man, who may insult men, women and children, and be excused for so doing because he is drunk. If a labor organization selects a committee to do a certain thing, and one member of the committee gets drunk, the others have no right to interfere with his personal liberty, but he does interfere with the liberty of every member of the committee. If there is a strike or difficulty in progress the man who drinks is the man who becomes involved in a disturbance at the bidding of the agent of the corporation, in order that a disturbance may be made the pretext for invoking the aid of the law. The sheriff's posse or the State militia usually follow a too free indulgence in personal liberty on the part of the man who will not allow his rights to be interfered with, while he is violating in a most shameful manner the rights of others.

On the evening of April 23, 1889, while going from Detroit, Mich., to Windsor, Ontario, across the ferry, a manufacturer of furniture, doing business in Detroit, introduced himself to the General Master Workman, and in course of his conversation said ·

I have had occasion to employ a number of men at one time or another, and have had no little trouble with them. My uncle, a very kind man, could not get along with the men as he ought to, and we had no end of little annoyances. On every pretext the men would send a committee into the office to complain of something or other until we became harassed beyond measure. I finally hit upon a remedy. I selected a member of the union and gave him $15, and told him next time we had any trouble with the men to take the most prominent ones to a saloon, and with that $15 to treat the crowd. He did as he was told, and when they tried to hold a meeting that night they were so drunk that they did not know what they assembled for; they became so mixed up that they adjourned without accomplishing anything, and before they got around to it again it was too late. I found out how to manage my men, and since then have had no trouble with them, for I know how to head them off. I know that you may not like to hear that this can be done, but it is true, and I now have complete mastery over the workmen in our employ.

That confession of heartless immorality was made without solicitation, and during its recital the man who had disgraced his manhood in debauching his employes in the manner described experienced a pride in explaining how he had outwitted the men who were employed by him.   Here is a living illustration of the evil effects which follow a love of drink.   It must not be supposed that it is a liking for liquor that induces men to frequent the saloons.

The love of the beautiful is as strong in workingmen as in others, and the majority of them cannot afford to make their homes attractive.   There are "fishers of men" whose duty it is to preach the word of God, but they open the doors of the house of God but once or twice a week.   During their discourses they seldom attack the vices of the rich, although all who attend know that they have vices.   The short-comings of the poor are arraigned in burning language.   Once a week is this gone through with, and to the poor the church doors are closed until Sunday comes again.

The home is scantily furnished, and that he may meet with his fellow-men to talk over the events of the day the workman goes upon the street each evening; no church door is open; no reading-room or public place in which he can enjoy himself, and chat, laugh and pass away the hour.   The only door open to him, the only place where he may act without restraint is in the saloon, the door of which is always open, the walls of which are tastily provided with pictures, and the trappings of which are displayed to the best advantage.   Mirrors, paintings, statues, easy chairs and comfortable sofas are at his disposal, and everything is conducted in the most democratic manner; rich and poor stand equal so long as the pennies hold out to purchase drink.   The "fishers of men" do not display their bait so temptingly as do the fishers of dimes and dollars, and it is no wonder that many men are allured away from the home and the church after the visit to the gilded saloon.

Few of the wealthy people who rail against strong drink and the evil effects of the saloon are really sincere in their professions of friendship for the poor drunkards; their philanthropy will never cause them to erect reading-rooms, billiard halls or coffee houses for the entertainment of those who would not enter the saloon if such institutions existed.   It is only while retaining his senses that the drinker enjoys the pleasure of his visit to the saloon, and it often happens that he drinks while there simply because he feels that he must do so while enjoying the hospitality of the rum-seller.

The scantily furnished apartments of the workman, lacking the attractiveness of the saloon, cause the workman to leave his home of an evening for the purpose of visiting the saloon.   This is given in evidence to prove that poverty drives men to drink, but it does not prove the charge by any means.   Were other doors open to him he could bring his wife and children with him, but they must not accompany him to the saloon for fear of its contaminating influences.

There is no good reason why poverty should cause a man to drink, and there are thousands of reasons why its presence should restrain him from indulging in the use of intoxicants. Why should poverty make a drunkard of a man? Is it because he is poor that he must do something which will make him poorer? Is it to hide from himself the knowledge of his poverty that the poor man drinks? If so, does he not know that the awakening will find him poorer than before? Will those who say that it is poverty which causes men to drink admit that when the poor man gets drunk he expects to remain so forever? Unless they do, they cannot advance any good reason why he should for a time, and a very short time, lose sight of his misery.

It is said that when a man is drunk he feels happy and rich. Will that be advanced as a reason why a poor man should drink? Will those who take the ground that poverty begets drunkenness admit that those who drink for such a cause are fools? for none but a fool would do that which would make him poorer because he was already poor, and none but an ignorant man would attempt to drive away his poverty by a means which would make him forget it for but a moment, only to add to it when the forgetfulness had passed away.

That poverty begets drunkenness is true, but the number of those who have been reduced to poverty through strong drink is far greater than those who have been made drunkards through poverty. The most fertile source of drunkenness is to be found in the American habit of "treating." It is considered no disgrace to accept a glass of rum from a friend or an acquaintance. To offer a drink to a friend is considered good taste and hospitable. A drink will be accepted without a remonstrance or protest. Should the price of a drink be tendered to a man he would be insulted, and a breach of etiquette would be charged to the person who offered it.

It is a false notion of friendship that causes men to recede from the stand which they have taken against the use of liquor when asked to take a drink. Poverty has done a great deal to make drunkards of men and women, but treating has made more drunkards than all other causes combined. To refuse to accept a drink when it is offered will subject the refuser to ridicule and insult. To the weak-minded it is easier to take the drink and break a good resolution than it is to refuse the proffered hospitality, and thus incur the displeasure of a friend.

Drunkenness in all its varied forms is condemned by the Order of the Knights of Labor. Liquor-selling and the habit of treating are discountenanced, and the members of the Knights of Labor are taught that the person who either sells or gives strong drink to his fellow-man is not worthy of membership in the organization. By keeping it constantly before the members that it is wrong to sell or give strong drink, it is taught that to patronize those who do sell or give liquor away is also wrong.

From a purely business standpoint the Knights of Labor are justified in excluding the liquor-seller, and in making odious the habits of the rum-drinker. It is unnecessary to give the statistics which would show what percentage of the earnings of labor go to the support of the rum traffic, for that has been done by others in works devoted exclusively to the cause of temperance, but it is not putting the case too strong to say that the workingmen of America have spent enough money for rum to buy for each head of a family in the United States and Canada, who toils for a living, a comfortable, well-furnished home.

The liquor habit has a direct bearing on the wage of the employe in more ways than one. The habits of the drinker not only reduce the comforts of the home by useless and criminal spendings, but they frequently bring about a reduction of wages. The use of liquor degrades and brutalizes the workman; it blunts his finer feelings and makes him careless of the surroundings and welfare of his family. His employer, when he notices the condition to which the use of strong drink has reduced the workman, will take it for granted that the greater the compensation paid to such a man the greater will be the amount spent for rum. Here again the personal liberty cry of the drinker militates against the majority, for the majority of workingmen do not drink to excess, but one man among a hundred who does get drunk will reduce the wages of the other ninety-nine. Employers, as a rule, are always willing to avail themselves of an opportunity to reduce wages, and the workman who reels past the door of the employer day after day is taken as the rule instead of the exception.

It is said that the workmen are a degraded set who will not appreciate an act of kindness or good wages, and as a consequence their earnings may as well be reduced as not, for the savings of the home will be no greater than if the merest pittance were paid. Another argument made use of is: the smaller the pay, the less will the workman spend for rum. In nine cases out of ten, where wages are reduced because of drunkenness, it follows that the drunken employes are the exception instead of the rule; but the sober, industrious workman must surrender more of comfort, more of the necessities and more of the dignity which belongs to man because of the habits of drunkenness and consequent improvidence of his fellow-workman who does use liquor.

The only argument used by the apologists of rum-drinking by workingmen that has any weight is that it cheers and brightens the surroundings of the rum-drinker for a short time at least. That is not true, and not one instance can be adduced to prove the assertion. No man who has ever emerged from a fit of drunkenness has ever acknowledged that he felt the better for his debauch, or that he felt better while drunk, or that it made his surroundings more cheerful to become drunk; and if any such statements have been made they are untrue. If for a time the surroundings of the drunkard appeared to be more cheerful, he soon awoke to find that it was only a delusion. If he felt better while drunk, he awoke to find that that feeling was only imagination, for it vanished with a return to reason. But while the surroundings of a man may appear more cheerful while drunk, it is an undeniable fact that they do not so appear to the wife and family of the drunkard, and a more cowardly act cannot be perpetrated by a man than to impose humiliation, disgrace and sorrow on a defenseless woman and children for a momentary gratification of the appetite.

The use of strong drink weakens a man in mind and body; it breeds disease; it has wrought untold misery on the human family, or that portion of it that has to toil for a living; and never has the use of liquor done a single thing to elevate or ennoble the workers of this or any other land. Every argument is against the use of liquor. The facts are all against it, and evidence of all kinds and statistics innumerable all go to prove that the use of liquor by working people is wrong, and does infinite harm to those who drink and those who come in contact with them.

While the Order of the Knights of Labor is not a temperance society so far as prohibiting members from the use of liquor is concerned, it has done more, possibly, than any other society to make workingmen see the enormity of rum-drinking. Those who advocate temperance in the Knights of Labor are not fanatics, but they are sincere in desiring to elevate the workingman to a more exalted station in life, and to make it easier for his family to secure the benefits of education and science. For these reasons the seller of rum cannot become a member of the Knights of Labor.

BUILDING THE STRUCTURE.

Steadily, steadily, step by step,
  Up the venturous builders go;
Carefully placing stone on stone—
  Thus the loftiest temples grow.
Remember the brotherhood, strong and true,
  Builders and artists, and bards sublime,
Who lived in the past and worked like you,
  Worked and waited a wearisome time.—*The Quiver.*

The second regular session of the General Assembly of the Knights of Labor convened at St. Louis, Mo., on January 14, 1879. There were but twenty-three representatives present, although there were twenty-six District Assemblies in existence. The Districts organized during the time which elapsed since the adjournment of the Reading General Assembly were:

D. A. 15, Elmira, N. Y., organized immediately after the Reading session.

D. A. 16, Scranton, Pa., which was originally organized under the number which was given to the District Assembly of West Virginia.

D. A. 16 was founded by U. S. Stephens in August, 1878.

D. A. 17, organized January 23, 1878, at St. Louis, Mo.

D. A. 18, organized at Hazleton, Pa., February 22, 1878.

D. A. 19, organized at Charleston, W. Va., March 15, 1878.

D. A. 20, organized April 30, 1878, at Mahanoy City, Pa.

D. A. 21, organized May 3, 1878, at Mt. Holly, N. J.

D. A. 22, organized August 15, 1878, at La Salle, Ill.

D. A. 23, organized October 7, 1878, at Coalton, Ky.

D. A. 24, organized November 10, 1878, at Chicago, Ill.

D. A. 25, organized November 7, 1878, at Frostburg, Md.

D. A. 26, which was organized January 11, 1879, just four days prior to the session of the General Assembly in St. Louis.

The most important action taken at that session was to change the time of holding the General Assembly from January to September. The vote which the Order at large was instructed to take by the special session which convened in Philadelphia in June, 1878, was not decisive. It did not indorse the proposition to make public the name of the Order, but the convention decided to allow such localities as wished to work openly to do so. When that session adjourned the officers for the ensuing term were:

Grand Master Workman—Uriah S. Stephens.
Grand Worthy Foreman—T. V. Powderly.
Grand Secretary—Charles H. Litchman.
Assistant Grand Secretary—James McGinniss, Newport, Ky.
Grand Treasurer—William H. Singer, St. Louis, Mo.

The General Executive Board consisted of the following-named representatives:

John McCaffrey, Philadelphia, Pa.
E. S. Marshall, Mobile, Ala.
Thomas Kavanaugh, Chicago, Ill.
James H. Coon, Des Moines, Iowa.
Newell Daniels, Milwaukee, Wis.

When the third regular session convened in Chicago, Ill., on September 2, 1879, Mr. Stephens was not present. The excessive strain under which he labored during the twenty months of his official career left him broken in health and finances. The Order was indebted to him for part of his salary, and indeed it could not afford adequate compensation for the work done. Night and day he labored to add to the strength of the Order. His salary was but $400 a year. He sent his report in manuscript to the Secretary, Mr. Litchman, who read it to the convention. In a letter to the Secretary he stated that his choice for Grand Master Workman lay between Richard Griffiths of Chicago, Ill., and T. V. Powderly of Scranton, Pa.

Four District Assemblies were organized between the St. Louis and Chicago Conventions:

D. A. 27, February 14, 1879, at Shamokin, Pa.
D. A. 28, organized May 10, 1879, at Des Moines, Iowa.
D. A. 29, July 19, 1879, at Helena, Ala.
D. A. 30 of Massachusetts, organized August 13, 1879.

Philip Van Patten, representing L. A. 280 of Cincinnati, Ohio, presented the following:

Resolved, That workingwomen may become members of this Order and form Assemblies under the same conditions as men.

Although a majority voted for the proposition, it failed to become a law. The rules required that all amendments to the Constitution should have two-thirds of the votes of the convention in the affirmative in order to become law. The attention of the Order was called to this inconsistency in the laws, and it was directed that representatives to the following session be instructed to come prepared to vote on the admission of women. The Preamble called upon members to endeavor " to secure for both sexes equal pay for equal work," and it was but equity to permit women to share in the effort to accomplish this much-desired result.

The officers elected at Chicago were:

Grand Master Workman—T. V. Powderly.
Grand Secretary—Charles H. Litchman.
Assistant Grand Secretary—Gilbert Rockwood, Boston, Mass.
Grand Treasurer—Dominic Hammer, Doylestown, Ohio.

The General Executive Board consisted of the following:

Edward A. Stevens, Chicago, Ill.
Philip Van Patten, Cincinnati, Ohio.
Michael A. Leary, Mahanoy Plane, Pa.
David Fitzgerald, West Elizabeth, Pa.
Cornelius Curtin, La Salle, Ill.

The salary of the Grand Master Workman was continued at $400 a year; that of the Grand Secretary was also continued at the rate paid the previous year, $800.

The fourth session of the General Assembly was called to order in Pittsburg, Pa., on Tuesday, September 7, 1880. There were present representatives from forty-two District Assemblies and over two hundred Local Assemblies, which were attached direct to the General Assembly.

The following Districts were organized during the year:

D. A. 31, Mobile, Ala.	D. A. 37, Leadville, Col.
D. A. 32, New Albany, Ind.	D. A. 38, Chapman, Ohio.
D. A. 33, O'Fallon, Ill.	D. A. 39, Fairmount, W. Va.
D. A. 34, Kanawha, W. Va.	D. A. 40, Houtzdale, Pa.
D. A. 35, Bellaire, Ohio.	D. A. 41, Baltimore, Md.
D. A. 36, Du Bois, Pa.	D. A. 42, Arnot, Pa.

The officers elected at the Pittsburg session were:

Grand Master Workman—T. V. Powderly.
Grand Secretary—Charles H. Litchman.
Assistant Grand Secretary—Gilbert Rockwood.
Grand Treasurer—Dominic Hammer.

The General Executive Board stood as follows:

James L. Wright, Philadelphia, Pa.
Frederick Turner, Philadelphia, Pa.
Daniel McLaughlin, Braidwood, Ill.
Henry G. Taylor, New York City, N. Y.
Robert Price, Lonaconing, Md.

The salary of the Grand Master Workman remained as before, $400; that of the Grand Secretary was advanced to $900; and that of the Assistant Grand Secretary was fixed at $750.

A committee was appointed at this session to prepare a ritual for the government of Assemblies of women, and a resolution adopted that women be admitted as soon as it was printed.

The most important action taken by the fifth regular session of the General Assembly of the Knights of Labor which met at Detroit, Mich., on Tuesday, September 6, 1881, was to declare the name of the Order to be public property after January 1, 1882. Up to this time the letter-heads and other printed matter of the Order did not bear the name of the organization. The five stars, by which the name was designated from the organization of the first Assembly, were discontinued and the words "noble and holy" omitted from future publications. The Grand Master Workman was instructed to issue an address to the world on January 1, 1882, proclaiming that there was such an organization in existence as the Order of the Knights of Labor.

The committee appointed at the previous session to prepare a ritual for the government of Assemblies of women made no report; the Grand Master Workman deciding that women should be admitted on equality with men, and that no separate form of ritual or Constitution was necessary. From the close of that session dates the admission of women to the Order of the Knights of Labor. But one new District Assembly appeared on the roll as presented by the Grand Secretary at the Detroit Convention, No. 43 of Erie, Col.

The salaries of the Grand Officers were not changed at that session. Up to that time the obligation by which members were bound to obey the laws of the Order consisted of an oath which pledged them to absolute secrecy. The oath was stricken out, and a word of honor, binding the member to secrecy, was substituted.

The officers for the ensuing year were as follows:

Grand Master Workman—T. V. Powderly.
Grand Secretary—Robert D. Layton, Pittsburg, Pa.
Assistant Grand Secretary—Gilbert Rockwood.
Grand Treasurer—A. M. Owens, Clarksburgh, W. Va.
Grand Statistician—Theodore F. Cuno, New York.

The General Executive Board was made up of the following:

T. V. Powderly.
Robert D. Layton.
James Campbell, Pittsburg, Pa.
Myles McPadden, Pittsburg, Pa.
Archibald Cowan, Coal Bluff, Ohio.

The sixth regular session was held in New York, beginning Tuesday, September 5, 1882. Six new District Assemblies were represented. Their numbers and headquarters are appended :

D. A. 44, Rochester, N. Y.
D. A. 45 (the first National Trade District ever organized), composed of telegraphers, with headquarters at Pittsburg, Pa.
D. A. 46, Buffalo, N. Y.
D. A. 47, Cleveland, Ohio.
D. A. 48, Cincinnati, Ohio.
D. A. 49, New York City, N. Y.

Much of the time of the convention was taken up in an investigation of a boycott which the Grand Statistician had placed on the Glen Cove Starch Company of Long Island, N. Y. A great deal of ill-feeling was created while the investigation was in progress. Provision was made in the law for a Co-operative Board of five to take charge of all rules, regulations and laws relating to co-operation. The New York session was called upon to mourn the death of Uriah S. Stephens, Past Grand Master Workman, and the Grand Treasurer, A. M. Owens. Mr. Owens died on December 9, 1881, and Mr. Stephens on February 13, 1882.

The officers elected at that convention for the ensuing year were:

Grand Master Workman—T. V. Powderly.
Grand Worthy Foreman—Ralph Beaumont.
Grand Secretary—Robert D. Layton.
Assistant Grand Secretary—Gilbert Rockwood.
Grand Treasurer—Richard Griffiths.
Grand Statistician—Francis B. Egan.

Members of the General Executive Board :

David Healy, Rochester, N. Y.
John S. McClelland, Hoboken, N. J.
James Campbell, Pittsburg, Pa.
Robert W. Price, Cincinnati, Ohio.
Henry C. Traphagen, Cincinnati, Ohio.

The Co-operative Board consisted of the following-named representatives :

George Holcombe, Trenton, N. J.
John H. Sanderson, Trenton, N. J.
Jacob Folsom, Lonaconing, Md.
John Murray, Shawnee, Ohio.
Anthony Jaquette, Mt. Pleasant, Pa.

At the New York session a plan of benefit insurance was adopted and placed in charge of Charles H. Litchman as Insurance Secretary. The salaries of officers were fixed for the year as follows: That of the

Grand Master Workman $400, as before, that officer refusing to serve if the salary was increased; the Grand Secretary received a salary of $1,200; the Assistant Grand Secretary $1,200; the Grand Treasurer $100. The Grand Master Workman was called away from the convention by the death of a relative before he read his annual report or address, and did not return until a few hours before the adjournment of the session. During his absence the officers for the ensuing term were elected.

The seventh regular meeting of the General Assembly convened in Cincinnati, Ohio, on Tuesday, September 4, 1883. The number of new Districts organized during the year was fifteen; their numbers and official headquarters are as follows:

D. A. 50, Detroit, Mich.	D. A. 58, Edwardsport, Ind.
D. A. 51, Newark, N. J.	D. A. 59, Oneida, N. Y.
D. A. 52, Brooklyn, N. Y.	D. A. 60, Utica, N. Y.
D. A. 53, San Francisco, Cal.	D. A. 61, Hamilton, Ont.
D. A. 54, ———	D. A. 62, Bloomington, Ill.
D. A. 55, Muskegon, Mich.	D. A. 63, Rochester, N. Y.
D. A. 56, Pittsburg, Pa.	D. A. 64, New York City, N. Y.
D. A. 57, Chicago, Ill.	

The strike of the Telegraphers' District, which took place during the previous summer, occupied no small share of the attention of the assembled delegates; that District was on the eve of disbanding as a result of the strike, and took but little part in the affairs of the Order afterward.

The officers elected for the ensuing year were:

General Master Workman—T. V. Powderly.
General Worthy Foreman—H. A. Coffeen, Danville, Ill.
General Treasurer—Richard Griffiths.
General Secretary—Frederick Turner.
Secretary of Insurance Association—H. L. McGaw, Pittsburg, Pa.

The General Executive Board stood as follows:

Frank K. Foster, Cambridge, Mass.
John S. McClelland, Hoboken, N. J.
John Murray, Shawnee, Ohio.
James Campbell, Pittsburg, Pa.
Thomas B. Barry, East Saginaw, Mich.

The members of the Co-operative Board were:

Henry E. Sharpe, Eglinton, Mo.
George Holcombe, Trenton, N. J.
Ralph Beaumont, Addison, N. Y.
Will J. Vale, Hamilton, Ontario.
Oliver M. Boyer, Louisville, Ky.

Up to the adjournment of the Cincinnati General Assembly the officers of the Order were styled "Grand Officers;" by a vote passed at that convention the use of the word "Grand" was abolished and "General" substituted. It was considered that the word "Grand" savored too much of aristocracy, and that "General" would be more in accord with the spirit of the Order. Mr. Layton refused to be a candidate for re-election to the office of General Secretary. Messrs. Rockwood and Turner contested for the place; the former was defeated by a majority of two votes and retired from office., The Order lost the official aid of one of the most valuable men that ever did service in its cause. Mr. Rockwood removed from Pittsburg to Washington, where he soon after accepted a position in the Government Printing Office.

The salary of the General Master Workman was raised to $800 at that session. A motion was made to increase it from $400 to $2,000; it received a majority vote, but was declared rejected by the General Master Workman because it lacked two-thirds of all votes cast. The General Master Workman refused to allow his salary to be raised to even $1,000, and at his recommendation it was fixed at $800. The salary of the General Secretary was continued at $1,200; he was authorized to appoint his chief clerk at a salary of $1,000 per year. After the adjournment of the General Assembly, Mr. Turner appointed Henry G. Taylor of New York as his chief clerk. The salary of the General Treasurer was fixed at $100. The salary of the Secretary of the General Executive Board was fixed at $1,200. Up to this time the Secretary of the Board was not constantly employed in the service of the Order; by resolution he was directed to devote his whole time to the work of his office. John S. McClelland was elected Secretary of the Board. The General Statistician was ordered to be paid $300 per annum.

On September 1, 1884, the eighth regular convention of the Order met in Philadelphia. Twelve District Assemblies were instituted between the adjournment of the Cincinnati session and the opening of the Philadelphia General Assembly:

D. A. 65, Albany, N. Y.	D. A. 71, St. Louis, Mo.
D. A. 66, Washington, D. C.	D. A. 72, Toledo, Ohio.
D. A. 67, Nashville, Tenn.	D. A. 73, Jackson, Mich.
D. A. 68, Troy, N. Y.	D. A. 74, Saginaw, Mich.
D. A. 69, Stilson, Kan.	D. A. 75, Brooklyn, N. Y.
D. A. 70 (shoemakers), Philadelphia, Pa.	D. A. 76, Grand Rapids, Mich.

The Constitution underwent a radical change at this session, and the first alteration made in the Preamble of Principles of the Order, since the first General Assembly, was effected in 1884. It was at this session that National Trade Assemblies were first recognized in the Knights of Labor.

The officers for the ensuing year were:

General Master Workman—T. V. Powderly.
General Worthy Foreman—Richard Griffiths.
General Secretary-Treasurer—Frederick Turner.
General Auditor (a position created at that session)—John G. Caville, New York City, N. Y.
Secretary of Insurance Association—Homer L. McGaw.

The General Master Workman and General Secretary-Treasurer were members of the General Executive Board by virtue of their office. The other members elected at Philadelphia were:

John W. Hayes, New Brunswick, N. J.
Joseph R. Buchanan, Denver, Col.
William H. Bailey, Shawnee, Ohio.

The Co-operative Board consisted of:
John Samuel, St. Louis, Mo.
O. M. Boyer, Louisville, Ky.
John J. McCartney, Baltimore, Md.
Peter D. Cattanoch, Troy, N. Y.
Hugh Cameron, Lawrence, Kan.
Henry Mente, Ithaca, N. Y.

The salary of the General Master Workman was raised to $1,500 a year, and he was directed to spend sixteen weeks in the field, four weeks in each section of the country. The salaries of the other officers were allowed to remain as before. At that session the time of holding the meetings of the General Assembly was changed from September to October.

———

The next session was held in Hamilton, Ontario, on October 5, 1885. Since the close of the Philadelphia Convention nineteen District Assemblies were organized:

D. A. 77, Lynn, Mass.
D. A. 78, covering the State of Texas, with headquarters at Austin.
D. A. 79, covering the State of Minnesota, with headquarters at Minneapolis.
D. A. 80, Coal Valley, Pa.
D. A. 81, Williamsport, Pa.
D. A. 82, Union Pacific employes, with headquarters at Denver, Col.
D. A. 83, Manistee, Mich.
D. A. 84, Richmond, Va.
D. A. 85, New York City, N. Y.
D. A. 86, covering the State of Maine, with headquarters at Portland, Me.
D. A. 87, Freeland, Pa.
D. A. 88, Bay City, Mich.
D. A. 89, Erie, Col.
D. A. 90, Trenton, N. J.

D. A. 91 (shoemakers), New York City, N. Y.

D. A. 92 (colored), Richmond, Va.

D. A. 93, Moberly, Mo.

D. A. 94, Philadelphia, Pa.

D. A. 95, Hartford, Conn.

T. V. Powderly, Richard Griffiths, Frederick Turner, John G. Caville, Homer L. McGaw, John W. Hayes and William H. Bailey were re-elected to the positions which they occupied during the previous term. Thomas B. Barry was elected to the position vacated by Joseph R. Buchanan. Three vacancies occurred on the Co-operative Board. Henry Mente and Hugh Cameron were re-elected, and John P. McGaughey of Minneapolis, Minn., was selected to take the place vacated by O. M. Boyer. The salaries of the General Officers were fixed at the same rates as were paid the year previous.

A great deal of time of the meeting was taken up in discussing co-operation, but no definite steps were taken to put any particular plan in operation. The failure to make a success of the Cannelburgh mine, and the recommendation to sell it, had a dampening effect on the convention.

The black-listing of members of the Order along the Wabash Railway System came in for a large share of attention.

The number of members reported in good standing at Hamilton was 104,335. It is more than likely that there were not over 90,000, for representation to the General Assembly was based on the number of members in good standing, and in some instances District Assemblies paid taxes on many who were not in good standing in order to be credited with a larger delegation than they would otherwise have. The convention adjourned after an eight days' session.

The rapid succession of strikes, boycotts and lockouts which followed the close of the Hamilton General Assembly necessitated the calling of a special session of that body on May 25, 1886. The convention remained in session nine days. The time was occupied in discussing the best means of meeting the constantly arising troubles in the labor world. Trade unions and Knights of Labor were clashing in many localities; the anarchist outbreaks caused alarm in some quarters; employers, without discrimination, classed trade unionist, Knight of Labor and anarchist as one; and the black list preceded the strike in some places and followed it in others.

It is safe to say that neither labor organization, manufacturer nor employer should be held accountable for the bitter feeling which was occasioned during the year 1886. Both sides were feverish; each side availed itself of every opportunity to take advantage of the other. In the excitement of the hour workmen who were employed by just and sympathetic manufacturers resented what they considered indignities, but which in many instances were only the inevitable results of the actions of others apart from their employers. Employers who had hitherto shown a disposition to treat their workmen fairly found themselves imposing restrictions upon their employes which they never thought of before. In other places concessions were made and mutual understandings were arrived at between employes and employers; but, on the whole, the tendencies of the times were not conducive to the continuance of a lasting friendship between workmen and their employers.

Many trade unions that had almost surrendered their existence were fanned into new life through the efforts of Knights of Labor. The agitation kept up by that organization stimulated others, and soon a jealousy sprung up between them—a rivalry as to which should do certain things threatened to destroy many effective associations. The Knights of Labor were justified in believing that their Order should assume the right to take charge of and settle disputes between employer and employe, since the trade unions of the past had almost died away and were no longer in position to interfere when the rights of the workmen were being interfered with. The clashing between local bodies and the jealousies between leaders have been prolific of more strife between labor organizations since 1886 than between capital and labor. Workmen, who had no hope of securing the benefits of organization, have, through the instrumentality of the Knights of Labor, been organized into Trade Assemblies until but few of the callings in America are now without organizations of their own.

The Cleveland session had to face the demand for a recognition of organizations that, up to that time, were unable to obtain recognition for themselves; and with every strike turned over to the Order, no matter by whom originated, it became necessary to augment the power of the General Officers that they might successfully cope with the troubles then brewing. It was voted to elect six members of the convention to act as an auxiliary to the General Executive Board, and the following were selected:

James E. Quinn, New York.
W. H. Mullen, Richmond, Va.
Hugh Cavanaugh, Cincinnati, Ohio.
David R. Gibson, Hamilton, Ont.
Joseph R. Buchanan, Denver, Col.
Ira B. Aylsworth, Baltimore, Md.

With these assistants the General Executive Board performed its labors until the assembling of the representatives at Richmond.

When the Richmond General Assembly convened on October 4, 1886, the representation was so large as to be almost unmanageable. The Philadelphia session of 1884 had 126 representatives in attendance; that of Hamilton, in 1885, had 146; while the Richmond General Assembly accorded seats to 658 representatives. The membership, as reported by the General Secretary-Treasurer, had increased from 104,335 in October, 1885, to 702,924 for October 1, 1886. The membership never exceeded 600,000 in good standing. The same methods by which a large representation was secured in 1885 were resorted to in 1886. No scrutiny was observed, and, indeed, it was not possible to carefully examine all who came with credentials. The number of new Districts organized during the year was eighty, as follows:

D. A. 96, Rockport, Ky.
D. A. 97, Washington, D. C.
D. A. 98, Butte City, Montana.
D. A. 99, Providence, R. I.
D. A. 100, Paterson, N. J.
D. A. 101, Employes of Gould system of railroads, with headquarters at Sedalia, Mo.
D. A. 102, New Orleans, La.
D. A. 103, New Brunswick, N. J.
D. A. 104, Cohoes, N. Y.
D. A. 105, Atlanta, Ga.
D. A. 106, Indianapolis, Ind.
D. A. 107, Kansas City, Kan.
D. A. 108, Milwaukee, Wis.
D. A. 109, Des Moines, Iowa.
D. A. 110, Mahanoy City, Pa.
D. A. 111, Duke Centre, Pa.
D. A. 112, St. Joseph, Mo.
D. A. 113, South Norwalk, Conn.
D. A. 114, Montreal, Canada.
D. A. 115, Seattle, Wash. Ter.
D. A. 116, Knoxville, Tenn.
D. A. 117, Downs, Kan.
D. A. 118, Shenandoah, Pa.
D. A. 119, South Bend, Ind.
D. A. 120, Petersburg, Va.
D. A. 121, Dayton, Ohio.
D. A. 122, Elizabeth, N. J.
D. A. 123, Norfolk, Va.
D. A. 124, Manchester, N. H.
D. A. 125, Toronto, Canada.
D. A. 126, New York City, N. Y.
D. A. 127, Wilmington, Del.
D. A. 128, New York City, N. Y.
D. A. 129, Williamstown, Pa.
D. A. 130, Reading, Pa.
D. A. 131, Key West, Fla.
D. A. 132, Chattanooga, Tenn.

D. A. 133, Memphis, Tenn.
D. A. 134, Big Rapids, Mich.
D. A. 135, composed of Miners and Mine Laborers, with headquarters at New Straitsville, Ohio.
D. A. 136, Chicago, Ill.
D. A. 137, Bellaire, Ohio.
D. A. 138, St. Thomas, Canada.
D. A. 139, Savannah, Ga.
D. A. 140, Los Angeles, Cal.
D. A. 141, Columbus, Ga.
D. A. 142, Springfield, Mo.
D. A. 143, Glass-blowers, with headquarters at Milwaukee, Wis.
D. A. 144, New Haven, Conn.
D. A. 145, Texarkana, Texas.
D. A. 146, Hastings, Neb.
D. A. 147, Albany, N. Y.
D. A. 148, Olean, N. Y.
D. A. 149, Glass-blowers, with headquarters at Brooklyn, N. Y.
D. A. 150, Creston, Iowa.
D. A. 151, Altoona, Pa.
D. A. 152, Syracuse, N. Y.
D. A. 153, Norristown, Pa.
D. A. 154, Pittsburg, Pa.
D. A. 155, Canton, Pa.
D. A. 156, Watertown, N. Y.
D. A. 157, Jeffersonville, Ind.
D. A. 158, Menominee, Mich.
D. A. 159, South Easton, Pa.
D. A. 160, Trenton, N. J.
D. A. 161, Middletown, N. Y.
D. A. 162, Rocklin, Cal.
D. A. 163, Carson City, Nevada; organization never completed.
D. A. 164, Clinton, Iowa.
D. A. 165, Eureka, Cal.

D. A. 166, Iron Mountain, Mich.
D. A. 167, Wichita, Kan.
D. A. 168, Harrisburg, Pa.
D. A. 169, Corry, Pa.
D. A. 172, Columbus, Ohio.
D. A. 173, Birmingham, Ala.
D. A. 174, Windsor, Ontario.
D. A. 175, Lamar, Mo.; organization never completed.
D. A. 176, Augusta, Ga.
D. A. 178, Springfield, Mo.

Numbers were assigned to D. A.'s 170, 171 and 177 before the Richmond session, but the work of organization was not completed until after the adjournment of that body.

The trouble between the Order and the trade unions took up much of the time of the session. A resolution was passed which obliged members of the Cigarmakers' International Union to leave the Order.

The General Executive Board was increased from five to seven members. The office of General Secretary-Treasurer was divided, and a Treasurer and Secretary provided for in the laws. The Secretary was no longer to be a member of the General Executive Board. When the session adjourned the General Officers were:

General Master Workman—T. V. Powderly.
General Worthy Foreman—Richard Griffiths.
General Secretary—Charles H. Litchman.
General Treasurer—Frederick Turner.

The office of Secretary of Insurance was abolished, and the duties of that office were intrusted to the General Treasurer.

The General Executive Board stood as follows:

Thomas B. Barry, East Saginaw, Mich.
John W. Hayes, New Brunswick, N. J.
William H. Bailey, Shawnee, Ohio.
Albert A. Carlton, Somerville, Mass.
Thomas B. McGuire, New York City, N. Y.
Ira B. Aylsworth, Baltimore, Md.

The General Co-operative Board stood:

John P. McGaughey, Minneapolis, Minn.
Hugh Cameron, Lawrence, Kan.
John Samuel, St. Louis, Mo.
Henry Mente, Ithaca, N. Y.
Louis C. T. Schleber, Lynn, Mass.
J. M. Broughton, Raleigh, N. C.

The length of the term of office of General Officers was extended from one to two years. The salary of the General Master Workman was fixed at $5,000 a year; that of the General Secretary and General Treasurer at $2,000 each. The compensation allowed to members of the General Executive Board was $4 per day when on duty.

The convention remained in session sixteen days. That part of the

Constitution relating to the General Assembly and the officers thereof was amended, but the remainder of it was referred to a committee to sit during recess. Over four hundred documents were presented at that session, enough to consume the time of a deliberative body for at least two months. The committee was instructed to go over the documents relating to changes in the laws and prepare a Constitution, to be submitted to the Order at large for adoption.

While the convention was in session the pork-packers' strike in Chicago was in progress, and, acting on the impulse of the moment, the body voted to send a member of the General Executive Board to the scene, not to involve the Order in the trouble but to keep it separate and apart from it, and, if possible, settle the difficulty without the aid of the Order. Thomas B. Barry was selected by those who represented Chicago; he was ordered to go, and did not return to the convention before adjournment was reached.

The General Executive Board was ordered to expend $50,000 in the purchase of a headquarters, and to purchase a home for the family of Past Grand Master Workman Stephens, to cost not less than $5,000. Both of these duties were performed by the Board, and in the purchase of a headquarters but $45,000 were expended on the building, the fitting up and repairing coming within the $50,000 limit.

At this convention it was decided to take steps to organize the women of America, and a General Investigator of Woman's Work was elected at the request of the women who were present as representatives. Mrs. Leonora M. Barry of Amsterdam, N. Y., was elected and entered upon the discharge of her duties almost as soon as the convention adjourned.

A number of strikes and lockouts were in progress at the time. The General Assembly passed a vote to render aid to some of them, and all who were engaged in a difficulty of any kind at once applied for assistance. The funds of the Order were never calculated to be spent for strike purposes, but in the excitement of the hour, and acting on the impulse of the moment, the vote was passed which took over $400,000 out of the treasury inside of one year. The results of that convention convinced all who attended it that a smaller representation was necessary in order to insure good order, harmony, good legislation and good results. One representative for every one thousand members in good standing was allowed prior to the Richmond session, and one for every three thousand members has been allowed ever since.

The Minneapolis General Assembly convened with 188 representatives in attendance. The session began on October 4 and ended on the 19th. The new Districts organized between the Richmond and Minneapolis sessions were:

D. A. 170, Janesville, Wis.
D. A. 171, Texarkana, Ark.
D. A. 177, Norwich, N. Y.
D. A. 179, Dover, N. H.
D. A. 180, Chillicothe, Mo.
D. A. 181, Filemakers' National Trade Assembly, with headquarters at Providence, R. I.
D. A. 182, Hamilton, Ohio.
D. A. 183, Nashville, Tenn.
D. A. 184, Pottsville, Pa.
D. A. 185, New Albany, Ind.
D. A. 186, Kingston, N. Y.
D. A. 187, Charleston, S. C.
D. A. 188, Terre Haute, Ind.
D. A. 189, Lithographers, with headquarters at New York City, N. Y.
D. A. 190, Textile-workers, with headquarters at Philadelphia, Pa.
D. A. 191, St. Louis, Mo.
D. A. 192, Macon, Ga.
D. A. 193, Lynchburg, Va.
D. A. 194, Morgan City, La.
D. A. 195, Fort Wayne, Ind.
D. A. 196, Sunbury, Pa.
D. A. 197, Jersey City, N. J.
D. A. 198, Machinery Constructors, with headquarters at New York City, N. Y.; since transferred to Cleveland, Ohio.

D. A. 199, New Castle, Pa.
D. A. 200, Rutland, Vt.
D. A. 201, Peoria, Ill.
D. A. 202, Hyde Park, Ill.
D. A. 203, Nanaimo, British Columbia.
D. A. 204, Winnipeg, Manitoba.
D. A. 205, Salt Lake City, Utah.
D. A. 206, East St. Louis, Mo.
D. A. 207, St. Catharines, Ontario.
D. A. 208, Birmingham, England.
D. A. 209, Leadville, Col.
D. A. 210, Paper-hangers' National Trade Assembly, with headquarters at New York City, N. Y.
D. A. 211, Galveston, Texas.
D. A. 212, Philadelphia, Pa.
D. A. 213, Mahanoy City, Pa.
D. A. 214, Media, Pa.
D. A. 215, Pulaski City, Va.
D. A. 216, Shoemakers' National Trade Assembly, with headquarters at Boston, N. Y.
D. A. 217, Harrisburg, Pa., Iron and Steel Workers' National Trade Assembly.
D. A. 218, Portland, Oregon.
D. A. 219, Graham, N. C.
D. A. 220, Brooklyn, N. Y.
D. A. 221, Hot Springs, Ark.

A remarkable feature of the session was the attendance, on the second day, of Michael Davitt, who addressed the assembled representatives during recess. The Farmers' Alliance was in session in Minneapolis at that time, and the chief officers of both organizations took part in a public meeting held under the auspices of the workingmen of Minneapolis.

The principal action of the session was the resignation of the General Officers. Acting under instructions from other sources than the Order of the Knights of Labor, Messrs. Bailey and Barry of the General Executive Board made reckless charges of extravagance against the other officers. Mr. Bailey had conceived a dislike for the General Secretary, and carried his ill-will so far as to include all who did not take sides with him in opposing the object of his hatred. Mr. Barry was intimately and warmly associated with the anarchist element, and had conceived a hatred for the General Master Workman because of that official's opposition to the meddling of the anarchists with the Knights of Labor. According to his own admission, Mr. Barry was at one time, and may yet be, the holder of the white card of the International Workingmen's Association and a member of a group of that society, although he denied it when asked if it were true.

Joseph R. Buchanan, who had previously represented D. A. 89 of Colorado, came with credentials to again represent that District Assembly, but his Local Assembly was not in good standing, and had not been for many months. He was not admitted to a seat, and the radical element, who recognized Mr. Buchanan as a champion, took offense at the action of the General Assembly.

The vote against asking for clemency for the condemned anarchists drove George Schilling, Charles F. Sieb, George F. Murray and several others to desperation, and they determined to form a Provisional Committee to purify the Order. When the resolution passed by which the General Officers were requested to resign, Messrs. Powderly, Griffiths, Litchman, Turner, Hayes, Carlton, Aylsworth and McGuire handed in their resignations. Messrs. Bailey and Barry, not willing to risk a re-election, refused to tender theirs, and those already in were not accepted.

There was no election of officers at that session, nor were any changes made in the make-up of the official staff of the Order. The time of holding meetings of the General Assembly was changed from October to November.

The Indianapolis Convention was called to order on November 13, 1888, and continued in session until the 27th of that month.

The new District and National Trade Assemblies represented at the Indianapolis session were:

D. A. 222, Silk-workers' National Trade Assembly, Paterson, N. J.

D. A. 223, Paragould, Ark.

D. A. 224, Philadelphia and Reading Railroad employes, since disbanded.

D. A. 225, Cigarmakers' National Trade Assembly.

D. A. 226, Surface Street-car Employes' National Trade Assembly, New York City, N. Y.

D. A. 227, Spartansburg, S. C.

D. A. 228, Gloversville, N. Y.

D. A. 229, Kylertown, Pa.

D. A. 230, Bookbinders' National Trade Assembly, with headquarters at New York City, N. Y.

D. A. 231, Garmentcutters' National Trade Assembly, with headquarters at New York City, N. Y.

D. A. 232, Indiana, Pa.

D. A. 233, Brinkley, Ark.

D. A. 234, Little Rock, Ark.

D. A. 235, Belleville, Ontario.

D. A. 236, Uxbridge, Ontario.

D. A. 237, Coudersport, Pa.

D. A. 238, Brinkley, Ark.

D. A. 239, Pine Bluff, Ark.

D. A. 240, Leather-workers' National Trade Assembly, with headquarters at Chicago, Ill.

D. A. 241, Berlin, Ontario.

D. A. 242, Little Rock, Ark.

D. A. 243, New Iberia, La.

D. A. 244, Fort Smith, Ark.

D. A. 245, Sawmakers' National Trade Assembly, Philadelphia, Pa.

D. A. 246, Albany, N. Y.

D. A. 247, Carriage-workers' National Trade Assembly, Cincinnati, Ohio.

D. A. 248, Dudley, England.

D. A. 249, Spokane Falls, Wash. Ter.

D. A. 250, Type-founders' National Trade Assembly, Cleveland, Ohio.

D. A. 251, Watch-case Makers' National Trade Assembly, New York City, N. Y.

D. A. 252, Brass-workers' National Trade Assembly, New York City, N. Y.

D. A. 253, New York City, N. Y.

The General Executive Board had occasion, during the year, to expel Thomas B. Barry from the Board and from the Order. He did not recognize or respect the decree of the Board, and presented himself at the opening of the General Assembly. The General Master Workman refused to open the session while he was in the convention, and he was obliged to retire. The action of the General Executive Board in expelling him was indorsed. It was clearly proven that his sympathies were entirely with those who opposed the Order. Both Barry and Bailey were in correspondence with officials of the International Workingmen's Association during the year, the object being to turn Local Assemblies of the Order into Provisional Committee Assemblies, in open defiance of the laws of the Knights of Labor.

The power was vested in the General Master Workman to nominate eight members of the convention, the body to select four from the number, these four, together with the General Master Workman, to constitute the General Executive Board. The office of General Secretary-Treasurer, which had been abolished at the Richmond session, was again created, and the offices of General Secretary and General Treasurer combined. When the General Assembly adjourned the General Officers were:

General Master Workman—T. V. Powderly.

General Worthy Foreman—Morris L. Wheat, Colfax, Iowa.

General Secretary-Treasurer—John W. Hayes.

General Instructor of Woman's Work—Mrs. L. M. Barry.

The General Executive Board, exclusive of the General Master Workman, stood:

John Devlin, Detroit, Mich.

J. J. Holland, Jacksonville, Fla.

John Costello, Pittsburg, Pa.

A. W. Wright, Toronto, Ontario.

The General Co-operative Board was reduced to three members, and consisted of Morris L. Wheat, Henry A. Beckmeyer of New Jersey, and John O'Keefe of Rhode Island.

The salary of the General Master Workman was fixed at $5,000 as before; that of the General Secretary-Treasurer at $2,000; that of the members of the General Executive Board was fixed at $4 per day. The salary of the General Instructor was ordered to be the same as that of the members of the General Executive Board.

The first representative of the Order from a foreign country appeared at this convention, Alberte Delwarte of Charleroi, Belgium. The General Master Workman was elected to represent the Order at the Paris Exposition of 1889.

The General Executive Board was instructed to work for the passage of that system of ballot reform which will afford the greatest protection to the voter.

The General Assembly of 1889 convened in Atlanta, Ga., November 12, and continued in session until the 20th. This was perhaps the most important session ever held, for it witnessed the reception as fraternal delegates of three members of the Farmers' Alliance: Colonel L. F. Livingstone, Reuben F. Gray and Harry Brown. Before adjournment the convention elected a committee of three to attend the National Convention of the Farmers' Alliance in St. Louis, Mo., December 4, 1889, and extend the fraternal greetings of the General Assembly to that body. That committee consisted of Ralph Beaumont, A. W. Wright and the General Master Workman.

On December 5, 1889, the above-named committee waited upon the Farmers' organizations in convention assembled at St. Louis, Mo. The various associations of Farmers of the South and Southwest had already consolidated, and the convention of the Farmers' Alliance of the Northwest, then in session, was considering the advisability of uniting forces with their Southern co-workers. Both bodies received the committee from the Knights of Labor very cordially. On December 6 the combined committees of Knights and the Alliance came to an agreement, which was submitted to the convention and adopted with practical unanimity. The following is the agreement:

ST. LOUIS, December 6, 1889.

Agreement made this day between the undersigned committee representing the National Farmers' Alliance and Industrial Union on the one part and the undersigned committee representing the Knights of Labor on the other part, witnesseth:

The undersigned committee representing the Knights of Labor, having read the demands of the Farmers' Alliance and Industrial Union which are embodied in this agreement, hereby indorses the same on behalf of the Knights of Labor, and, for the purpose of giving practical effect to the demands herein set forth, the Legislative Committee of both organizations will act in concert before Congress for the purpose of securing the enactment of laws in harmony with the demands mutually agreed. And it is further agreed, in order to carry out these objects, that we will support for office only such men as can be depended upon to enact these principles into statute law uninfluenced by party caucus.

The demands hereinbefore referred to are as follows:

I. That we demand the abolition of national banks and the substitution of legal-tender Treasury notes in lieu of national bank notes, issued in sufficient volume to do the business of the country on a cash system; regulating the amount needed on a per capita basis as the business interests of the country demand; and that all money issued by the government shall be legal tender in payment of all debts, both public and private.

II. That we demand that Congress shall pass such laws as shall effectually prevent the dealing in futures of all agricultural and mechanical productions, pursuing a stringent system of procedure in trials as shall secure the prompt conviction and imposing such penalties as shall secure the most perfect compliance with law.

III. That we demand the free and unlimited coinage of silver.

IV. That we demand the passage of laws prohibiting the alien ownership of land, and that Congress take early action to devise some plan to obtain all lands now owned by aliens and foreign syndicates; and that all lands now held by railroads and other corporations in excess of such as is actually used and needed by them be reclaimed by the government and held for actual settlers only.

V. Believing in the doctrine of equal rights to all and special favors to none, we demand that taxation, national or State, shall not be used to build up one interest or class at the expense of another. We believe that the money of the country should be kept as much as possible in the hands of the people, and hence we demand that all revenues—national, State or county—shall be limited to the necessary expenses of the government, economically and honestly administered.

VI. That Congress issue a sufficient amount of fractional paper currency to facilitate exchange through the medium of the United States mail.

VII. That the means of communication and transportation shall be controlled by and operated in the interest of the people, as is the United States postal system.

For the better protection of the interests of the two organizations it is hereby agreed that such seals or emblems as the National Farmers' Alliance and Industrial Union may adopt will be recognized and protected in transit or otherwise by the Knights of Labor, and that all seals and labels of the Knights of Labor will in like manner be recognized by the Farmers' Alliance and Industrial Union.

[Signed,]

S. B. ERWIN, *Chairman;*
U. S. HALL, *Secretary;*
J. D. HAMMOND,
B. H. CLOVER,
J. R. MILES,
N. A. DUNNING,
J. D. HATFIELD,
D. K. NORRIS,
R. F. PECK,
W. S. MORGAN,

F. M. BLUNT,
M. PAGE,
W. H. BARTON,
S. M. ADAMS,
J. B. ALEXANDER,
STUMP ASHBY,
R. C. BETTY,
J. H. TURNER,
A. S. MANN,

*Committee on Demands of the National
Farmers' Alliance and Industrial Union.*

T. V. POWDERLY,
A. W. WRIGHT,

RALPH BEAUMONT,

Committee Representing the Knights of Labor.

No officers were elected at the Atlanta session.

The fourth section of the Preamble underwent a radical change and is now worded as follows:

IV. The land, including all the natural sources of wealth, is the heritage of all the people, and should not be subject to speculative traffic. Occupancy and use should be the only title to the possession of land. The taxes upon land should be levied upon its full value for use, exclusive of improvements, and should be sufficient to take for the community all unearned increment.

New District Assemblies were organized during the year at Glasgow, Scotland, and Lockport, N. Y., and a National Trade Assembly at Bay City, Mich.

In the latter part of the year 1888, Brother W. W. Lyght, who had been a very active member in Montreal, Canada, left for Australia. He took with him a commission as Organizer, and succeeded in establishing the first Local Assembly in the antipodes, at Melbourne, in May, 1889. This Local Assembly did not make much headway at first, but it soon increased in membership, and the good work has already been spread broadcast. Local Assemblies are being organized at many points.

Just before the Atlanta session of the General Assembly information was received that an organization called the Knights of Labor had been formed in Auckland, New Zealand, but that the only instructions they had to guide them was part of a copy of the JOURNAL OF THE KNIGHTS OF LABOR. They asked how they could be affiliated with the Order in America. Full instructions were sent them, and they were put in communication with Brother Lyght at Melbourne. He visited New Zealand in February, 1890, and succeeded in firmly establishing the Order in Auckland, Wellington and Christchurch. Since then there have been seven other Local Assemblies founded, and the expectation is that this number will be more than doubled in the near future.

Denver, Col., was selected as the place to hold the General Assembly of 1890, and on November 13 the session convened.

The most important event of this convention was the adoption of a resolution authorizing the General Master Workman to issue a call to the other industrial organizations of the United States to send representatives to a conference to adopt a political platform. The resolution is as follows:

It is a conceded fact by every thoughtful mind that most of the objects set forth in the Preamble of the Knights of Labor can only be secured by independent political action.

Therefore your committee recommends that the General Master Workman correspond with the presidents or other chief officers of other industrial and reform organizations, with the view to the holding of a National Reform Industrial Conference, on the basis of the platform adopted at the St. Louis Conference of December, 1889, the conference to be held at as early a date as possible, so that a solid and harmonious union of the industrial and reform forces of the country may be consummated that will enact the principles of our Preamble into statute law.

Your committee further recommends that this General Assembly elect three fraternal delegates to the Supreme Council of the National Farmers' Alliance to be held at Ocala, Fla., on December 3 next, and instruct their delegates to present to that body a proposition to hold a National Reform Industrial Convention some time in the ensuing year.

And your committee further recommends that this General Assembly puts itself on record by the adoption of those recommendations, as binding the Order of the Knights of Labor to carry out any pledges made by its officers and delegates in these conferences, and further binding the members of the Order to the support of any political tickets put in the field on a platform formulated in a National Reform Industrial Convention held as above provided for.

And your committee further recommends that our brothers of the Dominion of Canada and the Canadian Provinces take similar action.

The twentieth section of the Preamble was changed to read: "To secure for both sexes equal rights."

The salary of the General Master Workman was reduced from $5,000 to $3,500, at his own request.

The officers elected for the ensuing term were:

General Master Workman—T. V. Powderly.
General Worthy Foreman—Hugh Cavanaugh.
General Secretary-Treasurer—John W. Hayes.

The members elected on the General Executive Board were:

John Devlin, Michigan.
A. W. Wright, Canada.
J. J. Holland, Florida.
John Davis, Kansas.

The Co-operative Board was abolished and the duties of that body were vested in the General Executive Board.

The Woman's Christian Temperance Union was represented by Mrs. Anna Steele, Mrs. M. E. Brazee, State Vice-President; Mrs. M. A. Cassels, President Arapahoe County Woman's Christian Temperance Union; Mrs. J. B. Belford, Mrs. E. C. Benton, Mrs. A. W. Hogle and Mrs. T. M. Chase. These ladies acted as fraternal delegates and conveyed the greetings of the body they represented.

A committee consisting of the same members who had served in the same capacity the year previous was appointed to confer with the National Farmers' Alliance and Laborers' Union at their convention in Ocala, Fla., on December 3, 1890.

New District Assemblies were organized during the year at Sheffield, England; Montreal, Canada; Quebec, Canada; and a Territorial Assembly in New Mexico.

In this chapter is given the merest outline of the work done at the various sessions of the General Assembly of the Knights of Labor. To properly record the really important measures that receivêd attention would take up more space than is contained within the covers of this book. The great strikes which took place have not been touched upon, for the reason that to do justice to the subject a volume as large as this would not suffice, and it is the intention, at no distant day, to publish, in a separate volume, an account of the principal strikes of the past ten years, giving the origin of each, the incidents during progress, and the results attained. For that reason they are not discussed in this volume. The important action of the General Assembly on the chief points of the Preamble are discussed elsewhere in these pages, and for that reason this chapter includes only the official work of the different conventions.

SOCIAL EQUALITY.

We see religion's conflicts and war's terrible munitions—
See advances and repulses, see contentions and transitions,
And Humanity's great struggles toward loftier conditions—
For *man* is marching on.

During the session of the General Assembly in Richmond, Va., an episode occurred which caused a great deal of excitement in that city, and came near resulting in bloodshed. Previous to the convention, William H. Mullen of Richmond requested Hon. Fitzhugh Lee, Governor of Virginia, to tender an address of welcome to the representatives of the Order on the assembling of the convention. The Governor kindly consented to do so, and made preparations accordingly. When D. A. 49 of New York elected representatives to the convention, one of the number chosen was a colored man, Frank J. Ferrell. In making arrangements for hotel accommodations for the New York delegation, the agent of D. A. 49 did not state that there would be any colored men among them, and when the representatives arrived in Richmond, and appeared at the hotel selected, they were told that Mr. Ferrell would not be admitted because of his color. Without hesitation the representatives of D. A. 49 withdrew in a body, and secured quarters where there would be no objections to any one of their number. J. E. Quinn, then Master Workman of that District, stated the facts in the case to the General Master Workman, and requested that officer to assign to Mr. Ferrell the duty of introducing Governor Lee to the General Assembly. The General Master Workman did not favor the proposition and urged that it be abandoned. In the discussion which took place at the hotel where the General Officers were staying, the General Master Workman said to Mr. Quinn :

I do not believe that it would be an act of courtesy on our part to violate any recognized rule of this community, and it would not be pleasant for either the Governor or the convention to attempt to set at defiance a long-established usage. I know a man who feels that he is the equal of Governor Lee, and I think he is just as good a man in every respect; if Brother Ferrell will consent to introduce this man to the convention when the time comes, I think it will be as acceptable to him, in fact I believe he will esteem it a greater honor than to introduce even the Governor of Virginia.

When asked to name the person of whom he spoke, the answer which Mr. Quinn received was: "The General Master Workman of the Knights of Labor."

With the understanding that the Governor was to be introduced by the General Master Workman, and that officer in turn introduced by Mr. Ferrell, the convention was called to order. The program was carried out to the letter, and, when the very excellent and well-received address of welcome was delivered by Governor Lee, Mr. Ferrell mounted the platform and said :

It is with much pleasure and gratification I introduce to you Mr. T. V. Powderly of the State of Pennsylvania, who will reply to the address of welcome of Governor Lee of this State, which is one of the oldest States in the arena of political influence of our country. He is one of the thoughtful men of the nation, who recognizes the importance of this gathering of the toiling masses in this our growing Republic. As Virginia has led in the aspirations of our country in the past, I look with much confidence to the future, in the hope that she will lead in the future to the realization of the objects of our noble Order. It is with extreme pleasure that we, the representatives from every section of our country, receive the welcome of congratulation for our efforts to improve the condition of humanity. One of the objects of our Order is the abolition of those distinctions which are maintained by creed or color. I believe I present to you a man above the'superstitions which are involved in these distinctions. My experience with the noble Order of the Knights of Labor and my training in the District have taught me that we have worked so far successfully toward the extinction of these regrettable distinctions. As we recognize and repose confidence in all men for their worth in society, so can we repose confidence in one of the noblest sons of labor—T. V. Powderly—whom I now take the pleasure of presenting to you.

The response to the address of welcome having been delivered by the General Master Workman, the convention was opened under the forms and usages of the Knights of Labor, and all visitors excluded.

On the boat which brought the New York delegation to Richmond was a dramatic company, which opened up for a week's stay at one of the Richmond theatres on the evening of the first day's session of the General Assembly. The leading man of the company extended an invitation to the representatives of D. A. 49 to attend the play, and it was accepted. The entire delegation, including Mr. Ferrell, went in a body to the theatre. When it became known that a colored man was admitted to one of the choicest seats in the theatre all interest in the play was lost, and many left the building vowing vengeance on the intruder who had so recklessly defied one of the rules of Richmond life. The next evening the attendance at the theatre was very slim, many theatre-goers having determined to boycott it while that particular company occupied the boards. Outside of the building an angry mob assembled, armed with revolvers and other weapons, for the purpose of preventing one negro from entering the theatre. Neither Mr. Ferrell nor any of the New York representatives went to the theatre for the reason that they were nearly all assigned to duty on some committee of the General Assembly, or to attend some of the Local Assemblies in session in the city that evening. The excitement ran high for many days, and on several occasions men who claimed to be residents of Richmond appeared at the hotel where the General Officers were stopping and threatened to do violence to some of the delegates. On Sunday, October 10, the information was conveyed to the General Master Workman that the armory building, where the convention held its sessions, was to be mobbed on the following evening. The information was made on good authority. The officers of the regiment, whose headquarters were in the armory building, held consultations with some of the General Officers and assured them that there would be no trouble. Sunday evening the General Master Workman sent a note to the Chief of Police informing him of the state of affairs, and requesting him to call at the hotel. After a consultation with the Chief of Police, it was resolved to pay no attention to the threats which were made each day as the representatives went to and from the armory. The Southern press was much exercised over the condition of affairs, and many unjust editorials were written on statements which were sent out from Richmond by sensational writers. On Monday the General Master Workman felt called upon to reply to some of the aspersions cast upon the General Assembly. He prepared a statement for publication and gave it to the Richmond *Dispatch*. It appeared in the issue of October 12, but no other paper copied it. Many extracts were taken from it, and garbled to suit the views of the editors of the papers who published them; but the whole of the article was never published outside of Richmond. It is given in full below:

RICHMOND, Va., October 11, 1886.

Much has been said and written concerning the events which have transpired in the city of Richmond during the past ten days. As I am responsible for a great deal of the agitation, it is but proper that I should be permitted to speak to as large an audience as that which listened to those who have criticised, misconstrued and distorted the words and the idea intended to be conveyed by my utterances of October 4, when Francis Ferrell introduced me to the meeting assembled in the armory. I stated to the meeting that it was at my request that Mr. Ferrell, a representative of the colored race, introduced me; it was left to me to make the selection, and I did it after mature deliberation and careful thought. I have not seen or heard an argument since then that would cause me to do differently to-day. Critics have seen fit to decide what I meant by selecting this man to introduce me, and they have asserted that my action must be regarded in the light of an attack upon the laws of social equality. A part of the press of the South has attacked, in a most unjustifiable manner, a man who, under the flag and Constitution of his country, selected another man, and a citizen of the Republic, to perform a public duty in a public place. In acknowledging his introduction I referred to the prejudice which existed against the colored man. If previous to that day I had any doubts that a prejudice existed, they have been removed by the hasty and inconsiderate action of those who were so quick to see an insult where none was intended.

WHY FERRELL WAS SELECTED.

My sole object in selecting a colored man to introduce me was to encourage and help to uplift his race from a bondage worse than that which held him in chains twenty-five years ago—viz.: mental slavery. I desired to impress upon the minds of white and black that the same result followed action in the field of labor, whether that action was on the part of the Caucasian or the negro. Two years ago, in an address delivered in this city, I said to the people of Richmond: "You stand face to face with a stern, living reality; a responsibility which cannot be avoided or shirked. The negro question is as prominent to-day as it ever was. The first proposition that stares us in the face is this: The negro is free; he is here, and he is here to stay. He is a citizen, and must learn to manage his own affairs. His labor and that of the white man will be thrown upon the market side by side, and no human eye can detect a difference between the article manufactured by the black mechanic and that manufactured by the white mechanic. Both claim an equal share of the protection afforded to American labor, and both mechanics must sink their differences or fall a prey to the slave labor now being imported to this country." I was not criticised for saying that, and yet it was as susceptible of criticism as my words on October 4. I did not refer to social equality, for that cannot be regulated by law. The sanctity of the fireside circle cannot be invaded by those who are not welcome. Every man has the right to say who shall enter beneath his roof; who shall occupy the same bed, private conveyance, or such other place as he is master of. I reserve for myself the right to say who I will or will not associate with. That right belongs to every other man. I have no wish to interfere with that right.

PERSONAL LIBERTY AND SOCIAL EQUALITY.

My critics have forgotten that personal liberty and social equality stand side by side. They would deny me the right to make my own selection as to which of the assembled representatives should perform a certain duty. Had I selected the colored man to introduce Governor Lee, it would have been quite another thing. It is, perhaps, unfortunate that our coming was at a time when political excitement ran high, and all things served as excuses for those who wished to use them. When I heard that there was a likelihood of trouble because Mr. Ferrell attended a place of amusement, I asked him not to subject himself to insult by going where he was not welcome. He told me that he had no intention of again going to that or any other place where his presence would give rise to comment. Until that time I did not know that colored men were denied admittance to theatres in this city.

A WORD TO THE CRITIC.

While I have no wish to interfere with the social relations which exist between the races of the South, I have a strong desire to see the black man educated. Southern labor, regardless of color, must learn to read and write. Southern cheap labor is more a menace to the American toiler than the Chinese, and this labor must be educated. Will my critics show me how the laws of social equality will be harmed by educating the black man so that he may know how to conduct himself as a gentleman? Will they explain how a knowledge of the laws of his country will cause a man to violate the laws of social equality? Will they, in a cool, dispassionate manner, explain to me whether an education will not elevate the moral standard of the colored man? and will they tell me that such a thing is not as necessary with the blacks as with the whites?

STARVATION WAGES.

Will it be explained to me whether the black man should continue to work for starvation wages? With so many able-bodied colored men in the South who do not know enough to ask for living wages, it is not hard to guess that while this race continues to increase in numbers and ignorance prosperity will not even knock at the door, much less enter the home of the Southern laborer; and that country which has an abundance of ill-fed, ill-bred laborers is not, nor cannot be, a prosperous one. Will my critics stop long enough to tell me why the United States Senate allowed a colored man to *introduce,* before the Vice-President of the United States, measures for the benefit of his State? Were the laws of social equality outraged when the House of Representatives permitted colored men to take seats in it? Why did other Southern representatives not leave and return to their homes when that was done?

THE COLORED DELEGATES WILL NOT INTRUDE.

There need be no further cause for alarm. The colored representatives to this convention will not intrude where they are not wanted, and the time-honored laws of social equality will be allowed to slumber on undisturbed. We have not done a thing since coming to this city that is not countenanced by the laws and Constitution of our country, and, in deference to the wishes of those who regard the laws of social equality as superior to the laws of God and man, we will not, while here, avail ourselves of all of those rights and privileges which belong to us. The equality of American citizenship is all that we insist on, and that equality *must* not, *will* not, be trampled upon.

AS TO HOSPITALITY.

Now a word as to hospitality. We are here under no invitation from any one. We came of our own free-will and accord, and are paying our own way; therefore, gratuitous insults, such as those offered by a few mischievous meddlers, are not in order, and do not admit of defense, even though given in behalf of the laws of social equality. I do not hold the people of Richmond responsible for the ill-advised, churlish action of a few who saw a menace in our every move. The treatment received at the hands of the citizens generally has been most cordial. If, during our stay, any representative shall conduct himself in an unbecoming manner, he alone will be held responsible for his action.

TO THE KNIGHTS.

To the convention I say: Let no member surrender an iota of intellectual freedom because of any clamor. Hold fast to that which is true and right. The triumph of noise over reason is but transient. Our principles will be better known, if not to-day it may be to-morrow; they can bide their time, and will some day have the world for an audience. In the field of labor and American citizenship we recognize no line of race, creed, politics or color. The demagogue may distort, for a purpose, the words of others, and for a time the noise of the vocal boss may silence reason, but that which is right and true will become known when the former has passed to rest and the sound of the latter's voice has forever died away. Then it will be known that the intelligent, educated man is better qualified to discern the difference between right and privilege, and the unwritten law of social equality will be more rigidly observed than it is to-day.

T. V. POWDERLY.

After the publication of that letter the excitement died away, and the representatives met with no further annoyance. The General Master Workman received many insulting letters from residents of Richmond, who, evidently, scorned to read the truth, and drew for their information on the store of prejudice which they had treasured up against allowing the negro to avail himself of the rights of citizenship. One lady, wrought to a high pitch of anger, sent a postal card bearing the following amusing proposition:

T. V. POWDERLY:

Dear Sir:—As you are so much in sympathy with the negro, will you please call over and fill our coachman's place until he gets well? Inquire on Church Hill.

MISS ————.

Many similar missives were conveyed to him during his stay in Richmond. There were people in that city who were not in sympathy with the element which acted so discourteously toward the visiting strangers but they made no outward sign of their disapproval of the course pursued by those whose foolish prejudices construed an act with which it was none of their business to meddle into an insult to their noble blood.

Violation of the rules of social equality formed no part of the thought or intentions of the General Master Workman when he selected Mr. Ferrell to introduce him to the General Assembly. Neither was it his desire to cater to the sentiment of D. A. 49, or Mr. Quinn, the Master Workman of that District. His only wish was to do something to encourage the black workman, and cause him to feel that, as a factor in the field of production, he stood the equal of all other men.

It was not reserved for the coming of the General Assembly of the Knights of Labor to do violence to the laws of social equality in Richmond or the Southern States. That had been done years before the Knights of Labor ever gained a foothold in the South, but in a far different way. Social equality is recognized in the South by many of those who prate the loudest against it. The slave-owners of long ago leveled the distinctions between the races, and some of their children and children's children honor the practice to the present day.

One has only to stand on a street corner, or at the door of one of the churches where colored people attend, to be convinced that Caucasian blood flows through the veins of thousands who, for certain reasons, dare not boast of pride of ancestry.

Had the laws of social equality been rigidly practiced in secret as they are boasted of in public by the aristocracy of the South, more of respect would be due to those who affect to scorn the man who would maintain the rights of a race whose crime is its color, and whose fault is that long years of slavery has transmitted the curse of ignorance to its children of the present day. The best evidence of the insincerity and hypocrisy of the Southern aristocrat is written upon the half-white faces of the hundreds of thousands of young men and women in whose veins flow, in mingled current, the blood of the former slave and that of the best families of the South.

It is not the negro alone who stands ostracised in the South by the remnant of the Bourbon element, which still exists to protest against the progress of the Southern States. The white man who works is held in no higher esteem than the black man, and his ignorance is taken advantage of when he is patted on the back and told that he " is better than the negro."

No labor advocate seeks to interfere with the social relations of the races in the South, for it is the industrial, not the race, question we endeavor to solve, and the intellectual status of the black and white laborer must be improved if either one is to prosper.

Of the two races in the South at the present time, the negro is making the most energetic struggle for an education. If the whites would not fall behind in the race they must learn that moral worth, not wealth, is the true standard of individual anα national greatness.

CONCLUSION.

But let the free-winged angel Truth their guarded passes scale,
To teach that right is more than might, and justice more than mail.
— *Whittier*.

Day follows the darkest night; and when the time comes, the latest fruits also ripen.—*Schiller*.

We pray "Thy kingdom come." But not by prayer
Alone will it be built of breath in air.
In life thro' labor must be brought to birth
The kingdom, as it is in heaven, on earth.—*Gerald Massey*.

The full extent of the good that has been done by the Order of the Knights of Labor will never be known. It is not within the bounds of human possibility to detail the many acts that have gone to benefit the millions. One fact attests the value of the Order: Its enemies have attacked it, belied its aims and purposes, and have opposed its advances as they never did those of any organization since the world began. Had the Knights of Labor been weak and unworthy of notice, this would not have been done. Had our mission not caused consternation among the enemies of human liberty, they would not have united to oppose the Order. The various acts of State Legislatures in the interest of the masses, the public opinion that has been created on the subject of labor, the education of philosophers, doctors, clergymen, scientists and others on the industrial question, have not been in vain.

But the mission of the Order is not yet complete. Having worked up a sentiment in favor of the measures advocated in its Preamble, it still remains to put them into practical operation, and that duty rests with us to perform. The call has been sounded, the warning has been given; those who knew nothing of the danger which threatened us now realize its full importance. The great work is still ahead of us. We must look to the future for what we have been contending for in the past.

As it was in the beginning, so it is to-day with labor. It is still in the grasp of heartless wealth, that instrument which, if properly used and directed by advanced ideas, can be made the servant of industry. The volume of wealth is in the hands of task-masters, who use it to build up fortunes for those who already have enough for their own comfort and too much for their country's good. Labor's ranks to-day contain more of keenly-felt poverty than ever before, when we consider the advancements which have been made in all that go to make

354

the pathway of mankind smoother. Those who labor bend from morn till night as of old. They toil on and on as when "the sword was law." But go among them and talk to them of the rights to which they were born, and not so many will stare in open-eyed wonder as would have done so thirty years ago. A revolution has taken place; others are to come. It need occasion no surprise if revolution after revolution shall arise in the days to come, gathering strength as they come and go, for when men have rights they will seek for them by the aid of that light which is held before their eyes. It is too close to the time when the evening gun of the nineteenth century shall sound in the ears of mankind to attempt to turn back the tide of education which is setting in.

Workingmen will find out, as certain as fate, what governments and nations owe to them; they will find out that which is of far greater importance: what they owe to themselves; and when the education shall have become more universal, he who speaks for humanity will not be called an agitator, a disturber, a breeder of discord or a fanatic—he will be known as a saviour. For long ages men who arose here and there in the march of labor's hosts to point out to them the path which leads to that higher civilization have been tied hand and foot by those for whom they plead, scourged as by scorpions by those whom they sought to serve, and at last were nailed to the cross of ingratitude between the two thieves—ignorance and wealth.

Poor struggling humanity! ever striving for something better, lifts its blood-shot eyes to heaven and gives forth, from the bottom of its tortured heart, the agonizing cry, "How long, O God, how long," will the idler, gambler, money-changer and speculator gather what we sow? How long will profligacy rule in high places? How long will it be in the power of a few to hold the millions of dollars above the reach of the millions of men who need? How long will men, who have ceased to trust in the wisdom and goodness of God, be permitted to create trusts and combinations which bind to earth the aspirations, the hopes and the interests of the many of earth that the few may revel in wealth, the full sum of which they cannot count during their earthly existence.

The fiat has gone forth that the toiler will not have to wait long for relief. Other eyes than his own are opened to his condition; other men are watching and other hands are assisting to build his castle of the future. His cause has been espoused by men who are with, but not of, him. Men of education, of thought, of ideas, of favorable condition in life; men who are to a great extent independent of monopoly or its influences, who have sufficient means of their own to enable them to live comfortably, are to-day ranged along-side of the laborer in his struggle for right.

The benefits of education and research are being conferred on the toiler by men who are the fortunate possessors of these advantages. In the eleven years of its existence under the General Assembly, men have entered the Order of the Knights of Labor poor, ignorant and friendless. They knew but little concerning their own condition, and nothing whatever about that of their neighbors. Through the instrumentality of the Order these men have acquired an education; natural ability, which lay dormant within them, was stimulated, and they studied, struggled and persevered until they passed the boundary line which separates the dependent from the independent workman. All over America are men, who are either Knights of Labor or who were such at one time, who have learned to know the wants of humanity through the teachings of the Order.

The enemy of human liberty is stronger and better fortified than ever before, but it is standing face to face with a far more formidable adversary than entered the lists against it since Magna Charta was granted. Men who toil for a master dare not raise the voice in their own behalf, but other men dare to, and do, speak out from pulpit and forum, through magazine and daily press for the toiling one. The number of labor's advocates is growing greater day by day. They are becoming more aggressive, add their weight and influence to the education now winding its way among the hills and valleys of the labor world, and we have a mighty leviathan at work, against whose effort monopoly, trust and combine will struggle in vain.

It is feared by some that before this labor agitation is at an end we will witness a revolution, not a peaceful one, doing its patient work among the masses, but a terrible, life-destroying revolution, which will cause cities and towns to weep tears of blood. There need be no fear of that if justice, immutable justice, is again seated on the bench now usurped by corporate power. What just man need fear a revolution ? How much worse can a nation be with a bomb in every man's hand than to have every man's hand bound in chains ? Who would not prefer a nation of men who would rather fight than be slaves to a nation of creatures who would rather be slaves than fight ?

Again, if every hope is taken from the laborer, if he is to continue on the down-track until his home is a hovel, his hearthstone a grave and his country a prison, what great debt will he owe to the nation that will cause him to keep the peace under such circumstances ? Why should he care for the feelings of others when no one cares for him ? Of what avail to tell him to respect the law when the law has permitted his fellow-man to rob him of everything this earth holds dear ? Of what avail to preach patience to the laborer while the ear-drum is receiving the sound of wailing distress from those whom God sent to gather within the circle of his protecting care ? Of what avail to longer cry, " Servants, obey your masters," when it is written in the full light of heaven's day that many of the masters are devils incarnate, whose only God is gold, and whose reward for labor is hell upon earth? The day must come when the Word of God, in all that that Word implies, must be preached among men again. The sound of the hammer which drove the nails through the quivering flesh of the God of the lowly, nineteen centuries ago, has not been heard in many a church for ages. The voice of agony has been drowned in the clink of the dollar until Murray Hill becomes the shrine before which many worship instead of Mount Calvary.

If the Sermon on the Mount were preached in many a church to-day, and the identity of the divine author concealed, fashionable pews would be emptied, the minister of God would be censured and warned never again to repeat the ravings of an utopist. In the church where the minister is the only friend to the poor, it shows that he has preached in vain not to have made more converts to the doctrine of Christ crucified.

But the world is changing. It is growing better, for men are searching for the truth. They have listened to the voice which arose above the din during the past few years in its plea for justice. When the Knights of Labor began their mission of education, all who advocated reform in land laws, in the regulation of transportation, in the issue of currency, were denounced as being insane or enemies to society. When the Knights of Labor began to direct the attention of the masses to the tendency of legislation, the various States were enacting tramp laws, conspiracy laws and restrictive measures of all kinds.

Only the poor and lowly spoke for the lowly and the poor. Those who began the agitation for the practical operation of the principles of Knighthood were sneeringly told that they " were seeking to bring the millennium," or that "mankind is not good enough to maintain such a state of society as would then exist." Others charged the advocates of Knighthood with being " visionaries and lunatics." No Knight of Labor ever advised his neighbor to " sell what thou hast and give to the poor," yet those who opposed the doctrines of Knighthood affected to be believers in and followers of the meek and lowly Jesus who gave that advice.

If what we are told of heaven is true, it is an abode of bliss; where love reigns supreme; where poverty, sin, death and crime are unknown; where all things are enjoyed in common by all the inhabitants thereof.

Surely no Knight of Labor has ever presumed to ask that this earth should become better than such a heavenly place, and yet those who oppose us, who tell us that we are wrong, that we are asking for too much, kneel down to say to God: " Thy kingdom come. Thy will be done on earth, as it is in heaven." They cannot be right in both instances; they must be insincere in one or the other; and as their visible effort is directed against the fulfillment of the prayer which habit, not conviction, forces from their lips, we must believe that away down in their hearts they feel that Christ was wrong, or that He made an exception of them when He preached the Sermon on the Mount.

"Visionaries and lunatics" have striven for the happiness of human kind since the world began; their reward has been the cross and stake; but their words have lived in letters of everlasting light to illumine the pathway of others who could not believe that prayers, teachings, sermons and precepts should all advise a rule of action which directed men to heaven, while the actions of those who exercised unlimited power through the possession of wealth tended to drive men to a hell of poverty and crime.

If prayers mean anything, those who say them should believe what they whisper when alone by the bedside or in the solitude of the closet. If prayers are right, their teachings should be lived up to. No Knight of Labor asks for more than that. But, notwithstanding the opposition shown in the beginning, the work of Knighthood went on, the education in the principles of right and justice became general, and to-day we have "single-tax" men, "nationalists," social reformers of every kind, advocating the measures which were first brought to the attention of the whole people by the Knights of Labor. Had it not been for the work done by the Order, it is more than likely that the pressure would have become so great, the turning of the screw of oppression so rapid, that those who would not listen to the voice of the poor would ere this have heard the roar which would have drowned the cry for mercy of him who had none for the laborer. It is far better to heed the voice of warning, while men can be reasoned with, than to wait until the workman becomes the brute, which the systems now crumbling to earth would have made of him. The historian of the future will record that the revolution inaugurated by the Knights of Labor, and carried forward by the force of thought and ideas, won more for the cause of human liberty than the revolutions which spilled the blood of humanity's advocates through all the centuries of time.

APPENDIX.

THE HOMESTEAD LAW.

AN ACT to secure homesteads to actual settlers on the public domain.

Be it enacted by the Senate and House of Representatives of the United States of America in Congress assembled, That any person who is the head of a family, or who has arrived at the age of twenty-one years, and is a citizen of the United States, or who shall have filed his declaration of intention to become such, as required by the naturalization laws of the United States, and who has never borne arms against the United States government or given aid and comfort to its enemies, shall, from and after the first of January, eighteen hundred and sixty-three, be entitled to enter one quarter-section or a less quantity of unappropriated public lands, upon which said person may have filed a pre-emption claim, or which may, at the time the application is made, be subject to pre-emption at one dollar and twenty-five cents, or less, per acre; or eighty acres, or less, of such unappropriated lands, at two dollars and fifty cents per acre, to be located in a body, in conformity to the legal subdivision of the public lands, and after the same shall have been surveyed; provided, that any person owning or residing on land may, under the provisions of this act, enter other land lying contiguous to his or her said land, which shall not, with the land so already owned and occupied, exceed in the aggregate one hundred and sixty acres.

SEC. 2. *And be it further enacted,* That the person applying for the benefit of this act shall, upon application to the register of the land office in which he or she is about to make such entry, make affidavit before the said register or receiver that he or she is the head of a family, or is twenty-one or more years of age, or shall have performed service in the army or navy of the United States, and that he has never borne arms against the government of the United States or given aid and comfort to its enemies, and that such application is made for his or her exclusive use and benefit, and that said entry is made for the purpose of actual settlement and cultivation, and not, either directly or indirectly, for the use or benefit of any other person or persons whomsoever; and upon filing the said affidavit with the register or receiver, and on payment of ten dollars, he or she shall thereupon be permitted to enter the quantity of land specified; provided, however, that no certificate shall be given or patent issued therefor until the expiration of five years from the date of such entry; and if, at the expiration of such time, or at any time within two years thereafter, the person making such entry—or if he be dead, his widow; or in case of her death, his heirs or devisee; or in case of a widow making such entry, her heirs or devisee, in case of her death—shall prove by two creditable witnesses that she or they have resided upon and cultivated the same for the term of five years immediately succeeding the time of filing the affidavit aforesaid, and shall make affidavit that no part of said land has been alienated, and that he has borne true allegiance to the government of the United States; then, in such case, he, she or they, if at that time a citizen of the United States, shall be entitled to a patent, as in other cases provided for by

359

law; and provided further, that in case of the death of both father and mother, leaving an infant child or children under twenty-one years of age, the right and fee simple shall inure to the benefit of said infant child or children; and the executor, administrator or guardian may, at any time within two years after the death of the surviving parent, and in accordance with the laws of the State in which such children for the time being have their domicil, sell said land for the benefit of said infants, but for no other purpose ; and the purchaser shall acquire the absolute title by the purchase, and be entitled to a patent from the United States, on payment of the office fees and sum of money herein specified.

SEC. 3. *And be it further enacted,* That the register of the land office shall note all such applications on the tract books and plats of his office, and keep a register of all such entries, and make return thereof to the General Land Office, together with the proof upon which they have been founded.

SEC. 4. *And be it further enacted,* That no lands acquired under the provisions of this act shall in any event become liable to the satisfaction of any debt or debts contracted prior to the issuing of the patent therefor.

SEC. 5. *And be it further enacted,* That if, at any time after the filing of the affidavit, as required in the second section of this act, and before the expiration of the five years aforesaid, it shall be proven, after due notice to the settler, to the satisfaction of the register of the land office, that the person having filed such affidavit shall have actually changed his or her residence, or abandoned the said land for more than six months at any time, then and in that event the land so entered shall revert to the government.

SEC. 6. *And be it further enacted,* That no individual shall be permitted to acquire title to more than one quarter-section under the provisions of this act; and that the Commissioner of the General Land Office is hereby required to prepare and issue such rules and regulations, consistent with this act, as shall be necessary and proper to carry its provisions into effect, and that the registers and receivers of the several land offices shall be entitled to receive the same compensation for any lands entered under the provisions of this act that they are now entitled to receive when the same quantity of land is entered with money, one-half to be paid by the person making the application at the time of so doing, and the other half on the issue of the certificate by the person to whom it may be issued; but this shall not be construed to enlarge the maximum of compensation now prescribed by law for any register or receiver; provided, that nothing contained in this act shall be so construed as to impair or interfere in any manner whatever with the existing pre-emption rights; and provided further, that all persons who may have filed their applications for a pre-emption right prior to the passage of this act shall be entitled to all privileges of this act; provided further, that no person who has served, or may hereafter serve, for a period of not less than fourteen days in the army or navy of the United States, either regular or volunteer, under the laws thereof, during the existence of an actual war, domestic or foreign, shall be deprived of the benefits of this act on account of not having attained the age of twenty-one years.

SEC. 7. *And be it further enacted,* That the fifth section of the act entitled " An act in addition to an act more effectually to provide for the punishment of certain crimes against the United States, and for other purposes," approved the third of March, in the year eighteen hundred and fifty-seven, shall extend to all oaths, affirmations and affidavits required or authorized by this act.

SEC. 8. *And be it further enacted,* That nothing in this act shall be so construed as to prevent any person who has availed him or herself of the benefits of the first section of this act from paying the minimum price, or the price to which the same may have graduated, for the quantity of land so entered at any time before the expiration of the five years, and obtaining a patent therefor from the government, as in other cases provided by law, on making proof of settlement and cultivation as provided by existing laws granting pre-emption right.

BURLINGAME TREATY.

CHINA, 1868.

ADDITIONAL ARTICLES TO THE TREATY BETWEEN THE UNITED STATES AND
CHINA OF JUNE 18, 1858, CONCLUDED JULY 28, 1868. RATIFICATIONS
EXCHANGED AT PEKIN, NOVEMBER 23, 1869.

*Additional Articles of the Treaty between the United States of America and the Ta
Tsing Empire of the 18th of June, 1858.*

WHEREAS, Since the conclusion of the treaty between the United States of
America and the Ta Tsing Empire (China) of the 18th of June, 1858, circumstances
have arisen showing the necessity of additional articles thereto, the President of
the United States and the August Sovereign of the Ta Tsing Empire have named
for their plenipotentiaries, to-wit: The President of the United States of America,
William H. Seward, Secretary of State, and his Majesty the Emperor of China,
Anson Burlingame, accredited as his Envoy Extraordinary and Minister Pleni-
potentiary, and Chih-Kang and Sun Chia-Ku, of the second Chinese rank, associated high envoys and ministers of his Majesty; and the said plenipotentiaries,
after having exchanged this full power found to be in due and proper form, have
agreed upon the following articles:

ARTICLE I.

His Majesty the Emperor of China, being of the opinion that, in making concessions to the citizens or subjects of foreign powers of the privileges of residing
on certain tracts of land, or resorting to certain waters of that empire for purposes
of trade, he has by no means relinquished his right of eminent domain over said
land and waters, hereby agrees that no such concession or grant shall be construed to give to any power or party which may be at war with or hostile to the
United States, the right to attack the citizens of the United States or their property within the said lands or waters. And the United States for themselves
hereby agree to abstain from offensively attacking the citizens or subjects of any
power or party or their property with which they may be at war on any such
tract of land or waters of the said empire. But nothing in this article shall be
construed to prevent the United States from resisting any attack by any hostile
power or party upon their citizens or their property. It is further agreed that if
any rights or interest in any tract of land in China has been, or shall be hereafter,
granted by the government of China to the United States, or their citizens, for
purposes of trade or commerce, that grant shall in no event be construed to divest
the Chinese authorities of their rights of jurisdiction over persons and property
within said tract of land, except so far as that right may have been expressly
relinquished by treaty.

ARTICLE II.

The United States of America and his Majesty the Emperor of China, believing
that the safety and prosperity of commerce will thereby best be promoted, agree
that any privilege or immunity in respect to trade or navigation within the
Chinese dominions which may not have been stipulated for by treaty shall be
subject to the discretion of the Chinese government, and may be regulated by it
accordingly, but not in a manner or spirit incompatible with the treaty stipulations of the parties.

ARTICLE III.

The Emperor of China shall have the right to appoint consuls at ports of the
United States, who shall enjoy the same privileges and immunities as those
which are enjoyed by public law and treaty in the United States by the consuls
of Great Britain and Russia, or either of them.

ARTICLE IV.

The twenty-ninth article of the treaty of the 18th of June, 1858, having stipulated for the exemption of Christian citizens of the United States and Chinese converts from persecutions in China on account of their faith, it is further agreed that citizens of the United States in China of every religious persuasion, and Chinese subjects in the United States, shall enjoy entire liberty of conscience, and shall be exempt from all disability or persecution on account of their religious faith or worship in either country. Cemeteries for sepulture of the dead, of whatever nativity or nationality, shall be held in respect and free from disturbance or profanation.

ARTICLE V.

The United States of America and the Emperor of China cordially recognize the inherent and inalienable right of man to change his home and allegiance, and also the mutual advantage of the free migration and emigration of their citizens and subjects respectively from the one country to the other for purposes of curiosity, of trade or as permanent residence. The high contracting parties, therefore, join in reprobating any other than an entirely voluntary emigration for these purposes. They consequently agree to pass laws making it a penal offense for a citizen of the United States or Chinese subjects to take Chinese subjects either to the United States or to any other foreign country, or for a Chinese subject or citizen of the United States to take citizens of the United States to China or any other foreign country, without their free and voluntary consent, respectively.

ARTICLE VI.

Citizens of the United States visiting or residing in China shall enjoy the same privileges, immunities or exemptions in respect to travel or residence as may there be enjoyed by the citizens or subjects of the most favored nation; and, reciprocally, Chinese subjects visiting or residing in the United States shall enjoy the same privileges, immunities and exemptions in respect to travel or residence as may there be enjoyed by the citizens or subjects of the most favored nation. But nothing herein contained shall be held to confer naturalization upon citizens of the United States in China, nor upon the subjects of China in the United States.

ARTICLE VII.

Citizens of the United States shall enjoy all of the privileges of the public education under the control of the government of China; and, reciprocally, Chinese subjects shall enjoy all of the privileges of the public educational institutions under the control of the United States which are enjoyed in the respective countries by the citizens or subjects of the most favored nations. The citizens of the United States may freely establish and maintain schools within the Empire of China at those places where foreigners are permitted to reside; and, reciprocally, Chinese subjects may enjoy the same privileges and immunities in the United States.

ARTICLE VIII.

The United States, always disclaiming and discouraging all practices of unnecessary dictation and intervention by one nation in the affairs or domestic relations of another, do hereby disclaim and disavow any intention or right to interfere in the domestic administration of China in regard to the construction of railroads, telegraphs or other national internal improvements. On the other hand, his Majesty the Emperor of China reserves to himself the right to decide the time and manner and circumstances of introducing such improvements within his dominions. With this mutual understanding it is agreed by the contracting parties that if at any time hereafter his Imperial Majesty shall determine to construct, or cause to be constructed, works of the character mentioned within the empire, and shall make application to the United States, or any other

Western power, for facilities to carry out that policy, the United States will in that case designate and authorize suitable engineers to be employed by the Chinese government, and will recommend to other nations an equal compliance with such application, the Chinese in that case protecting such engineers in their persons and property, and paying them a reasonable compensation for their services.

In faith whereof the respective plenipotentiaries have signed this treaty, and thereto fixed the seals of their arms.

Done at Washington this twenty-eighth day of July, in the year of our Lord one thousand eight hundred and sixty-eight.

[SEAL.]   WILLIAM H. SEWARD.
                        ANSON BURLINGAME.

[SEAL.]   CHIH KANG.
                        SUN CHIA-KU.

ALIEN LABOR LAW.

Be it enacted by the Senate and House of Representatives of the United States of America in Congress assembled, That from and after the passage of this act it shall be unlawful for any person, company, partnership or corporation, in any manner whatsoever, to prepay the transportation, or in any way assist or encourage the importation or migration of any alien or aliens, any foreigner or foreigners, into the United States, its Territories, or the District of Columbia, under contract or agreement, parole or special, express or implied, made previous to the importation or migration of such alien or aliens, foreigner or foreigners, to perform labor or service of any kind in the United States, its Territories, or the District of Columbia.

SEC. 2. That all contracts or agreements, express or implied, parole or special, which may hereafter be made by and between any person, company, partnership or corporation, and any foreigner or foreigners, alien or aliens, to perform labor or service, or having reference to the performance of labor or service by any person in the United States, its Territories, or the District of Columbia, previous to the migration or importation of the person or persons whose labor or service is contracted for into the United States, shall be utterly void and of no effect.

SEC. 3. That for every violation of any of the provisions of section one of this act, the person, partnership, company or corporation violating the same by knowingly assisting, encouraging or soliciting the migration or importation of any alien or aliens, foreigner or foreigners, into the United States, its Territories, or the District of Columbia, to perform labor or service of any kind under contract or agreement, express or implied, parole or special, with such alien or aliens, foreigner or foreigners, previous to becoming residents or citizens of the United States, shall forfeit and pay for every such offense the sum of one thousand dollars, which may be sued for and recovered by the United States, or by any person who shall first bring his action therefor, including any such alien or foreigner who may be a party to any such contract or agreement, as debts of like amount are now recovered in the Circuit Courts of the United States; the proceeds to be paid into the treasury of the United States; and separate suits may be brought for each alien or foreigner being a party to such contract or agreement aforesaid. And it shall be the duty of the district attorney of the proper district to prosecute every such suit at the expense of the United States.

SEC. 4. That the master of any vessel who shall knowingly bring within the United States on any such vessel, and land, or permit to be landed, from any foreign port or place, any alien laborer, mechanic or artisan, who, previous to embarkation on such vessel, had entered into contract or agreement, parole or special, express or implied, to perform labor or service in the United States, shall be deemed guilty of a misdemeanor, and on conviction thereof shall be punished by a fine of not more than five hundred dollars for each and every such alien laborer, mechanic or artisan so brought as aforesaid, and may also be imprisoned for a term not exceeding six months.

SEC. 5. That nothing in this act shall be so construed as to prevent any citizen or subject of any foreign country, temporarily residing in the United States, either in private or official capacity, from engaging, under contract or otherwise, persons not residents or citizens of the United States to act as private secretaries, servants or domestics for such foreigner temporarily residing in the United States as aforesaid; nor shall this act be so construed as to prevent any person or persons, partnership or corporation from engaging, under contract or agreement, skilled workmen in foreign countries to perform labor in the United States in or upon any new industry not at present established in the United States; provided, that skilled labor for that purpose cannot be otherwise obtained; nor shall the provisions of this act apply to professional actors, artists, lecturers or singers, nor to persons employed strictly as personal or domestic servants; provided, that nothing in this act shall be construed as prohibiting any individual from assisting any member of his family, or any relative or personal friend, to migrate from any foreign country to the United States for the purpose of settlement here.

SEC. 6. That all laws or parts of laws conflicting herewith be, and the same are hereby, repealed.

Approved February 26, 1885.

SUPPLEMENT TO ALIEN LABOR LAW.

Be it enacted by the Senate and House of Representatives of the United States of America in Congress assembled, That an act to prohibit the importation and immigration of foreigners and aliens under contract or agreement to perform labor in the United States, its Territories and the District of Columbia, approved February twenty-sixth, eighteen hundred and eighty-five, and to provide for the enforcement thereof, be amended by adding the following:

"SEC. 6. That the Secretary of the Treasury is hereby charged with the duty of executing the provisions of this act, and for that purpose he shall have power to enter into contracts with such State commission, board or officers as may be designated for that purpose by the governor of any State to take charge of the local affairs of immigration in the ports within said State, under the rules and regulations to be prescribed by said Secretary; and it shall be the duty of such State commission, board or officers so designated to examine into the condition of passengers arriving at the ports within such State in any ship or vessel, and for that purpose all or any of such commissioners or officers, or such other person or persons as they shall appoint, shall be authorized to go on board of and through any such ship or vessel; and if in such examination there shall be found among such passengers any person included in the prohibition in this act, they shall report the same in writing to the collector of such port, and such persons shall not be permitted to land.

"SEC. 7. That the Secretary of the Treasury shall establish such regulations and rules, and issue from time to time such instructions, not inconsistent with law, as he shall deem best calculated for carrying out the provisions of this act; and he shall prescribe all forms of bonds, entries and other papers to be used under and in the enforcement of the various provisions of this act.

"SEC. 8. That all persons included in the prohibition in this act, upon arrival, shall be sent back to the nations to which they belong and from whence they came. The Secretary of the Treasury may designate the State Board of Charities of any State in which such board shall exist by law, or any commission in any State, or any person or persons in any State, whose duty it shall be to execute the provisions of this section, and shall be entitled to reasonable compensation therefor, to be fixed by regulation prescribed by the Secretary of the Treasury. The Secretary of the Treasury shall prescribe regulations for the return of the aforesaid persons to the countries from whence they came, and shall furnish instructions to the board, commission or persons charged with the execution of the provisions of this section as to the time of procedure in respect thereto, and may change such instructions from time to time. The expense of such return of the aforesaid persons not permitted to land shall be borne by the owners of the vessels in which they came. And any vessel refusing to pay such expenses shall not thereafter be permitted to land at or clear from any port of the United States; and such expenses shall be a lien on said vessel; that the necessary expense in the execution of this act for the present fiscal year shall be paid out of any money in the treasury not otherwise appropriated.

"SEC. 9. That all acts and parts of acts inconsistent with this act are hereby repealed.

"SEC. 10. That this act shall take effect at the expiration of thirty days after its passage."

Approved February 23, 1887.

AIMS AND PURPOSES OF THE ANARCHISTS.

[From the Chicago *Star*, April 25, 1887.]

REVOLUTION OF 1889.

ANARCHISTIC PREPARATIONS FOR THE BLOODY EVENT—HOW THE GROUPS WERE TO BE DRILLED AND TAUGHT FOR THE WORK—TEXT OF THE INSTRUCTIONS —TACTICS OF THE LEADERS.

The announcement that a committee has been appointed by Burnette G. Haskell to effect a union of the Red and Black Internationalists and the Socialistic Labor Party into one national socialistic organization is one that to the initiated is fraught with some significance.

The International Workingmen's Association was organized in London in 1864 by an assemblage of representative workingmen from all the principal cities of Europe. Its first general convention was held in Geneva in 1866, when the plan of organization and declaration of principles as drafted by Dr. Carl Marx were adopted in preference to those proposed by Mazzini and Bakounine. While the principles proposed by Marx were perfectly satisfactory to these leaders, it was Marx's idea that progress could be made only through education and agitation, and he would listen to no other methods of propaganda. These methods Mazzini and Bakounine considered wholly inadequate, even puerile. Mazzini's connection with the carbonari of Italy had made him thoroughly an adherent of the doctrine of force. Bakounine, who claimed to be a Russian prince, was also an advocate of a desperate policy. Space forbids an extended resume of the discussion, but the convention adopted the policy outlined by Marx.

The strike of the Paris bronze-workers in 1867 was sustained by money from London obtained through the International groups, and by a force policy successfully engineered by Bakounine and his adherents. From that time on the advocates of force gained ground, especially in France, where Blanqui's maxim, "Buy lead, and you'll get bread," seemed to be the motto of nearly all the Internationalists. At the congress of the Internationalists held at Hague in 1872, Bakounine was expelled from the association, and took with him thirty delegates. With these thirty delegates he organized the "Black" International as distinguished from the "Red," as the followers of Marx were called. In their declaration of principles they said: "We reject all legislation, all authority, and all privileged, licensed, official and legal influence, even though arising from universal suffrage, convinced that it can turn only to the advantage of a dominant minority of exploiters against the interest of the immense majority in subjection to them. Such is the sense in which we are really anarchists."

Bakounine declares: "I demand the destruction of all States, national and territorial, and the foundation on their ruins of the International State of Laborers." .The Black's reject the educational methods of the Reds, and declare for force, destruction, devastation.

The Blacks have increased very rapidly in France and Belgium, but have made but little progress in other European countries.

The Red International was introduced in the United States almost immediately after the war. Its plan of organization is by groups—eleven forming a group. The first, or student's degree, is accompanied by a red card. Red-card members are instructed in the principles of socialism, must take a certain course of reading; after which they stand an examination, which, if satisfactory, entitles them to a white card. Before entering the course red-card members are assured that the International Workingmen's Association is not anarchistic nor counsels the use of force. White-card members are members of the Executive Committee. From among these are picked those to whom blue cards are given. Blue-card members are the counselors and directors of affairs.

The course of study for American red-card members is radically different from that organized in Europe. Burnette G. Haskell, who was made Secretary of the North American Section, included in the books to be read those of Krapotkine, Bakounine, and many other avowed anarchists. It was always the object of Haskell to unite the Reds and Blacks in America. The "private and confidential" instructions to white-card members, or executive members, prepared by Haskell, say:

"PRELIMINARY INSTRUCTION.

"Having received the necessary information certifying you as a socialist, we take pleasure in inclosing to you your white card, the possession of which constitutes you a member of the Central Committee of the International Workingmen's Association for your particular locality. This is in accordance with the socialist idea, which maintains, first, that no person should have any control over the movement until he is a scientific socialist; and, second, that all who are such socialists should have equal voice and hand in the conduct of the movement.

"As a member of this Central Committee the following may be outlined as your duties:

"1. To urge forward the work of education among the general public of your locality by addresses, propaganda and personal argument.

"2. To endeavor to force or cause the capitalistic press of your locality to give prominence to socialistic ideas.

"3. To aid and support the labor press, and especially to obtain support and subscribers for the *Enquirer*, our official organ.

"4. To report all matters of interest to your State Secretary (if one exists; if not, to the Bureau of Information).

"5. To do all in your power to enforce federation among all trade unionists, to aid local labor organizations, and to urge upon the Knights of Labor a consistent and harmonious work in radical ideas.

"6. To endeavor, in your proselyting among the various societies, to secure as converts, first, those who are the most intellectual and who have developed as the leaders of their respective organizations.

"7. To insist, whenever opportunity presents, upon the absolute necessity of harmony between all schools of socialism, and to deprecate any quarrels founded upon personalities or minor points of doctrine.

"8. To educate yourselves thoroughly so as to be competent to meet at once and prove the falsity of all lies that are told concerning us; as for instance the following lie: 'The socialists desire to overthrow the present government by force.' Answer: 'No. They predict by the light of science merely that an armed conflict between the insolent rich and the ignorant poor is near at hand; that that battle will end in chaos unless at the proper time the socialists interfere and by their aid secure a just system of society; and that when they do interfere they propose to do so effectively.'

"9. To endeavor (even though without much hope of its being successful) to secure the gradual interference of the State in production and distribution.

"10. To aid such co-operative enterprises as will really do good.

"11. To grasp the whole situation as it now stands and endeavor to fit yourself for a leader in the revolution and a scientific organizer of the new society."

Then follows, under the head of "General Suggestions," the following somewhat definite suggestions:

"We desire to deal with the probable future of the social revolution, and in doing so we propose to touch briefly upon its conduct and the subsequent reorganization of society flowing from it. We believe that the entire lack of a definite idea of the proper scheme of action to be pursued has in past times of insurrection been the greatest stumbling-block to success. And we see no way to avoid similar failures in the future unless we at least consider the question now.

"First, then, we all admit that the operation of the competitive system itself will force its own downfall at some time or other. Those of us who have carefully consulted and compared the statistics of invention, production, exchange and labor believe, with Krapotkine, that ten years absolutely cannot pass without the outbreak. The idea is very general, in both France and England, that the historic year of 1889 will see the first serious trouble, and to that end every energy is being bent. The theory of our movement is the creation in every country of so strong an agitation that combination between governments to suppress the revolts in one land will be impossible because of the necessity of looking after their home affairs; the uprising in those lands which are best prepared for success follows and may be either simultaneous or consecutive. In Europe, England will probably be the first to strike; but the beacon-fires there will be answered at once, we know, from the hills of Spain, the plains of Italy, the fields of Germany, Russia and Austria, and the valleys of France. The movement in Europe will be guided by wise heads and careful hands, and of its success we have no doubt whatever.

"It is in America that we need to understand what the future may hold. The impression seems to be general that we here will occupy in '89 a place similar to that held by England in 1848, that of the conservative reactionary country. This view is certainly held by many of the wealthy people of Europe, who are backing their belief, as we all know, by extensive purchases of American lands. But we think this impression is ill founded. The revolution in every land can only be postponed by keeping the people contented. And our position now is entirely different from that of England in 1848. So long as old markets existed or new ones could be opened it was possible to keep the people employed. Where are the new markets now? Even the pitiful substitutes such as are so eagerly sought in the Congo are not available for American productions. It seems indeed to threaten that in America the course of events will tend, as it has in the past in Europe. Some particular localities may be aroused and will take independent action; the conservative centres will be drawn upon for force to suppress the uprisings, and the end will be failure—this certainly unless we foresee and provide against such an event. What then ought we to do?

"We believe we ought first of all to urge the organization of the International Workingmen's Association and federation of all socialists irrespective of the schools to which they belong; that this federation ought to arrange a system of correspondence by which they can consult fraternally regarding disputed points of doctrine and proper methods of harmonious action.

"That the first active duty of the International Workingmen's Association should be to secure in every town, city and county of the country at least one good socialist who should act as a revolutionary agent in the distribution of propaganda and the making of converts.

"If we set actively to work with these ends in view we believe this much could easily be accomplished within the coming year.

"Nothing else would then remain to be done save work of education and preparation until such time as circumstances permitted decisive action.

"We do not approve of quarrels with the S. L. P., I. A. A., nor the Henry George men. Let them continue to teach their own peculiar ideas if they so desire, but let us urge them to federate with all others of the reform school.

"The circumstances which may permit decisive action will probably be these:

"In 1887 the present panic will approach a climax. It will be wide-spread and alarming, accompanied by closed factories, starving workers, rioting and the use of military force. It may even, complicated by a bitter class feeling, result in a suppression of the rights of free speech, meeting and press.

"Until then, unless the whole people are aroused, it is the duty of the wise socialist to hold aloof from riots in special localities. The time is not yet ripe for success; we have counted our heads and we know it. To strike this year would be to uselessly slaughter our best people and put back the cause a hundred years. No; at present we must be wise as serpents but harmless as doves. We must take advantage of it for agitation and education only. We must speak much and act not at all. *When the working people are hungry their brains weaken.* One year of panic means a trebling of our forces at the very least. And while with our present 100,000 American socialists forcible action is impossible, with 400,000 (which the next panic will give us if we manage wisely) we hold the game in our own hands!

"We have perhaps until 1889, four years, in which to perfect our plans. That year in Europe will surely bring grave results. In America, if figures lie not, another panic, greater and more wide-spread than the preceding, will be upon us. Then, and not till then, may we risk a cast of the iron dice. Then may we strike and strike to win!

"Let us say, then, that the probabilities are in favor of our having in 1889, in the United States, at least half a million earnest socialists. Let us say they are divided somewhat as follows:

"Chicago, 25,000; New York, 25,000; in the New England factory States, 100,000; in the central coal and iron region, 100,000; in Colorado and the Western States, 50,000; on the Pacific coast, 50,000; in the Atlantic and Southern cities altogether, 100,000; and scattered at various points in towns and villages, 50,000 more.

"The panic comes, the public is excited, outbreaks occur, the large centres revolt, the places where but a few socialists exist are made points for rallying of the conservative elements. In these small places it should be made the duty of the socialists there presiding, secretly and with all the aid of science in *destructive warfare*, to raise sufficient turmoil to keep the conservative busy at home. Meanwhile in large centres bold measures should be taken. Our people should head, lead and control the popular revolt; should seize the places of power; should lay hands upon the machinery of government. Once installed in power the Revolutionary Committee should follow this course of action. Decrees somewhat as follows should at once be promulgated and enforced:

I.

"Decreed: That private title in fee simple to lands, mines and the natural raw materials of production is abolished and the possessory title thereto vested in the commonwealth.

"Decreed: That rent for the use of houses and lands is declared illegal and action for its recovery barred; except that in all cases the landlord shall have the right of demanding compensation for such improvements whose original cost has not been repaid in rent, until such time as the cost is so repaid.

"Decreed: That the books wherein the titles of private persons to lands are recorded and preserved by the State be burned.

"Decreed: That personal occupancy and use of any piece of land gives a right of tenancy from the State to the occupier as against any other person free of rent, at the pleasure of the State.

"Decreed: That a department of lands be created to carry out this decree.

II.

"Decreed: That it is the right of every individual who supports the commonwealth to receive from it an opportunity to labor.

"Decreed: That a department of production be organized, whose duty it shall be to carry out this decree.

"Decreed: That the title to all machinery of production shall vest in the commonwealth. And that the individual manufacturers now claiming to 'own' such machinery shall turn such over to the State officials without compensation, when it shall appear that the profits have, in times past, paid back to said owner the first cost thereof; but otherwise upon a compensation equal to a difference between said first cost and the profits gained.

"Decreed: That profit is abolished, and that the department of production shall turn over its manufactured goods to the department of distribution at cost.

"Decreed: That nothing herein shall prevent any manufacturer who has not received back in profits the cost of his enterprise from continuing his business, if he so pleases, in competition with the State.

III.

"Decreed: That a department of distribution be organized.

"Decreed: That the stock on hand of all wholesale and retail dealers is confiscated to the commonwealth without compensation, in cases where their profits have paid back their original capital; but otherwise upon payment of the difference between the first capital and the amount of profit returns.

IV.

"Decreed: That a department of statistics be organized, whose duty it shall be to ascertain the productive capacity of the people and also their probable wants, and to certify the same to the proper departments.

V.

"Decreed: That a department of education be organized; that all printing establishments be placed under their charge; that kindergarten, athletic, mechanical, industrial and technical schools be organized.

VI.

"Decreed: That interest for money be abolished. That money be abolished. That a department of exchange be organized. That cost be declared the limit of price; and that temporarily (until proper statistics are obtained showing the true relations of the various classes of labor to each other), in State employ, the time of one man shall be held on equivalent value to that of any other. That clearing houses be established upon this principle, and that the payment of workers and delivery of goods to the holders of labor notes be made upon the same principle. That until proper statistics are obtained goods shall be sold at thirty-three per cent. less than their ruling retail price under the old profit system, and wages shall be fixed at a rate equivalent to $5 a day.

VII.

"Decreed: That subdepartments of public justice, art, agriculture, transportation and communication be organized:

"Decreed: That one year from date the first election for public functionaries shall be held, and that a provisional department to formulate a just system therefore be now organized.

"Etc., etc., etc., etc., etc., etc.

"Each centre of insurrection having pursued this course, immediate steps should then be taken to federate the various localities. A congress should be called and the national organization effected.

"The system thus set in operation would gather strength and power every hour and day, and long before the year had passed when the people with a free ballot were to pass upon the work, its beneficent results would be felt by every citizen. The plebiscit would then but give it the sanctity of popular approval, and no power on earth could then for any length of time withstand its triumphant progress.

"In concluding these necessarily crude and fragmentary remarks, we beg to emphasize our belief that the Pacific coast particularly, by reason of its peculiar population, its natural wealth, its position (such that a few determined men could isolate it from the balance of the world for months of time), and the agitation already started over its whole area, is peculiarly fitted to be the first to lead off in active work when the time for that work shall come.

"'Workingmen of the world, unite! You have a world to win and but your chains to lose!'

"FINAL WORDS.—1. Central committees will take measures to provide themselves with a regular agitation and expense fund.

"2. They will remit monthly to their State Secretary, for the postage, circulars and other expenses of his office, five cents for each white-card member on their roll.

"As soon as practicable you ought to put your State Secretary in a position of independence by paying him a salary, and requiring him to devote his whole time to the work.

"3. They will remit also to the bureau of information a similar sum for similar purposes.

"4. The State Secretary and State Executive are elected to hold during good behavior, subject to recall at any time by the blue-card members of their State. The National Secretary and National Executive may be elected similarly by the blue-card members of the United States.

"5. Such men as have been for years prominent socialists or workers in the cause may be recommended by any central committee for a blue-card without having made the actual converts required by the rules.

"The blue-card members are designed as the revolutionary force, and it is expected they will exercise their best thoughts in study and consideration of the points that ought to be dealt with. In future, by congresses and correspondence, plans will undoubtedly be formulated that will cover every emergency.

"As it is of the utmost importance that only those who are tried, trusted and true shall hold the 'blue-card,' you are urged to the most careful scrutiny of all new applicants for the same in your locality. Do not recommend any who are not of the very best material. Mere numbers are not so much of an object as men.

"At present the most important work is organization, and to this every energy should be bent.

"During the year 1885 all white-card members are instructed to write and forward to headquarters carefully-written essays upon the subjects named below. At the end of the year abstracts of each essay or class of essays will be submitted by referendum to the consideration of all white-card members:

"1. How may the new social order be organized and administered; *i. e.*, how may the change be brought about with the least jar?

"2. What should be our proper course of action in times of panic, revolt, revolution?

"3. What are the best means of offense and defense? How may the success of the revolution be assured?

"4. Our policy in times of revolution.

"In centres of insurrection—how controlled—seizure of public buildings—control of the press, telegraph, railroads, shipping—occupancy of armories—organization of the people—arming—arrest of prominent capitalists—seizure of military stores—guarding against disorder—the rationing of the people—prevention of arson, murder, theft—reorganization of society—means of preventing stagnation of business—free justice—no rent—work for all—organization and federation of the new society.

"At conservative points—formation of secret revolutionary committees—proclamations of intention—forcibly preventing departure of forces to aid capital at other points, etc., etc.

"Arrangements have been made to commence, before the end of the year, the circulation of brochures containing, *in extenso*, what accumulated knowledge we already have concerning newly discovered means of practically applying dynamite to organized (not sporadic) revolutionary warfare. But this is not a matter for haste. Organization should be the watchword for the hour.

"You should be, as well, particularly active in labor organization. Every white-card member ought to be, in fact, a leader. If possible, he should control some trade union or organization, moulding it carefully and steadily into such shape that it may be of use in the time of struggle.

"Every white-card member should thoroughly understand that it may be upon his efforts alone—upon his fidelity and persistence—that the successful issue of the revolution depends. He must, for the sake of the cause, watch his fellow white-card members, must advise with, strengthen, purify, and aid them upward."

This is the Red International in America as directed by Burnette Haskell! A great number of dainty morsels might be quoted, but are omitted for lack of space.

The Blacks, or the International Anarchist Association, as an organization, was introduced into America, in Pittsburg in 1883, as the International Working People's Association. It issued a long manifesto, which ended up as follows:

"If there ever could have been any question on this point, it should long ago have been dispelled by the brutalities which the bourgeois of all countries—in America as well as in Europe—constantly commit, as often as the proletariat anywhere energetically move to better their condition. It becomes, therefore, self-evident that the struggle of the proletariat with the bourgeois will be of a violent, revolutionary character.

"We could show by scores of illustrations that all attempts in the past to reform this monstrous system by peaceable means, such as the ballot, have been futile, and all such efforts in the future must necessarily be so for the following reasons:

"The political institutions of our time are the agencies of the propertied class; their mission is the upholding of the privileges of their masters; any reform in your own behalf would curtail these privileges. To this they will not and cannot consent, for it would be suicidal to themselves.

"That they will not resign their privileges voluntarily we know; that they will not make any concessions to us we likewise know. Since we must then rely upon the kindness of our masters for whatever redress we have, and knowing that from them no good may be expected, there remains but one resource—force! Our forefathers have not only told us that against despots force is justifiable because it is the only means, but they themselves have set the immemorial example.

"By force our ancestors liberated themselves from political oppression, by force their children will have to liberate themselves from economic bondage. 'It is therefore your right, it is your duty,' says Jefferson, 'to arm!'

"What we would achieve is, therefore, plainly and simply:

"1. Destruction of the existing class rule, by all means; *i. e.*, by energetic, relentless, revolutionary and international action.

"2. Establishment of a free society based upon co-operative organization of production.

"3. Free exchange of equivalent products by and between the productive organizations without commerce and profit-mongery.

"4. Organization of education on a secular, scientific and equal basis for both sexes.

"5. Equal rights for all without distinction to sex or race.

"6. Regulation of all public affairs by free contracts between the autonomous (independent) communes and associations, resting on a federalistic basis.

"Whoever agrees with this idea let him grasp our outstretched brother hands!
"Proletarians from all countries, unite!

"Fellow-workmen, all we need for the achievement of this great end is organization and unity!

"The day has come for solidarity. Join our ranks! Let the drum beat defiantly the roll of battle: 'Workmen of all countries, unite! You have nothing to lose but your chains; you have the world to win!'"